The
INSTANT
EXPERT
Guide

Finance:
Essentials for the
Successful Professional

Pierre G. B

Australia • Canada • United States

THOMSON

First trade edition, 2002

Photo Credit: Pages 2, 28, 68, 106, 134, 166, 194, 228, 270, 310, 350: © PhotoDisc, Inc.

Copyright © 2002 South-Western, a division of Thomson Learning, Inc. Thomson Learning™ is a trademark used herein under license.

ISBN: 0-538-72613-X

Adapted from *Finance for Non-Financial Managers* published by Nelson Thomson Learning, © 2001

Printed in the United States of America
1 2 3 4 5 6 07 06 05 04 03 02

For permission to use material from this text or product, contact us by
Tel: 800-730-2214
Fax: 800-730-2215
Web: www.thomsonrights.com

For more information, contact South-Western Publishing, 5191 Natorp Boulevard, Mason, OH, 45040. Or you can visit our Internet site at www.swep.com.

Finance:

Essentials for the Successful Professional

HOW TO USE THIS BOOK

Finance: Essentials for the Successful Professional is for managers and others who have little experience in the field of finance. It is aimed primarily at those who wish to broaden their understanding of financial analysis, improve their decision-making skills, or upgrade old skills in the fields of financial management and accounting.

Finance is a function that is far too important to be left only to financial specialists. Financial activities should be practiced by nonfinancial managers who are responsible for resources and interested in improving the financial performance and destiny of their organizations.

This book will be particularly useful to:

1. People who plan to work in areas such as business management, marketing, production, human resources, engineering, or research and development.
2. Managers who want to learn how to analyze financial statements in a more comprehensive way and use them as decision-making instruments.
3. Entrepreneurs of small- and medium-sized businesses who feel the need to develop fundamental skills in financial control and financial planning.
4. Independent professionals such as lawyers, engineers, and medical practitioners, who want to develop the financial side of their profession.

One of the most important objectives of this book is to make the various topics presented in each chapter intelligible to all readers at different levels of education and experience. Managers, entrepreneurs, and prospective employees in business will find this book instrumental in learning the essentials of financial statement analysis and capital budgeting techniques.

Readers will find *Finance: Essentials for the Successful Professional* informative and enjoyable. Using a common-sense approach, supported by many tables, figures, examples, and illustrations, various financial management concepts and techniques are presented in a simple way. There is no need to present finance as an abstract or obtuse subject. Properly explained and presented, finance can be easily understood and, more importantly, applied to business situations so that nonfinancial managers and entrepreneurs can be more effective.

Each chapter is introduced by an opening vignette that presents the more important financial topics covered in the chapter. This helps readers understand more completely the link between the theory and its applications. All introductory vignettes are connected to each other. This unique feature enables the reader to visualize how all concepts covered in the book can be logically linked to analyze financial statements and to make decisions to improve a company's bottom line.

Spreadsheet templates are included on a disk. The templates provide the framework for solving many of your essential financial problems. The templates can be used to analyze real-world financial data.

TABLE OF CONTENTS

CHAPTER 1

Overview of Financial Management

*A*fter spending ten years with different organizations, Len and Joan Edwards decided to open their own retail business, CompuTech Sales and Services. While Len worked for several computer retail stores, Joan was employed as a sales representative for a multinational computer organization. They believed that their combined experience would be important for their success.

However, before making their final decision, they decided to speak to a long-term friend and entrepreneur, Bill Murray who had operated a successful retail business for the past twenty-five years. The purpose of the meeting was to obtain advice before launching their business. The following summarizes Bill's comments:

"The two most important factors for any business to be successful are its products/services and its management. The products or services that you want to sell must be in demand, and you must possess management and administrative skills if you are to realize your goals and objectives. To measure your success, you will need operating and financial information. Although an accountant can help you set up your bookkeeping and accounting systems, you have to make sure that you can analyze your financial statements. Reading financial statements is as important to a business owner as reading the instruments on the dashboard is to a race car driver. Similar to the driver, who is able to read these instruments, analyzing financial statements will help you see how well your business is doing and will help you analyze what decisions you need to make to improve the financial performance of your retail operations.

"To succeed, your business will have to generate a healthy profit (efficiency) and be able to pay its bills on time (liquidity). In addition, your business must show signs of continuous growth in all segments such as sales and profit (profitability) and make sure that you do not overburden your business with too much debt (stability).

"You will encounter three types of business decisions. The first type relates to launching your business, known as **investing decisions**. This is not the only investing decision that you will make. If your business prospers, you will be faced with a series of investing decisions such as expanding your business, opening up new retail outlets, buying equipment for your business, and so on. **Operating decisions** are the second type of business decisions. They have to do with your day-to-day operations. You will be continually faced with decisions such as pricing, advertising, hiring new employees, buying office supplies, and so on. Through your budgeting exercise, you will have to make sure that you keep your operating costs as low as possible in order to maximize your profit (efficiency). The third type of decisions are financing decisions. Once you know exactly how much it will cost you to start your business, you will have to invest your own money in the business and approach lenders for financial support. All these different sources of financing bear a cost. You have to make sure that your business generates enough profit (return) to pay for financing your business (cost)."

Both Len and Joan knew they needed to learn more about the concepts that Bill Murray had introduced to them. They wanted to learn as much as possible to help them realize their dream.

This chapter examines in more detail the recommendations made by Bill Murray. In particular, it focuses on four key topics:

- Why is financial management so important for business owners and managers?
- Who is really responsible for the finance function of a business?
- What financial objectives should be formulated by business owners and managers?
- What types of decisions are usually faced by business managers?

Introduction

Financial management has undergone major changes in recent decades. Initially, finance consisted mainly of raising funds to purchase the assets needed by a business. This was understandable because, when finance emerged as an organizational function back in the 1920s, financial management focused almost exclusively on legal matters: acquisitions, corporate offerings, mergers, formation of new businesses, reorganizations, recapitalizations, bankruptcies, and business consolidations. Finance concentrated mostly on the external activities of a business, such as raising funds, rather than on internal activities, such as finding methods to allocate funds effectively within the business. Originally, activities such as cost accounting, credit and collection, budgeting, financial planning, financial accounting, and working capital management were not an important part of the manager's "tool kit." Only in the past several decades has attention been turned to developing analytical and decision-making techniques geared to assist managers in improving the effectiveness of their investing, operating, and financing decisions. Put simply, in the beginning, more attention was paid to administering the right-hand side of the balance sheet (raising funds from investors; that is, lenders and shareholders).

Today, although the management of the right-hand side of the balance sheet is still considered important, financial management has focused increasingly on the left-hand side of the balance sheet (finding ways to manage more efficiently all assets of a business, such as cash, accounts receivable, and inventories, and on improving the productivity of capital assets). Finance has assumed unprecedented importance as a management function. Today, improving a company's bottom line is a major managerial challenge. There are several reasons for this change in focus.

First, on the *economic front,* the recessions of the early 1980s and the early 1990s were considered by many economists as deeper and broader than any other downturns experienced since the Great Depression. As a result, the cost of operating businesses came under intense scrutiny. During the 1980s, managers began to realize that the North American economy was not only undergoing another shift in the business cycle, but that it had reached a certain level of maturity. Managers began to downsize their organizations in an effort to make them more efficient, responsive, and productive.

Second, on the *political side,* governments began to open their national borders and push industrial strategies to make their companies and industries leaders in world markets. The *North American Free Trade Agreement (NAFTA),* which took effect in 1994, forced managers to rethink their cost structure, improve their manufacturing capabilities, and sharpen their marketing strategies.

Third, with more global and open *world economies,* companies were forced to make structural changes to their organizations (removing organizational layers and introducing cross-functional teams and network organizations) in order to make them more responsive to market demand. For example, Wal-Mart has certainly changed the cost structure of many retailers by reducing prices.

Fourth, *technological changes* have compelled managers to alter their company's operations dramatically by producing new and/or better products or services, reducing their operating costs, modifying the size of their plants, and integrating operating activities. Technological change is taking place in all sectors of organizations. For example, the reengineering of manufacturing facilities have resulted in increased quality at reduced costs. The use of computers, the Internet, and company intranets have revolutionized the way workers gather information and communicate with each other. The Internet is increasing competition and, in some cases, lowering production costs.

Fifth, the *product life cycle* is now measured not in years, but in months. Whenever a company introduces a product or service into the market, "time risk," that is, the number of months or years it should take a company to recover its investment, has to be measured in order to determine an acceptable price structure.

Sixth, on the manufacturing side, managers not only had to find more innovative ways to produce their goods and provide services more efficiently, but had to be concerned about *quality objectives.* Many US firms have turned to total quality management and measuring the quality of their products and services against world standards. For example, getting certification from the *International Standards Organization* (ISO) enables a company to improve its chance of success in world markets.

All these changes put a strain on the company's profitability, or bottom line. When operating managers make investing, operating, and financing decisions, they have to gauge how these decisions affect their bottom lines.

What Is Financial Management?

Financial management ensures that a company uses its resources in the most *efficient* and *effective* way: maximizing the income generated by a business, which ultimately increases the value of a business (its net worth or shareholders' equity). What was called finance in the past is now referred to as **financial management**, reflecting the current emphasis on the importance of having *all* operating managers in a business participate in making important decisions that affect the financial destiny of their respective organizational units and the company as a whole.

Financial management deals with two things: first, *raising funds*, and second, *buying and utilizing assets* in order to earn the highest possible return. An important objective of financial management is to make sure that the assets used in business produce a return that is higher than the cost of borrowing. It would be pointless for a business to raise funds from investors at a cost of 10 percent and invest them in assets that generate only 7 percent. As shown in **Figure 1.1**, the objective of financial management is to ensure that the return on assets generated by a business (here, 15 percent) is higher than the cost of money borrowed from investors—that is, lenders and shareholders (here, 11 percent).

In the article, America's Wealth Creators[1], *Fortune* annually lists 200 companies as the largest wealth creators (out of a pool of 1,000 large companies). The 1999 ranking is based on market value added (MVA) defined as the difference between the amount of funds that capital investors have put into a company and the money that they can take out. The article also shows companies with the highest economic value added (EVA), which is defined as the after tax net operating profit minus the cost of capital. The following shows the five largest wealth creators measured by MVA.

FIGURE 1.1 Relationship between ROA and Cost of Financing

Balance Sheet

Assets	Investors
Return on Assets	Cost of financing
15%	11%

MVA Rank	Company	Market Value Added (million $)	Economic Value Added (million $)	Capital (million $)	Return on Capital	Cost of Capital
1	Microsoft	$328,257	$3,776	$10,954	56.2%	12.6%
2	General Electric	285,320	4,370	65,298	19.3	11.9
3	Intel	166,902	4,280	23,626	35.4	12.9
4	Wal-Mart Stores	159,444	1,159	36,188	13.2	9.8
5	Coca-Cola	157,536	2,194	13,311	31.2	11.2

Financial management, then, focuses on five important questions:

1. *How are we doing?* Managers, short- and long-term lenders, shareholders, suppliers, and so on want to know about a company's financial performance; Is the company profitable? What is the return on its investment? Is it efficient and keeping its costs under control? Is the company adding value to its shareholders? The company's scorecard, that is, financial statements are the documents that give answers to these questions.

2. *How much cash do we have on hand?* Knowing how much cash a company has on hand is important to determine its liquidity. Can it meet its payroll? Pay its suppliers on time? Service its debt? How much cash can be generated internally, that is, from operations within the next months or years? Managers must know how much cash the business has on hand and how much it will have in the future in order to determine how much it will want to borrow from external sources such as lenders and shareholders.

3. *What should we spend our funds on?* Money can be spent on (1) operating activities such as salaries, advertising, freight, supplies, and insurance. (2) Working capital assets such as inventories and accounts receivable, or (3) capital assets such as machinery and equipment. Managers must determine if its operating costs are efficient and whether the money that will be spent on capital assets for automation and expansion will generate a return that is higher than the cost of capital, and equally important, if it will compensate for the risk. Since money can be invested in different projects

bearing different risk levels, the return to be earned from various investments must show different economic values. The greater the risk, the greater must be the potential return.

4.   *Where will our funds come from?* Once managers have identified how much money the company needs and how much cash it now has on hand, they have to determine where the business can be obtained in the future. Should funds come from suppliers; bankers; or long-term investors such as shareholders, venture capitalists, or insurance companies?

5.   *How will the business be protected?* The most important responsibility of managers is to protect the investors' interests, while maximizing their share value (MVA). It is important to recognize that managers are employed by shareholders and should therefore act on their behalf. However, managers have to reconcile the legitimate and sometimes conflicting objectives of various interest groups such as unions, lenders, employees, customers, suppliers, communities, and government agencies. Since shareholders have a specific legal status, managers must ensure that their interests are not compromised.

Who Is Responsible for the Finance Function?

As shown in the organizational chart in **Figure 1.2**, finance activities are carried-out by three individuals or groups: the treasurer, the controller, and operating managers.

The **controller** establishes the accounting and financial reporting policies and procedures, maintains the accounting, auditing, and management control mechanisms, and analyzes financial results. Together with operating managers, the controller prepares annual budgets and financial plans and determines financial objectives and standards to ensure efficiency and adequate returns. This *controllership function* has to do with how funds are spent and invested to satisfy consumer needs and shareholder interests.

FIGURE 1.2   Responsibility of Financial Management

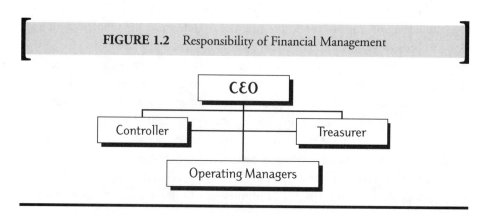

The **treasurer**—that is, the person responsible for raising funds—looks after investors, plans investment strategies, analyzes tax implications, and gauges the impact of internal and external events on a firm's capital structure, that is the relationship between long-term debt and shareholders' equity. The treasurer also regulates the flow of funds, determines dividend payments, recommends short- and long-term financing strategies, and cultivates relations with investors. In short, the treasurer is responsible for the accounts shown on the right (or liability and shareholders' equity) side of the balance.

Financial management is also practiced by *operating managers* (or line managers) in various organizational units such as marketing, manufacturing, research and development, and general administration. These managers are responsible for analyzing operating and financial data, making decisions about asset acquisitions, improving the operating performance of their respective organizational units and of the company as a whole. In some businesses all members of cross-functional teams have input into financial management decisions. In this book we will use operating managers to mean both groups unless otherwise stated.

Table 1.1 shows a list of typical activities of the finance function under the oversight of the controller (controllership functions) and the treasurer (treasury functions).

TABLE 1.1   The Finance Function

Functions of the Controller	Functions of the Treasurer
◆ General accounting	◆ Raising capital
◆ Cost accounting	◆ Investor relations
◆ Credit and collection	◆ Short-term financing
◆ Management information system	◆ Dividend and interest payments
◆ Accounts payable	◆ Insurance
◆ Corporate accounting	◆ Analysis of investment securities
◆ Internal auditing	◆ Retirement funds
◆ Budgets and analysis	◆ Property taxes
◆ Payroll	◆ Investment portfolio
◆ Systems and procedures	◆ Cash flow requirements
◆ Planning	◆ Actuarial
◆ Controlling	◆ Underwriting policy and manuals
◆ Interpreting financial reports	◆ Tax administration
◆ Evaluation and consultation	
◆ Preparing reports for government agencies	
◆ Preparing reports on capital assets	

Financial Objectives

The financial objectives of a firm include efficiency, liquidity, profitability, and stability. Each of these has a specific meaning in the world of finance.

Efficiency

Efficiency means the productivity of assets, that is, the relationship between profits generated and assets employed. The objective is to ensure that a company's assets are used efficiently and produce an acceptable rate of return. High profits satisfy investors and indicate that the assets of a business are working hard. The more profit a company earns, the more cash it can invest in the business to finance its growth and to purchase capital assets. For example, **Figure 1.3** shows a company that earns $0.08 on every dollar's worth of sales revenue, known as return on sales. Of this profit, $0.05 is reinvested in the business through retained earnings. With this money, the firm invests $0.02 in working capital such as accounts receivable and inventory (for day-to-day operating purposes) and $0.03 in capital assets to purchase equipment and machinery (for long-term growth purposes). The balance of the money ($0.03) can be used for external uses. In this example, the shareholders will receive $0.02 to compensate for their investment in the business, and $0.01 will be used to repay the principal on the debt. If, in the future, the return on sales declines, the company will have less internally generated funds to help its growth, to invest in capital assets, and to satisfy its shareholders.

Liquidity

Liquidity is a company's ability to meet its short-term financial commitments. If a business increases its sales, it will inevitably increase its working capital accounts such as inventory, accounts receivable, and cash required to pay its employees, suppliers, and creditors on time. (As shown in **Figure 1.3**, the amount of $0.02 is invested working capital accounts.) If a company wants to grow but shows a reduction in its return on sales performance, it will have less cash from internal opera-

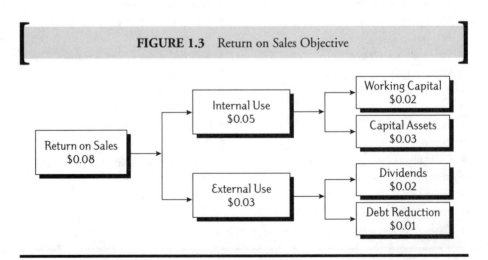

FIGURE 1.3   Return on Sales Objective

tions to invest in working capital accounts, and may have to rely on short-term borrowings in order to keep growing. Too much borrowing reduces a company's profit (because of interest charges) which further contributes to a reduction in return on sales.

Profitability

Profitability means growth in all segments of a business: sales volume, profits, dividend payments, capital assets, shareholders' equity, and working capital. If a company's return on sales deteriorates, it may not be able to generate the funds internally to finance its growth. Consequently, it would have difficulty investing in capital assets such as equipment and machinery in order to expand its operations and improve its productivity. (Recall that in **Figure 1.3**, an amount of $0.03 is invested in capital assets.) Again, if the company wants to invest in capital assets, it may have to borrow (if internally generated cash is not sufficient) from long-term lenders and shareholders to finance the purchase.

Stability

Stability refers to the financial structure of a business. Here, financial management ensures a balance between the funds provided by creditors and those provided by shareholders (relationship between debt and shareholders' equity). If a business continues to borrow from lenders, it may have a high debt to equity ratio and, as a result, may not be able to meet its short- and long-term debt obligations. If the company's return on sales is adequate, it will have enough cash to pay dividends to its shareholders and reduce the principal on its debt. (**Figure 1.3** shows $0.03 for external activities, $0.02 to pay dividends, and $0.01 to reduce the principal on the debt.) If the company does not produce an adequate return on sales, it may have to borrow more from lenders and consequently produce a negative effect on its stability.

The bottom line is this: If a company wants to maintain or improve its stability, it must never lose sight of the first objective, *earn a suitable return on sales.* If successful, profits (or retained earnings) can be used to increase its working capital, to purchase capital assets, to pay dividends, and to reduce its debt without relying too extensively on debt financing.

Business Decisions

Figure 1.4 shows the three types of decisions made by managers: investing decisions, financing decisions, and operating decisions.[2] For example, if managers want to invest $1.0 million in capital assets (*investing decisions*), the funds required to purchase these assets would come from two sources: internal and external. First, internal funds are generated by the business through operating decisions (income statement and improvement in the management of working capital accounts). Second, shareholders and lenders as a result of financing decisions provide external

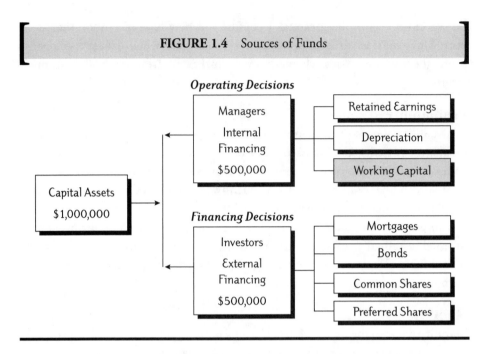

FIGURE 1.4   Sources of Funds

funds. As shown in the figure, if the company generates $500,000 from internal sources and obtains $500,000 from investors, the $1,000,000 in assets would be financed equitably.

The ideal situation is to finance, to the maximum, the purchase of capital assets with internally generated funds. For example, if the company purchases the $1.0 million in assets with $800,000 of internal funds, it would rely less on external funding and be able to enhance its financial stability.

Internal financing is obtained from retained earnings—that is, the profits generated by the business, depreciation and amortization that appear on the income statement as non-cash expenses—and by reducing working capital accounts such as accounts receivable and inventories. In **Figure 1.4**, the box representing working capital is shaded because managers can obtain funds only if they reduce accounts such as accounts receivable and inventory. An increase in these accounts would be considered a use or an application of funds. To illustrate, suppose that a plant manager wants to buy a $50,000 machine; this could be financed by a $50,000 reduction in inventory.

Figure 1.5 illustrates how the three types of business decisions appear on the balance sheet. On the left side are investments in current assets such as accounts receivable and inventories; capital assets such as buildings, machinery, and equipment; and other assets or intangible assets such as research and development, goodwill, and patents. Operating managers are responsible for these types investing decisions.

The right side of the balance sheet shows the **external financing** decisions related to the acquisition of funds from long-term lenders and shareholders.

Borrowing funds from investors is the responsibility of the chief executive officer (CEO), the chief financial officer (CFO), or the treasurer.

The center of the balance sheet shows to what extent operating decisions affect the balance sheet.[3] Operating decisions are the responsibility of all managers and include decisions that affect "every" account shown on the income statement. If managers make prudent operating decisions in marketing, manufacturing, production, administration, human resources, and so on, they will help generate higher profit levels and ultimately improve the return on sales. As mentioned earlier, higher income enables management to pay dividends and to reinvest the rest in the business through retained earnings (shareholders' equity).

Figure 1.5 also shows how the three types of business decisions affect a company's cash position. For instance, a decrease in the asset accounts (e.g., through selling an asset such as a truck or by reducing inventories) would be considered a source of funds. An increase in liability and equity accounts (through borrowing from banks or the injection of additional funds from shareholders) would also be considered a source. Income (or profit) generated by a business is also a source.

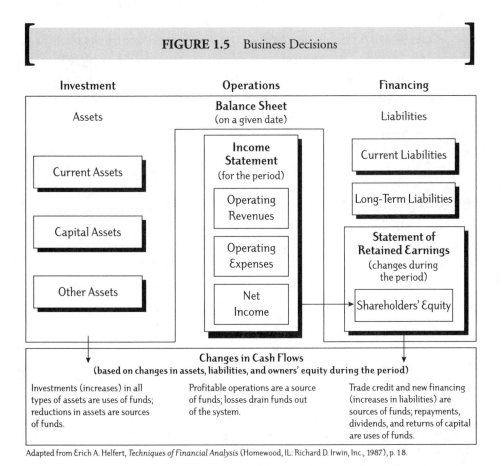

FIGURE 1.5   Business Decisions

Adapted from Erich A. Helfert, *Techniques of Financial Analysis* (Homewood, IL: Richard D. Irwin, Inc., 1987), p. 18.

This book will explore in detail these three types of business decisions. After studying the structure and analysis of financial statements in Chapters 2 and 3, we will discuss *investing decisions* in Chapters 6, 7, 10, and 11; *financing decisions* in Chapters 5 and 9; and *operating decisions* in Chapters 4 and 8.

Here is a brief overview of how these three types of business decisions can affect the financial performance (income statement) and financial structure (balance sheet) of a business.

Investing Decisions

As mentioned earlier, **investing decisions** deal with the accounts appearing on the left side of the balance sheet—that is, working capital accounts such as cash, accounts receivable, and inventory and capital assets such as machinery and equipment. As shown in **Figure 1.5**, investing decisions have an impact on a company's cash flow. Investing funds in working capital and capital assets reduces a company's cash position since it is considered a use of cash. However, a reduction in such assets, achieved by lowering inventory or accounts receivable or by selling unproductive capital assets, is a source of funds.

Let's now examine how current and capital asset decisions affect a company's cash flow performance.

Current Assets. Managing working capital means accelerating the movement of cash in a business. This movement of cash is referred to as the *cash conversion cycle*. The faster accounts receivable are collected or inventory is turned over, the more cash and profit a firm earns. Current assets are not productive assets, but they are necessary for a business to operate; it must sell on credit and carry a certain amount of inventory. However, it is necessary to determine the optimum amount of working capital that should be maintained. The faster working capital assets are transformed into cash, the faster the cash can be invested into more productive assets such as equipment and machinery.

Decisions related to managing cash determine the minimum level of cash that will satisfy business needs under normal operating conditions. Cash reserves (including marketable securities) should be sufficient to satisfy daily cash expenditures for such things as salaries, payments to suppliers, and payment of rent.

Cash reserve decisions are usually based on planning assumptions such as:

- The minimum level of cash balance required to meet on-going operating conditions.
- The amount necessary to absorb unforeseen expenditures.
- The level of cash required to take advantage of profitable business opportunities such as special discounts on purchases or anticipation of an increase in the price of raw materials.

It is important to keep cash at a minimum even when it is invested, it earns a relatively small return. It would therefore be more economically advantageous to invest excess cash into investment opportunities in order to earn a more attractive return.

Decisions related to accounts receivable deal with collecting receivables from customers as fast as possible. For example, if a business has slow-paying customers, management may decide to offer cash discounts off the original sale price to accelerate the cash flow and shorten the collection period. Before offering a discount, however, management will analyze the cost of offering the discount versus the interest earned as a result of receiving payment from the customers more quickly. Management needs to answer the following questions:

♦   What is the status of our accounts receivable (how many days are customers taking to pay)?
♦   What are the competitors' credit policies?
♦   How much will we lose in profit if we offer the discount?
♦   How much interest can be earned from the bank on the additional cash flow?

Let's take the example of a business that has $300,000 in accounts receivable on sales of $1,825,000 and is experiencing a 60-day average collection period. If management is able to reduce its receivables to 30 days, the company would have an extra $150,000 in cash that could be invested. If the investment yields 10 percent, the company can earn an extra $15,000 a year in profit. The following shows the calculation:

	Current Performance	Targeted Performance
Sales	$1,825,000	$1,825,000
Average daily sales (Sales ÷ 365)	$5,000	$5,000
Average collection period	60 days	30 days
Investment in accounts receivable ($5,000 × no. of days)	$300,000	$150,000
Reduction in accounts receivable	$150,000	
Incremental profit (@ 10%)	$ 15,000	

Decisions related to inventories deal with lowering the amount of raw materials, unfinished goods, and finished goods. Turning inventory rapidly can also improve a company's cash position and, ultimately, its profitability and return on investment. Several techniques can be used to make inventory decisions, including:

1. The *just-in-time inventory* management process, which is a supply system that attempts to reduce working inventories; and
2. The *economic ordering quantity* system, which determines the optimal number of units that should be ordered each time goods are purchased from suppliers.

As with managing accounts receivable, the intent is to invest as little as possible in inventory since it is also considered a non-productive asset.

To illustrate, let's take the example of a business that buys $1,000,000 a year in raw materials and supplies and holds $250,000 in inventory. This means that the company's inventory turns four times a year ($1,000,000 ÷ $250,000). If management can reduce its inventory to $200,000 (turnover of five times a year) by using the just-in-time approach or the economic ordering quantity technique, the company will benefit from an extra $50,000 in cash. If this amount is invested in securities earning 10 percent interest, the company would earn an additional $5,000 in profit. The following shows these calculation:

	Current performance	Targeted performance
Cost of goods sold	$1,000,000	$1,000,000
Inventory turnover	4 times	5 times
Inventory level	$ 250,000	$ 200,000
Reduction in inventory		$50,000
Incremental profit (@ 10%)		$ 5,000

Capital Assets. Decisions dealing with capital (or fixed) assets involve the purchase of equipment or machinery, and the more complicated decisions such as plant expansion, plant modernization to increase productivity, or investment in new facilities. These types of decisions are usually made during the capital budgeting exercise. Here, management must examine the relationship between the cash invested in such assets and the anticipated cash that can be generated in the future by these assets. For example, if someone invests $100,000 in US Savings Bonds and earns $10,000 in interest, the investor would earn 10 percent. The same applies when managers invest in capital assets. They want to measure two things: the expected return on assets and how the return compares to the cost of capital.

Here is an example of how investment decisions in capital assets are calculated. Let's say that a company invests $1.0 million in the following assets:

Land	$ 100,000
Buildings	400,000
Machinery & equipment	400,000
Working capital	100,000
Total investments	$1,000,000

Let's also assume that this investment produces $120,000 in after-tax profit each year. The following shows the calculation:

Sales revenue	$2,000,000
Cost of goods sold	1,200,000
Gross margin	800,000
Operating expenses	560,000
Profit before taxes	240,000
Income taxes	120,000
Profit after taxes	$ 120,000

Several capital budgeting techniques are used to gauge the economic desirability of such investments. For example, the return on assets calculation relates profit after taxes to investment in assets. It is calculated as follows:

$$\frac{\text{Profit after taxes}}{\text{Investment in assets}} = \frac{\$120,000}{\$1,000,000} = 12\%$$

This means that the $1.0 million investment generates a 12 percent after-tax return. Managers must also consider whether the investment is worth the risk. Before making a decision, they would determine the *cost of capital.* For example, if the company borrows the entire amount from lenders at an after-tax cost of 5 percent, the company would earn 7 percent more than the cost of borrowed funds.

The *project's risk* would also be considered. Managers would have to gauge whether a 12 percent return on this particular investment is worth the risk. If this investment was in the high-risk category, such as an investment in an untried product, management may want to earn at least 35 percent to 40 percent to justify the investment. However, if the project is low-risk, such as the expansion of an existing plant, it could require a much lower return on investment.

Financing Decisions

As shown in **Figure 1.5**, **financing decisions** deal with the accounts listed on the right side of the balance sheet—that is, funds borrowed from short-term and long-term lenders and provided by shareholders. Financing decisions examine the best way funds can be raised from investors (lenders and shareholders). Financing decisions deal with four elements: **matching principle**, sources and forms of financing, cost of financing, and financing mix.

The Matching Principle. Essentially, *matching* explores the selection of the most appropriate financing source when buying an asset. This means that short-term funds should be used to finance current assets while long-term funds should buy the more permanent assets such as capital assets. For example, it would not make much sense to buy a house on a credit card such as MasterCard or Visa! Simply put, the matching principle calls for relating the maturity of the sources of funds and the maturity of the uses of funds.

Sources and Forms of Financing. A business can obtain money from many sources and in different forms. *Sources* are institutions that provide funds and include commercial banks, investment bankers, equipment vendors, government agencies, private venture capital companies, suppliers, trust companies, life insurance companies, mortgage companies, individuals, and shareholders. *Forms* are the financing instruments used to buy the assets. They include short-term loans (secured or unsecured), term or installment loans, revolving loans, lease financing, mortgages, bonds, and preferred or common shares.

Cost of Borrowed Funds. Another important element in financing decisions is determining the cost of raising funds from different sources. This is critical because borrowed funds are used to purchase assets, and managers want to make sure that the *return generated by the assets exceeds the cost of capital.* Determining the cost of capital usually precedes the capital budgeting exercise.

In actual practice, the cost of capital deals with the more permanent forms of financing such as mortgages, bonds, and preferred and common shares. These are often called "capital funds;" thus, their cost is known as *cost of capital.* In the earlier example of a $1.0 million investment in capital assets, managers would have to determine the cost of each loan and the weighted cost of capital. For instance, if the business borrows $400,000 from a mortgage company at 12 percent, $300,000 from bondholders at 13 percent, and the rest ($300,000) from shareholders at 15 percent,[4] the composite weighted after-tax cost of capital would be 8.8 percent. Since interest charges on mortgage and bond financing are tax-deductible and the company is in a 50 percent tax bracket, such financing options are more attractive than shareholder financing since dividends are paid with after-tax profits. The calculation is as follows:

Sources	Amount ($)	Before-tax cost (%)	After-tax cost (%)	Proportion	Weighted cost of capital (%)
Mortgage	$ 400,000	12.0	6.0	.40	2.4
Bonds	300,000	13.0	6.5	.30	1.9
Shares	300,000	15.0	15.0	.30	4.5
Weighted cost of capital	$1,000,000			1.00	8.8

Financing Mix. Another important component of financing decisions is determining the proportion of funds that should be raised from lenders versus owners. As shown in the previous example, it would be advantageous to borrow as much as possible from lenders because it is the least expensive option (6.0 percent). However, since lenders do not want to take all the risks related to the investment decisions, they will insist that an appropriate amount of funds be provided by shareholders.

Equally important in financing decisions is a firm's ability to repay its debt obligation. If both the economy and the industry sectors are in a strong growth position, the company will generate healthy profits and be able to repay its loan without difficulty and borrow more funds from lenders rather than shareholders. However, if the economic indicators and the marketplace indicate slow growth, less money borrowed from lenders would be more advantageous and less risky.

Operating Decisions

As shown in **Figure 1.5**, **operating decisions** deal with the accounts appearing on the income statement such as sales revenue, cost of goods sold, and selling and administrative expenses. As shown in the figure, effective operating decisions improve net income, which in turn enhances a shareholders' equity position.

Profit can be improved in a number of ways. First, as discussed earlier, investment and financing decisions can have a positive impact on a company's profit performance. There is interplay between investing, financing, and operating decisions. Let's look at one example. If management decides to purchase a $50,000 forklift truck (investment decision) that will have a ten-year life span, the treasurer will have to determine how this truck will be financed (financing decision). Financing $30,000 of it by debt bearing a 10 percent interest charge and the rest through equity will reduce the company's before-tax profit by $8,000 (annual depreciation charge of $5,000 plus $3,000 in interest charges). This cost would have to be compared to any operating savings generated by the forklift truck.

Budgeting Techniques. Operating decisions can also increase a company's income in many ways. Some decisions cut across all organizational functions and activities affecting the income statement, such as improving employee productivity, reducing waste, and eliminating useless activities. The following paragraphs discuss budgeting approaches used by managers that can help improve profitability.

Demassing is a recession-driven technique that was widely used during the sharp economic downturn in early 1980. The purpose of this approach was to remove headquarters' staff and entire management layers and professional positions from organizational charts. Organizations were simply flattened. It has been reported that more than a third of US middle-management positions were eliminated in 1981–82 as a result of demassing exercises.

Planned downsizing is similar to demassing except that it is a more systematic way of cutting overhead costs. Guidelines used in planned downsizing include:

- matching organizational structure with strategies;
- pinpointing excess staff in the control and support organizational units;
- evaluating the effectiveness of staff performance;
- performing a zero-based evaluation by questioning everything;
- introducing norms and ratios such as allowing one staff position per 100 employees or maintaining computer-related expenses below 1 percent;
- using strategic concepts such as product life cycles and value added to determine staff size;
- enforcing sunset laws by closing down, decentralizing, or contracting out mature or aging activities before starting new ones; and
- flattening organizational pyramids by asking pertinent questions such as: How many management layers are really necessary? How many people can one manager manage? How can a manager's span of control be increased?

Productivity indicators are essential for measuring the performance of organizational units. It is often said that organizational units without clearly defined goals are difficult to manage. Productivity indicators must first be identified for each organizational unit before the units can be made more productive. If organizational efficiencies and effectiveness for the most important activities performed by managers and employees are measured and used as goals, they can improve productivity and ultimately the bottom line because:

- Productivity is more likely to improve when expected results are measured.
- Productivity increases rapidly when expected benefits are shared with those who will produce them.
- The greater the alignment of employee expectations (needs) with organizational objectives (targets), the greater the motivation to accomplish both.

- When productivity objectives are placed on a time scale, there is a greater likelihood of achieving the objectives.

Rewarding simplification instead of needless complication can also produce positive financial effects. For example, some years ago, Sir Simon Marks, Chairman of the Board of Marks and Spencer of Britain, began questioning the work of individual employees within his stores and found that numerous bureaucratic and seemingly meaningless tasks were being done. He then led a campaign to simplify work procedures and to reduce the volume of bureaucratic forms. At the conclusion of his major reorganization, it was estimated that more than 22 million forms weighing more than 100 tons had been eliminated. As a result, he was able to improve the bottom line by millions of dollars.

Cutting back useless activities and replacing them with productive work adds value to financial statements. For instance, the Dallas-based oil and gas producer Oryx is estimated to have saved $70 million in operating costs by eliminating rules, procedures, reviews, reports, and approvals that had little to do with the company's real objective of finding more hydrocarbons.

Rewarding quality work instead of fast work can also increase operating margins and the bottom line. Doing work too quickly and too cheaply often inadvertently becomes costly because quality suffers. Several of the payoffs of improving quality include lower costs, increased productivity, worker pride, and customer loyalty. At H.J. Heinz, for example, the managers became acolytes of the Philip Crosby tome *Quality Is Free*, which states that by making things right the *first time* you save money on inspection, wastage, and rework. At one Heinz plant in Puerto Rico, production lines were slowed down, 400 hourly workers and 15 supervisors were hired, and the entire workforce was retrained. Four more lines were installed to take some of the load off each worker and to increase volume. All told, the plant increased labor costs by $5 million but cut out $15 million in waste for a net savings of $10 million annually.

Empowering workers through team building and communication can also produce synergistic effects on a company's operating performance. Empowerment is more than a trendy slogan; it has produced positive financial results. Working in teams creates a great sense of interdependence. Some plants have increased productivity substantially just by giving workers the option to decide how to perform their work. Workers learned to inspect their own work, management listened more actively to their suggestions, and employee dignity was greatly elevated.

Organizational Units. Some costs on the income statement touch on specific organizational units such as marketing, production, engineering, human resources, and administration. These organizational units are sometimes referred to as revenue centers, cost centers, profit centers, or investment centers. Specific operating decisions affecting these types of units also have positive effects on profitability at three profit levels: gross margin, operating income, and income after taxes.

Gross margin. Decisions that affect the gross margin are the revenue and cost of goods sold accounts. *Revenue* is made up of decisions affecting output (number of units) and selling price. Decisions that have to do with the marketing variables determine, to a large extent, sales output and market share performance. Effective marketing decisions can improve a company's sales performance and, ultimately, its revenue. There are a number of ways management can determine the most appropriate selling price. These are mark-up percentages, cost-plus pricing, suggested retail price, psychological pricing, discounts, price lining, and geographic pricing policies.

For manufacturing businesses, cost of goods sold represents a substantial percentage (as much as 80 percent) of a company's total expenses. For this reason, a great deal of attention is devoted to making a company's manufacturing operations more efficient by modernizing its plants (mechanization or automation), reducing waste, improving employee morale, and empowering workers.

Operating income. Decisions affecting operating income are found in two categories of expenses: selling and administration. Many of the operating budgeting techniques explained earlier, such as planned downsizing, cutting useless activities, and empowering workers, are examples of how profit can be improved. In the past, incremental or traditional budgeting was used to prepare budgets. To justify the amount of budget or funds to be allocated, input-oriented budgeting techniques (emphasis on activities and functions or on objects of expenditures such as salaries, telephone, travel, and training) were frequently used. Today, more businesses are using results-oriented budgeting techniques in which productivity measures or some form of standards are applied to help justify and approve budget proposals. When preparing operating budgets, two broad operating decisions are often explored: economy and levels of service.

These types of decisions deal with *cost–benefit analysis* and the focus is on doing a job in the most economical manner. Here are some common issues relating to such decisions: Should we have this activity or job done by our staff or should it be contracted outside? Should we lease or buy this equipment? Should we automate our office? Should we rearrange the workflow?

Zero-based budgeting, popularized in the early 1970s, places the burden on managers to justify their budgets. Today, we talk about reengineering and activity-based budgeting. This budgeting process calls for identifying different *levels of service* that can be offered by overhead units such as finance, human resources, engineering, accounting, and administration and pinpointing a cost for each. When unit managers have identified each level of service, they are in a much better position to identify the cost of each. This approach makes it easier for management to link budget proposals to corporate priorities and objectives.

Income after taxes. Other accounts that affect the income after taxes are interest earned and interest charges. The treasurer has the primary responsibility for making decisions regarding the most appropriate sources and forms of financing and investing funds in investment securities that offer the highest yield.

Finance for the Nonfinancial Manager

People often think of finance as a function performed by accountants, book-keepers, treasurers, controllers, or financial analysts. Although these people play a key role in financial management and the financial planning process, *all managers* are really financial managers, because every business decision made by them affects, directly or indirectly, the financial performance of their organizations.

It is important that all managers responsible for resources or budgets become familiar with the language of finance and with the different tools available for analyzing business performance and for making business decisions. A manager who lacks these skills will not be in a position to contribute fully and effectively to improving the operational and financial performance of his or her responsibility center and that of the organization.

By becoming familiar with the language and concepts of finance and being able to use financial tools, such as capital budgeting techniques, ratio analysis, operational and financial break-even analysis, cost-benefit analysis, and reading financial statements, a manager will be in a better position to improve his or her decisions and to communicate more effectively with other members of the organization.

Understanding finance also helps managers become more disciplined, because it can force them to express their plans in *measurable terms* and to assess the impact their decisions have on the financial well-being of the firm. Managers, who make an effort to understand the language of finance, and make a point of using financial concepts and techniques, will increase their effectiveness.

Decision-Making in Action

The management committee of Flint Ltd. is considering investing $1.0 million in capital assets for expansion purposes, and an additional $200,000 for working capital requirements (i.e., accounts receivable, inventory). Currently, the profit after taxes generated by the company is $500,000 which represents a 5 percent return on sales of $10.0 million. The investment proposal was presented to the board of directors for consideration and approval.

To finance the $1.2 million investment, Flint's CFO explained that a certain portion of the expansion would be financed by internal sources. He indicated that (1) the sales revenue for the budget year would show a 10 percent increase over the current year, and that (2) the return on sales (as a result of cost cutting activities particularly in manufacturing) would be increased to 7 percent. He also indicated that the allowance for depreciation would be $50,000.

The CFO explained that the profit was to be allocated as follows:

- Sixty percent (60%) for internal use; half of the funds would be allocated towards working capital and the rest on the new capital project.
- Forty percent (40%) would be used for external purposes of which 60 percent would be used to pay dividends and the rest, to reduce the principal on the debt.

Based on the feasibility study prepared by the controller's department, he explained that the capital expansion would generate $200,000 a year in profit after taxes (income tax rate is at 50 percent). However, in order to finance the purchase of these assets, he would have to raise capital funds from a lending institution at a cost estimated at 10 percent (before tax). The shareholders were prepared to invest $200,000 towards the capital project and that an amount of $100,000 would be obtained from the bank for financing the working capital requirements. The shareholders are looking for at least a 12 percent return on their investment.

The members of the board of directors indicated that if the project generated 15 percent, they would consider approving it. However, before giving the go ahead, they wanted answers to the following questions:

Question 1: How much cash would be generated internally (operating activities)?

Question 2: How much cash would have to be raised from external sources (financing activities)?

Question 3: How would the return on assets (investing activities) compare to the cost of capital (financing activities)?

The CFO provided the following explanation to these questions:

1. An amount of **$462,000** would be generated internally based on the following:

   - Sales revenue for the budget year will be $11,000,000 (a 10 percent increase over the current year);
   - A 7 percent return on sales would generate $770,000 in profit after taxes;
   - Of the profit, 60 percent, or $462,000, would be reinvested in the business in the form of retained earnings and the remaining 40 percent, or $308,000, would be used externally. This means that $184,800 (or 60 percent), would be used for the payment of dividends and $123,200 (or 40 percent) for the payment of the debt.

2. External financing would be as follows: **$200,000 from shareholders and $388,000 from long-term lenders**. The following shows the calculation.

   a. Funds generated from operating activities:

After tax profit		+ $ 462,000
Depreciation		+ 50,000
Subtotal		+ 512,000
Working capital requirements	− $200,000	
Working capital loan	+ 100,000	− 100,000
Funds generated from operating activities		+ $ 412,000

   b. Investing activities

Capital assets	− $1,000,000
Shortfall	− $ 588,000

   c. Financing activities

Shareholders	+ $200,000	
Long-term debt	+ $388,000	+ $ 588,000
Net difference		$ 0

3. **Return on assets is 16.7 percent and the cost of capital is 7.38 percent.** The calculations are as follows:

   a. Return on assets:

   $$\frac{\text{Profit}}{\text{Total assets}} = \frac{\$200,000}{\$1,200,000} = 16.7\%$$

   b. Cost of capital

Source	Amount	Proportion	After-tax cost	Weighted Cost
Owners' equity	$200,000	.34	12.0%	4.08%
Long-term debt	388,000	.66	5.0	3.30
Total capital raised	$588,000	1.00		7.38%

   The board of directors would probably approve the project for the following reasons:

   1. The project's return on assets compared to the cost of capital is favorable (16.7 percent compared to 7.38 percent).

   2. The project's return on assets exceeds the board's expectations (16.7 percent return on assets compared to 15 percent return on investment).

   3. The project would be financed in the following way:
      - 41 percent ($412,000) from internal funds and 59 percent ($588,000) from external funds (shareholders and long-term lenders).
      - 41 percent of the total debt raised to finance the project would amount to only $488,000 (a $100,000 short-term loan and a $388,000 long-term loan) while 59 percent or $712,000 would be funded by ownership interest ($512,000 provided from cash flow from operations and $200,000 from the shareholders).

Summary

The role of financial management is not limited to raising capital dollars; it also extends to finding ways to use funds more effectively within a business. The main factors that have contributed to making financial management critical include global competition, shorter product life cycles, and technological advancement.

Financial management focuses on four basic objectives: *efficiency* (productivity of assets); *liquidity* (ability to meet current debt obligations); *profitability* (improvement of the financial health of the business); and *stability* (appropriate balance between the funds provided by the owners and the creditors).

The finance functions are usually divided between the controller, who is responsible for the internal financial activities of a business, and the treasurer, who is responsible for the external financial activities. If financial management is to be effective, financial activities should also be performed by operating managers.

Business decisions can be grouped under three broad categories: investing decisions, financing decisions, and operating decisions.

Investing decisions deal with the accounts appearing on the left side of the balance sheet, that is, the management of the working capital accounts such as cash, accounts receivable, and inventory and the acquisition of capital assets such as equipment. Investing decisions have an impact on a company's funds flow. Investments in working capital or in capital assets are a drain on a company's cash position. However, reductions in such assets, achieved by either reducing inventory or accounts receivable or selling unproductive capital assets, are sources of funds.

Financing decisions deal with the accounts appearing on the right side of the balance sheet: funds borrowed from short-term and long-term lenders and provided by shareholders. Financing decisions look at the best way to raise funds from different investors.

Operating decisions deal with the accounts appearing on the income statement, such as revenue, cost of goods sold, and selling and administration expenses. Effective operating decisions can only improve net income and in turn, enhance a firm's equity position and return on investment.

CHAPTER 2

From Scorekeeping to Financial Statements

*A*fter their discussion with Bill Murray, Len and Joan Edwards did some additional homework in light of Bill's comments. They felt that Bill's advice about pinpointing operational and financial objectives was critical for formulating operational plans that would help them succeed.

They also felt that it was important for them to learn how to set up a bookkeeping and accounting system. They knew that relevant and timely information was critical for analyzing all aspects of their retail operations and for making key decisions. They asked Bill Murray if he knew an accountant. He suggested Mary Ogaki, an accountant with a professional designation, CPA, and experience in counseling small businesses.

Len contacted Mary to set up an appointment. During their first meeting, Len and Joan indicated to Mary that they were looking for an integrated information system that would provide them with different types of operational and financial data. They would need a cash register that could generate reports about their sales, purchases, inventory, costs, and so on. Len made the following comments:

> "As far as I'm concerned, the cash register should be considered the most important instrument in our business. It should provide us with operational daily, weekly, and monthly data. Anything that we buy and sell should be entered in the cash register. With a good software program integrated to our cash register, we should be able to know exactly what product is moving and when, the amount of inventory we have in stock at all times, when we should be ordering goods from suppliers, how much profit we make on each product

line, how many sales each salesperson in the store makes, and so on. In addition, we need an accounting software program that could provide us with financial statements such as the balance sheet, the income statement, and the statement of cash flows. This software should also help us prepare our monthly operating budget."

Mary Ogaki was impressed with the kind of information that they were looking for. With regards to the accounting software, she indicated that accounting software programs available on the market would provide them with the type of financial information that they were looking for. Mary indicated that she would be prepared to investigate this matter further and meet with them to recommend specifically, on the basis of their requirements, the type of programs and reports they should get.

However, before leaving, Mary asked Len and Joan to think about the type of accounts or ledgers that they would like to see on their financial statements. As Mary pointed out, "this is the first step that you have to go through in the bookkeeping and accounting process. Once you know the information that you want to analyze and help you to make your decisions, it will be easy for me to determine the type of operational and financial reports that should produced".

Mary also recommended that they should take a basic course in accounting just to be familiar with some of the fundamentals of accounting and financial terms and concepts. She indicated that although it was important for them to have an accountant prepare their financial statements yearly for income tax purposes, they should be able to read and analyze their own financial statements. Just like a pilot who reads instruments in his aircraft, owners and managers of any business should be able to understand and interpret their own financial statements. This point simply validated what Bill Murray told them during their first meeting.

This chapter examines in detail some of the points made by Mary Ogaki. In particular, it focuses on three key topics:

- The more important accounting terms and concepts.
- The key steps involved in the bookkeeping and accounting process.
- The information that should be included in financial statements.

Introduction

Managers, owners, lenders, investors and short-term creditors want to know the financial health of the firm. At times, they want to analyze reports (or scorecards) that summarize the financial condition of the business. The financial performance is presented in a report called the *income statement,* also known as "statement of operations," "profit and loss statement" and "statement of earnings." The financial structure of a business is presented in another report called the *balance sheet,* also referred to as the "statement of financial condition" or "statement of financial position."

The term **financial statements** is generally used to reflect the fact that several financial reports such as the balance sheet, the income statement, the statement of retained earnings, and the statement of cash flows are included in annual reports. This chapter examines the meaning of these financial statements, what they contain, and their structure.

Accounting is considered the language of business; it is used to present financial information about business activities. It shows the results of managerial decisions dealing with all segments of a business such as marketing, manufacturing, administration, engineering, human resources, and distribution. Accounting is the methodology that gives data about the financial structure and financial performance of a business.

Every day, hundreds or even thousands of activities take place in a business: goods are sold on a cash or credit basis; materials are purchased; salaries, rent, and utility bills are paid; customers pay their accounts; and payments are made for goods previously purchased. If managers want to know, on a daily, monthly, or yearly basis, the financial results of all these transactions, they must have them collected and recorded in a logical and methodical manner. For example, if managers want to know:

- The profit position of their business, they will refer to the *income statement.*
- How much the business owns or owes, they will refer to the *balance sheet.*
- How much money the business has accumulated and the amount of dividends that was paid to their shareholders this year, they will look at the *statement of retained earnings.*
- How much cash was generated or used by different organizational functions of the business, they will look at the *statement of cash flows.*

These reports give financial results of all transactions that have taken place in a business between two calendar dates, also known as accounting periods, or fiscal periods.

Managers who want to know how their business performed in the past, how it is doing now, and what decisions they should make to improve its financial position must refer to a variety of reports. For example, they will refer to the *operational reports,* produced by a management information system, and the *financial reports,* produced by bookkeeping and accounting systems. This chapter gives an overview of the methodology used by accountants for preparing these financial statements. The ultimate objective of financial management is to help managers *analyze* financial statements and to make sound financial decisions.

Financial management embraces four broad activities: bookkeeping, accounting, analysis, and decision-making. Let's briefly examine each of these activities.

Bookkeeping involves collecting, classifying, and recording information that arises from the multitude of transactions taking place in a business. As will be discussed later in this chapter, these transactions are first recorded in books of original entry known as *journals* and are subsequently recorded in books of final entry known as *ledgers*.

Accounting is the activity that arranges the information into separate and distinct financial statements, such as the balance sheet and the income statement. Since these financial statements are structured in a standardized format, they can be easily read, understood, and analyzed. For instance, if you want to know what a business owns, you look at the asset component of the balance sheet; if you want to know how much a business owes and the nature of its liabilities, you look at the liability and shareholders' components of the balance sheet. These financial statements are prepared on the basis of *generally accepted accounting principles* (GAAP). Accounting is a profession, with certain requirements and standards of education, accreditation, and conduct. In order to measure the financial affairs of a business, accountants have to follow established rules, procedures, and standards. These rules govern how accountants measure, process, and communicate financial information.

Analysis consists of interpreting financial statements. The data presented on the financial statements should be considered not merely as statistics, but as information that should be examined carefully to see how well (or poorly) a business is doing. For example, the reader may want to know about a company's:

- Profit position. (How much profit is the company generating? What is the ROA?)
- Accounts receivable and inventories. (Are they at reasonable levels?)
- Relationship between the current assets and current debts. (Is it acceptable?)
- Long-term debt. (Is it in line with the amount of money the owners have put into the business?).

Finally, there is *decision-making*. It is not enough to record, arrange, and analyze data. To make decisions to improve the financial performance and financial structure of their businesses, managers must use financial information. For example, the information will help to:

- Set the right price.
- Establish the most appropriate credit policy.
- Maintain an optimal inventory level.
- Assess the financial viability of capital investments for new plants or the expansion or modernization of existing ones.
- Determine the most appropriate source of funds needed to finance their operations.

This chapter discusses bookkeeping and accounting; financial statement analysis and decision-making will be examined in later chapters.

The Bookkeeping and Accounting Process

Managers need information to plan and to control their operations. Once managers have formulated their operational and financial objectives and prepared their strategic and operational plans, management implements the plans and compares performance with projections.

Operating and financial data that are presented clearly and logically make it easy for managers to review and analyze performance and to make decisions to solve problems or take advantage of opportunities. The planning and controlling management functions cannot be performed effectively if managers are deprived of such basic operational and financial information. Therefore, the purpose of bookkeeping and accounting activities is to make sure that managers are provided with the *right kind* of information at the *right time*.

Let's first examine the activities involved in bookkeeping and accounting. As shown in **Figure 2.1**, *bookkeeping* is the clerical activity aimed at systematically recording financial transactions incurred by a business, on a day-by-day basis, in sets of books known as journals and ledgers. *Accounting*, on the other hand, involves the preparation of financial statements such as the income statement, the statement of retained earnings, the balance sheet, and the statement of cash flows. Accounting is a more specialized, creative, and comprehensive activity because accountants must present data in financial statements to inform managers, creditors, shareholders, and government agencies about the financial performance of a business.

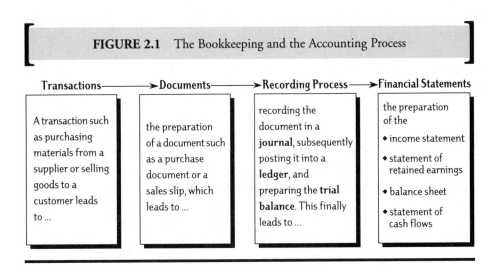

FIGURE 2.1 The Bookkeeping and the Accounting Process

Transactions ──────→ Documents ──────→ Recording Process ──────→ Financial Statements

A transaction such as purchasing materials from a supplier or selling goods to a customer leads to ...	the preparation of a document such as a purchase document or a sales slip, which leads to ...	recording the document in a **journal**, subsequently posting it into a **ledger**, and preparing the **trial balance**. This finally leads to ...	the preparation of the ◆ income statement ◆ statement of retained earnings ◆ balance sheet ◆ statement of cash flows

Bookkeeping

Bookkeepers use a **chart of accounts**, which establishes the categories a business uses to record transactions. It is much like the accounts that an individual has at home such as: bank book, car, house, trailer, Visa, clothing, food, insurance, salary, vacations, etc. The number of accounts that a business sets up depends largely on the needs and desires of management.

Bookkeeping involves collecting, classifying, and reporting transactions taking place each day in different departments of a business. Some transactions take place in the sales department, others in the accounts receivable department or manufacturing plant. All business transactions are recorded under five major groupings or *accounts*:

◆   *Assets*, what a business owns.
◆   *Liabilities*, what it owes to creditors.
◆   *Equity*, the amount of assets owned by shareholders.
◆   *Revenue*, amounts earned as a result of selling its goods or services.
◆   *Expenses*, costs to produce and sell its goods or services.

The Accounting Equation

To understand how the accounting system works, it is important to see the interplay between these five types of accounts. Each time a business transaction takes place, at least two accounts are affected. This is referred to as **double-entry accounting**. For example, when a business buys a truck with borrowed funds from a banker, both an asset and a liability account are affected. If a business pays its mortgage with cash, both its asset and liability accounts are also affected. If shareholders invest money in a business and the funds are used to buy a truck, two accounts are also affected, assets and equity.

In its simplest form, the financial picture of a business can be expressed by the following equation, referred to as the **accounting equation**:

$$\text{Assets} = \text{Liabilities} + \text{Equity}$$

It can also be expressed in the following way:

$$\text{Assets} - \text{Liabilities} = \text{Equity}$$

For the moment, we'll assume that both the revenue and the expense accounts are part of the equity account. Let's examine several transactions to see how this equation works. If a person invests $100,000 in a start-up operation, this money would first be deposited in a bank account and the business owner would own all of the assets. After this first transaction, the financial position of the business would be as follows:

Assets	=	Liabilities	+	Equity
$100,000	=	$ 0	+	$100,000

Let's assume that the next day the business buys a $30,000 truck and pays $10,000 in cash and borrows $20,000 from the bank. This means that the company would increase its asset accounts to $120,000 (the truck account would show an increase of $30,000 and the bank account would be reduced by $10,000, down to $90,000); the business would also owe $20,000 to a creditor (the bank). After this second transaction, the accounting equation would read as follows:

Assets	=	Liabilities	+	Equity
$120,000	=	$20,000	+	$100,000

In recording business transactions, bookkeepers use the rules of debit and credit. There are some very basic rules that determine whether an account should be debited or credited. These rules can be summarized as follows:

	Assets	=	**Liabilities**	+	**Equity**
Debit	Increases		Decreases		Decreases
Credit	Decreases		Increases		Increases

There are two types of accounts that determine whether a business finds itself in a profit or a loss situation: revenues and expenses. These accounts affect equity. Equity increases if a business makes a profit and decreases if a business incurs a loss. Any change in the revenue and expense accounts also affects the accounting equation. For example, if a business sells $1,000 worth of goods for cash, its financial worth—that is, the equity account (through the revenue account)—increases by $1,000; the company is "wealthier" by that amount. Assets increase by the same amount. In order to produce the goods it sells, raw materials have to be purchased from suppliers and expenses such as salaries have to be paid to employees. If the purchase of raw materials amounts to $700 and the payment for salaries is $100, it means that the company took $800 from its bank account (asset) and reduced its financial worth or equity (through the expense accounts) by the same amount. The effect of these transactions on the financial position of the business would be as follows:

Assets	=	Liabilities	+	Equity
$120,000	=	$20,000	+	$100,000
+ 1,000	=	—	+	1,000
121,000	=	20,000	+	101,000
− 800		—		− 800
120,200	=	20,000	+	100,200

Notice that the equation is always in balance. The rules of debit and credit also extend to the revenue and expense accounts. They apply to revenue and expenses as follows:

	Revenues	**Expenses**
Debit	Decreases	Increases
Credit	Increases	Decreases

As shown in **Figure 2.2**, a credit in equity or revenue accounts increases the wealth of a business. Conversely, a debit in the expense or equity accounts reduces the wealth of a business.

The Accounting Cycle

There are several steps involved from the time that a transaction is processed in a business to the time that it is reported in one of the financial statements. This bookkeeping and **accounting cycle** includes five steps.

Step 1: The first step is a business *transaction* (e.g., investing money in a business, buying a truck, selling goods, paying salaries).

Step 2: Each transaction is accompanied by a *document* (e.g., a deposit slip from the bank, a sales slip, a purchase document, a check stub).

Step 3: Through the bookkeeping system, each transaction is recorded in a journal. As indicated earlier, each business transaction affects at least two accounts. In the double-entry accounting system, all accounts must always be in balance, and an arithmetic error is automatically identified by a lack of balance. Each transaction has a debit and credit part. The word **debit** refers to the left side of an account; the word **credit**, to the right side. As shown in **Figure 2.2**, at the end of an accounting period, the asset and expense accounts have *debit balances* and the liability, equity, and revenue accounts have *credit balances.*

To illustrate, here is how the previously mentioned bookkeeping transactions would be debited and credited in their respective accounts.

A debit takes place when there is:

1. An increase in an asset account (e.g., a deposit of $100,000 in the bank account or the acquisition of a $30,000 truck).

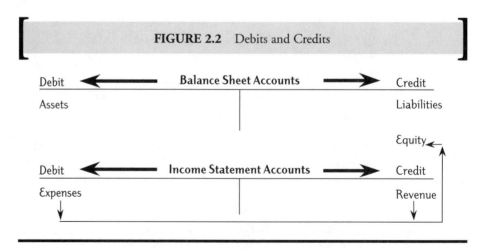

FIGURE 2.2   Debits and Credits

2. A decrease in a liability or equity account.
3. A decrease in a revenue account.
4. An increase in an expense account (e.g., purchase of $700 worth of materials and payment of $100 in salaries).

A credit takes place when there is:

1. A decrease in an asset account (e.g., withdrawal of $10,000 from the bank).
2. An increase in a liability or equity account (e.g., borrowing $20,000 from the bank).
3. An increase in a revenue account (e.g., selling $1,000 worth of goods).
4. A decrease in an expense account.

Transactions are first recorded in *journals*, which are sometimes referred to as the books of original entry. Bookkeepers record transactions in journals in chronological order—that is, as they happen. **Table 2.1** shows how the journal entries of the four transactions mentioned previously would be recorded. The process of recording transactions in the journal is called **journalizing**. As shown in the table, the total of all debit entries amounts to $131,800, which equals the sum of all credit entries.

Step 4: The fourth step in the process is to transfer the amounts recorded in the journals into *ledgers*. Journals do not show the outstanding balance of each account after each transaction has been recorded. For this purpose, a second set of books called ledgers is created. A ledger is very much like a checkbook register. It shows all amounts debited and credited in each account and includes a running balance.

TABLE 2.1 The Journals

		Dr.	Cr.
Transaction 1	Cash	$100,000	
	Equity		$100,000
Transaction 2	Truck	$ 30,000	
	Cash		$ 10,000
	Bank loan		$ 20,000
Transaction 3	Cash	$ 1,000	
	Revenue		$ 1,000
Transaction 4	Purchases	$ 700	
	Salaries	$ 100	
	Cash		$ 800
Total		$ 131,800	$ 131,800

Ledgers are known as books of final entry. All transactions recorded in journals are subsequently transferred to the appropriate ledger accounts; this process is called **posting**. Ledgers provide a running balance for each account. **Figure 2.3** shows how each of the four journal transactions mentioned previously would be posted in their respective ledgers. The ledgers here are shown in the form of T-accounts.[1] Ledger accounts are usually given a number to facilitate the process of recording the transactions, whether the recording is done manually or electronically.

Step 5: The fifth and final step in the bookkeeping and accounting cycle is called "closing the books." It is done at the end of an accounting period (i.e., the end of a month or the end of a fiscal year). To ensure that all transactions recorded during the period are error-free—that is, the sum of all debits equals the sum of all credits—the outstanding account balances are listed under the appropriate column in the **trial balance**.

As shown in **Table 2.2**, the trial balance is done by listing, in parallel columns, the accounts with debit balances and the accounts with credit balances. Once this has been done, the debit and credit columns of the trial balance are added. If the debit column equals the credit column, it means that there should be

FIGURE 2.3   The Ledgers

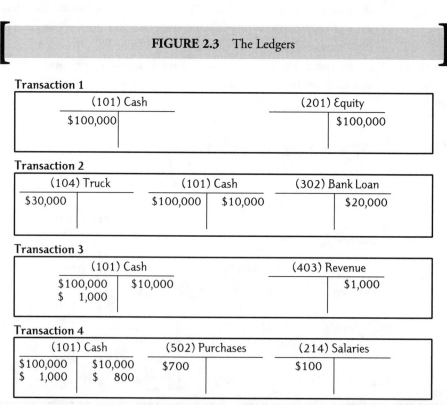

TABLE 2.2   The Trial Balance

	Debit	Credit
Cash	$ 90,200	
Truck	30,000	
Bank loan		$ 20,000
Equity		100,000
Sales revenue		1,000
Purchases	700	
Salaries	100	
Total	$ 121,000	$ 121,000

---

no arithmetical errors; all accounts are in balance. Since the ledger accounts are used to prepare the financial statements, the trial balance is taken before the statements are prepared.

Identifying Errors

Some of the most common errors that will cause inequality in trial balance totals are:

- One of the columns of the trial balance was added incorrectly.
- One amount of an account balance was improperly recorded on the trial balance.
- A debit balance was recorded on the trial balance as a credit (or vice versa).
- An account was omitted from the trial balance.
- One side of an account was computed incorrectly.
- An erroneous amount was posted as a debit or as a credit in an account.
- A debit entry was recorded as a credit, or vice versa.
- A debit or a credit entry was omitted.

Some errors will not result in an inequality on the trial balance, including:

- Failure to record an entire transaction.
- Recording the same erroneous amount for both the debit and the credit.
- Recording the same transaction more than once.
- Recording one part of a transaction in the wrong account.

Accounting

The function of **accounting** governs the way the four financial statements shown in **Figure 2.4** are prepared. The *American Institute of Certified Public Accountants* (AICPA) provides some **generally accepted accounting principles (GAAP)** regarding the way in which the accounts should be presented on the income

FIGURE 2.4   The Financial Statements

The Income Statement

Sales revenue − Cost of goods sold 1. = Gross Margin
− Selling and general expenses 2. = Operating income
− Interest expenses + Other revenue 3. = Income before taxes
− Income taxes 4. = Income after taxes

The Statement of Retained Earnings

1. Retained Earnings (Beginning Balance)
2. + Current-Year Earnings 3. − Dividends
4. = Retained Earnings (Ending Balance)

The Balance Sheet

1. Current Assets	4. Current Liabilities
2. Capital Assets	5. Long-Term Debts
3. Intangible Assets	6. Equity

The Statement of Cash Flows

1. Operating Activities
2. Financing Activities
3. Investing Activities
4. Cash Balance

statement, the statement of retained earnings, the balance sheet, and the statement of cash flows.

The **income statement** is much like a "moving picture." It shows the flow of revenues and expenses incurred by a business during a given period (e.g., one month or one year). As shown in **Figure 2.4**, the income statement shows income (profit[2]) at four levels.

- The first level is *gross margin*, which is calculated by deducting the cost of producing or obtaining the goods sold from sales revenue.
- The second level is *operating income*, which is calculated by deducting operating expenses such as selling and administrative expenses from the gross margin.
- The third level, *income before taxes*, is calculated by adding other revenue to the operating income, and by deducting other charges from this balance.
- The fourth level is the **income after taxes**. It is also often referred to as the "owners' section," since income after taxes actually belongs to the shareholders, to be paid in dividends or to be retained in the business for reinvestment purposes or for reducing debt.

As shown in **Figure 2.4**, the **statement of retained earnings** shows the amount of income retained in a business since it was started. It also identifies the income earned and dividends paid during a current operating year, and the amount of earnings remaining in the business at the end of the period.

The **balance sheet** is a "snapshot" of a company's financial position or financial condition. As shown in **Figure 2.4**, this statement is divided into six sections. The left side shows what the business owns, or its assets. Asset accounts are grouped under three headings.

* *Current assets* are accounts that are more liquid or can be converted into cash quickly (e.g., accounts receivable, inventory, marketable securities, and prepaid expenses).
* *Capital assets* (also referred to as fixed or plant assets) include accounts such as land, buildings, machinery, and equipment, which are not liquid and are used by the business over an extended period of time.
* *Intangible assets*, such as goodwill and patents, may also appear on the asset side of the balance sheet.

The right side shows what a business owes to its creditors (lenders) and what the shareholders (owners) own. Liabilities are also grouped under two headings.

* *Current liabilities* are loans that come due within a 12-month period and include accounts such as accounts payable, term loans, and accrued expenses.
* *Long-term debts* such as long-term loans, bonds, and mortgages are loans that are to be paid beyond the current accounting period.

The right side of the balance sheet also shows the *equity* account, which are funds provided by the shareholders to a business.

The **statement of cash flows** shows the sources and uses of cash during the accounting period. As shown in **Figure 2.4**, this statement is divided into four sections.

* *Cash flows from operating activities* shows the sources and uses of cash generated by the business itself (i.e., income after taxes).
* *Cash flows from financing activities* includes items such as long-term loans and shareholders' participation.
* *Cash flows from investing activities* includes transactions such as the purchase or sale of assets.
* *Cash balance* shows the effects that all changes registered under the three activities have had on the cash account.

Figure 2.5 gives a visual comparison of the relationship between the balance sheet and the income statement. As indicated earlier, the income statement is much like a movie, that is, what went on "during" an operating period (say from January 1 to December 31). This is the reason why the income statement heading

FIGURE 2.5   Relationship between the Income Statement and the Balance Sheet

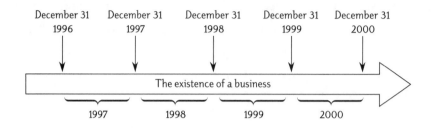

includes: *For the period ended December 31.* On the other hand, the balance sheet shows a "picture" of the financial position of a business at a given point in time (say December 31). For this reason, the balance sheet heading includes: *As of December 31.*

There is a parallel between an individual and a business in terms of its evolution (in the first case, the weight, in the second, the wealth). Suppose that both John Pound and ABC Inc. were born and started, in 1960 respectively. At the end of the first year, John weighed 20 pounds and ABC Inc. had accumulated $100,000 in income after taxes. Each year, during the next forty years, John's daily activities (among others) were to eat (intake of food and drinks) and to exercise (burn calories). On the other hand, ABC Inc. made sales revenue and incurred expenses. In both cases, 40 (one for each year) 12-month movies were produced. For ABC Inc., the information would be recorded on the income statement. Also, at the *end* of each year, John weighed himself to find out how many pounds he gained (or lost) and recorded the results in his diary. In the case of ABC Inc., the accumulated gains would be recorded in the balance sheet. The number of pounds that John gained (or lost) each year would be added (or subtracted) to the previous year's weight. In the case of ABC Inc., each time it generated a profit (or loss) it would also be added or subtracted from the previous year's balance sheet.

Now, assuming that on January 1, 2000, John's weight was 170 pounds (beginning of the year) and increased to 180 pounds (end of the year); his weight would have increased by 10 pounds. However, assume that during the twelve-month period, John actually gained 15 pounds, but the extra five pounds was removed through liposuction just before he stepped on the scale. The removal of excess pounds would be equivalent to what is paid in dividends and recorded in the statement of retained earnings. Similar to the evolution of John's weight pattern, ABC Inc.'s earnings and dividends would also be recorded in the same fashion on the three financial statements. This information would be recorded as follows:

	John Pound	ABC Inc.
Beginning of year (January 1, 2000)		
On the scale	170 pounds	
Last year's balance sheet		$ 1,000,000
Change during the year		
Changes in calories	+ 15 pounds	
Income statement (income)		+ $200,000
Adjustment during the year		
Liposuction	− 5 pounds	
Net change	+ 10 pounds	
Statement of retained earnings (dividends)		− $100,000
Statement of retained earnings (net change)		+ $100,000
End of year (December 31, 2000)		
On the scale	180 pounds	
This year's balance sheet		$ 1,100,000

Let's now examine three financial statements in more detail. **Tables 2.3**, **2.4**, **2.5**, and **2.7** show Eastman Technologies Inc.'s income statement, statement of retained earnings, balance sheet, and statement of cash flows, respectively.

The Income Statement

Everyone associated with a business wants to know if it is making a profit. If so, how much. The income statement summarizes the sales revenue and expenses for a period of time (could be for one month, for six months, or for a year). The income statement is to be read in *a step-down* fashion. As shown in **Table 2.3**, the income statement shows four levels of profitability: (1) the gross margin, (2) the operating income, (3) the income before taxes, and (4) the income after taxes. The accounts shown on the income statement can be grouped in three distinct sections.

1. The *operating section* shows the gross margin and the operating income.
2. The *non-operating section* shows income before taxes.
3. The *owners' section* shows the income after taxes or the amount left to the owners.

   Operating Section. This section includes the gross margin and the operating income.

   Gross margin. The gross margin (also referred to as gross profit) is calculated by subtracting the cost of goods sold from net sales or revenues.

Net sales	$2,500,000
Less cost of goods sold	1,900,000
Equals gross margin	$ 600,000

[

TABLE 2.3   The Income Statement

]

Eastman Technologies Inc.
Income Statement
For the Year Ended December 31, 2000

Operating Section

Net sales		$2,500,000
Cost of goods sold		1,900,000
Gross margin		**600,000**
Operating expenses		
Selling expenses:		
Sales salaries	$140,000	
Advertising expenses	20,000	
Total selling expenses	160,000	
Administrative expenses:		
Office salaries	170,000	
Rent	20,000	
Depreciation	40,000	
Total administration expenses	230,000	
Total operating expenses		390,000
Operating income		**210,000**

Non-Operating Section

Other income	20,000	
Other expenses (interest)	35,000	15,000
Income before taxes		**195,000**

Owners' Section

Income taxes		97,500
Income after taxes		**$ 97,500**

Net sales or sales revenue is what a business earns for the sale of its products and/or services. It represents items actually delivered or shipped to customers during the fiscal period. The term *net* sales or net revenue is used because allowances for sales discounts and sales returns have been adjusted from gross sales. Net sales are the amount a company has received or expects to receive after allowing for discounts off list prices, sales returns, prompt payment discounts, and other deductions from the original sales prices. Sales taxes are not included in the net sales revenue amount. Essentially, net sales are the amount that a business receives in order to cover all operating expenses and to generate a profit.

Cost of goods sold (also known as cost of sales) is the cost incurred in making or producing the goods that were sold. It is by far the largest expense in the income statement for a manufacturing enterprise. It includes three major items: materials purchased from suppliers, transportation cost or freight-in for goods shipped from suppliers to the company's plant, and all expenses associated with the manufacturing process to make the goods, such as wages of factory workers and depreciation on the plant's equipment and machinery.

Gross margin is the difference between cost of goods sold and net sales. Basically, it is the profit a business makes after paying for the cost of making the goods. It is called gross margin because no other types of expenses have been deducted and it represents the amount of money left over to pay for general expenses such as selling and administration. Gross margin is the starting point for earning an adequate income after taxes.

Operating income is sometimes called operating earnings or earnings before interest and taxes (EBIT). Deducting operating expenses, such as selling and administration expenses, from the gross margin gives the operating income. Generally, operating expenses include all expenses other than the cost of goods sold, interest, and income tax. There are sometimes hundreds of operating expenses included in this category ranging from salaries of office workers and managers (a large amount) to legal fees (usually a small amount).

Selling expenses are incurred to promote, sell, and distribute goods and services. These expenses include advertising, sales salaries, sales commissions, trade shows, sales supplies, delivery expenses, and sales promotions.

Administrative expenses are all other expenses that are not directly related to producing and selling goods. They include expenses incurred by administrative units such as human resources, accounting, legal, finance, information systems, insurance, and depreciation on office equipment (a non-cash expense). When equipment is first purchased, it was a *capital expenditure*. For such purchases, a useful life is usually estimated. A useful life is the number of years that a business thinks the asset will be used before it wears out or is replaced by new technology. The asset is then depreciated over its useful life, meaning that its cost is spread over a number of years.

By subtracting these operating expenses from the gross margin, we obtain the second level of profit, operating income. This level of profitability is directly affected by decisions made by operating managers; therefore, managers are directly accountable for the "operating income" performance.

Gross margin	$600,000
Less operating expenses	390,000
Equals operating income	$210,000

Non-Operating Section. This section deals with income and expenses that are not directly connected with the mainstream operating activities of a firm. It includes three types of items: (1) interest income and interest charges, (2) extraordinary items, and (3) nonrecurring items.

- ◆   *Interest income* includes interest earned on investments and *interest charges* paid for borrowed funds.
- ◆   *Extraordinary items* are unusual and infrequent gains (revenue) or losses (expenses) for a given year. They are occurrences unrelated to the usual activities of the business and not expected to occur again. An example is loss from a fire.
- ◆   *Nonrecurring items* are unusual or infrequent. For example, a business may sell a major capital asset and record a gain. Or a business may record a restructuring charge for the cost of downsizing employees who receive severance packages. These unusual gains or losses are therefore reported separately from the ongoing, continuing operations of a business. The logical reason for this is that irregular gains or losses would complicate the analysis and forecasting of the financial performance of a business.

Operating income		$210,000
Plus other income	$20,000	
Less other expenses	35,000	15,000
Equals income before taxes		$195,000

As shown, the company's other expenses exceed the other income by $15,000 and consequently reduce the operating profit to $195,000. This amount, called income before taxes, is used for three purposes: to pay income taxes, to pay dividends to shareholders, and to reinvest in the business.

Owners' Section. This section deals with the amount of money left to the shareholders; that is, "the bottom line."

Income taxes. This is the total amount of taxes due to federal and state governments on the taxable income earned by the business during the current period. It is calculated by multiplying the taxable income for the period by the appropriate tax rate (in this case, 50%). Income tax expense does not include other types of taxes, such as payroll and property taxes that are included in operating expenses.

Income before taxes	$195,000
Less income taxes	97,500
Equals income after taxes	$ 97,500

Income after taxes. This is the profit that belongs to the shareholders. In this case, Eastman Technologies Inc. earned $97,500 in income. It is the responsibility of the board of directors to decide how much of this amount will be paid to the shareholders in dividends and how much will be left in the business in the form of retained earnings. The portion of the income after taxes paid to shareholders and retained in the business appears on the next statement, called the statement of retained earnings.

The Statement of Retained Earnings

The **statement of retained earnings** (used in the case of corporations) is relatively simple to prepare. It is an important statement because it links the income statement and the balance sheet. Retained earnings represent the amount of money kept by a company after it pays dividends to its shareholders. This statement shows:

1. The amount of accumulated earnings at the start of the fiscal period (that is, the money that was not distributed to the shareholders). This amount should agree with the retained earnings figure appearing in the previous year's balance sheet.
2. The total net income (or loss) after taxes for the current operating year.
3. Any amount paid to the shareholders in the form of dividends.
4. The amount left in retained earnings at the end of the fiscal year. This amount determines the retained earnings figure that will appear in the company's current year's balance sheet.

Table 2.4 shows Eastman's statement of retained earnings for the year 2000. It should be noted that the net earnings of $97,500 for the year 2000 was obtained from the income statement in **Table 2.3**, and the $255,000 retained earnings as at December 31, 2000, is the same as the amount shown on the balance sheet (see **Table 2.5**).

The Balance Sheet

Table 2.5 shows Eastman's balance sheet. It shows the position of the company as of December 31, 2000 and 1999. The balance sheet gives a report about the health of a business at the close of an accounting period. Each separate item reported on the balance sheet is called an account. Every account has a name and a dollar amount, which is called its balance, reported at the end of the accounting period.

TABLE 2.4   The Statement of Retained Earnings

Eastman Technologies Inc.
Retained Earnings Statement
For the Year Ended December 31, 2000

Retained earnings (beginning balance)		$205,000
Earnings for the year	$97,500	
Dividends	47,500	50,000
Retained earnings (ending balance)		$255,000

> **TABLE 2.5**   The Balance Sheet

Eastman Technologies Inc.
Balance Sheets
December 31

Assets	2000	1999
Current Assets		
Cash	$ 22,000	$ 18,000
Prepaid expenses	60,000	55,000
Accounts receivable	300,000	280,000
Inventory	218,000	185,000
Total current assets	**600,000**	**538,000**
Capital assets (at cost)	1,340,000	1,050,000
Accumulated depreciation	140,000	100,000
Capital assets (net)	1,200,000	950,000
Total Assets	$1,800,000	$1,488,000
Liabilities		
Current liabilities		
Accounts payable	$ 195,000	$175,000
Notes payable	150,000	135,000
Accrued expenses	20,000	18,000
Taxes payable	80,000	70,000
Total current liabilities	**445,000**	**398,000**
Long-term debts	**800,000**	**600,000**
Total liabilities	**1,245,000**	**998,000**
Common shares	300,000	285,000
Retained earnings	255,000	205,000
Shareholders' equity	**555,000**	**490,000**
Total liabilities and equity	$1,800,000	$1,488,000

We will begin by discussing the meaning and significance of the major balance sheet accounts. As summarized on the next several pages, the balance sheet is made up of assets, liabilities, and shareholders' equity, also known as net worth. As shown on Eastman's balance sheet (**Table 2.5**), the total of all assets amounts to $1,800,000 and equals the liability and equity side of the balance sheet. Usually, the balance sheet's assets, liabilities, and equity accounts are presented under several headings such as current assets, capital assets, investments, intangible assets, current liabilities, long-term debts, and shareholders' equity.

Assets. Assets are the physical items (tangible) or rights (intangible) owned by a business. Assets have a monetary value attached to them and usually appear under two distinct headings: current assets and capital assets. Some businesses with other assets, such as investments and intangible assets will show them separately.

Current assets. Current assets are defined as cash or other assets expected to be turned into cash, usually in one year or less, that is, during the operating cycle. They include cash, marketable securities, accounts receivable, notes receivable, inventories, and prepaid expenses. It is common to list these assets on the balance sheet in order of liquidity. For instance, since cash is more liquid than marketable securities, it will be listed first. Similarly, since notes receivable can typically be converted into cash more quickly than inventory, they will be listed before inventory.

Cash includes all funds such as bills, coins, and checks that are on hand or readily available from the bank account. A certain reservoir of cash is usually kept on hand in order to pay current bills and to take advantage of specific opportunities, such as cash discounts.

Marketable securities include items such as term deposits or shares that can be readily converted into cash (in less than one year) and are regarded as an added reservoir of cash. The company buys these securities to obtain a greater return than on money in its bank account.

Accounts receivable represents money owed to the company by its regular business customers for the purchase of goods or services, and can be collected within a reasonable time period (usually between 30 to 90 days). To reduce the size of the cash tied-up in this account, some businesses formulate credit policies and collection procedures to minimize the time it takes to turn receivables into cash.

Notes receivable are written promises that have a specific maturity date. A note receivable may be the result of the settlement of one account by a customer who does not have the cash to pay the account according to the company's credit terms. If a company believes that some accounts will not be collected, it will open an account called "allowance for uncollectible accounts." Since this account is a "negative" asset account, it will be deducted from the regular accounts receivable to reflect the true value of that account.

Prepaid expenses are payments made for services that have not yet been received. It is an operating expense that is recorded before services were received. Rent, insurance, or property taxes are typical examples of such items. For example, Eastman may pay $8,000 for its insurance premium on June 30. If this is a one-year insurance policy and Eastman's accounting cycle closes on December 31, half of the premium, that is $4,000, will be recorded as a prepaid expense. This amount will be expensed during the next accounting period. If Eastman decides to cancel its policy on December 31, the insurance company will owe Eastman $4,000. This is why such items are regarded as assets. Another example is annual property taxes paid at the start of the taxation year and allocated over all the months covered by the property taxes.

The *inventory* account describes the monetary value of the material it has purchased or goods it has manufactured. Usually, a manufacturer has three types of inventory accounts.

- *Raw materials* represent the goods purchased from various suppliers to be used for manufacturing purposes.
- *Finished goods* are the products ready for sale.
- *Work-in-process* includes the goods or materials tied up in various stages of the production process, somewhere between raw materials and finished goods.

Since inventory is not a source of income, management makes an effort to keep it at low levels or to move it as fast as possible. Inventory is recorded at cost and not the price the firm hopes to sell it for.

Capital assets. Capital assets (also called fixed or plant assets) are items that are considered permanent and are to be used over an extended period of time (many years). The word "used" is important because it characterizes the major difference between current assets and capital assets. Capital assets have a limited life span (building, equipment, machinery) or an unlimited one (land). They are usually listed on the balance sheet at "book value." Book value equals the original purchase price less accumulated depreciation. Accumulated depreciation is the sum of all annual depreciation since the purchase of the capital asset.

Capital assets (other than land) have a finite life span and wear out over a number of years. Because of this, a company will allocate a certain amount of the total value of the capital asset over many years; this allocated amount is called *depreciation.* For example, if a building with an original cost of $600,000 has a 20-year physical life span, $30,000 will be allocated as an expense each year. Although this $30,000 is not a cash outlay, it is considered an expense and shown as such (as was indicated earlier) on the income statement. If the building has been used for four years, the balance sheet will show an accumulated depreciation of $120,000 deducted from the original price of the capital asset. The difference between the gross capital assets and the accumulated depreciation is called "net capital assets" or "book value."

Investments. Investments are similar to marketable securities, except that they are invested for a longer period. They include items such as bonds and shares of stock purchased from other companies.

Intangible Assets. Intangible assets represent values of trademarks, goodwill, franchises, and patents. These items have no physical value, but represent a real, measurable value to the owners of a business. Goodwill, for example, arises when a firm purchases another firm for a price that is higher than the value of the tangible assets. This difference represents the potential earning power resulting from its name or reputation. Also, company trademarks such as Coca-Cola, McDonald's arch and Microsoft are worth millions of dollars.

Liabilities. Liabilities represent the debts of a business. They are the credit that persons or other businesses have extended to a business in order to provide some financial assistance for purchasing the assets. Liabilities are divided into two distinct groups: *current liabilities* and *long-term debts.*

Current Liabilities. Current liabilities are what a business has to pay its creditors; monies that are owed to them within a short time (less than one year). Normally, such debts are used to finance the current assets. Current liabilities include accounts payable, notes payable, accrued expenses, and taxes.

Accounts payable usually represent the most current debts of a business. This is the money owed to suppliers of goods or services that were purchased on credit.

Notes payable are written promises to repay a specified sum of money within a short period time (less than one year).

Accrued liability accounts represent what a company owes for services received but not yet paid or an expense incurred but not yet recorded. Normally, a business records expenses as soon as the invoice is received for operating costs, even though it doesn't pay the invoice until several weeks later. However, certain unpaid expenses when a business closes its books must be identified. For instance, if employees are paid every second week and the company closes its books on December 31, it would have to record that it owes (as a liability) to its employees salaries for the week prior to December 31. The following are typical examples of accrued liabilities.

- Accumulated vacation and sick leave pay.
- Interest on debt that hasn't come due by year-end.
- Property taxes that should be charged for the year, but have not been paid yet.
- Warranty and guarantee work on products already sold that will be done during the following year.

Accrued expenses are the opposite of prepaid expenses. It is a service that has been received, but not paid for and not included in the accounts payable.

Long Term Debts. Long-term debts include accounts that are not due for at least one year. They include items such as mortgages, contracts, or long-term notes and loans, such as bonds. These items are used to finance the purchase of capital assets. A mortgage is a long-term obligation for which a company has pledged certain capital assets (land and buildings) to serve as collateral. This assures lenders that the value of some assets will be made available to them if the company ceases to operate, or if it is sold or liquidated. A long-term note is similar to notes payable (current liabilities) except that this item is to be repaid beyond a one-year period.

Shareholders' Equity. Shareholders' equity is another way of financing a business. This money comes from the owners of a business in the form of a capital account (if it is a sole proprietorship), partner's account (if it is a partnership), or capital shares (if it is a corporation).

Capital shares represent the amount of money that is put into the business by the shareholders. These could be common shares (certificates of ownership in a company) or preferred shares (shares that rank ahead of common shares in their claims on dividends and in their claim on assets in the event of liquidation).

Retained earnings represent the profits or income generated by the business for which the owners have not claimed the amount in the form of dividends. This represents the profits that have been accumulated and reinvested in the business to finance the purchase of current or capital assets or to pay off debts. If a company makes a profit in a given year, the amount in the retained earnings account shown on the current year's balance sheet is greater than the amount shown on the previous year's balance sheet. Conversely, if it incurs a loss, the retained earnings account declines accordingly.

The Statement of Cash Flows

Let's begin by saying that cash flow can be examined at two levels: micro and macro. At the micro level, cash flow looks at short-term operating statements such as the monthly cash receipts and disbursements incurred by a business. The financial tool used to determine cash flow at this level is called the cash budget. The objective is to make sure that the company has enough cash on hand to pay the company's ongoing bills (e.g., salaries, purchases, advertising, etc.) and debts as they come due. On the other hand, if the company has enough cash reserve, the treasurer would invest the surplus in short-term securities. This type of analysis and decision-making has to do with liquidity.

At the macro level, cash flow deals with insolvency and the ability of a business to:

1. Generate cash from its operations (profit plus depreciation and the management of working capital accounts).
2. Pay all of its debts (both short- and long-term) and dividends.
3. Purchase capital assets (capital budget).

While the operating cash receipts and disbursements show the liquidity performance of a business, the information dealing with solvency appears in the statement of cash flows. That information has to do with operating activities, investing activities, and financing activities.

Preparing the statement of cash flows is a relatively complex task, but interpreting it is somewhat easy and of great importance to stakeholders. To prepare this statement, the financial information has to be drawn from (1) the balance sheet, (2) the income statement, and (3) the statement of retained earnings.

Operating Activities

Operating activities deal with the flow of funds generated by the business itself (internally generated funds). Three important items in this section are income after taxes, depreciation, and the net change in non-cash working capital accounts.

Income after Taxes and Depreciation. Eastman Technologies Inc. earned $97,500 in income after taxes in 2000 (see **Table 2.3**). By adding back $40,000 in depreciation to this figure, the company generated $137,500 in cash. Depreciation is added back to income after taxes since this account is a book entry and does not represent a cash outflow.

Net Change in Non-cash Working Capital Accounts. The statement of cash flows may include a listing of the cash flow generated by a company's individual working capital accounts. **Table 2.6** shows whether individual working capital accounts are sources of cash or uses of cash. Non-cash working capital accounts include all current assets (excluding cash), and all current liability accounts. These accounts are all drawn from the balance sheet. These accounts and the amount of change from 1999 to 2000 are listed in the operating activities section of the statement of cash flows shown in **Table 2.7**.

Investing Activities

Investing activities show the source or use of cash for buying or selling capital assets. As shown in **Table 2.7**, Eastman invested $290,000 in capital assets. In practice, the actual capital asset accounts must be examined to identify the amounts of asset purchases and sales.

Financing Activities

Financing activities deal with the flow of cash from the sale of shares, the repayment of long-term debts, the borrowing of long-term debts, and the payment of dividends. With the exception of the payment of dividends, which is obtained from

---

TABLE 2.6   Eastman Technologies Inc.
Changes in Non-Cash Working Capital Accounts

Sources

Increase in accounts payable	$20,000	
Increase in notes payable	15,000	
Increase in accrued expenses	2,000	
Increase in deferred taxes	10,000	$47,000

Drawn from working capital accounts in the balance sheet (current assets and current liabilities)

Uses

Increase in accounts receivable	$20,000	
Increase in inventory	33,000	
Increase in prepaid expenses	5,000	58,000

> ## TABLE 2.7   Statement of Cash Flows

Eastman Technologies Inc.
Statement of Cash Flows
For the Year Ended 2000

Cash Flow from Operating Activities

Net income from operations	$ 97,500	
Add: Depreciation	40,000	
Increase in accounts payable	20,000	
Increase in notes payable	15,000	
Increase in accrued expenses	2,000	
Increase in deferred taxes	10,000	
	87,000	
Deduct: Increase in accounts receivable	(20,000)	
Increase in inventory	(33,000)	
Increase in prepaid expenses	(5,000)	
	(58,000)	
Cash provided by operating activities		$ 126,500
Cash Flow from Financing Activities		
Payment of dividends	(47,500)	
Long-term debt	200,000	
Common shares	15,000	
Cash provided by financing activities		167,500
Cash Flow from Investing Activities		
Purchase of capital assets	(290,000)	
Cash used by investing activities		(290,000)
Cash Balance		
Increase (decrease) in cash		4,000
Cash at beginning of year		18,000
Cash at end of year		$ 22,000

the statement of retained earnings, this information is taken from the balance sheet. As shown in **Table 2.7** under the heading "Cash Flows from Financing Activities," Eastman Technologies Inc. obtained a total of $167,500. First, the company paid $47,500 in dividends (see **Table 2.4**); second, it borrowed $200,000 from its long-term lenders; and finally, the shareholders invested $15,000 in the business.

Cash Balance

The cash balance is reconciled at the bottom of the statement of cash flows. The increase (or decrease) from operating, investing, and financing activities is added (or subtracted) from the cash balance at the beginning of the year. The cash balance at the end of the year must match the cash balance shown on the balance sheet.

The Auditor's Report

All companies traded in the public markets must have their financial statements audited. Auditors review the financial statements prepared by management and issue an opinion. The **auditor's report** includes:

1. The auditors' opinion on the financial statements.
2. A statement that the financial statements are prepared in accordance with generally accepted accounting principles applied on a basis consistent with that of the preceding year.
3. A description of the scope of the examination (the audit itself). It usually comments on the accounting procedures and any tests made to support the accounting records, and presents evidence to show that they were made in accordance with generally accepted auditing standards.

The following is a typical auditor's statement that appears in annual reports.

We have audited the balance sheets of ABC Ltd. as at December 31, 1999 and December 31, 2000 and the income statements, the statement of retained earnings, and the statement of cash flows for the years then ended. These financial statements are the responsibility of the company's management. Our responsibility is to express an opinion on these financial statements based on our audits.

We conducted our audits in accordance with generally accepted auditing standards. Those standards require that we plan and perform an audit to obtain reasonable assurance whether the financial statements are free of material misstatement. An audit includes examination, on a test basis, of evidence supporting the amounts and disclosures in the financial statements. An audit also includes assessing the accounting principles used and significant estimates made by management, as well as evaluating the overall financial statement presentation.

In our opinion, these financial statements present fairly, in all material respects, the financial position of the company as at December 31, 1999 and December 31, 2000 and the results of its operations and the changes in its financial position for the years then ended in accordance with generally accepted accounting principles.

The auditor's report and the company's financial statements are presented in a company's annual report. A typical annual report contains more than financial statements. It also includes additional information, that is, footnotes to financial statements. These footnotes are essential to financial statements; in fact, they are an integral, inseparable part of an annual report. Without footnotes, financial statements would be incomplete since they provide inadequate disclosure about relevant information so that the shareholders can make informed decisions and at the same time protect their interests. The two types of footnotes disclose:

- ◆ The main accounting methods used by the business.
- ◆ Information that cannot be incorporated in the main body of the financial statements (i.e., details regarding stock ownership, long-term operating leases, maturity dates, interest rates, collateral or other security provisions, lawsuits pending, and company's employee's retirement and pension plans.

Analysis

Once the financial statements have been drawn up, the information can be analyzed and interpreted. Many techniques exist for analyzing financial statements. What is important, however, is to ensure that the right type of information has been gathered and put together in a way that will assist managers, creditors, and shareholders in analyzing the data in a meaningful way.

Here are typical analytical techniques that will be examined in Chapter 3.

- ◆ *Horizontal analysis*, which compares a company's financial structure and profitability over time. Two or more years are required for this type of analysis.
- ◆ *Vertical analysis*, which helps financial analysts compare different numbers on a balance sheet and income statement (through ratios) in a more meaningful way.
- ◆ *Ratio analysis*, which expresses different sets of numbers contained in financial statements as ratios: liquidity ratios, leverage ratios, activity ratios, and profitability ratios.
- ◆ *Break-even analysis*, which shows the relationship between revenues, expenses (fixed and variable), and profits.
- ◆ *Operational analysis*, which uses information contained in financial statements and management information reports to evaluate the efficiency, effectiveness, and productivity of a business.

Decision-Making

This last activity of financial management gets to the heart of the management process—decision-making. Bookkeeping, accounting, and analysis are the key steps in financial management because they provide important information to management and assist them in making prudent decisions. Decision-making techniques will be explored in more depth in subsequent chapters. The information contained in financial statements and the analysis of this data provide answers to the following questions.

- ◆ How much money should we borrow?
- ◆ Should we borrow on a short-term or a long-term basis?
- ◆ How much inventory should be kept on hand?

- ◆ Should we buy or lease an asset?
- ◆ Should we invest in this project? Expand this operation? Modernize our plant?
- ◆ How much credit should we extend?
- ◆ How fast should our company grow?
- ◆ What size of capital commitments should our company tackle this year? Next year?
- ◆ What level of risk does this project present?
- ◆ How should we administer our working capital assets?
- ◆ What is the optimal level of capital structure?
- ◆ What price should we set for our products?
- ◆ How can we compare the financial results of different projects coming from various divisions, and how can we rate them?

These are typical questions managers ask, and they will be discussed throughout this book. Before moving on to the analysis and decision-making chapters, a few important concepts associated with financial statements should be reviewed and understood. They are:

- ◆ The accounting methods (cash method versus accrual method)
- ◆ The depreciation methods, capital cost allowance, and amortization
- ◆ Deferred taxes
- ◆ Income after taxes (or profit) versus cash flow
- ◆ Working capital

Accounting Methods

There are two ways of reporting financial statements: the cash method and the accrual method.

The **cash method** keeps a record of cash receipts from sales and disbursements of expenses. In this case, the business recognizes revenue when cash or its equivalent is received, without regard to when the goods or services are delivered. Expenses are treated in a similar way. At the end of an accounting period, the expenses are deducted from revenues, and the excess gives the net income or loss for the period. This accounting method is limited to small businesses that conduct most transactions in cash. For this reason, all financial reports or statements discussed in this book, unless otherwise stated, use the accrual method.

The **accrual method** disregards the receipt and disbursement of cash. It records revenue when goods are sold or services rendered. For example, if a business makes a sale, for cash or credit, or buys goods for cash or on credit, it assumes that the revenues and the expenses have been incurred. Although a sale is made on credit (and cash has not been received) or goods are purchased from suppliers on credit (and payment has not been made), the income statement shows the respective revenue and expense transactions in the appropriate accounts. The most important accounts that differentiate cash basis from accrual basis are accounts receivable and accounts payable.

The main purpose of the accrual method is to obtain a measure of the results of business operations by allocating, to each fiscal period, the appropriate revenue and expense items. In accounting, this process is called "matching expenses with revenues." This concept is important in order to reflect, in a realistic way, the true income or profit generated by a business during a particular operating period.

Depreciation Methods, MACRS, and Amortization

Depreciation is used to spread the cost of using a capital asset over a period of years. For tax purposes, an accelerated cost recovery system, similar to depreciation, is used to allocate the expense of capital assets over a number of years. Amortization, like depreciation, is used to spread the cost of an intangible asset over a period of years.

Depreciation

Depreciation is defined as the estimated decrease in the book value of a capital asset, fixed asset, or long-lived asset. It is computed annually over the estimated useful life of the asset. It has nothing to do with the market value of the asset. For example, a truck may last 3 years; a building, 20 years; and furniture, 15 years. Although a truck may be purchased for cash in a particular year, since it will be used for 3 years, the business will apportion the cost over this 3-year useful life of that asset.

There are different ways of calculating depreciation. Two commonly used methods are the straight-line method and the sum-of-the-years'-digits method. Let's examine how these two depreciation methods are calculated.

Straight Line Method. This method is the most widely used and the simplest to calculate. It allocates an equal portion of the capital asset to be depreciated each year over the asset's estimated useful life. It is calculated as follows:

$$\text{Depreciation} = \frac{\text{Purchase cost} - \text{scrap/salvage value}}{\text{Estimated useful life in years}}$$

For example, if an asset costs $100,000 and has a useful life of five years and no salvage value, the yearly depreciation amount will be $20,000.

$$\text{Depreciation} = \frac{\$100,000}{5} = \$20,000$$

The yearly depreciation, the net asset book value, and the percent depreciated value of the asset are presented as follows:

Year	Depreciation	Net Asset Book Value	% Depreciated
0	—	$100,000	0%
1	$ 20,000	80,000	20
2	20,000	60,000	40
3	20,000	40,000	60
4	20,000	20,000	80
5	20,000	—	100
Total	$100,000		

Sum-of-the-Years'-Digits Method. This method is an accelerated way of calculating depreciation. It is based on the sum of the digits of the estimated life of an asset, which is used as the common denominator. The numerators of the fractions are the years in the asset's life. Using the same $100,000 asset purchase to illustrate this method of calculation, the arithmetic works this way:

1. If the life of the asset is 5 years, each individual year would be listed as follows: 1, 2, 3, 4, and 5; if it is 10 years, it would go from 1 to 10.
2. The sum-of-the-digits for each year would be added as follows: $1 + 2 + 3 + 4 + 5 = 15$.
3. A fraction is identified for each year as follows: 1/15, 2/15, 3/15, 4/15, and 5/15.
4. Each fraction, starting with the last year, is multiplied by the original $100,000 investment. The calculation to find the depreciation is therefore done in the following way:

$$\text{Cost} \times \frac{\text{Number of years of depreciation remaining}}{\text{Sum of total digits of the asset's useful life}}$$

Year	Fraction		Cost of the asset		Depreciation	Net Book Value	% Depreciated
1	5/15	×	$100,000	=	$ 33,333	$66,667	33.3%
2	4/15	×	100,000	=	26,667	40,000	60.0
3	3/15	×	100,000	=	20,000	20,000	80.0
4	2/15	×	100,000	=	13,333	6,667	93.3
5	1/15	×	100,000	=	6,667	—	100.0
Total					$100,000		

MACRS

In the 1980s, legislation resulted in significant changes to the tax code. The Internal Revenue Service (IRS) publishes tables to be used for recording depreciation for tax purposes. The current system being used is referred to **MACRS**, which stands for Modified Accelerated Cost Recovery System. Businesses want to pay the lowest amount of tax possible. Using the MACRS tables, businesses record for tax purposes the cost of the asset on an accelerated basis.

All assets are assigned to categories. Most capital assets, except buildings, fall in to the five-year or seven-year categories. The cost recovery on buildings occurs over a longer period of time. The following table shows the cost recovery percentage assigned to each year of the asset's life for the five-year and seven-year categories.

Depreciation Rate for Cost Recovery under MACRS

Year	5-year	7-year
1	20.00%	14.29%
2	32.00	24.49
3	19.20	17.49
4	11.52	12.49
5	11.52	8.93
6	5.76	8.92
7		8.93
8		4.46

Notice that the recovery period runs a year longer than stated category length. The table assumes that the asset was placed in service by the business at the middle of year. The remaining depreciation is claimed in the final year.

Although the IRS does allow businesses to use straight-line depreciation for tax purposes, most businesses choose to use the MACRS system since it reduces the amount of tax to be paid in the early years of the asset's life. Businesses, like individuals, seek to pay the smallest amount possible in taxes.

Amortization

Amortization is also a tax-deductible expense. It applies to intangible assets such as goodwill, patents, franchise fees, trademarks, legal and architectural fees, and research and development. Basically, amortization is to intangible assets what depreciation is to capital assets. Tax rules for deducting amortization vary depending on the type of intangible asset. Most intangibles are amortized over a period of 5 to 15 years. Most amortization occurs on a straight line basis.

Deferred Taxes

Because companies use depreciation rates that are different from the MACRS rates used to calculate income taxes, businesses pay less tax in the first several years of the asset utilization. Eventually, the company will owe this additional amount to the government. These are referred to as **deferred taxes** and appear as a liability on the company's balance sheet.

Using the $100,000 example, the five-year straight-line depreciation rate (equivalent to 20%), and the MACRS rate, the deferred taxes would be calculated as follows:

Years	MACRS	Straight-line Depreciation @ 20%	Difference between MACRS and Straight-line Depreciation	Difference in Annual Deferred Taxes (tax rate @ 50%)	Difference Cumulative Deferred Taxes
1	$20,000*	$20,000	—	—	—
2	32,000	20,000	$ 12,000	$ 6,000	−$6,000
3	19,200	20,000	− 800	− 400	− 5,600
4	11,520	20,000	−8,480	−4,240	− 1,360
5	11,520	20,000	−8,480	−4,240	—
6	5,760	—	5,760	2,880	2,880

* Only one-half year of depreciation is allowed in first year.

Notice that in the first year, the depreciation and MACRS rates produce the same amount of depreciation. Therefore, no deferred tax occurs until the second year. As shown in **Table 2.8**, depreciation is used as an expense while MACRS is used to calculate the company's income taxes. The first column is used to calculate the company's income taxes using MACRS for Year 2. Column 3 shows the company "profit and loss statement" for the year when using the company's five-year depreciation rate (or 20%), while column 2 shows the company's "income statement." The depreciation expense, the actual income taxes paid in that year, and the amount of deferred taxes that the company owes to the government all appear in the statement. The income after taxes in columns 2 and 3 are the same ($40,000); the only difference between the two columns is the timing of payment of the taxes. The company paid $6,000 less in taxes due to a higher MACRS rate. Therefore, the company owes this amount to the government in the form of deferred taxes. It is like an interest-free loan.

Income After Taxes Versus Cash Flow

We have defined **income** (or profit) as the excess of revenues over expenses. Income tells you how efficient a business is. On the other hand, **cash flow** is the result of the income after tax plus depreciation. The calculation is relatively simple. If we refer to **Table 2.3**, Eastman's Income Statement, the cash flow calculation is done as follows:

Net income after taxes	$ 97,500
Depreciation	40,000
Cash flow	$137,500

Depreciation is added to net income after taxes because it is the only expense item on the income statement that is *not* a cash outlay. Depreciation is nothing more than an accounting or book entry; it is not a check made out to "Depreciation Inc." or cash paid to someone called "Mr. Depreciation." Since depreciation is regarded as a book entry and not a cash outlay, it should be added to the net income after taxes to determine the true amount of cash that was generated by a business. In the case of Eastman, the cash inflow from operations in 2000 is $137,500.

	1 Accountant's Worksheet	2 Income Statement	3 P & L Statement
TABLE 2.8 The Income Statement and the Profit and Loss Statement in Year 2			

	1 Accountant's Worksheet	2 Income Statement	3 P & L Statement
Revenue	$300,000	$300,000	$300,000
Cost of sales	150,000	150,000	150,000
Gross margin	150,000	150,000	150,000
Operating expenses	50,000	50,000	50,000
MACRS/Depreciation	32,000	20,000 ⟵	20,000
Total expenses	82,000	70,000	70,000
Income before taxes	68,000	80,000	80,000
Taxes—Current (50%)	34,000 ⟶	34,000	
—Deferred	6,000 ⟶	6,000	40,000
	40,000	40,000	40,000
Income/profit after taxes	$ 28,000	$ 40,000	$ 40,000

Cash flow is important because it gives the business operator an idea of the debt repayment ability of the business. Sometimes cash flow can be even more important to a business than income; while the business may be losing money (income- or profit-wise), the business may still have money or cash to pay its debts.

Working Capital

Working capital includes the current accounts listed on the balance sheet, that is, current assets and current liabilities. Every account shown on the balance sheet labeled current, such as cash, accounts receivable, notes receivable, accounts payable, and notes payable, is part of working capital. People often think of a business in terms of land, buildings, equipment, and machinery—its "hard assets"—but, in many industries, close to 50 percent of the assets are current assets. Many businesses fail because of poor working capital management—for example, carrying an inventory that is too large or financed at too high an interest rate. Working capital represents the focal point of the "operating cycle" of a business. Goods are sold for cash or on credit, and when the company collects its receivables from its customers, the cycle ends. For many businesses the control of working capital is the key to successful and profitable operation. The objective is to shorten the working capital cycle. In general, the faster the cycle, the more profitable the business. Referring to Eastman's balance sheets in **Table 2.5**, working capital accounts include the following items:

Eastman Technologies Inc.
Working Capital as of December 31, 2000

Current assets		Current liabilities	
Cash	$ 22,000	Accounts payable	$195,000
Prepaid expenses	60,000	Notes payable	150,000
Accounts receivable	300,000	Accrued expenses	20,000
Inventory	218,000	Taxes payable	80,000
Total current assets	$600,000	Total current liabilities	$445,000

Net working capital is defined as the difference between current assets and current liabilities. Eastman's net working capital is computed as follows:

Current assets	$600,000
Less current liabilities	445,000
Equals net working capital	$155,000

Working capital management means the management of individual current asset and current liability accounts to ensure that there is a good relationship between them. Because of the importance of working capital management, Chapter 10 is devoted entirely to this topic.

Decision-Making in Action

The CEO of Oxford Manufacturing Inc. was reviewing the December 31, 2001 financial statements prepared by the company's controller. The controller points out that these financial statements must be prepared in accordance with generally accepted accounting principles in order to make it easy for managers, lenders, owners, etc. to understand, interpret, analyze their content and to make enlightened decisions.

The CEO noticed that the income statement in **Table 2.9** contained three levels of income: gross margin, operating income and income after taxes. The first level of income (gross margin) shows how much profit was earned by Oxford after paying for the cost of manufacturing them: that is, purchases, freight-in, and all other expenses related to producing them in the plant. The second level of income (operating income) shows the amount of profit that Oxford made after deducting, from sales revenue, all operating expenses (cost of goods sold and operating expenses). This level is the level of income that managers are *accountable* for since they are directly responsible for making decisions related to sales revenue and operating expenses. These two income levels deal with the *operating section* of the income statement.

The third level of income (income after taxes) is in two sections. The first is referred to as the *non-operating section* and shows how much other income and other expenses were added (or deducted) to the operating income. Essentially, this

TABLE 2.9 Income Statement

Oxford Manufacturing Inc.
Income Statement
For the Year Ended 2001

Sales revenue	$ 5,100,000
Cost of goods sold	3,800,000
Gross margin	**1,300,000**
Operating expenses	
Selling	270,000
Administrative expenses	270,000
Depreciation	60,000
Total operating expenses	600,000
Operating income	**700,000**
Other income/expenses	
Other income	22,000
Other expenses	50,000
Income before taxes	672,000
Taxes	260,000
Income after taxes	**$ 412,000**

section deals with all interest earned (or interest paid), nonrecurring expenses and extraordinary expenses. After deducting this amount from the operating income, the company is left with income before taxes. The second deals with the *owners' section* and shows how much income tax is deducted from income before taxes. The shareholders, through the board of directors, decide what to do with this third level of income: pay dividends or reinvest the income in the business in the form of retained earnings.

The CEO noticed that although Oxford earned a profit of $412,000, it generated $472,000 in cash ($412,000 + $60,000 for depreciation which is a *noncash expense*).

He also noticed that the second financial statement, the statement of retained earnings in **Table 2.10** had little value to his managers but showed important information about the amount of profit that was invested back into Oxford since it was started. He noticed that as of January 1, 2001, a total of $1,310,000 had been reinvested in Oxford. During the operating year, $155,674 was paid in dividends to shareholders and deducted from the $412,000 earnings (or income after taxes) and the balance of $256,326 was reinvested in Oxford. At the end of the operating year, Oxford had accumulated $1,566,326 in retained earnings. This same amount also appears in the current year's balance sheet under the heading, Shareholders' equity.

TABLE 2.10   Statement of Retained Earnings

Oxford Manufacturing Inc.
Statement of Retained Earnings
For the Year Ended 2001

Retained earnings (beginning balance)		$1,310,000
Earnings	$412,000	
Dividends	155,674	
		256,326
Retained earnings (ending balance)		$ 1,566,326

The third financial statement is the balance sheet shown in **Table 2.11**. The CEO noticed that this financial statement was divided into two sections: what Oxford owns (assets) and what it owes to its creditors (liabilities) and shareholders (equity).

The *asset* section was further subdivided into three sections. The first grouping of accounts are *current assets* or those assets that can be converted into cash within the operating year. The second grouping of accounts are *capital assets* such as land, buildings, machinery and equipment. Since these assets are used over an extended period of years, the original cost of the assets can be depreciated over their respective useful lives. The worth of these tangible assets in the company books is recorded as net capital assets. The third grouping of accounts is *intangible assets* and includes goodwill, patents, and so on.

Two groups of individuals finance the assets listed on the company's books: creditors and shareholders. This is the reason why the liability and shareholders' section of the balance sheet is divided into two sections: liabilities and share-holders' equity. The *liability section* also contains two subgroups, *current liabilities* and *long-term debt*. Current liabilities help finance current assets. These liabilities must be paid within the next operating year (twelve months). The second group lists the long-term debts. These liabilities help to finance the purchase of the capital assets. These debts will be paid in future years. The *shareholders' section* also contains two subgroups: capital shares and retained earnings. *Capital shares* is the amount of money that was invested in the business by the shareholders themselves. *Retained earnings* is the amount of money that was reinvested in the business since it was started. This money belongs to the shareholders, but they decided to leave it in the business in order to finance the purchase of capital assets and also help the business fund its growth (working capital).

The fourth financial statement, the statement of cash flows, shows how cash was used for or provided by operating, investing, and financing activities.

Table 2.12 indicates that $367,000 in cash was provided by operating activities and $644,326 was provided by financing activities. Investing activities showed a $1,000,000 use of cash. As a result of these activities, there was an increase of $11,326 in cash for the year.

TABLE 2.11   Comparative Balance Sheet

Oxford Manufacturing Inc.
Comparative Balance Sheet
At December 31, 2001 and 2000

Assets	2001	2000
Current assets		
Cash	$ 46,326	$ 35,000
Marketable securities	50,000	50,000
Prepaid expenses	25,000	30,000
Accounts receivable	550,000	450,000
Inventory	850,000	750,000
Total current assets	1,521,326	1,315,000
Capital assets (at cost)	3,450,000	2,450,000
Accumulated depreciation	710,000	650,000
Captial assets (net)	2,740,000	1,800,000
Intangible assets	65,000	65,000
Total assets	$4,326,326	$3,180,000
Liabilities		
Current liabilities		
Accounts payable	$ 170,000	$ 130,000
Accrued expenses	50,000	50,000
Current portion of long-term debt	40,000	40,000
Working capital loan	400,000	350,000
Total current liabilities	660,000	570,000
Long-term debts	1,600,000	900,000
Total liabilities	2,260,000	1,470,000
Shareholders' equity		
Common shares	500,000	400,000
Retained earnings	1,566,326	1,310,000
Total shareholders' equity	2,066,326	1,710,000
Total liabilities and shareholders' equity	$ 4,326,326	$3,180,000

TABLE 2.12 Statement of Cash Flows

Oxford Manufacturing Inc.
Statement of Cash Flows
For the Year Ended 2000 and 2001

Cash Flow from Operating Activities

Income after taxes	$ 412,000	
Add: Depreciation	60,000	
Decrease in prepaid expenses	5,000	
Increase in accounts payable	40,000	
Increase in working capital loan	50,000	
	155,000	
Deduct: Increase in accounts receivable	(100,000)	
Increase in inventory	(100,000)	
	(200,000)	
Cash provided by operating activities		$ 367,000

Cash Flow from Investing Activities

Purchase of capital assets	(1,000,000)	
Cash used by investing activities		(1,000,000)

Cash Flow from Financing Activities

Payment of dividends	(155,674)	
Long-term debt	700,000	
Common shares	100,000	
Cash provided by financing activities		644,326

Cash Balance

Increase (decrease) in cash		11,326
Cash at beginning of year		35,000
Cash at end of year		$ 46,326

Summary

This chapter has dealt with the process of constructing financial statements, the structure of the income statement, the statement of retained earnings, and the balance sheet.

The basic activities involved in financial management are:

1. *Bookkeeping*, which is the process of collecting, classifying, and recording raw information resulting from a multitude of different transactions that take place in a business;
2. *Accounting*, which is the activity that arranges all information into distinct financial statements;
3. *Analysis*, which involves the interpretation of financial statements; and
4. *Decision making*, which is the process of using information for the purpose of improving the financial performance of a business.

Four key financial statements were reviewed. The *income statement* presents the operating results; that is, revenues and expenses and income for a given period of time. The *statement of retained earnings* shows the changes that take place in retained earnings during a given fiscal period. It shows the income that was added to the earnings, the dividends paid, and the retained earnings at the end of the fiscal period. The *balance sheet* describes a company's financial position at a given moment in time and contains a list of the assets (what a company owns), liabilities (creditors who have a claim on the assets), and shareholders' equity (owners who also have a claim on the assets). The *statement of cash flows* reconciles the cash at the beginning and end of the year by examining the cash provided or used by operating, investing, and financing activities.

There are two accounting methods: the *cash method*, which recognizes revenue and expenses when cash or its equivalent is received or disbursed; and the *accrual method*, which records revenue when goods are sold or services rendered and when expenses are incurred.

Depreciation is an estimated decrease in the value of capital or long-lived assets. There are several ways of calculating depreciation, and two were presented in this chapter: the *straight-line method* and the *sum-of-the-years'-digits method*. These methods are used by individual business operators for the purpose of calculating income. MACRS is the cost recovery system established by the Internal Revenue Service, and is used by businesses in calculating their income taxes. *Amortization* is a rate used for allocating the cost of an intangible asset over a period of years.

Cash flow is the total of income after taxes plus depreciation. *Working capital* includes all items in the current asset and current liability accounts of a balance sheet. Net working capital is the difference between current assets and current liabilities.

CHAPTER 3

Financial Statement Analysis

Since CompuTech Sales and Services started, the Edwards have been obtaining the company's financial statements from their accountant Mary Ogaki each month. The data presented on the financial statements enables the Edwards to analyze their financial performance each month.

As Mary pointed out, the information presented on the various financial statements is critical to gauge the results of past decisions and to determine what has to be done in the future. The Edwards remember vividly the points made by Bill Murray regarding the requirements to maintain a liquid, stable, productive, and profitable business. This is exactly what the Edwards look at when analyzing their financial statements. CompuTech Sales and Services financial statements for year 2002 are presented in Exercise 44 at the end of this chapter.

The first requirement was to pay their current bills on time, that is to be "liquid." In 2002, CompuTech bought approximately $200,000 worth of goods from different suppliers. The Edwards always made a point to pay their invoices (usually within 30 days) on time. They felt that this was important if CompuTech was to maintain a healthy working relationship with their suppliers. Also, being in a favorable liquid position, the business could take advantage of cash and trade discounts. The business has close to $100,000 in bank loans. In order to maintain a certain level of "trustworthiness" with their banker, the Edwards make sure that all debt commitments are honored each month.

The second requirement is "stability," that is maintaining a certain level of debt that CompuTech can afford. The Edwards did not want too much debt for two reasons. First, the more debt that the business has to carry, the more costly it is. They realize that a heavy debt load has an adverse effect on profit performance, particularly if interest charges increase, even by 1 or 2 percent. The Edwards' strategy in 2002 is to reduce their debt load to allow them more leverage in the year 2003 to finance the opening of a new store.

The third requirement was "efficiency." To the Edwards, efficiency means getting the "biggest bang for each invested dollar." Efficiency means generating the highest level of revenue with the least amount of resources (assets). For example, they realize that dollars invested in accounts receivable ($45,000) and inventory ($65,000), although necessary, do not generate any profit. For this reason, they want to maintain their level of working capital accounts as low as possible. In total, CompuTech has $268,000 invested in assets and each dollar generates $1.57 in sales revenue ($420,000/$268,000). To find out whether CompuTech is productive or not, the Edwards have to obtain information from different sources (i.e., banks, industry associations, Dun & Bradstreet) to compare their firm's performance against the industry and other competing firms. This information is used as benchmarks for making decisions.

The last requirement for long-term growth and success is "profitability." This has to do with the level of profit CompuTech generates compared to sales revenue, assets, and equity. The Edwards realize the importance of making effective investment and operating decisions in order to maximize profitability. High profit level is a sign of efficiency. In 2002, for example, the Edwards expect to earn 7.86 cents for every sales revenue dollar ($33,000/$420,000). As far as they are concerned, return on sales is one of the most important financial objectives. Improving profitability can be achieved by increasing sales revenue and being vigilant in spending budget dollars (i.e., cost of goods sold and operating expenses). They know that the more profit the business earns, the better it can expand by using more internally generated funds and fewer external sources of funds.

This chapter examines the more important financial ratios used by businesses to measure a company's financial performance. In particular, it focuses on three key topics:

- Why financial ratios are important to measure a company's success.
- What financial ratios can be used to measure liquidity, debt, efficiency, and profitability.
- How benchmarks can be used to measure financial performance.

Introduction

An important tool used to gauge the financial health of a business is ratio analysis. Essentially, a financial ratio is the comparison or relationship between different numbers appearing on a balance sheet and/or an income statement. This relationship is usually expressed in terms of a *ratio* or a *percentage*.

Business managers, suppliers, investors, and market analysts do not look only at the make-up of financial statements, that is, the "cosmetics." Just because a balance sheet *balances* or is prepared by renowned accounting firms, does not mean that a business is in a healthy financial position. A person who knows how to read financial statements can readily detect whether a business is financially sound or suffers from financial anemia. Just like a medical doctor, trained to look at X-rays to detect whether patients are healthy or not, persons can also be trained to read financial statements and to draw meaningful conclusions from them.

After reading this chapter, it will be possible to analyze financial statements, that is, the balance sheet and an income statement and to gauge the financial soundness and profitability of any business.

Ratio analysis helps readers of financial statements assess the *financial structure* and *profitability* performance of businesses by exploring answers to the following questions.

- Is this company able to meet its current debt obligations?
- Are the company's assets being managed effectively?
- Are the business' accounts receivable and inventory at suitable levels?
- Will the company be able to meet its long-term debt commitments?
- Can the company service its debt comfortably?
- Is the company profitable?
- Is this business using its assets or resources efficiently?
- How does the company's financial structure and profitability compare with those of others in the same industry?
- Is the shareholders' return on investment satisfactory?
- Do investors have a high regard for the company?

This chapter analyzes financial statements, showing how to meaningfully compare numbers appearing on balance sheets and income statements. Here are a few examples of how numbers shown on financial statements can be compared and the reasons for the comparison.

Why compare...	**To see if the ...**
• Current liabilities *to* current assets	• company is able to meet its payroll and pay its suppliers on time.
• Accounts receivable *to* sales	• company can collect its receivables quickly enough.
• Inventory *to* cost of goods sold	• company's inventory is turning over quickly enough.
• Fixed charges *to* income	• business can service its debt.
• Total debt *to* total assets	• company has too much in debt.
• Total assets *to* sales	• company's assets are productive.
• Net income *to* sales	• company as a whole is efficient.

Why Use Ratios to Analyze Financial Statements

Managers analyze financial statements for two key reasons. First, to examine the *past* in order to gauge how well a business performed in terms of meeting its financial objectives, that is, efficiency, liquidity, profitability, and stability (see Chapter 1). Second, to formulate goals and strategies that will help improve the company's *future* financial performance. One important characteristic of good business goals are the elements of *precision* and *meaningfulness*. Financial ratios are considered vital instruments that can make financial analysis and decision-making useful and unambiguous.

Analyzing financial statements through ratios helps managers, market analysts, or investors find out what is *good* or *bad* about a business. While ratios only give *signals* about what is wrong or right, they can easily trigger a process that can help managers dig a little deeper in order to find answers to questions, to seek solutions for problems, or to improve performance.

Financial statements become valuable instruments when managers or analysts are able to make the connection between different accounts or groups of accounts shown on income statements and balance sheets. Furthermore, this information can be quite revealing when compared to competitors and industry norms that can be used as **benchmarks**. Once the analysis is completed, only then can corrective measures be taken to improve the financial performance.

The real value of financial statement analysis lies in the fact that it can be used to *help* predict a company's future financial performance. If the analysis is done effectively, managers can anticipate future conditions and, more importantly, establish a platform upon which decisions can impact favorably the future of their business.

The reasons why it is important to analyze financial statements can be grouped under four headings: (1) to maximize return, (2) to ensure liquidity, (3) to maintain solvency, and (4) to secure long-term prosperity.

Maximize Return

In business, the word **return** is synonymous with survival. To survive, a business must earn adequate *profit* and *cash flow* that will in turn earn a suitable return for investors, and provide adequate funds to finance its working capital requirements and to buy capital assets. Ratios such as return on sales, return on assets, and return on invested capital can readily tell whether a business is generating enough profit to satisfy its day-to-day operating needs and longer-term financial aspirations.

Profitability can be improved by:

♦   Increasing sales volume and/or unit selling price.
♦   Reducing operating expenses (i.e., cost of goods sold, selling, or administration).

◆   Reducing the use of borrowed capital (interest charges).
◆   Cutting back non-productive assets (i.e., working capital and capital assets).

As will be covered later in this chapter, the use of financial ratios through the common-size ratio analysis technique of the income statement can help set the stage to improve profitability and return performance. As shown below, converting all numbers in the income statement from dollar figures to percentages (or ratios) does this. Each line on the income statement is compared to sales revenue. Once the percentages or ratios have been calculated, the statement can be used to analyze past performance and can be compared to specific competitors and to industry-wide statistics. This analysis can readily help managers pinpoint operating efficiencies (or inefficiencies) and profitability.

% of sales revenue	1999	2000	2001
Sales revenue	100.0%	100.0%	100.0%
Cost of goods sold	80.0	81.0	79.0
Gross margin	20.0	19.0	21.0
Operating expenses	15.0	16.0	15.0
Income before taxes	5.0%	3.0%	6.0%

As shown above, it does not take the mind of a financial genius to observe that return on sales declined from 5 cents to 3 cents between 1999 and 2000. Managers have to find out the reasons for this deterioration in operating efficiencies. More importantly, they will have to formulate financial goals for the next year for each operating line on the income statement (e.g., 79 cents in cost of goods sold and 15 cents in operating expenses). Also, they will have to determine strategies and plans that will help realize the 2001 goals in order to improve their gross margin and income before tax performance. To illustrate the importance of this simple analysis, suppose that the sales revenue objective for the year 2001 is $10 million. A 6 percent return on sales would generate $600,000 in income before taxes. If the return on sales performance is maintained at the 2000 operating efficiency level (3.0% level), the income level would be reduced to $300,000. Common-size statement analysis helps to pinpoint what should be done for each account on the income statement in order to improve profitability and return.

Ensure Liquidity

In business, being liquid is just as important as generating an adequate return. What activity in business is more important than being able to pay customers, lenders, and employees on time? To operate with some degree of comfort, a business must have enough cash (**liquidity**) to pay its day-to-day operating expenses and retire other liabilities on schedule. It is always possible to defer a payment of some financial obligations (i.e., accounts payable or bank loan) because of a temporary cash shortage; however, taking advantage of that privilege can quickly lead to a financial downfall. An important ratio that can test a company's liquidity position is the relationship between all *current asset accounts* such as accounts receivable and inventories to all *current liability accounts* that must be paid also within a reasonable time period (within a year) such as accounts payable and accrued expenses.

Stakeholders that are interested in measuring liquidity are short-term lenders (providers of working capital loans), suppliers (bills), employees (salaries and wages), and owners (dividends).

Businesses that want to improve their profit performance (maximize return) must implement effective cash management strategies such as:

- Accelerating cash receipts by speeding up billing and collection processes.
- Delaying disbursements to maximize the use of cash.
- Reducing working capital requirements.
- Monitoring the operating cycle that can help gauge cash goals (i.e., number of days it takes from the purchase of inventory to collecting receivables from its customers).

Some of the financial ratios that can help in formulating cash management strategies include the cash ratio, the current ratio, the quick ratio, the working capital ratio, and the cash conversion cycle.

Maintain Solvency

Solvency can be defined as a company's ability to pay its debts. Solvency ratios attempt to determine if a business is overextended in debt. This is done by examining whether a firm has (or will have) the ability to pay its principal and interest obligations as they become due. Cash flow performance and capital structure (proportion of debt to equity) can help determine the solvency prospects of a company in order to avoid getting into financial trouble. There is no question that maintaining solvency is essential for any business. If a business defaults on its debt obligations, it can lead to legal proceedings that could easily put a strain on its day-to-day operations and even derail its operations.

Managers and investors are always on the alert for the threat of insolvency that applies to both current and longer-term operating conditions. When a business is *insolvent*, it means that its liabilities exceed assets and that it is operating with a negative equity. Nevertheless, if a company operates with a positive equity structure, it can still be insolvent if it has difficulty in *servicing* its debt payments. For this reason, financial measures are used to test whether a business is financially solvent. Solvency can be examined from two angles.

- *Financial structure* examines whether a company has too much debt compared to what owners have invested in the business (equity).
- *Debt-paying-ability* examines whether a business has the ability to service its debt with relative ease. Here, solvency is analyzed using short-term solvency tests such as the quick ratio and current ratio, and long-term solvency tests such as debt-service coverage and fixed-charge-coverage.

Testing the solvency conditions of a business is of prime interest to market analysts, investment portfolio managers, private investors, investment bankers, and other stakeholders. They will usually test a firm's solvency performance before deciding whether to make or renew a loan. These financial ratios can determine the financial profile of a firm in terms of its creditworthiness and judge whether it will have enough cash to pay its loans, interest, and dividends on time.

As will be covered later in this chapter, the use of financial ratios through the common-size ratios of the balance sheet can help set the stage for improving a business' financial structure. As shown below, converting all figures in the balance sheet from dollar figures to *percentages* (or ratios) does this. Here, every line on the balance sheet is compared to total liabilities and equity. Once the ratios have been calculated, they can be used to analyze performance over time, and performance compared to specific competitors and to industry-wide statistics.

% of liabilities and equity	1999	2000	2001
Current liabilities	20.0%	23.0%	21.0%
Long-term debt	40.0	42.0	39.0
Total debt	60.0	65.0	60.0
Shareholders' equity	40.0	35.0	40.0
Liabilities and equity	100.0%	100.0%	100.0%

As shown, by using the common-size analysis, the company's leverage structure has changed between 1999 and 2000. More debt as compared to shareholders' equity was used to finance the purchase of assets (65% compared to 60%). Management would therefore have to determine whether this financial structure should be maintained or altered. Detailed analysis would give answers regarding the level of margin of safety or protective cushion that owners' equity should provide for creditors, and whether there will be enough funds available from operations to pay the interest owed to lenders and other fixed charges such as lease payments.

Secure Long-term Profitability

The ability of a business to grow *smoothly* is always a concern for stakeholders. Growth funds come from several sources:

1. Internally generated funds (cash from operations).
2. Externally generated funds (from lenders and shareholders).
3. Reduced dividends.
4. Reduced investment in capital assets.

To be sure, the size of the market, a company's yearly growth rate, and the aggressiveness of management to increase its share of the market or even launch new products and operate in different markets will determine, to a large extent, how fast a business' sales revenue will increase. However, sales revenue is only one component of the puzzle. Sales revenue increments impact all lines on the income statement (e.g., cost of goods sold, selling expenses, and administrative expenses) and the balance sheet (e.g., accounts receivable, inventory, working capital loans, and long-term debt).

Typical questions that stakeholders usually ask are:

- Do we have sufficient resources to grow (physical, financial, human)?
- Where will growth funds come from—internal sources or external sources? How much will be needed?
- Do we have enough borrowing power to finance our growth?
- Will we have enough cash to service the new debt and equity (interest charges and dividends)?
- Will the incremental return on sales and earnings before interest and taxes (EBIT) be positive? If so, to what extent?

As shown below, the use of financial ratios or percentages through the horizontal analysis of the income statement and the balance sheet helps to visualize the proportion of growth patterns in all components of the financial statements between two comparable fiscal periods. This comparison could be done between:

- A month in the current year with the same month in the previous year.
- The current quarter and the same quarter last year.
- This year's 12-month operating results and last year's 12-month operating results.

% change over previous year	1999	2000	2001
Income statement accounts			
Sales revenue	11.5%	25.0%	25.3%
Cost of goods sold	12.1	19.5	10.4
Operating expenses	8.8	12.6	17.5
Income after taxes	10.4	93.2	81.4
Balance sheet accounts			
Current assets	9.5%	17.8%	3.2%
Capital assets	21.3	38.2	32.4
Total assets	14.3	26.3	17.0
Current liabilities	8.5	14.4	2.4
Long-term debt	14.6	41.0	−14.0
Total debt	12.1	24.8	−5.4
Shareholders' equity	15.3	27.8	40.9
Total liabilities and equity	14.3	26.3	17.0

As shown, horizontal analysis gives a clear indication of the growth patterns (past and future) for various accounts appearing on financial statements. It reveals, for example, that a 25.3 percent increase in sales revenue for the forecast period (2001) will generate an 81.4 percent increase in income after taxes. It will also require a 17 percent increase in total assets, and most of the growth funds will come from shareholders' equity (new capital from shareholders or increase in retained earnings). These numbers are very informative and revealing. They certainly give managers or investors the opportunity to ask questions about whether the growth rate for each element on the financial statements is feasible.

Now that we have an understanding of the reasons why ratios are important to analyze financial statements and to help make important operating, financing, and investing decisions, let's now examine the more commonly used financial ratios, what they measure, and how they are calculated.

Financial Ratios

As discussed in Chapter 2, the purpose of the initial two steps in financial management (bookkeeping and accounting) is to prepare financial statements. The next two steps involve the *analysis* of business performance for the purpose of assessing financial strengths and weaknesses, and making investing, financing, and operating *decisions*.

When looking at a balance sheet or an income statement, it is relatively easy to gauge how much profit a business has made, how much debt it owes to its creditors, or the amount of funds owners have invested in it. However, in order to evaluate business performance in more depth and with more precision, managers and business investors use **financial ratios** to gauge liquidity, debt coverage, asset management, profitability, and market value.

Hundreds of ratios can be used to gauge financial performance and management competence. Using too many ratios to evaluate a business's financial performance can, however, confuse more than enlighten. Some ratios are deficient because they (1) can mislead, (2) do not give a complete picture of a financial situation, (3) do not have a practical application, or (4) show in a roundabout manner what other ratios show more clearly. For example, what would be the point of comparing current liabilities to owners' equity, or selling expenses to capital assets? The real objective of ratio analysis is to reduce the large number of accounts (or items) contained in financial statements to a relatively small number of *meaningful relationships*. Important relationships (ratios) depend to a large measure on the purpose of the ratios selected and should relate components in which a *logical decision-making relationship* exists between the two elements.

Ratios can be regarded as diagnostic tools. Just as a doctor measures various characteristics of the blood, a person evaluating a company measures the various relationships of numbers shown on financial statements. To be sure, a high or low value of some characteristics of the blood is seldom a disease in itself, but more likely the symptom of a disease. Likewise, the study of numbers shown on financial statements reveals symptoms of problems or of management errors that need to be corrected.

As indicated earlier, a ratio is simply a comparison of one account to another to express the size of an item in relation to the other. For instance, one can express the number of sunny days to rainy days during a given month simply by:

- Dividing the number of sunny days (say 15) by the number of rainy days (15) for a ratio of 1.
- By dividing the total number of sunny days (say 15) by the total number of days during the month (30) for a ratio of 0.50 or 50 percent.

This chapter examines sixteen ratios that can be grouped under three categories.

- *Balance sheet ratios* relate two balance sheet accounts.
- *Income statement ratios* show the relationship between two items on the income statement.
- *Combined ratios* relate numbers on the balance sheet to the numbers on the income statement.

Balance sheet, income statement, and combined ratios can also be regrouped under five other categories in order to measure a company's financial performance.

a. *Liquidity ratios* measure the ability of a firm to meet its future cash obligations—that is, to meet its short-term obligations.
b. *Debt/coverage* ratios are used to evaluate the capital structure—that is, the proportion of funds a business borrows from creditors and owners to finance the purchase of assets, and the firm's ability to service its debt.
c. *Asset-management ratios* evaluate how efficiently managers use the assets of a business.
d. *Profitability ratios* measure the overall operating effectiveness of a business by comparing profit level to sales, to assets, and to equity.
e. *Market-value ratios* are used to assess the way investors and stock markets react to a company's performance.

The sixteen ratios identified in **Table 3.1** will be defined and examined within the context of Eastman Technologies Inc.'s income statement and balance sheet shown in **Tables 2.3** and **2.5** respectively in Chapter 2.

Liquidity Ratios

Liquidity ratios examine the accounts shown on the upper portion of the balance sheet—that is, the relationship between current assets and current liabilities. These two grouping of accounts are referred to as *working capital*. By referring to **Table 2.5**, we can calculate Eastman's net working capital in 2000 as follows:

Current assets	$600,000
Current liabilities	445,000
Net working capital	$155,000

These ratios measure the short-term solvency and help judge the adequacy of liquid assets for meeting short-term obligations as they come due. The $155,000 in net working capital is the level of funds Eastman has to operate with on a day-to-day basis—that is, to pay on time its accounts payable, short-term bank loans,

> **TABLE 3.1**   Commonly Used Financial Ratios

A. **Liquidity Ratios**
   1. Current ratio (times)
   2. Quick ratio (times)

B. **Leverage Ratios**
   3. Debt-to-total-assets (%)
   4. Debt-to-equity (times)
   5. Times-interest-earned (times)
   6. Fixed-charge-coverage (times)

C. **Asset-Management Ratios**
   7. Average collection period (days)
   8. Inventory turnover (times)

   9. Capital assets turnover (times)
   10. Total assets turnover (times)

D. **Profitability Ratios**
   11. Profit margin on sales (%)
   12. Return on sales (%)
   13. Return on total assets (%)
   14. Return on equity (%)

E. **Market-Value Ratios**
   15. Earnings per share ($)
   16. Price/earnings ratio (times)

and weekly operating expenses such as wages and salaries. Businesses experience financial difficulty because they cannot pay obligations as they come due and not merely because they are not profitable.

The most commonly used liquidity ratios are the current ratio and the quick ratio.

Current Ratio. The **current ratio**, also referred to as the working capital ratio, is calculated by dividing current assets by current liabilities. It is an excellent way to gauge business liquidity because it measures to what extent current assets exceed current liabilities. A common rule of thumb suggests that an acceptable current ratio should be around 2 to 1; that is, every dollar's worth of current liabilities should be backed up by at least two dollars' worth of current assets. This makes sense because if the firm could liquidate current assets for only one-half of their value stated in the balance sheet, it would still have adequate funds to pay all current liabilities. Nevertheless, a general standard for this ratio is not useful because it fails to recognize that an appropriate current ratio is a function of the nature of a company's business and would vary with different operating cycles of different businesses. It is more pertinent to use *industry averages* than *overall standards.* Eastman's current ratio is computed as follows:

$$\frac{\text{Current assets}}{\text{Current liabilities}} = \frac{\$600,000}{\$445,000} \quad 1.35 \text{ times}$$

This means that Eastman has $1.35 of current assets for every dollar of current liabilities. This ratio falls short of the 2 to 1 acceptable ratio. However, the current ratio has a general weakness in that it ignores the composition of the current asset accounts, which may be as important as their relationship with current liabilities. Therefore, before judging the liquidity position of a business, it is always prudent to examine other factors, such as the ratio of the industry in which it operates, the composition of the company's current assets, and the season of the year. For example, a business that has a 2 to 1 current ratio with 80 percent of its current assets in inventory would not be as liquid as a company in the same industry that has a 1.5 to 1 ratio and only has 30 percent of its current assets in inventory. Therefore, current ratio analysis must be supplemented by other working capital ratios such as the quick ratio.

Quick Ratio. The **quick ratio**, also called the acid-test ratio, measures the relationship between the more liquid current asset accounts such as cash, marketable securities, and accounts receivable to the current liability accounts. This ratio complements the current ratio because the problem in meeting current liabilities may rest on slowness or even in the inability to convert inventories into cash to meet current obligations particularly in periods of economic disturbance. This is a more severe measure of the short-term liability-paying ability of a business since the least liquid current asset, inventory, is not included in the calculation because this account takes more time to be converted into cash. This ratio does assume that receivables are of good quality and will be converted into cash over the next twelve months.

Eastman's quick ratio, which includes cash ($22,000), prepaid expenses ($60,000), and accounts receivable ($300,000), is calculated as follows:

$$\frac{\text{Quick assets}}{\text{Current liabilities}} \quad = \quad \frac{\$382,000}{\$445,000} \quad = \quad 0.86 \text{ times}$$

Generally, an acceptable quick ratio is in the 1 to 1 range. This means that Eastman's second liquidity position also does not appear to be acceptable. However, before passing final judgment on Eastman's liquidity position, it would be preferable to evaluate the company's historical working capital performance and compare it to industry standards or norms.

Leverage Ratios

These ratios deal with debt—that is, the funds borrowed by a business to finance the purchase of its assets. It is a lot like a house purchase for which funds come from two sources, mortgage holders and the buyer. Two questions are usually asked when gauging indebtedness. First, what should be the best mix of funds provided by lenders and the buyer to buy assets? This mix is measured by debt ratios. Second, will the business be able to service its contractual loan agreement—that is, pay the interest and principal each month? This ability is measured by coverage ratios. The most commonly used debt/coverage ratios are debt-to-total-assets ratio, debt-to-equity ratio, times-interest-earned ratio, and fixed-charge-coverage ratio.

Debt-to-Total-Assets Ratio. The **debt-to-total-assets ratio** (also called debt ratio) measures the proportion of all debts (current and long-term) injected into a business by lenders to buy assets shown on the balance sheet. The more debt employed by a firm, the more highly leveraged it is. This ratio is calculated by dividing total debts by total assets.

This ratio is important to lenders because they want to make sure that shareholders invest a sufficient amount of funds in the business in order to spread the risk more equitably. For Eastman, the ratio is computed as follows:

$$\frac{\text{Total debts}}{\text{Total assets}} = \frac{\$1,245,000}{\$1,800,000} = 69\%$$

This means that 69 percent of Eastman's assets are financed by debt, and thus lenders bear the greatest portion of risk. This suggests that creditors may have difficulty in collecting their loan from the business in the event of bankruptcy or liquidation. Generally, when this ratio exceeds 50 percent, creditors may be reluctant to provide more debt financing. However, as with all other ratios, it is important to assess the type or nature of the assets owned by the business, since that may very well influence how far lenders will go in funding the operations. The assets of the business appearing in the books, for example, may be much less than its market value. Also, a business may obtain more funds from lenders to construct a plant in an industrial park located in a large metropolitan area, than one located in an economically depressed region.

Debt-to-Equity Ratio. The **debt-to-equity ratio** is actually redundant if the debt-to-total assets ratio is used since the two ratios convey the same information. The debt-to-equity ratio is explained here because financial publications that provide industry average ratios for comparison purposes often cite the debt-to-equity ratio instead of the debt-to-total assets ratio. Therefore, it is important to be familiar with this measure. This ratio also shows whether a company is using debts prudently or has gone too far and is overburdened with debt that may cause some problem. It is important to show the relative proportions of lenders' claims and of ownership claims since it is used as a measure of *debt exposure*. It is expressed as either a percentage or as a proportion. Companies with debt-to-equity ratios above 1 are probably relying too much on debt.

In the case of Eastman, the ratio works out to:

$$\frac{\text{Total debts}}{\text{Total shareholders' equity}} = \frac{\$1,245,000}{\$\ 555,000} = 2.24 \text{ times}$$

Eastman uses over two dollars in borrowed funds compared to each dollar provided by shareholders. The ratio therefore shows that a considerable amount of funds is being financed by debt rather than by equity and that the company would find it difficult to borrow additional funds without first raising more equity capital. Management would probably be subjecting the firm to the risk of bankruptcy if it sought to increase the debt-to-equity ratio any further by borrowing additional funds. For this reason, it would be advantageous for Eastman to start thinking about trying to lower its total debt and/or increase owners' equity over the next year in an effort to improve its financial structure.

Times-Interest-Earned Ratio. The **times-interest-earned ratio** (**TIE**) measures to what extent a business can *service* its debt, or the business's ability to pay back the loan as agreed. Take the example of a potential homeowner who is seeking a loan to buy a $200,000 house. The bank would be interested not only in the value of the house in relation to how much the home buyer is prepared to put into the house, but also the buyer's ability to repay the loan on a month-to-month basis. An acceptable ratio is around 30 percent; that is, for every dollar's worth of salary, the loan repayment should not exceed 30 percent of the buyer's gross salary. For example, if a home buyer earns $5,000 a month, the mortgage payment should not be greater than $1,500 (or 30%). If the buyer is in the 40 percent tax bracket, $1,500 would go for loan payments, $2,000 would be used to pay income taxes, and the remaining $1,500 would be left for monthly living expenses. The higher the loan repayment in proportion to the buyer's gross salary, the less she or he would have left to pay for on-going living expenses.

This is what the times-interest-earned ratio reveals. It is determined by dividing earnings before interest and taxes (EBIT) by interest charges. The ratio measures the extent to which operating income can decline before the business is unable to meet its annual interest costs.

This ratio shows the number of dollars of income (earnings) before interest and taxes that is available to pay each dollar of interest expense. To calculate TIE, add income before taxes ($195,000) and interest charges ($35,000) and divide the sum by interest charges. The $230,000 sum would be equivalent to the home-buyer's $5,000 gross salary. The higher the ratio the greater the business' ability to pay all interest charges as agreed.

The calculation is always done on a before-tax basis, because interest charges are a tax-deductible expense. Referring to **Table 2.3**, the Eastman's ratio is computed as follows:

$$\frac{\text{Income before tax} + \text{Interest charges}}{\text{Interest charges}} = \frac{\$195,000 + \$35,000}{\$35,000} = 6.57 \text{ times}$$

To interpret times-interest-earned, consider that with each $6.57 earnings before interest and taxes, Eastman pays $1.00 towards interest and is left with $5.57 in earnings before taxes. Since the company is in the 50 percent tax bracket, Eastman pays:

$2.78 in income taxes and is left with $2.79 to:
1) pay dividends,
2) the principal on the loan, and
3) reinvest in the business as retained earnings.

Here is another way of describing this ratio.

EBIT	$6.57
Interest charges	1.00
EBT	5.57
Income taxes (50%)	2.78
EAIT	$2.79

The lower the ratio, the riskier it is. To illustrate, if the times-interest-earned ratio is reduced to 3.0, it means that the company would be left with only $2.00 (after paying the interest charges) to pay income taxes, the principal on the loan, and dividends, and to reinvest in the business (i.e., retained earnings). A comfortable times-interest-earned ratio is generally in the 4.0 to 5.0 range. An acceptable ratio is around 3.0 to 4.0 times.

This ratio complements the debt ratios by providing additional information about the company's ability to meet debt obligations. However, it still does not present a complete picture. The ultimate question is whether or not the company can meet its commitments to *all* creditors. Thus, a ratio based on *all* fixed charges is helpful.

Fixed-Charge-Coverage Ratio. This ratio is similar to the times-interest-earned ratio. However, it is more inclusive in that it recognizes that many firms incur long-term obligations under scheduled lease payments. The total of those obligations, that is, lease payments plus interest charges, makes up a firm's total annual fixed charges. The fixed-charge-coverage ratio is calculated by dividing the sum of the income before taxes and all fixed charges, by fixed charges. Fixed charges are regarded as unavoidable outlays. The Eastman ratio is computed as follows:

$$\frac{\text{Income before tax} + \text{Interest charges} + \text{Lease payments}}{\text{Interest charges} + \text{Lease payments}} = \frac{\$195{,}000 + \$35{,}000 + \$20{,}000}{\$35{,}000 + \$20{,}000} = 4.55 \text{ times}$$

With the growth of long-term lease arrangements, investors are increasingly interested in this ratio. As you can see in the calculation of Eastman's ratio, less profit will be available to pay dividends and to reinvest in the business.

Asset-Management Ratios

Asset-management ratios, sometimes referred to as activity ratios, operating ratios, or management ratios, measure the *efficiency* with which a business uses its assets or resources (i.e., inventories, accounts receivable, capital assets) to earn a profit. The intent of these ratios is to answer one basic question: Does the amount of each category of asset shown on the balance sheet seem too high or too low in view of what the firm has accomplished or wants to accomplish in the future? The more commonly used asset-management ratios are

- Average collection period
- Inventory turnover
- Capital assets turnover
- Total assets turnover

Average Collection Period. The **average collection period** (**ACP**) measures how long a firm's average sales dollar remains in the hands of its customers. A longer collection period automatically creates a larger investment in assets and may even indicate that the firm is extending credit terms that are too generous. However, management must balance its needs to collect receivables quickly with the competitive credit practices of other companies. The company does not want to lose sales simply because its credit policies are too restrictive. The main point is that investment in accounts receivable has a cost. Excess accounts receivable means that too much debt or shareholders' equity is being used by the business for receivables, and the business is not as capital-efficient as it could be.

The average collection period is calculated in two steps. The first step is calculating the average daily sales, which is done by dividing the total annual net sales by 365 days. Eastman's average daily sales is $6,849 ($2,500,000 ÷ 365). The second step is dividing the average daily sales into accounts receivable. Eastman's average collection period is 44 days and is calculated as follows:

$$\frac{\text{Accounts receivable}}{\text{Average daily sales}} = \frac{\$300,000}{\$6,849} = 44 \text{ days}$$

If Eastman were able to collect its receivables within 30 days, the company would reduce its accounts receivable by $95,886 ($6,849 × 14 days) and thus make this amount available to be invested in more productive assets. The question for Eastman is: How long should sales credit be? The manager responsible has to decide whether the average collection period is getting out of hand. If so, actions would have to be taken to shorten credit terms, shut off credit to slow payers, or step up collection efforts.

Inventory Turnover. **Inventory turnover** (also called inventory utilization ratio) measures the number of times a company's investment in inventory is turned over during a given year. For a company that buys merchandise and then sells it to customers, turnover is measured from the time an item is purchased until it is sold. Since a company's balance sheet does not show individual items, this ratio looks at the total *average* annual turnover rate. The higher the turnover ratio, the better, since a company with a high turnover requires a smaller investment in inventory than one producing the same level of sales with a low turnover rate. However, a company cannot keep inventory at too low a level or it will miss sales. If customers come to purchase items that are out of stock, they will likely purchase the items from a competitor.

Cost of goods sold, rather than sales revenue, should be used as the numerator for calculating the inventory turnover ratio since the denominator (inventory) is valued at cost and the purpose is to assess the adequacy of the physical turnover of that inventory.

Since a company's sales revenue takes place over a 12-month period (moving picture concept) while inventory level is computed at a specific point in time (still photography concept), the *average inventory* for the year may be used. Quarterly and even monthly inventory can also be used.

This ratio indicates the efficiency in turning over inventory and can be compared with the experience of other companies in the same industry. It also provides some indication of the adequacy of a company's inventory for the volume of business being handled. If a company has an inventory turnover rate that is above the industry average, it means that a better balance is being maintained between inventory and cost of goods sold. As a result, there will be less risk for the business of being caught with top-heavy inventory in the event of a decline in the price of raw materials or finished products. Here is how Eastman's ratio is calculated.

$$\frac{\text{Cost of goods sold}}{\text{Inventory}} = \frac{\$1,900,000}{\$218,000} = 8.7 \text{ times}$$

Eastman turns the average item carried in its inventory 8.7 times during the year. To be sure, not every item in the company's stock turns at the same rate. Some turn over more rapidly, while others have a slower turnover rate. Nevertheless, the overall average provides a logical starting point for positive inventory management. If Eastman were able to turn over its inventory faster, say up to 10 times a year, it would reduce its inventory from $218,000 to $190,000 ($1,900,000 ÷ 10) and thus add an extra $28,000 to the company's treasury.

Capital Assets Turnover. The **capital** (or **fixed**) **assets turnover ratio** (also called fixed assets utilization ratio) measures how intensively a firm's capital assets such as land, buildings, and equipment are used to generate sales. A low capital assets turnover implies that a firm has too much invested in capital assets relative to sales. The ratio is basically a measure of efficiency. The following shows how Eastman's capital assets turnover ratio is calculated.

$$\frac{\text{Sales}}{\text{Capital assets}} = \frac{\$2,500,000}{\$1,200,000} = 2.1 \text{ times}$$

This means that the company generates $2.10 worth of sales for every dollar invested in capital assets. If a competing firm has a $3.00 ratio, it implies that it is more productive since every dollar invested in capital assets produces an extra $0.90 in sales. If a business shows a weakness in this ratio, its plant may be operating below capacity and managers should be looking at the possibility of selling the less productive assets.

There is one problem with the use of capital assets turnover for comparison purposes. If the capital-assets turnover ratio of a firm with assets that were acquired many years ago are compared to a company that has recently automated its operations to make them more efficient or productive, the more modern firm will have a much lower ratio than the old and less productive company.

Total Assets Turnover. This ratio measures the turnover or utilization of all of a firm's assets, that is both capital assets and current assets. It indicates the efficiency with which assets are used. A low ratio means that excessive assets are employed to generate sales and/or that some assets (capital or current assets) should be liquidated or reduced. This ratio is very useful as an initial indicator of a problem with sales or an excessive accumulation of assets. When managers see that this ratio is too low, they may have to modify their sales objectives and plans, examine the growth in the marketplace and competitors, or determine if their asset base is too large. Eastman's total assets turnover is as follows:

$$\frac{\text{Sales}}{\text{Total assets}} \quad = \quad \frac{\$2,500,000}{\$1,800,000} \quad = \quad 1.4 \text{ times}$$

In this case, the company produces $1.40 worth of sales for every dollar invested in total assets. If Eastman is able to reduce its investment in accounts receivable and inventory and/or sell a division or capital assets which are a burden on the company's operating performance, it would increase the total assets turnover ratio and thus would prove to be more productive.

Profitability Ratios

Profitability ratios deal with bottom-line performance and measure the extent to which a business is successful in generating profit relative to sales, investment in assets, and equity. These ratios show the level of business efficiency and effectiveness and reflect the results of a large number of policies and decisions. Therefore, profitability ratios show the combined effects or operating results of liquidity, asset management, and debt management. The most commonly used profitability ratios are: profit margin on sales, return on sales, return on total assets, and return on equity.

Profit Margin on Sales. **Profit margin on sales** or net operating margin (operating income) is computed by dividing net operating income by sales. This ratio is an excellent measure of a firm's ability to make any financial gains since the calculation excludes non-operating items, such as interest and other income that are not part of the mainstream operating activities of a business. The main purpose of this ratio is to assess the effectiveness of management in generating operating income. Eastman's profit margin on sales is as follows:

$$\frac{\text{Operating income}}{\text{Sales}} \quad = \quad \frac{\$210,000}{\$2,500,000} \quad = \quad 8.4\ \%$$

In the case of Eastman, the company generates 8.4 cents in operating income for every dollar's worth of sales.

Return on Sales. **Return on sales** represents an important measure of a company's financial performance after recognizing its interest charges and income tax obligation. This ratio gauges the firm's overall ability to *squeeze* profits from each sales dollar. This ratio measures the overall profitability of a business and is calculated by dividing income after taxes by sales. Profit-seeking businesses are keenly interested in maximizing their return on sales, since this bottom-line figure represents funds either distributed to shareholders in the form of dividends or retained and reinvested in the business. Eastman's return on sales is calculated as follows:

$$\frac{\text{Income after taxes}}{\text{Sales}} = \frac{\$97,500}{\$2,500,000} = 3.9\%$$

For every dollar's worth of sales, Eastman earns 3.9 cents in income after taxes. The higher the ratio, the more beneficial it is to the wealth of the business and to its shareholders. For effective analysis, this ratio should also be compared to historical company performance, used as a platform for planning purposes, and compared to industry average or specific firms competing in the industry.

The return on sales ratio has a limitation in that it is based on income after deduction of interest expenses. If the company has increased its debt substantially, this may result in a decrease in income after taxes because of the interest expense deduction, even if the return on the shareholders' investment has actually increased. The profit margin on sales overcomes this problem and provides another view of profitability.

Return on Total Assets. This ratio measures profit performance in relation to assets committed. This ratio might be viewed as a measure of the efficiency of total asset usage. It is calculated by dividing net income after taxes by total assets. Eastman's return on total assets is computed as follows:

$$\frac{\text{Income after taxes}}{\text{Total assets}} = \frac{\$97,500}{\$1,800,000} = 5.4\%$$

To have any meaning, this ratio should also be compared to the industry average or to competing firms.

Return on Equity. This ratio relates the income after taxes to owners' equity. This ratio is critical to shareholders since it shows the yield they earn on their investments. It also allows shareholders to judge whether the return made on their investment is worth the risk. Eastman's return on equity ratio is calculated as follows:

$$\frac{\text{Net income}}{\text{Owners' equity}} = \frac{\$97,500}{\$555,000} = 17.6\%$$

This means that for every dollar invested in the business by the shareholders, they earn 17.6 cents. By most standards, this profit performance would be judged relatively good.

Market-Value Ratios

Up to this point, we have examined *financial statement ratios,* that is ratios that are calculated by using information drawn from financial statements. The next two ratios deal with **market-value ratios** that are used to analyze the way investors and stock markets are reacting to a company's performance.

These ratios would be impossible to calculate for Eastman or any company whose stock is not actively traded on a stock market such as the New York Stock Exchange (NYSE). Only public companies have to report market-value ratios at the bottom of their financial statements. To be sure, if a company's liquidity, asset-management, leverage, and profitability ratios are all good, the chances for its market ratios would be excellent, and its share price would also be on the high side.

Market-value ratios relate the data presented on a company's financial statements to financial market data and provide some insight into how investors perceive a business as a whole including its strength in the securities markets. The more commonly used market-value ratios are earnings per share and price/earnings ratio.

Earnings per Share. **Earnings per share** is calculated by dividing the net income after preferred dividends—that is, net income available to common shareholders by the number of shares of common shares outstanding. Assuming that Eastman has 40,000 shares outstanding in 2000, the calculation would be as follows:

$$\frac{\text{Income to common shareholders}}{\text{Number of shares outstanding}} = \frac{\$97,500}{40,000} = \$2.44$$

Earnings per share is a measure that both management and shareholders pay attention to because it is widely used in the valuation of commons shares, and is often the basis for setting specific strategic goals and plans.

Price/earnings ratio, abbreviated as P/E, is one of the most used ratios in share value and securities analysis. The P/E shows how much investors are willing to pay per dollar of reported profits. The P/E ratio is the market price of common shares divided by the earnings per common share. In the case of Eastman, we assume that in 2000, the company's common share market price was $30.00. Daily newspaper stock market pages include EPS and P/E ratio, and are considered primary stock valuation criteria. The price/earnings ratio is calculated as follows:

$$\frac{\text{Price per common share}}{\text{Earnings per common share}} = \frac{\$30.00}{\$2.44} = 12.3 \text{ times}$$

Eastman's 12.3 P/E ratio is more meaningful when it is compared to the P/E ratios of other companies. If a competitor is generating a P/E ratio of 10, it means the Eastman's P/E ratio is above the competitor and suggests that it could be regarded as somewhat less risky, or having better growth prospects, or both.

Table 3.2 summarizes Eastman's sixteen key ratios.

Common Size Ratios

One of the most frequently used approaches in probing a balance sheet and an income statement is to compare the individual items on a statement between two successive years. The comparison is made using percentages. Statements showing these percentages are called "common-size statement analysis" or "vertical analysis."

As shown in **Table 3.3**, each component of Eastman's balance sheet related to assets is expressed as a percentage of *total assets*, and each component related to liabilities and shareholders' equity is expressed as a percentage of *total liabilities* and *shareholders' equity.* Common size ratio analysis is interesting to use for comparing the performance of one business to another or one division to another, because it ignores the difference in the size of the individual accounts. All elements are converted on comparable terms—that is, percentages.

TABLE 3.2   Eastman Technologies Inc.'s Financial Ratios

Liquidity ratios

1. Current Ratio

$$\frac{\text{Current assets}}{\text{Current liabilities}} = \frac{\$600,000}{\$445,000} = 1.35 \text{ times}$$

2. Quick Ratio

$$\frac{\text{Quick assets}}{\text{Current liabilities}} = \frac{\$382,000}{\$445,000} = 0.86 \text{ times}$$

Leverage Ratios

3. Debt-to-Total Assets Ratio

$$\frac{\text{Total debt}}{\text{Total assets}} = \frac{\$1,245,000}{\$1,800,000} = 69\%$$

4. Debt-to-Equity Ratio

$$\frac{\text{Total debt}}{\text{Shareholders' equity}} = \frac{\$1,245,000}{\$555,000} = 2.24 \text{ times}$$

5. Times-Interest-Earned Ratio

$$\frac{\text{Income before taxes} + \text{Interest charges}}{\text{Interest charges}} = \frac{\$195,000 + \$35,000}{\$35,000} = 6.57 \text{ times}$$

6. Fixed-Charge-Coverage Ratio

$$\frac{\text{Income before taxes} + \text{Interest charges} + \text{Lease payment}}{\text{Interest charges} + \text{Lease payment}} = \frac{\$195,000 + \$35,000 + \$20,000}{\$35,000 + \$20,000} = 4.55 \text{ times}$$

Asset Management Ratios

7. Average Collection Period

$$\frac{\text{Accounts receivable}}{\text{Average daily sales}} = \frac{\$300,000}{\$6,849} = 44 \text{ days}$$

8. Inventory Turnover

$$\frac{\text{Cost of goods sold}}{\text{Inventory}} = \frac{\$1,900,000}{\$218,000} = 8.7 \text{ times}$$

9. Capital Assets Turnover

$$\frac{\text{Sales}}{\text{Capital assets}} = \frac{\$2,500,000}{\$1,200,000} = 2.1 \text{ times}$$

10. Total Assets Turnover

$$\frac{\text{Sales}}{\text{Total assets}} = \frac{\$2,500,000}{\$1,800,000} = 1.4 \text{ times}$$

Profitability Ratios

11. Profit Margin on Sales

$$\frac{\text{Operating income}}{\text{Sales}} = \frac{\$210,000}{\$2,500,000} = 8.4\%$$

12. Return on Sales

$$\frac{\text{Income after taxes}}{\text{Total assets}} = \frac{\$97,500}{\$2,500,000} = 3.9\%$$

13. Return on Total Assets

$$\frac{\text{Income after taxes}}{\text{Total assets}} = \frac{\$97,500}{\$1,800,000} = 5.4\%$$

14. Return on Equity

$$\frac{\text{Net income}}{\text{Owners' equity}} = \frac{\$97,500}{\$555,000} = 17.6\%$$

Market-Value Ratios

15. Earnings Per Share

$$\frac{\text{Income to common shareholders}}{\text{Number of shares}} = \frac{\$97,500}{\$40,000} = \$2.44$$

16. Price/Earnings Ratio

$$\frac{\text{Price per common share}}{\text{Earnings per common share}} = \frac{\$30.00}{\$2.44} = 12.3 \text{ times}$$

Common size ratio analysis also reveals the change in mix between several elements of a balance sheet and between two consecutive balance sheets. For example, **Table 3.3** shows that, in 1999, current assets represented 36.16 percent out of every asset dollar of the company. In 2000, this ratio declined to 33.33 percent. Examining the individual percentages, we see that prepaid expenses

---

TABLE 3.3   Common Size Ratio Analysis of the Balance Sheet

Eastman Technologies Inc.
Balance Sheets as of December 31

Assets	2000	%	1999	%
Current Assets				
Cash	$ 22,000	1.22	$ 18,000	1.21
Prepaid expenses	60,000	3.33	55,000	3.70
Accounts receivable	300,000	16.67	280,000	18.82
Inventory	218,000	12.11	185,000	12.43
Total current assets	**600,000**	**33.33**	**538,000**	**36.16**
Capital assets (at cost)	1,340,000	74.44	1,050,000	70.56
Accumulated depreciation	140,000	7.78	100,000	6.72
Capital assets (net)	**1,200,000**	**66.67**	**950,000**	**63.84**
Total Assets	$1,800,000	100.00	$1,488,000	100.00
Liabilities				
Current liabilities				
Accounts payable	$ 195,000	10.83	$ 175,000	11.76
Notes payable	150,000	8.33	135,000	9.07
Accrued expenses	20,000	1.11	18,000	1.21
Taxes payable	80,000	4.44	70,000	4.70
Total current liabilities	**445,000**	**24.72**	**398,000**	**26.75**
Long-term debts	**800,000**	**44.44**	**600,000**	**40.32**
Total liabilities	**1,245,000**	**69.17**	**998,000**	**67.07**
Common shares	300,000	16.67	285,000	19.15
Retained earnings	255,000	14.17	205,000	13.78
Shareholders' equity	**555,000**	**30.83**	**490,000**	**32.93**
Total liabilities and equity	$1,800,000	100.00	$1,488,000	100.00

---

dropped from 3.70 percent to 3.33 percent. In addition, it shows that accounts receivable and inventory, which represent a greater percentage of the total assets, also declined. The same analysis can be performed for each component in the liability and shareholders' equity accounts.

Common size ratio analysis of the income statement provides the same type of information. As shown in **Table 3.4**, each component of Eastman's income statement is converted to a percentage of net sales. Eastman's income performance improved from 1999 to 2000. In 2000, for every dollar in sales, it made 3.9 percent (or cents) compared to 3.3 percent (or cents) in 1999. Although the overall profitability performance of the company improved, it is evident that some accounts improved and others deteriorated. For example, the cost of goods sold went from 77.5 percent

TABLE 3.4   Common Size Ratio Analysis of the Income Statement

Eastman Technologies Inc.
Income Statements for the Years Ended December 31, 2000 and 1999

	2000	% of sales	1999	% of sales
Net sales	$2,500,000	100.0	$2,250,000	100.0
Cost of goods sold	1,900,000	76.0	1,743,000	77.5
Gross margin	600,000	24.0	507,000	22.5
Operating expenses				
Selling expenses:				
Sales salaries	$ 140,000	5.6	128,000	5.7
Advertising expenses	20,000	0.8	19,000	0.8
Total selling expenses	160,000	6.4	147,000	6.5
Administrative expenses:				
Office salaries	170,000	6.8	155,000	6.9
Rent	20,000	0.8	20,000	0.9
Depreciation	40,000	1.6	30,000	1.3
Total administration expenses	230,000	9.2	205,000	9.1
Total operating expenses	390,000	15.6	352,000	15.6
Operating income	210,000	8.4	155,000	6.9
Other income	20,000	0.8	18,000	0.8
Other expenses (interest)	35,000	1.4	23,000	1.0
	15,000	0.6	5,000	0.2
Income before taxes	195,000	7.8	150,000	6.7
Income taxes	97,500	3.9	75,000	3.3
Income after taxes	$ 97,500	3.9	$ 75,000	3.3

to 76.0 percent, which improved the company's margin from 22.5 percent to 24.0 percent. Salary and lease accounts improved, while depreciation showed an increase.

Common size ratio analysis enables management to compare financial statements from one year to the next and between companies or operating divisions. The analysis allows management to answer the following types of questions.

- Is our company's capital structure in line with that of the industry?
- Is the ratio of the company's current assets to total assets favorable?
- Is the investment in capital assets in the right proportion?
- Are the manufacturing costs too high?
- Are the operating expenses too high?
- Is the ratio of income after taxes to sales adequate?

Horizontal Analysis

Horizontal analysis is performed by listing two consecutive financial statements, side by side, and then comparing the differences between the two periods. The comparison shows the growth or decline in each component of a financial statement, both in absolute dollars and as a percentage. For example, if sales in 1999 was $900,000 and in 2000 was $990,000, horizontal analysis will show the $90,000 increase and a 10 percent growth.

Tables 3.5 and 3.6 show horizontal analysis for Eastman's balance sheet and income statement respectively. In **Table 3.5**, Eastman's balance sheets show signif-

---

TABLE 3.5   Horizontal Analysis of the Balance Sheet

Eastman Technologies Inc.
Balance Sheets at December 31, 2000 and 1999

Assets	2000	1999	Amount of change	% of change
Current Assets				
Cash	$ 22,000	$ 18,000	$ 4,000	22.2
Prepaid expenses	60,000	55,000	5,000	9.1
Accounts receivable	300,000	280,000	20,000	7.1
Inventory	218,000	185,000	33,000	17.8
Total current assets	**600,000**	**538,000**	**62,000**	**11.5**
Capital assets (at cost)	1,340,000	1,050,000	290,000	27.6
Accumulated depreciation	140,000	100,000	40,000	40.0
Capital assets (net)	**1,200,000**	**950,000**	**250,000**	**26.3**
Total Assets	$1,800,000	$1,488,000	312,000	21.0
Liabilities				
Current liabilities				
Accounts payable	$ 195,000	$ 175,000	20,000	11.4
Notes payable	150,000	135,000	15,000	11.1
Accrued expenses	20,000	18,000	2,000	11.1
Taxes payable	80,000	70,000	10,000	14.3
Total current liabilities	**445,000**	**398,000**	**47,000**	**11.8**
Long-term debts	**800,000**	**600,000**	**200,000**	**33.3**
Total liabilities	**1,245,000**	**998,000**	**247,000**	**24.7**
Common shares	300,000	285,000	15,000	5.3
Retained earnings	255,000	205,000	50,000	24.4
Shareholders' equity	**555,000**	**490,000**	**65,000**	**13.3**
Total liabilities and equity	$1,800,000	$1,488,000	$312,000	21.0

icant changes in certain accounts. For example, current assets show an 11.5 percent growth while total net capital assets increased by 26.3 percent. The lower part of the balance sheet shows an increase of 11.8 percent in Eastman's current liabilities, an increase of 33.3 percent in its long-term debts, and a 13.3 percent increase in total shareholders' equity.

Table 3.6 shows a 30 percent increase in income after taxes. Individual components that have contributed to this significant increase are registered in sales, which show a larger increase than the cost of goods sold (11.1 percent versus 9.0 percent). Although salaries increased by only 9.4 percent, interest expense increased by a hefty 52.2 percent.

[**TABLE 3.6**   Horizontal Analysis of the Income Statement   ]

Eastman Technologies Inc.
Income Statement for the Years Ended December 31, 2000 and 1999

	2000	1999	Amount of change	% of change
Net sales	$2,500,000	$2,250,000	$250,000	11.1
Cost of goods sold	1,900,000	1,743,000	157,000	9.0
Gross margin	**600,000**	**507,000**	**93,000**	**18.3**
Operating expenses				
Selling expenses:				
Sales salaries	$ 140,000	128,000	12,000	9.4
Advertising expenses	20,000	19,000	1,000	5.3
Total selling expenses	160,000	147,000	13,000	8.8
Administrative expenses:				
Office salaries	170,000	155,000	15,000	9.7
Rent	20,000	20,000	—	—
Depreciation	40,000	30,000	10,000	33.3
Total administration expenses	230,000	205,000	25,000	12.2
Total operating expenses	390,000	352,000	38,000	10.8
Operating income	**210,000**	**155,000**	**55,000**	**35.5**
Other income	20,000	18,000	2,000	11.1
Other expenses (interest)	35,000	23,000	12,000	52.2
	15,000	5,000	10,000	200.0
Income before taxes	195,000	150,000	45,000	30.0
Income taxes	97,500	75,000	22,500	30.0
Income after taxes	**$ 97,500**	**$ 75,000**	**$ 22,500**	**30.0**

Using Benchmarks to Analyze Financial Statements

The most popular term for learning from others is benchmarking. **Benchmarking** is the process of searching for the best practices among competitors or non-competitors that have led to their superior performance. It is looking for companies that are doing "something excellent" and learning about their best practices, and then adapting them for your own company. By aspiring to be as good as the best in the industry, managers can set their own ambitions.

Reading industry and trade journals and attending trade shows and public symposia help to keep managers and employees aware of what others are doing and give them ideas for how to improve their own company's practices. Benchmarking should at least help managers and employees to think more creatively.

Benchmarking can be used from three angles: comparing a company to specific competitors, comparing a company to industry, and using trend analysis.

Comparing a Company to Specific Competitors

The first step for benchmarking is to select, from trade journals or periodicals, the companies that are showing the best financial results in their respective industries for managing their resources. For example, teams in various sectors of a company could embark on benchmarking journeys and try to find solutions to improve various aspects of the company's financial statements, such as improving current asset management.

For example, *Standard and Poor's Compustat Services, Inc.* produces all types of historical and current financial ratios about individual firms and industries. If a company wants to improve its working capital accounts, debt structure, or profit performance, as a starting point it should pay a visit to the *Report Library* and look for those companies that excel in various activities of the financial statements. The next logical step would be to analyze and ask questions about why performance is superior.

Table 3.7 shows a partial list of the type of financial information that can be drawn from the *Standard and Poor's Compustat Inc.'s Report Library* on a company basis and industry-wide basis.

As shown in the table, there is certainly no lack of information that can be drawn from annual financial reports for comparative purposes. If a business is in the food industry, information can be drawn for all public corporations. Those companies that show excellent ratios can be studied further.

Comparing a Company to an Industry

To be of value, the study should be limited to the ratios of businesses in the same sector or industry. To illustrate how ratios can be used as measurement tools, let us examine **Table 3.8** and compare Eastman's 16 ratios to those of the industry in general.

TABLE 3.7   Benchmarking the Corporation

Partial List of Financial Information that Can be Drawn from the *Compustat Report Library*

Income Statement Reports
- Annual Income Statement – Eleven Years
- Comparative Income Statement
- Comparative Composite Income Statement
- Trend Income Statement
- Common Size Income Statement
- Quarterly Common Size Income Statement
- Twelve-Month Moving Income Statement

Balance Sheet Reports
- Annual Balance Sheet – Eleven Years
- Annual Balance Sheet – With Footnotes
- Composite Historical Annual Balance Sheet
- Trend Balance Sheet
- Common Size Balance Sheet
- Quarterly Trend Balance Sheet

Statement of Cash Flows
- Statement of Cash Flows (Annual and Quarterly)
- Cash Statement by Source and Use (Annual and Quarterly)
- Twelve-Month Moving Statement of Cash Flows
- Working Capital Statement (Annual and Quarterly)

Ratio Reports
- Annual Ratio
- Quarterly Ratio
- Comparative Annual Ratio

Market Reports
- Daily Market Date – Seven Days
- Daily Adjusted Prices

Summary Reports
- Profitability
- Trend – Five Years

Earnings Estimate Reports
- Standardized Unexpected Earnings – Current
- Analysts' Coverage

Graphics Library
- Fundamental Financial Data
- Six-Month and One-Year Daily Price
- Company Segment Pie Chart
- Geographic Segment Pie Chart
- Ten-Year Monthly Price/Earnings

	TABLE 3.8 Comparative Ratio Analysis of Eastman Technologies Inc. with Industry		

Ratios	Eastman Technologies Inc.	Industry
A. Liquidity Ratios		
1. Current ratio (times)	1.35	2.00
2. Quick ratio (times)	0.86	1.25
B. Leverage Ratios		
3. Debt-to-total assets (%)	69	55
4. Debt-to-equity (times)	2.24	1.52
5. Times-interest-earned (times)	6.57	6.0
6. Fixed-charge-coverage (times)	4.55	4.12
C. Asset-Management Ratios		
7. Average collection period (days)	44	53
8. Inventory turnover (times)	8.7	6.3
9. Capital assets turnover (times)	2.1	4.3
10. Total assets turnover (times)	1.4	2.1
D. Profitability Ratios		
11. Profit margin on sales (%)	8.4	6.2
12. Return on sales (%)	3.9	2.4
13. Return on total assets (%)	5.4	4.4
13. Return on equity (%)	17.6	14.3
E. Market-Value Ratios		
15. Earnings per share ($)	2.44	2.11
16. Price/earnings ratio (times)	12.3	10.0

By looking at **Table 3.8**, it is possible to see whether Eastman's management should be satisfied or concerned about the financial structure and profitability position of its business.

On *liquidity,* Eastman appears to be in a difficult position compared to the industry. Maybe there is no reason for concern if the company is able to meet its current commitments on time. If the current ratio was too high, say 3.5 or 4.0, it could mean that the company had money tied up in assets that had low earning power, since cash or marketable securities are low profit generators. A high liquidity ratio could also mean that management should reduce inventories and accounts receivable, and put the proceeds into more productive uses.

On *leverage,* the company appears to be in a more precarious position than the industry. This means that the creditors are more exposed; that is, they bear a greater amount of risk. Although Eastman has a higher debt ratio, its fixed debt commitments are slightly better than industry (6.57 compared to 6.0). Nevertheless, the high debt-to-total-assets ratio and debt-to-equity ratio suggests that Eastman has reached, if not exceeded, its borrowing capacity.

On *asset-management ratios,* Eastman is doing a good job with the management of its current assets, but shows signs of weakness in the administration of the capital and total assets. Both the average collection period and the inventory turnover indicate that management is keeping the accounts receivable and inventory at minimum levels. These ratios are also in line with the liquidity ratios that deal with the current portion of the assets shown on the balance sheet. The capital assets turnover and total assets turnover indicate that, overall, the business has too many assets (mainly capital assets) for the level of sales. It also means that the capital assets are not working hard enough. The only way to correct this situation is by increasing sales or by liquidating, if possible, some of its capital assets.

On *profitability,* Eastman is doing well on all counts. Profit margin and income after taxes in relation to sales, assets, or equity is healthy. The profit level is particularly encouraging, despite the fact that capital assets and debt burden are higher than the industry.

On *market-value,* Eastman is also doing well. Both the earnings per share and price/earnings ratio exceed those of the industry.

Trend Analysis

Comparing one set of figures for a given year to those of the industry gives a good picture of the financial structure and profitability level of a particular business. However, this analysis does not give a full picture of the situation, since it does not take into account the element of time. Comparative analysis gives a snapshot view of the financial statements at a given point in time; it is like still photography. For a more complete picture, ratios of one company should be compared to those of industry over a period of several years, like a motion picture; this would show whether the financial statements are improving or deteriorating.

Trend analysis is illustrated in **Figure 3.1**. Four of Eastman's ratios are compared with industry over a four-year period (from 1997 to 2000); they are the current ratio, debt to total assets, capital assets turnover, and return on total assets.

Eastman's *current ratio* has always been inferior to that of industry. It widened between 1997 and 2000, and reached a 0.65 spread in 2000 (1.35 versus 2.00). This means that the company decreased the level of receivables and inventory, or increased its current liabilities. Although the current ratio is a good indicator of current asset management, management and creditors may want to learn more about individual current asset accounts by looking at average collection period and inventory turnover.

The *debt-to-total-assets ratio* has deteriorated over the years. While Eastman finances 69 cents of each asset by debt, the industry is at only 55 cents. The debt ratio position started to weaken in 1997 and continued to deteriorate.

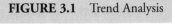

FIGURE 3.1   Trend Analysis

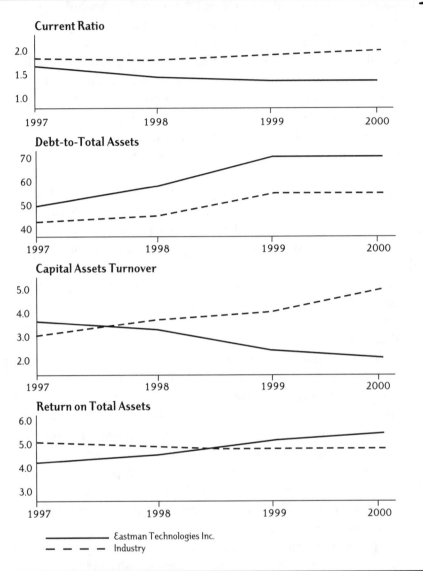

The company probably invested large sums of money in capital assets that, as can be seen in the capital assets turnover, are not being very productive in relation to industry.

Eastman's *capital assets turnover* followed the same trend as that of the debt ratio. Although the management of current assets has been good over the last four years, the acquisition of capital assets during the 1997–2000 period indicates that Eastman has a surplus of non-productive capital assets. This means that management of Eastman should examine closely all capital asset accounts to see what can be done to improve the ratio. If management sees a growth trend in sales, it might not want to change anything; however, if sales are projected to improve only marginally, it may have to sell some of the capital assets in order to make all assets work at full capacity.

Return on total assets shows a strong position. Eastman is operating at a level one point higher than industry (5.4 versus 4.4). The profitability position of Eastman surpassed that of industry in 1998; industry's trend declined over the four-year period, while Eastman's profit position during the same period improved considerably. In short, Eastman's profitability position is healthy despite the fact that the debt ratio and the capital assets turnover are weaker than industry.

The Du Pont Financial System

The **Du Pont system** is a financial analysis system that has achieved international recognition. Du Pont brought together the key financial ratios in a logical presentation to assist management in measuring their return on investment (ROI). The system shows the various components affecting ROI, such as net income, capital and current assets, and the most important figures appearing on the income statement and the balance sheet. **Figure 3.2** shows a modified and simplified version of the Du Pont financial system.

The numbers in the upper portion of the diagram deal with balance sheet and income statement items, and show how current assets, such as cash, inventory, accounts receivable and capital assets, are employed. To obtain the total assets turnover, sales are divided by total assets.

The numbers in the lower portion of the diagram deal with income statement items. They give the income performance in relation to sales. By multiplying the total assets turnover by the operating margin, we obtain the return on investment figure.

Eastman's ROI was calculated by multiplying the 1.4 total assets turnover by the 8.4 operating margin. This gives an 11.8 percent *before-tax* ROI performance. If the company wants to increase this ratio, it may have to improve the capital assets turnover ratio and/or the operating margin.

Limitations of Financial Ratios

Although financial ratios can be effective tools for gauging financial performance and managerial effectiveness, they should not be used blindly. First, they should be used as only one instrument in the management tool kit. Essentially, a financial ratio gives an indication of the weak and strong points in a business. Ratios will not say why something is going wrong and what to do about a particular situation; they only pinpoint where a problem exists. For example, the inventory turnover may have gone from 10 to 7 over a period of three years, and the industry average

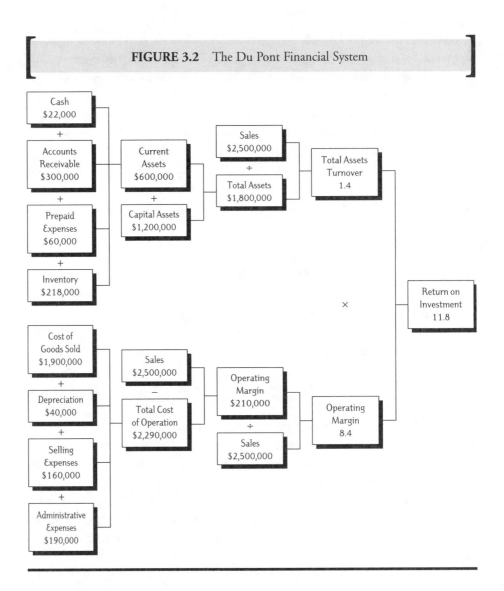

FIGURE 3.2   The Du Pont Financial System

may be at 9; this means that management will have to investigate further to see if there is a problem and what to do about it.

A second limitation of ratios emerges when a particular set of ratios in a business is compared to other businesses or industry averages. Although there are accepted accounting principles and conventions for constructing financial statements, several different numbers can be used to calculate a ratio. For example, when calculating the inventory turnover, one business may use the cost of goods sold as the numerator, while another may wish to use its sales figures. Even though both companies are part of the same industry and are equally efficient in the management of inventory, they will show different ratios. In another situation, a business may use the operating profit to calculate its total assets turnover, while another may use the net income after taxes. What is important to remember is that before ratios are compared, some of the numbers on the financial statements may have to be adjusted for comparison purposes.

Third, the fact that different operating methodologies can be used to run a business may render the comparison of financial ratios irrelevant. For instance, one business may lease most of its assets while another may own them. If this is the case, some of the ratios, such as debt-to-total-assets, fixed-charge coverage, total assets turnover, and return on total assets, would not be comparable.

A fourth limitation is the inflation factor. Inflation can make the ratio of a particular business look good or bad over time, when trends are examined. For example, inventory turnover may have deteriorated over a three-year period; the problem here may not be due to the increase in physical inventory, but rather, to a substantial increase in the cost of the goods. Also, an increase in return on total assets may not mean that the company is more efficient; it may reflect the fact that sales prices (and not volume) have increased rapidly and that the capital assets, which are shown on the financial statements at book costs, have remained unchanged.

Finally, since balance sheets reflect the financial situation of a business at a particular point in time, usually at the end of a fiscal period (e.g., as at December 31), this may indicate a weak ratio which might not be the case if the same calculation were done using the June figures. The balance sheet figures show the situation of a business only on one day out of 365. For instance, because of business cycles, inventories and accounts receivable may be high in December and low in June.

Although financial ratios have limitations, a business operator should not shy away from using them. As long as a manager knows how to use them, understands their limitations, and accepts the fact that they are used as indicators and as one of many management tools, he or she will be in a better position to use them wisely, effectively, and with some degree of caution.

Decision-Making in Action

Up to this point, we have covered quite a few financial concepts and techniques, such as ratios, common size ratio analysis, horizontal analysis, internal and external financing, sources and uses of funds, and depreciation as a source of cash. Let's now see how these financial concepts and techniques can be used to analyze financial information and, most important, to make decisions that will improve a company's bottom line and cash flow performance.

Referring to Eastman Technologies' financial statements, let's assume that management is formulating its financial objectives for 2001 and making the following projections:

Income statement objectives
- Sales will show a 15% growth.
- Cost of goods sold as a percent of sales revenue will improve to 75%.

♦ Operating expenses as a percent of sales revenue (excluding depreciation) will also improve to 13.2%.
♦ Depreciation expense will be $56,000.

Balance sheet objectives
♦ Accounts receivable turnover will be reduced to 37 days.
♦ Inventory turnover will be improved to 10 times.
♦ Shareholders will invest $100,000 in common shares in the company.
♦ Capital budget is estimated at $400,000.

Retained earnings statement objectives
♦ The board of directors wants to pay $50,000 in dividends.

If management wants to invest $400,000 in capital assets such as equipment and machinery, how much money will the company have to borrow from lenders? As shown in **Table 3.9**, the company will have to borrow $148,974. The following shows how this number was calculated.

♦ A 15% increase over the $2,500,000 sales in 2001 will bring in $2,875,000 in sales revenue.
♦ A 75% efficiency performance (as a percent of sales) at the production level (versus 76% in 2000) will produce $2,156,250 in cost of goods sold.
♦ Operating expenses, as a percent of sales, will decrease to 13.2 percent (versus 14.0 percent in 2000), or an estimated $379,500.
♦ Depreciation expense will reach $56,000 in 2001. Total operating expenses as a percent of sales revenue are therefore estimated at $435,500 and will be reduced to 15.1 percent of sales (versus 15.6 percent in 2000).
♦ The average collection period target of 37 days (compared to 44 days in 2000) will produce $8,551 in cash despite the 15 percent sales revenue increase. The calculation is as follows:

2000 accounts receivable	$300,000
2001 target of 37 days	
(average daily sales of $7,877 × 37)	291,449
Net change	$ 8,551

The projected balance sheet also shows inventory to generate an extra $2,350 in cash (turnover will improve to 10 times compared to 8.7 times). The calculation is as follows:

2000 inventory	$218,000
2001 target of 10 times	
(cost of goods sold, $2,156,500 / 10)	215,650
Net change	$ 2,350

As shown in the lower portion of **Table 3.9**, a total of $201,026 will be generated internally—that is, from operating activities. The company will invest

$400,000 in its capital budget. Since the operating activities will generate $201,026, the company will have to borrow $148,974 from long-term lenders, since shareholders will invest $100,000 in the business and be paid $50,000 in dividends. This means that to finance its capital budget, Eastman will generate 50 percent of the funds internally and the rest from external sources.

TABLE 3.9 Decision-Making in Action

	2000	2001	% of sales	Objectives
Income Statement Assumptions				
Sales revenue	$2,500,000	$2,875,000	100.0	15% growth
Cost of goods sold	1,900,000	2,156,250	75.0	
Gross margin	600,000	718,750	25.0	
Selling and administration expenses	350,000	379,500	13.2	
Depreciation	40,000	56,000	1.9	
Total operating expenses	390,000	435,500	15.1	
Operating income	210,000	283,250	9.9	
Other expenses/revenue	15,000	15,000	0.5	
Income before taxes	195,000	268,250	9.3	
Income taxes	97,500	134,125	4.7	
Income after taxes	97,500	134,125	4.7	

Balance Sheet Assumptions Related to Working Capital Accounts			
Accounts receivable	44 days	$291,449	37 days
Inventory turnover	8.7 times	215,650	10 times

Operating activities		
Income from operations	$ 134,125	
Depreciation	56,000	
Accounts receivable	8,551	
Inventory	2,350	
Total operating activities		$201,026
Financing activities		
Common shares	$100,000	
Dividends	(50,000)	
Long-term borrowing	148,974	198,974
Investing activities		(400,000)

Summary

Financial statements should be analyzed in order to maximize a company's return, ensure its liquidity, maintain its solvency, and secure its long-term prosperity.

Financial ratios can be grouped under five main categories. *Liquidity ratios,* such as current ratio and quick or acid test, measure a company's ability to meet its short-term debts. Second, the *leverage ratios,* such as debt-to-total assets, debt-to-equity, times-interest-earned, and fixed-charge-coverage, can be used to measure the extent to which a business is financed by debt as opposed to equity and how it is able to service its debt. Third, the *asset-management ratios,* such as average collection period, inventory turnover, capital assets turnover, and total assets turnover, measure how effectively managers utilize the assets or resources of a business. Fourth, the *profitability ratios,* such as profit margin on sales, return on sales, return on total assets, and return on equity, gauge management's overall effectiveness. Finally, *market-value ratios* make the relationship on the data presented on a company's financial statements to financial market data and include earnings per share and price/earnings ratio.

In order to derive the most value from financial ratios, management should compare its standards of performance to other companies in the same industry, or to industry averages. Also, since financial statements give the financial picture of a company at a particular point in time, financial trends should be assessed to see if financial structure and profitability are improving or deteriorating.

Analysts who constantly examine financial statements will look at them from different angles. To enhance the usefulness of financial statement analysis, these analysts will go through the common size ratio analysis and horizontal analysis.

CHAPTER 4

Profit Planning and Decision-Making

N ow that the Edwards have been in business for close to two years, they are continuously faced with on-going operating and investment decisions such as:

- Should we increase our advertising budget? By how much?
- Should we hire more part-time or full-time sales clerks? Should we let some go? How many?
- Should we introduce a new product line?
- Should we open a new retail outlet?
- Should we reduce our selling price for a product line? Increase it? By how much?
- Should we introduce a new service?

The Edwards realize that many of these decisions will be based on whether the increase in sales revenue will be adequate to generate sufficient profit. For example, if the amount spent on advertising increases by $2,000, how much more revenue should be generated in order to pay for this cost and to generate a profit? Although the Edwards had been making some of these decisions by using their instinct and good judgment, they were looking for a decision-making tool that could help "validate their feelings." Len had heard that break-even analysis is an effective decision-making tool. He therefore decided to meet with Mary Ogaki, his accountant, to learn more about how this tool could be used as a decision-making instrument to improve the quality of his decisions.

During the meeting, Mary made the following comments:

"Break-even analysis is an excellent and effective decision-making tool and very easy to apply. Before using this tool, however, what you need to do is to carefully differentiate your store's costs in terms of what is fixed and what is variable. You will surely have to draw on your cost accounting knowledge and skills. This is the most difficult task that you have to go through if you want to use the break-even technique as a reliable decision-making instrument. As you are fully aware, some of your costs are relatively easy to classify between fixed and variable. Costs such as the goods you buy from suppliers and sales commissions vary directly with sales revenue and for this reason, they are considered *variable*. The more you sell, the more you buy goods from suppliers. Also, costs such as leasing and office salaries do not vary with the level of sales activities (sales revenue). For that reason, they are considered *fixed*.

"Other costs, however, are more difficult to differentiate; for example, you may want to classify some of your sales clerks' salaries as fixed and some as variable. Advertising could also be considered fixed or variable. It all depends on how you look at these various costs. For instance, you may set a *fixed budget* for advertising a product line or you may increase your advertising budget if you sell more of a certain product line. Once you have determined exactly how each item (i.e., advertising, sales salaries) shown on your operating budget will be classified as fixed or variable, doing the break-even calculation is an exercise that can be done rather quickly and easily.

"The allocation of your store's overhead costs to each department is also an important element to consider when calculating the break-even point for different product lines. For example, you must decide how to distribute your interest charges, depreciation expense, and office salaries to each product line. You will have to go through this cost accounting allocation process if you want to utilize to the maximum the break-even technique."

Len felt that the break-even calculation would be an excellent tool and considered investing some time and effort in understanding cost accounting in order to improve the effectiveness of his decisions.

This chapter examines how break-even analysis can be used as a decision-making instrument. In particular, it focuses on the two topics:

1. The interplay between the various cost elements (fixed versus variable) involved in decision-making.
2. How break-even analysis can be used as an effective decision-making tool.

Introduction

If a business were operated without fixed costs such as rent and salaries, its managers would not have to be concerned about incurring a loss. In fact, managers of this unusual type of business would not have to go through detailed calculations to set prices for different products nor evaluate the level of risk associated with the business. If variable costs such as purchases and sales commission were the only element to be deducted from sales revenue to arrive at a profit, profit planning would be relatively simple. All that would be required would be to deduct a variable cost, say $5.00, from a $7.00 unit selling price to obtain a $2.00 profit. Whether a business sells 20 or 100,000 widgets, it would make a $2.00 profit on each unit. The absence of fixed costs would not only facilitate the preparation of profit plans and detailed operating budgets, but the business would operate at minimal or no risk. Under these operating conditions, chances for incurring a loss would be virtually non-existent.

Businesses do not operate under such favorable conditions. The fact that businesses have to pay on-going fixed costs creates an element of the *unknown*. Recognizing the fact that fixed costs must be paid, managers must have a complete knowledge of the number of widgets that should be sold. In addition, they should know the price at which each product should be sold, the exact costs that will be incurred for producing each widget, and the total costs that will be generated by the business if a given number of widgets are sold.

If managers are to plan their profit in a proficient manner, and measure precisely the risk they are prepared to take, they should be able to calculate, analyze, and compare the projected sales volume, the unit selling price for each product, and all costs associated with running the business. If, on the other hand, managers are unable to forecast their costs and revenues with reasonable accuracy, the chances for achieving a favorable profit level are minimized.

Relevance of Break-Even Analysis

Break-even analysis is a straightforward yet very powerful financial technique that can help managers to make a wide-range of important decisions that touch on many types of business activities.

Break-even analysis helps to analyze the effect of *pricing decisions* and volume levels on *levels of profit*. For example, if a software company decides to increase its unit-selling price by five percent with no change in variable costs and fixed costs, break-even analysis would make it easy for managers to determine whether the change will have a positive or negative impact on profitability. To be sure, the most difficult variable element to pin down in this particular analysis is the reaction of the competitors.

New product, new plant, new sales representative, new sales office, or new advertising campaign decisions are typical decisions that break-even analysis can help to make more carefully. For example, break-even analysis can help determine the incremental sales volume level that is required in order to justify an investment, given the projected unit selling price and operating costs.

Modernization or automation decisions can be made more clearly with break-even analysis since it can disclose profit implications. All that is required within the break-even analysis framework is to determine to what extent variable costs can be replaced by fixed costs. For example, if management wants to invest $1.0 million to automate a plant, additional costs (presumably most of them fixed) associated with the automation program would replace workers and reduce wages (variable costs). Break-even analysis helps to study the interplay between the various types of costs affecting a business and the impact they have on profit performance.

Expansion decisions involve the study of the impact that incremental volume has on profitability. When a business reaches full operating capacity at one of its plants, management must decide whether to use its resources to expand the existing plant or to build a new one. The key question surrounding the decision is this: Will both the incremental volume and cost levels have a positive (or negative) effect on profitability? To be sure, expansion programs impact variable costs, fixed costs, economies of scale, and profitability. Break-even analysis helps to analyze the interplay between each of these variables.

Profit decisions deal with what a company needs to do in order to achieve a certain level of profitability. For example, if a company is operating at a loss or below profit performance and wants to achieve a profit objective, say 10 percent return on investment, the break-even analysis tool will help company management decide on the following in order to achieve the objective.

◆   How many units should we sell?
◆   At what price should we sell our product or service?
◆   What should our fixed costs be?
◆   What should each unit cost?
◆   Which product or service should be pushed?

Cost Behavior

Calculating the profit generated by a product at different levels of production requires a total awareness of how volume, price, product mix, and product costs relate to one another. The tool used for analyzing the behavior of these different variables, how they relate to one another, and how they affect profit levels, is called **cost-volume-profit analysis**. The major advantage to understanding the cost-volume-profit concept is that it helps managers to figure out the interrelationships among all costs affecting profits.

To prepare profit and operating budgets, managers must classify all costs into two distinct groups: fixed costs and variable costs.

Fixed Costs

Costs that remain constant at varying levels of production are called **fixed costs**, also known as period costs, time costs, constant costs, or standby costs. Although there are subtle variations between each of these terms, they all have an element of "fixedness" and all must be paid with the passage of time. Such costs do not change as a result of variations in levels of production. Some of these costs are inescapable because they are essential for operating purposes. The following are typical examples of fixed costs:

- ◆ Rent
- ◆ Property taxes
- ◆ Protection service

- ◆ Interest on mortgage
- ◆ Office salaries
- ◆ Telephone

- ◆ Property insurance
- ◆ Depreciation
- ◆ Professional fees

Figure 4.1 shows the relationship between fixed costs and volume.

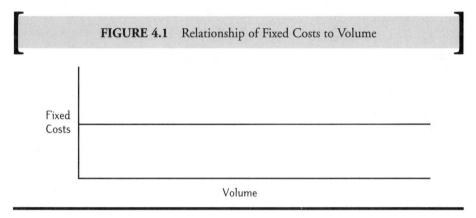

FIGURE 4.1   Relationship of Fixed Costs to Volume

Variable Costs

Costs that vary directly with fluctuations in production levels are referred to as **variable costs**, also known as direct costs, out-of-pocket costs, or volume costs. As the volume of a business increases, so do these costs. For example, if a business produces 100 widgets made of material A at a per-unit cost of $0.10, and of material B at $0.20, the firm would incur a total variable cost of $30. If the firm sells 1,000 units, the costs would increase to $300.

The reason such costs are called variable is because they vary almost automatically with volume. The following are typical examples of variable costs:

- ◆ Sales commission
- ◆ Materials
- ◆ Direct labor

- ◆ Overtime premiums
- ◆ Freight-out
- ◆ Packing materials

- ◆ Equipment rentals
- ◆ Fuel

Figure 4.2 shows the relationship between variable costs and volume.

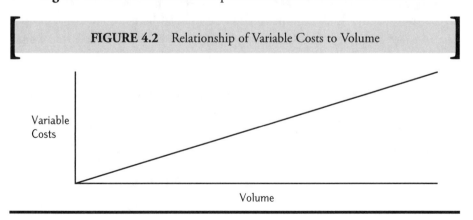

FIGURE 4.2   Relationship of Variable Costs to Volume

Semi-Variable Costs

While some costs vary directly and proportionately with volume, others have some characteristics of both fixed and variable costs; in other words, they possess different degrees of variability, or they change in a disproportionate way with changes in output levels. For this reason, these types of costs are considered **semi-variable** (or semi-fixed).

Let us take four examples. First, electricity in a house is a typical example. House owners surely have to pay a basic fixed cost each month (say $50.00) even if they don't use any electricity; in fact, the owner could be away on vacation for several months and still receive a $50.00 bill from the utility company. However, the owners would have to pay additional costs if they were at home using electrical equipment such as stove, toasters, heaters, dryers, and so on. This cost would vary according to the number of people living in the house and the extent to which electrical appliances are used. Second, a business owner may also pay a fixed rent to operate a business up to a certain volume level. When that level is reached, the owner may have no choice but to increase the space in order to meet increased production. If this is the case, these costs would be considered fixed for a specific lapse of time or period or up to a certain capacity or range of production. Third, a business owner may pay x dollars for raw material at y level of production, but when that level of operation is exceeded, less may be paid because of increased purchase discounts. Fourth, if a business owner wants to produce an extra volume of units with the same production crew, but after regular hours, time-and-a-half or double-time may have to be paid. These direct or variable costs would not vary proportionately with volume increments, and would surely not fit the linear cost pattern.

As shown in **Figure 4.3**, it is important to separate fixed and variable costs for different levels of volume. This helps to prepare operating budgets in a more proficient manner. Once the costs are identified under their respective categories, they can be related to specific levels of volume. One way of separating costs is by percentage of capacity. As shown in **Figure 4.4**, an owner may incur a total cost of $10.00 per unit (fixed and variable costs between periods A and B) up to 40 percent of capacity. At that point (B to C), costs will be increased by $2.00 per unit in order to exceed the 40 percent level of production capacity; this would bring total unit cost to $12.00. Between points C and D (up to 60 percent of capacity), costs remain the same (fixed costs will not change, while variable costs per unit can still vary proportionately with volume). Again, in order to go beyond the 60 percent capacity level, the owner may increase costs from $12.00 to $14.00. As shown on the chart, costs move from $14.00 to $16.00 (F to G) at the 80 percent capacity level and remain at that point (G to H) up to 100 percent capacity.

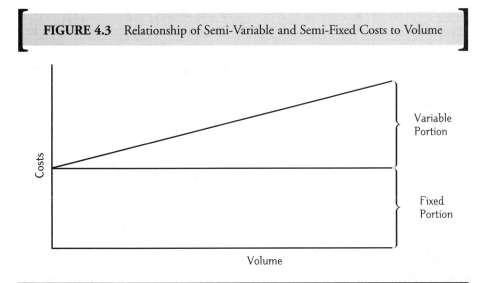

FIGURE 4.3   Relationship of Semi-Variable and Semi-Fixed Costs to Volume

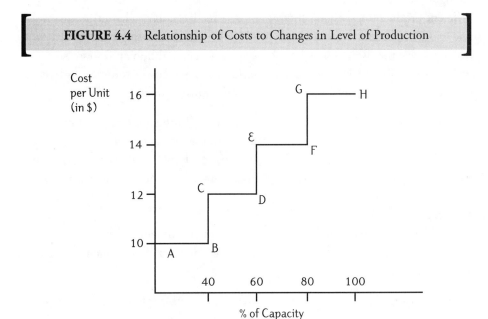

FIGURE 4.4   Relationship of Costs to Changes in Level of Production

Anatomy of Profit

If operating costs changed in the same proportion as that of revenue, or if profits had a *linear relationship* with costs or revenue, this chapter would be irrelevant. However, as indicated earlier, costs behave in a variety of ways with respect to revenue. If budgets and profit plans are to be prepared in a meaningful way, it is important for management to be completely familiar with the way costs change within specific time periods, at different levels of production, and even with changes in methods of operation.

Knowing the structure of costs and how they affect profits when volume changes enables management to make well-informed decisions. The cost-volume-profit analysis helps managers to establish prices in a more prudent way. Establishing accurate prices for a business is the key to achieving profit goals and, ultimately, to determining the success of a business.

The factors that affect profit levels are:

- Volume of production;
- Prices;
- Costs (fixed and variable); and
- Changes in product mix.

Managers who understand the interrelationships among the above factors and how they each affect profit can more readily realign their operations to changing market conditions. They can identify the relative profitability levels of different product lines, establish prices more effectively, have a better product mix, and most important, be in a better position to make operating changes that will best optimize the use of financial, physical, material, and human resources.

Specifically, analyzing the relationships among costs, volume, and profit enables a manager to answer fundamental questions, such as:

- How much volume do we need to sell before hiring another employee?
- At what sales volume should we change our method of operation; for example, should we maintain the existing warehouse or should we move to a larger one?
- Which products require streamlining, from a cost point of view, if we are to improve our profit performance?
- Should we change our product mix?
- When should we purchase another piece of equipment?
- Should we reduce the level of output of product A and increase that of product B?

One of the most effective techniques used in profit planning, solving problems, and making rational decisions is called *break-even analysis*.

Break-Even Analysis

Cost behavior can be understood more easily in a cost-volume-profit relationship when break-even analysis is used. The importance of break-even analysis is that it projects the impact of management decisions made today on future profit levels. This technique helps management to see, well in advance, profit performance resulting from changes in methods of operations. The break-even method gives a picture of the effect that changes in price, costs, and volume have on profit.

The break-even analysis deals with the **break-even point**, which can be defined as that point where, at a specific level of revenues, a business ceases to incur losses and begins to make a profit. In other words, it is at that level of operation where profit levels stand at *zero*, or where total revenues equal total costs. Before examining the break-even chart, let us look at other key concepts, namely, the contribution margin, relevant range, and relevant costs. These concepts will help us to further understand the mechanics of break-even analysis.

Contribution Margin Analysis

So far, fixed, variable, and semi-variable costs have been explained. These different concepts suggest that every time a business produces a unit, it increases its revenue and reduces the loss up to a point where total revenues equal total costs. If sales continue to climb past the break-even point, profits are realized. There is another way of looking at this. Each time a business produces a unit, the sales generated on each unit "contributes" to paying for fixed costs. Simply put, when variable costs are deducted from revenues, we are left with an amount which will be used to pay for fixed costs and then realize a profit. The difference between the revenue generated and the variable cost is called the **contribution margin**. The contribution margin is the level of profit that contributes to paying for fixed costs and, eventually, realizing a profit. For example, assume that John's monthly fixed expenses for his house, including mortgage payment, insurance payment, and utility payments, are $2,500. Let's also assume that John works on a commission basis and earns on average $25 an hour. It would take 100 hours for John to pay all his fixed expenses ($2,500 ÷ $25 per hour). In other words, every hour of work (or $25) *contributes* to paying the fixed expenses. If John works 101 hours, the money that he would earn during the last hour would contribute towards a surplus (profit). If John works 40 hours a week (or 160 hours a month), he would make a $1,500 surplus (160 hours × $25 = $4,000 − $2,500). Contribution margin is also known as marginal contribution, cash margin, or margin income.

Rearranging information shown on an income statement can help identify the contribution margin. **Table 4.1** shows how contribution margin relates to revenue, fixed and variable costs, and profit.

The contribution margin can also be expressed on a per-unit basis, as the difference between unit selling price and unit variable cost. This information becomes extremely valuable for decision-making purposes. If the contribution margin is positive, management knows how much money is earned on each unit sold, which will contribute to meeting fixed costs and realizing a profit. The contribution can also be expressed by a ratio called the marginal contribution ratio, contribution ratio, or marginal income ratio. The term that will be used in this chapter is **profit–volume (PV) ratio**.

Table 4.2 shows how to compute the contribution by using the PV ratio for varying volume levels. As shown in **Table 4.2**, the difference between revenues and variable costs gives a contribution of $250,000 or a PV ratio of 0.25

TABLE 4.1 The Income Statement and the Contribution Margin

Revenue		$1,000,000
Less variable costs:		
Direct material	$500,000	
Direct labor	250,000	
Total variable costs		750,000
Contribution margin		250,000
Less fixed costs		
Manufacturing	150,000	
Administrative	50,000	
Total fixed costs		200,000
Operating profit		$ 50,000

($250,000 ÷ $1,000,000). If revenue increases by 25 percent, to $1,250,000, the contribution becomes $312,500 and the PV ratio remains at 0.25 ($312,000 ÷ $1,250,000). If revenue drops to $600,000, contribution is $150,000, and the PV ratio is still 0.25 ($150,000 ÷ $600,000).

The contribution margin approach offers significant benefits for examining pricing alternatives. Management can readily determine the impact each increase or decrease in price has on volume, revenues, and profit; this analysis helps streamline production operations in order to reach optimum cost levels.

Relevant Range

Changes in the operating variable costs alter the PV ratio, which in turn affects the profit level. As was indicated earlier, fixed costs can change from period to period, or from one level of output to another. These costs must therefore be budgeted as accurately as possible, since they have a direct impact on the prof-

---

TABLE 4.2 Calculating the Contribution Margin Using the PV Ratio

	Base case	Ratio	Increased revenues	Decreased revenues
Revenue	$1,000,000		$1,250,000	$600,000
Variable cost	750,000	.75	937,500	450,000
Contribution margin	250,000	.25 (PV)	312,500	150,000
Fixed costs	200,000		200,000	200,000
Operating profit (loss)	$ 50,000		$ 112,500	$(50,000)

itability level of a firm in both the short term and the long term. Cost analysis for costs incurred within a specific time-span must be considered within a designated range of volume levels. This range is known as the **relevant range**. As indicated earlier, if the management of a business decides to increase its manufacturing capacity, additional costs will be incurred. These costs may be fixed such as the purchase of additional machinery or variable such as the overtime paid to workers. **Figure 4.5** shows graphically an example of relevant range. In this particular case, costs of $5,000 would be relevant for a volume of 0 to 1,000 units. From 1,000 to 2,000 units, costs of $10,000 would be incurred. If volume exceeds 2,000 units, different cost information ($15,000) would have to be integrated into the profit analysis.

Relevant Costs

Relevant costs arise when management has the option of choosing among several cost alternatives to operate a business. If there are cost variations among the options, they are called differential costs. For example, if management is currently spending $20,000 in operating costs for selling $50,000 worth of goods, two cost options may be analyzed for making a plant more cost-efficient and increasing profitability. As shown in **Table 4.3**, option A shows that an additional $10,000 in variable costs and $15,000 in fixed costs would be incurred. Option B shows an additional $14,000 in variable costs (less efficient than option A) and $13,000 in fixed costs (more efficient than option A). The table shows the differential between the two options. The $20,000 that is already spent for selling the $50,000 worth of goods is not taken into account in this analysis since it has already been spent. (These costs are sometimes referred to as sunk costs.) The only costs that are relevant for the purpose of this analysis are the uncommitted or unspent costs, which

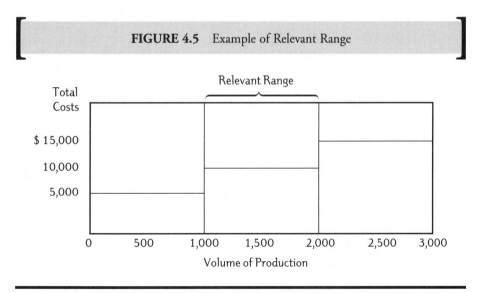

FIGURE 4.5   Example of Relevant Range

TABLE 4.3   Differential Costs between Two Cost Options

	Option A	Option B	Differential
Sales revenue	$50,000	$50,000	—
Current costs	20,000	20,000	—
Variable cost	10,000	14,000	$ 4,000
Fixed cost	15,000	13,000	(2,000)
Total relevant cost	25,000	27,000	2,000
Total cost	45,000	47,000	2,000
Profit	$ 5,000	$ 3,000	$ 2,000

The net cost or profit advantage of choosing option A is $2,000.

are $25,000 for option A and $27,000 for option B. These options should be analyzed because of the $2,000 cost differential. As shown in the table, option A gives a $5,000 profit compared to $3,000 for option B.

The Break-Even Chart

The **break-even chart** is a relatively simple way of picturing the effect of changes in revenue and cost on profitability. **Figure 4.6** shows the break-even chart for a firm that sells widgets. As shown, there are different parts in a break-even chart. They are:

- Sales revenue   line OD
- Revenue zone   area OED
- Fixed cost line   line AB
- Fixed cost zone   area AOEB
- Total cost line   line AC
- Total cost zone   area AOEC
- Profit zone   area ZCD
- Loss zone   area AOZ

As shown in the figure, the horizontal axis represents the number of units sold, while the vertical axis represents total sales revenue and total costs.

Fixed costs (line AB) are shown parallel to the unit volume line. Fixed costs are $100,000 and remain unchanged throughout the relevant range of units.

Sales revenue (line OD) slopes upward at an angle. As the company sells more units, sales revenue increases proportionately.

Total cost line (line AC) portrays a gradual slope that intersects the sales revenue line at the 1,000-unit mark. The line begins at $100,000 (fixed cost), and slopes at an angle that is less steep than the revenue line.

The *loss zone* (area AOZ) represents losses if the company sells fewer than 1,000 units. If the company's unit selling price is maintained at $200 and fixed costs and variable costs are kept at the stated levels, losses range from $100,000 at zero unit sales, to $100 at 999 units.

The *profit zone* (area ZCD) represents the profits made by the company. Any volume of sales over the 1,000-unit mark (horizontal axis) or $200,000 sales revenue (vertical axis) represents a profit to the company.

The cost schedule shown in **Table 4.4** was used to construct the break-even chart shown in **Figure 4.6**. The table shows numerically the change in profit at varying levels of sales units—from 200 to 1,600. For example, at 200 widgets with an average unit selling price of $200, the company's sales revenue amounts to $40,000. At any level of sales volume, the company's fixed costs remain unchanged at $100,000. If the unit variable cost is $100, the total variable cost is $20,000 at the 200-unit volume level. At that level, total costs (fixed and variable) amount to $120,000, and the company loses $80,000.

FIGURE 4.6   The Break-Even Chart

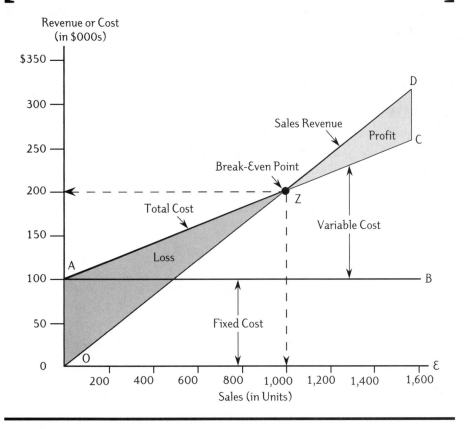

Sales Units	Unit Price	Sales Revenue	Fixed Cost	Variable Cost	Total Cost	Profit (Loss)
		TABLE 4.4 The Profit and Cost Schedule				
0	$200	0	$100,000	0	$100,000	$(100,000)
200	200	$ 40,000	100,000	$ 20,000	120,000	(80,000)
400	200	80,000	100,000	40,000	140,000	(60,000)
600	200	120,000	100,000	60,000	160,000	(40,000)
800	200	160,000	100,000	80,000	180,000	(20,000)
1,000	200	200,000	100,000	100,000	200,000	—
1,200	200	240,000	100,000	120,000	220,000	20,000
1,400	200	280,000	100,000	140,000	240,000	40,000
1,600	200	320,000	100,000	160,000	260,000	60,000

At 400 units, the loss is reduced to $60,000; at 1,000 units, sales revenue equals $200,000, fixed costs remain at $100,000, and variable costs are $100,000, for a total cost of $200,000. At that point, the company is showing neither a loss nor a profit, since costs equal sales revenues. It is at this particular sales volume level that break-even takes place. Additional volume will result in profits. With sales units reaching levels of 1,400 and 1,600, the company generates profits of $40,000 and $60,000, respectively.

Finding the Break-Even Point by Formula

The break-even chart gives a visual presentation of the different variables affecting profitability. However, if the intent is to establish the quantity and revenue break-even points, and the variables such as sales units, fixed costs, and unit variable costs are known, the graph can be formulated algebraically. The following information is needed for an algebraic solution:

$$SP = \text{selling price per unit}$$
$$VC = \text{variable cost per unit}$$
$$FC = \text{fixed cost}$$
$$N = \text{quantity of units sold at break-even}$$

By definition, at break-even, total revenue equals total cost. If:

$$\text{total revenue} = SP \times N$$
$$\text{and total cost} = (VC \times N) + FC$$

therefore break-even is:

$$(SP \times N) = (VC \times N) + FC$$

The above formula can also be presented in the following way:

$$N(SP - VC) = FC$$
$$\text{or } N = FC/(SP - VC)$$

By using the information from **Table 4.4**, we get:

$$FC = \$100,000$$
$$SP = \$200$$
$$VC = \$100$$

The contribution margin (SP − VC) is $100 (that is, $200 minus $100).

By applying the above information to the break-even algebraic formula, we get the following break-even results for both quantity and revenue.

Unit break-even point *(BEP) is:*

$$BEP = \frac{\text{Fixed cost}}{\text{Price per unit} - \text{Variable cost per unit}}$$

$$BEP = \frac{\$100,000}{\$200 - \$100} = \frac{\$100,000}{\$100} = 1,000 \text{ units}$$

Revenue break-even point *is calculated in two steps:*

Step 1:   Find the PV ratio or unit contribution

$$PV = \frac{\text{Unit contribution}}{\text{Unit selling price}} = \frac{\$100}{\$200} = 0.50$$

Step 2:   Find the revenue break-even point

$$BEP = \frac{\text{Fixed cost}}{PV} = \frac{\$100,000}{0.50} = \$200,000$$

If the break-even volume is multiplied by the unit selling price, the same answer is obtained: 1,000 units × $200 = $200,000.

Cash Break-Even

The break-even model can also be applied to solve cash management problems. Most costs, such as rent, salaries, utilities, insurance, raw materials, or telephone are cash outlays. There are, however, other costs that are non-cash items such as depreciation. Even though these non-cash items are treated as expenses, they do not entail an actual outflow of cash.

If we refer to the revenue and cost information in **Table 4.4**, and assume that the $100,000 fixed cost includes an amount of $25,000 for depreciation, the fixed cash disbursements would be $75,000.

In this case, the **cash break-even point** for both quantity and revenue would be calculated as follows:

Unit break-even point is:

$$\text{Cash BEP} = \frac{\text{Fixed cost} - \text{Depreciation}}{\text{Price per unit} - \text{Variable cost per unit}}$$

$$\text{Cash BEP} = \frac{\$100,000 - \$25,000}{\$200 - \$100} = \frac{\$75,000}{\$100} = 750 \text{ units}$$

Revenue break-even point is:

$$\text{Revenue cash BEP} = \frac{\text{Fixed cost} - \text{Depreciation}}{\text{PV}}$$

$$\text{Revenue cash BEP} = \frac{\$75,000}{0.50} = \$150,000$$

Profit Break-Even

Companies are interested in more than just breaking even. Some establish profit objectives to determine the sales units that should be sold in order to reach the stated objective. If this is the case, all that is needed is to modify the break-even formula. Referring to our base data shown in **Table 4.4**, and assuming that $10,000 is the objective, we can calculate the **profit break-even points** for both quantity and revenue as follows:

Unit break-even point is:

$$\text{Profit BEP} = \frac{\text{Fixed cost} + \text{Profit objective}}{\text{Price per unit} - \text{Variable cost}}$$

$$\text{Profit BEP} = \frac{\$100,000 + \$10,000}{\$200 - \$100} = 1,100 \text{ units}$$

Revenue break-even point is:

$$\text{Revenue profit BEP} = \frac{\text{Fixed cost} + \text{Profit}}{\text{PV}} = \frac{\$110,000}{0.50} = \$220,000$$

The various quantity and revenue break-even points are summarized below:

	Quantity (in units)	Revenue
Regular break-even	1,000	$200,000
Cash break-even	750	150,000
Profit break-even	1,100	220,000

Sensitivity Analysis

Any change in sales revenue, whether it comes from increased unit selling price, change in product mix, or a reduction in fixed or variable costs, will have favorable or unfavorable effects on a company's profitability. For example, referring to the base data in **Table 4.4**, a reduction of $20,000 in fixed costs (to $80,000) would reduce the break-even point to 800 units or $160,000 in sales revenue. Similarly, reducing variable costs to $80 (assuming that fixed costs are at the original level of $100,000) would reduce the break-even point to 833 units. A simultaneous decline of both costs would improve the company's profitability substantially and reduce the break-even point to 667 units. The opposite takes place if fixed and variable costs are increased. A change in unit selling price would also have an effect on profitability. If, for instance, the company faces a $20 per unit variable cost increase, and it wishes to maintain its break-even point at the 1,000 mark, the company would have to increase the unit selling price by $20 to $220. Obviously, this assumes that the increase in unit selling price would have no adverse effect on units sold.

Before deciding to make changes in the methods of operation, or to purchase new equipment, it is important to make a **sensitivity evaluation** of different break-even points representing changes in unit sales, selling price, unit variable costs, and fixed costs.

Where Break-Even Can Be Used

The break-even system can be used in just about any type of business or any area of a company's operations where variable and fixed costs exist and where products or services are offered. For example, a break-even chart can be applied in any of the following areas: company-wide, district or sales territory, service center, retail store, plant, production center, department, or product division.

Let us examine how the break-even points can be presented for four of the above operations: company-wide, district or sales territory, service center, and retail store.

Company-Wide

Figure 4.7 shows a company-wide break-even chart. It indicates the various components of all elements entering into the total cost line. For example, the chart shows the total company fixed costs (which include production, sales, general, and administrative expenses) and the variable costs (which include direct material and direct labor for various company operations), and income taxes and the net profit after income taxes. The break-even point is shown for both cash and profit, both before and after taxes.

District or Sales Territory

The break-even chart is also useful for analyzing whether it is economically attractive to open a sales office in a particular area. In this case, the fixed costs are rental charges, clerical staff, utilities, depreciation of office equipment, etc. Fixed costs would also include a portion of head office fixed expenses. The variable costs

FIGURE 4.7 Company-Wide Break-Even Chart

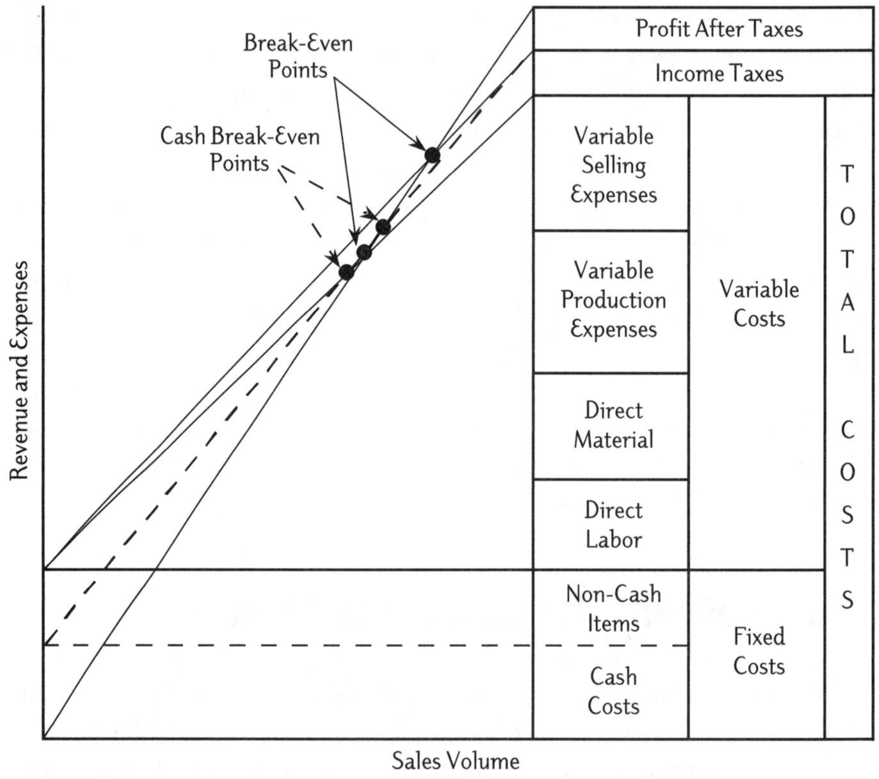

would consist of sales commissions, travel, and living allowances. The break-even chart for a district or sales territory is shown in **Figure 4.8**.

The break-even analysis may become useful for determining whether a sales office should be located in the center core of the business district, where high fixed costs would be incurred and variable costs would be minimized, or in an area remote from the city core, where fixed costs are lower and variable costs higher. In weighing the two possibilities, the marketing manager would have to consider the market potential, the market share objectives, and the sales revenue for the short and medium term.

Service Center

Break-even analysis works exceptionally well for activities that produce specific units of output. Here, fixed costs and direct costs can be related to specific levels of operation. Like a retail store, a service unit does not produce specific production units; while fixed costs can be readily identified, variable costs cannot be related to a specific level of operation. The break-even concept can be applied to service operations, but with subtle differences. The break-even chart for a service

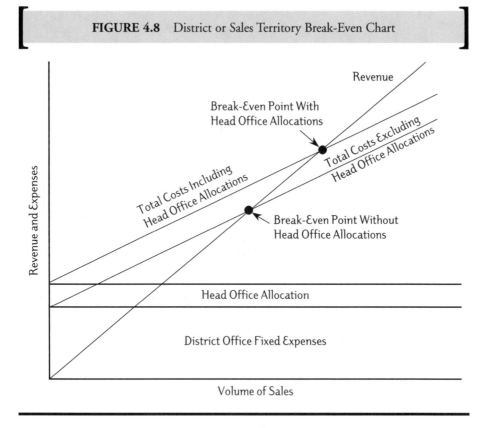

FIGURE 4.8 District or Sales Territory Break-Even Chart

center is shown in **Figure 4.9**. The vertical axis represents sales revenue and costs; the horizontal axis represents sales revenue. The dollar scale of the horizontal and vertical lines is identical since the break-even chart deals with dollar measurements in both instances. The fixed-cost line is parallel to the horizontal line, while the revenue line can have a 45° slant. The variable-cost line is not moved by the quantity of units sold, but rather by the PV ratio. For example, if the variable costs represented 20 percent of sales revenue, the line would increase by a factor of 0.20 every time a dollar sale is made.

Retail Store

As shown in **Table 4.5**, the break-even point can also be calculated for a retail store. First, we must determine the number of products that would be sold and the unit selling price for each. As shown in the table, the total revenue amounts to $500,000. Based on that forecast, variable costs, which include purchases and commissions, amount to $275,000 and $25,000, respectively. By deducting total variable costs from total sales revenue, we find that the store's contribution margin is $200,000. This margin contributes to pay for the $100,000 in fixed costs; the remaining $100,000 is profit. As indicated in the table, the store breaks even at $250,000, or 50 percent of its sales estimates.

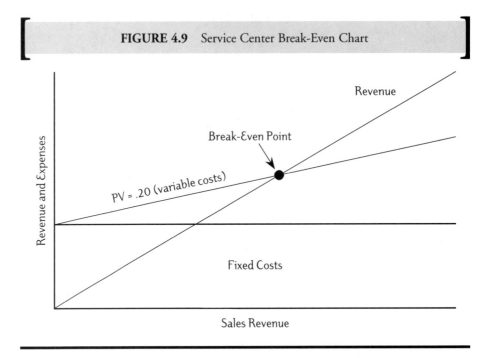

FIGURE 4.9   Service Center Break-Even Chart

TABLE 4.5   Retail Store Break-Even Point

	Suits	Jackets	Shirts	Ties	Socks	Overcoats	Total
No. of units	800	200	700	900	2,500	500	
Unit price	$300	$150	$ 50	$ 30	$ 80	$300	
Revenue							$500,000
Variable costs	%	%	%	%	%	%	
Purchases	%	%	%	%	%	%	275,000
Commissions							25,000
Total variable costs							300,000
Contribution margin							200,000
Fixed costs							100,000
Profit							$100,000

$$\frac{\text{Contribution margin}}{\text{Sales revenue}} = \frac{\$200,000}{\$500,000} = .40 \text{ or } \$0.40$$

$$\frac{\text{Fixed costs}}{\text{PV ratio}} = \frac{\$100,000}{.40} = \$250,000$$

Break-Even Wedges

Managers have different ways of structuring the cost profile of their businesses. They make their decisions based on two major factors: the level of risk they are prepared to take and the level of expected sales volume. Some managers may favor a high volume and a low PV ratio; others, a low volume and high PV ratio. Some may prefer high fixed costs and low variable costs while others prefer low fixed costs and high variable costs. **Figure 4.10** shows different possibilities.

For example, with an extremely high and stable level of sales, it would be preferable for Company A to build a highly automated plant with high fixed costs and low unit variable costs. Management of Company B is not as optimistic about sales levels; it would therefore favor a plant that is not as highly automated (lower fixed costs), but it would have to pay higher unit variable costs (direct labor). Company A would therefore have a competitive advantage over B, if the economy is strong and there is a large demand for the product. Profits are amplified when

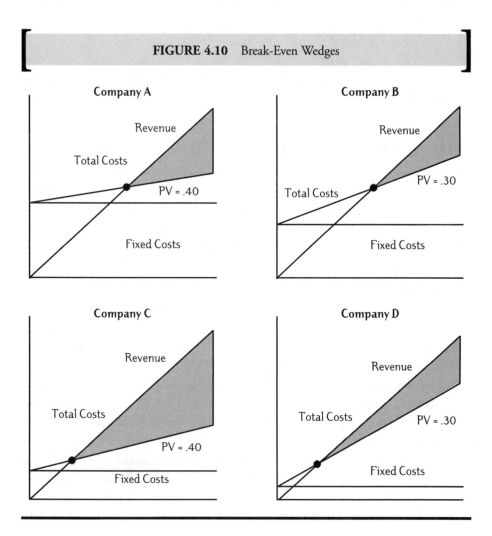

FIGURE 4.10   Break-Even Wedges

the company has reached its break-even point. If, however, the economy is weak and production levels are low, Company B would have a distinct competitive advantage over Company A because its fixed costs would be lower.

The figure shows four companies with different cost structures and PV ratios. Each company shows a different profit wedge. As indicated earlier, Company A and Company B have the same break-even points, but Company A has higher fixed costs and a higher PV ratio than Company B. Although Company A's profits are amplified after the break-even point, it is more vulnerable if sales volume falls short of the break-even point. As shown, the loss zone is more pronounced for Company A than for Company B.

Companies C and D have lower fixed costs. The sales revenue line is the same as those of Companies A and B, but the profit levels are reached earlier. For example, Company C's profit structure (PV ratio) is similar to that of Company A, but, Company C generates a profit on each sales dollar at a lower level of production. Profits generated by Companies B and D follow a similar pattern.

The major advantage of Companies A and C is that profits amplify faster once they have reached the break-even point (producing a wider wedge or bigger PV ratio). These companies are, however, more vulnerable to losses in a slow economy. Companies B and D have similar revenue and variable cost patterns (the slope of the lines are identical), which produce a similar wedge in the profit zone.

Other Cost Concepts

Managers classify costs in different categories. So far, we have made the distinction between fixed and variable costs, and have shown that there are also costs that can be classified as semi-fixed or semi-variable. Costs must be classified in separate and distinct categories when preparing a cost-volume-profit analysis. Let us examine other cost concepts and see how they can be used for purposes of analysis and control.

Committed Versus Discretionary Costs

Fixed costs can be grouped in two distinct categories: committed and discretionary.

Committed fixed costs are those that cannot be controlled and that must be incurred in order to operate a business. They include depreciation on buildings and equipment and salaries paid to managers.

Discretionary fixed costs are those that can be controlled by managers from one period to another if necessary. For example, expenditures on research and development, training programs, advertising, and promotional activities can be increased or decreased from one period to the next.

It is important to recognize the difference between committed and discretionary fixed costs for cost-volume-profit analysis purposes. As shown in **Figure 4.11**, for a difficult anticipated planning period, management may decide to cut back some discretionary costs in order to bring the break-even point from A to B.

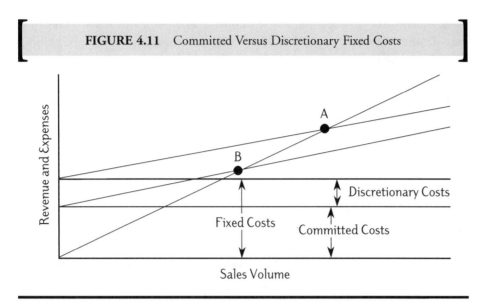

FIGURE 4.11 Committed Versus Discretionary Fixed Costs

Controllable Versus Non-Controllable Costs

Accountability is important in the management process. For this reason, it is vital to separate all costs that are within the control of a manager from those that are not.

Budgets are allocated to individual managers, and the managers are monitored to see whether they operate within these budget ceilings. If certain costs over which managers have control exceed the budget, the managers must explain why. Typical **controllable costs** for plant managers are maintenance, production supplies, overtime, waste, and equipment. Certain other costs are incurred over which they have no control; typical **non-controllable costs** are depreciation, insurance, supervisor's salary, and other overhead costs.

It is important to distinguish between these two types of costs for reporting purposes. On the manager's budget reports, costs should be grouped under these two categories, and managers should be held responsible only for variances over which they have control.

Direct Versus Indirect Costs

Costs may be direct or indirect. **Direct costs** are directly related to a specific activity, product, program, project, or objective. These costs would be avoided if an activity was eliminated or incurred if the activity was performed.

Indirect costs are not associated with a specific activity, product, program, project, or objective. Typical indirect costs include overhead, which is usually divided among different operating or production units. For example, **Table 4.6(a)** shows a company that produces three different products, each generating identifiable direct costs. A total of $90,000 in indirect costs or overhead costs is allocated equally ($30,000) to the products. As shown, products A and B are producing positive net results while product C is showing a $5,000 loss. Under these circumstances, management may contemplate the possibility of abandoning product C. If this is the case, the absorption of the $90,000 overhead (if these costs cannot be reduced with the abandonment of product C) would therefore have to be split between products A and B. As shown in **Table 4.6(b)**, this would reduce the profit position of these two products, and even produce a negative result for product B. In addition to apparently losing money on product B, the company would reduce its overall profitability from $45,000 to $20,000. The company would, therefore, be in a better position if it continued to manufacture product C.

Decision-Making in Action

Let's now examine how the break-even concept can be applied within the context of decision-making. The left side of **Table 4.7** shows the income statement of Widget Inc. As indicated, the company needs to earn a $100,000 profit. Management is considering the following questions.

1. Should we increase our selling price by 5 percent?
2. Should we increase our advertising budget by $30,000?
3. Should we hire a new sales representative? Cost is estimated at $60,000.

TABLE 4.6(A)   Direct and Indirect Costs

	Product A	Product B	Product C	Total
Sales	$100,000	$90,000	$75,000	$265,000
Direct costs	25,000	55,000	50,000	130,000
Indirect costs	30,000	30,000	30,000	90,000
Total costs	55,000	85,000	80,000	220,000
Profit	$ 45,000	$ 5,000	$(5,000)	$ 45,000

TABLE 4.6(B)   Direct and Indirect Costs

	Product A	Product B	Total
Sales	$100,000	$ 90,000	$190,000
Direct costs	25,000	55,000	80,000
Indirect costs	45,000	45,000	90,000
Total costs	70,000	100,000	170,000
Profit	$ 30,000	$(10,000)	$20,000

TABLE 4.7 Decision-Making in Action

Profit and Loss Statement		Rearranged Profit and Loss Statement		Average Unit Selling Price and Cost	
Sales revenue	$2,500,000	Sales revenue	$2,500,000	No. of units	250,000
Cost of goods sold	1,900,000	Variable costs		Unit selling price	$10.00
		Cost of goods sold	1,600,000	Unit variable cost	6.80
Gross margin	600,000	Selling	50,000		
		Administrative	50,000	Contribution margin per unit	$ 3.20
Selling expenses	300,000	Total variable costs	1,700,000		
Administrative	200,000				
Subtotal	500,000	Contribution margin	800,000		
Profit	$ 100,000	Fixed costs			
		Cost of goods sold	300,000		
		Selling	250,000		
		Administrative	150,000		
		Total fixed costs	700,000		
		Profit	$ 100,000		
		PV ratio	.32	PV ratio	.32

4. What would our break-even sales revenue be if we were to reduce our variable costs by 3 percent?

5. How much sales revenue must we achieve to earn an extra $20,000 profit?

To answer these questions, the Widget Inc. managers must first rearrange the profit and loss statement by putting under two distinct groupings all variable costs and all fixed costs. As shown under the rearranged profit and loss statement in the middle section of **Table 4.7**, it is assumed that the company's variable costs amount to $1,700,000 and generate $800,000 in contribution margin. Total fixed costs amount to $700,000. By regrouping the variable and fixed costs, it is possible to calculate the PV ratio. As shown, the PV ratio is .32 and is calculated by dividing the $800,000 contribution margin by the $2,500,000 sales revenue. This means that for every dollar's worth of sales, the company is generating $0.32 in contribution margin. The PV ratio is required to quickly answer the above-mentioned questions. For example, dividing fixed costs by the PV ratio shows that the company would have to sell $2,187,500 or 87.5 percent of its sales revenue objective.

The right side of **Table 4.7** presents the number of units sold and, for each unit, the selling price, variable cost, and contribution margin. The contribution is maintained at .32, or $3.20 per unit.

Now, let's answer the five questions referred to earlier.

Question 1: Should we increase our selling price by 5 percent?
If the selling price is increased by 5 percent, the unit selling price would be $10.50 and increase the contribution margin to $3.70 or 37 percent. Dividing the fixed costs, $700,000, by the new contribution margin shows that the company's new break-even point would be $1,891,892 or 75.7 percent of its sales revenue objective. But before increasing its selling price, the company would have to consider the effect of a change in the selling price on sales volume; that is, how many customers would be lost as a result of this change. The same arithmetic could be done for a 3 percent increase, a 2 percent decrease, and so on.

Question 2: Should we increase our advertising budget by $30,000?
If the advertising budget is increased by $30,000, total fixed costs would be increased to $730,000. Dividing these fixed costs by PV ratio (.32) shows that the break-even point would be increased to $2,281,250 (instead of $2,187,500), a difference of $93,750. Before increasing the advertising budget, management would have to determine whether the extra $30,000 expenditure would be able to generate an additional $93,750 in sales revenue. If it is estimated that the $30,000 would generate an extra $175,000 in sales revenue, then the higher advertising budget could be justified.

Question 3: Should we hire a new sales representative? Cost is estimated at $60,000.
The arithmetic here is similar to that of question 2. Fixed costs would increase to $760,000 and the new break-even point would rise to $2,375,000 (compared to the existing $2,187,500). This would require an additional $187,500 in sales revenue. Could the new sales representative generate this much revenue? If the sales revenue is not achieved during the first year, how about the second or third year?

Question 4: What would our break-even sales revenue be if we were to reduce our variable costs by 3 percent?
A 3 percent reduction would bring the total variable costs to $1,649,000 and increase the PV ratio to .34. The arithmetic is done as follows:

Sales revenue	$2,500,000
Variable costs	1,649,000
Contribution margin	851,000
PV ratio	.34

Here, the break-even point would be reduced to $2,058,824 (from $2,187,500) or 82.4 percent of the sales revenue objective (instead of the existing 87.5 percent).

Question 5: How much sales revenue must we bring in to earn an extra $20,000 profit?
If management wants to realize a $120,000 profit objective, sales revenue would have to be $2,562,500 ([$700,000 + $120,000] ÷ .32). This means that the company's sales revenue would have to be increased by 2.5 percent ($2,562,500 ÷ $2,500,000).

Summary

Break-even analysis can be used in business to make different types of decisions such as pricing decisions, new product decisions, modernization decisions, and expansion decisions. However, in order to make the right decision, management must have a complete knowledge of its business's operating cost structure.

Cost-volume-profit analysis consists of analyzing the interrelationships among volume of production, fixed costs, and variable costs. Fixed costs remain constant and do not vary with different levels of production. Variable costs vary in direct proportion to changes in level of output. There are also semi-fixed or semi-variable costs that vary at different levels of production.

Break-even analysis is the method that helps management determine at what point profit or loss takes place. The break-even point is the level of output where a business stops incurring a loss and begins to make a profit.

The contribution margin is the difference between the selling price of a product and the variable costs. This difference is used to pay for fixed costs, and to earn a profit.

The break-even chart gives a visual presentation of the interrelationships among revenues, variable costs, fixed costs, and total costs. The break-even point can be calculated using the following formula:

$$N = FC/(SP - VC)$$

The cash break-even point determines how many units a business must sell in order to pay for its cash expenses. The profit break-even point determines the number of units a business must sell in order to achieve a targeted profit objective.

Sensitivity analysis is used to gauge the various break-even points when there are changes in any one of the variables, such as unit selling price, volume of production, fixed costs, or variable costs.

Break-even analysis can be applied in many areas, including sales territories, retail stores, plants, departments, product divisions, production centers, and service centers.

Costs can also be broken down into committed fixed costs versus discretionary fixed costs, controllable versus non-controllable costs, and direct versus indirect costs.

CHAPTER 5

Cost of Capital and Capital Structure

*B*y the end of 2002, the Edwards are pleased with CompuTech's Sales and Service's financial performance. In fact, they exceeded their financial expectations. During that year, they decided to incorporate their business. It is now called CompuTech Inc. The Edwards are entering an important phase in their business development in order to further expand their retail business. The determining factor that limits the number of outlets they hoped to open is how much financing they would be able to obtain from lenders. They are also thinking of asking a few friends to invest in their business as shareholders.

One important element that could encourage lenders to invest in CompuTech is the quality of the collateral and the company's ability to service its debt. On the other hand, the factor that would entice potential shareholders to invest in the company is its ability to grow in terms of sales and earnings. The Edwards will have to demonstrate to potential shareholders that they have the ability to manage the company extraordinarily well and demonstrate that CompuTech would be able to generate substantial earnings.

The Edwards begin to prepare an investment proposal to be presented to different investors. They do not consider 2003 as too ambitious. They want to expand the working capital of their existing retail outlet and open another retail outlet. The amount of the investment is estimated at $350,000. The following shows how the Edwards propose to finance their expansion program.

	Uses	Sources
Working capital requirements	$ 99,000	
Short-term financing		$ 72,000
Capital assets	350,000	
Internal financing		157,000
Capital shares		70,000
Long-term debt		150,000
Total	$449,000	$449,000

One of the last points that the Edwards remembered during their initial conversation with their friend and entrepreneur Bill Murray was this: "You have to make sure that your business generates enough cash to pay for financing your business." Now that the Edwards are anticipating growth and expansion, they are beginning to realize the significance of Bill's statement. They need to make sure that sufficient cash is available from the business to pay the interest and dividends to the shareholders. They also have to make sure that earnings from their business will be sufficient to reinvest into their business for working capital requirements and for the purchase of capital assets such as a new store and equipment.

A quick analysis of their projected financial statements for 2003 indicates that CompuTech will generate a 12.1 percent return on assets. The Edwards have to make sure that the cost of the borrowed funds from different financing sources is less than the 12.1 percent ROA. In order to encourage shareholders to invest, they have to demonstrate a positive economic value added (EVA).

The Edwards have even more ambitious objectives for the longer term. They want to go public by 2010. This means that they have six to seven years to demonstrate that CompuTech has "real growth potential" with "powerful earnings." They are thinking of approaching venture capitalists in 2005 who would invest substantial sums of money in their business in the form of equity. They realize, however, that these types of investors are looking for 25 percent to 35 percent (if not more) return on their investments. If they want to attract these types of investors, CompuTech must demonstrate substantial growth and earnings potential.

This chapter examines two key concepts:

1. How cost of capital is calculated and used as a management tool.
2. The significance of leverage analysis and how it can be used to maximize return.

Introduction

This chapter examines two distinct but related topics: cost of capital and leverage. Let's begin by explaining the meaning and the significance of these two concepts.

Cost of capital deals with the cost of borrowing funds to finance a business. For example, someone who obtains a mortgage from the bank at 7 percent to finance a house would have a 7 percent cost of capital. Similarly, if an entrepreneur wants to start a business that requires $500,000 in capital, the first thing that she or he will do is to determine how much it will cost to raise these funds from various investors. These long-term investors could be lenders or shareholders. As shown on the following balance sheet, the cost to raise the $500,000 from investors to buy the assets is 13.1 percent. Also, assuming that the entrepreneur earns $100,000 in profit on a $500,000 investment in assets, the business would generate a 20 percent return on assets (ROA). As shown on the balance sheet, there is a positive 6.9 percent difference between the cost of borrowed funds (13.1 percent) and the amount that the entrepreneur expects to earn from the business (20.0 percent).

Balance Sheet

Assets	Investors
Return on assets	Cost of capital
20%	13.1%

The reason for comparing the ROA to the cost of capital is to ensure that the return generated from a particular investment justifies the cost of borrowed funds. This is how banks operate: they borrow money at a cost, and lend it for a return; they refer to this difference as the *spread*.

The following shows how the cost to raise funds from different investors is calculated. For example, the $100,000 amount borrowed from Source A represents 20 percent of the $500,000 amount and accounts for 2.0 percent of the total weighted cost of borrowing. This 13.1 percent is referred to as *cost of capital.*

Sources	Amount	Cost		Proportion		Weight
Source A	$100,000	10%	×	.20	=	2.0%
Source B	250,000	15	×	.50	=	7.5
Source C	150,000	12	×	.30	=	3.6
Total	$500,000					13.1%

Leverage, on the other hand, involves determining the most suitable operating and financial structure that will help increase financial performance. It focuses on the following questions: Should a business have more fixed costs than variable costs? What would be the right proportion? Should the business have more debt than equity? Again, what would be the best combination or proportion.

Sales volume is the important element that helps to decide on the most suitable operating and financial mix (or structure). In general, the more volume a business generates, the more management will be inclined to have a higher mix of fixed costs to variable costs. This was particularly critical when free trade agreements were signed with Canada and Mexico which gave wider access to markets for American businesses. With expanded markets, many businesses restructured their operating and financial structures in order to maximize both profitability and the wealth to their shareholders.

Finding the most suitable operating structure can help increase profitability. Here is how the concept works. If a business generates an increase in profit of 20 percent with a 10 percent increase in sales revenue, this means that the business has a 2.0 (or 2 to 1) operating leverage; that is, each time sales revenue increases by 10 percent, profitability is amplified by 20 percent. If management decides to change the composition of its operating cost structure and obtains a leverage of 3.0 (meaning that a 10 percent increase in sales generates a 30 percent increase in profit), it simply means greater *profit maximization*. The importance of calculating operating leverage is this: if Company A operates with a 3.0 leverage and Company B with a 2.0 leverage, Company A has a competitive advantage.

This chapter explains these two financial concepts, cost of capital and financial structure (or leverage analysis). But first, let's distinguish between the meaning of financial structure and capital structure.

Financial Structure and Capital Structure

As shown in **Figure 5.1**, **financial structure** means the way a company's total assets are financed by the "entire right-hand side of the balance sheet" (current liabilities, long-term debts, and shareholders' equity). **Capital structure**, on the other hand, represents the more permanent forms of financing such as long-term debt and equity (common shares, preferred shares, and retained earnings) which are normally used to finance capital (or fixed) assets. The shaded portion in the figure represents this portion of the financing package. Capital structure therefore

FIGURE 5.1   Financial Structure and Capital Structure

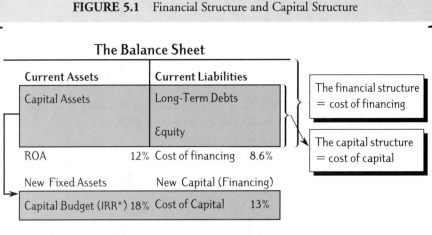

* IRR denotes internal rate of return, which is a capital budgeting technique used to gauge the financial viability of capital projects. The financial concept will be covered at the end of the chapter and in much detail in Chapters 6 and 7.

accounts for only a portion of a company's total financial structure. As shown, it excludes current liabilities.

Cost of Financing. **Cost of financing** calculates how much a business is charged to finance the assets that are shown on a company's balance sheet. As shown in **Figure 5.1**, let's assume that a company borrows funds from different financial institutions which cost 8.6 percent and earns 12.0 percent return on its assets (ROA); in this case, the company's cost of financing is *less* than what it earns. This produces positive results and undoubtedly only makes good business sense. However, if the cost of financing a business is *more* than its ROA, the shareholders would not be earning enough to justify the investments in capital assets.

Cost of Capital. Cost of capital is a different concept but it is calculated in a similar way. As indicated earlier, it deals with only the *permanent* forms of financing and has to do with the raising of *new* long-term capital to buy new capital assets. As shown in **Figure 5.1**, the company raises new capital funds from different financing sources (long-term debt and equity) at a cost of 13 percent (cost of capital). These funds are invested in new capital assets and generate an 18 percent return (IRR). This means that the cost of the newly acquired capital or permanent financing is less than the return expected to be earned on newly acquired capital assets. Again, this would make good business sense. In fact, the decision to borrow the capital funds at 13 percent in order to earn 18 percent would be considered favorable.

Cost of capital is associated with capital budgets since both have long-term implications. Bonds and mortgages, for example, are borrowed on a long-term basis (say 15 years) and are used to finance capital projects that also have long life spans (say 15 years). Referring to **Figure 5.1**, if the company's cost of capital is 13 percent, and it earns 18 percent return on assets, this means that the business would have a 5.0 percent positive spread every year during the next 15 years. If the spread was negative, the shareholders would make less on their investments. If this was the case, management would surely not go ahead with the investment decision.

Cost of Financing

Let's now examine the importance of cost of financing and how it is calculated. **Table 5.1** shows a company that raises $1,200,000 from seven different sources. Short-term financing or current liabilities account for $250,000 (or 20.8 percent) of the total financing package, long-term debts account for $500,000 (or 41.7 percent), and equity accounts for $450,000 (or 37.5 percent). The table also presents the cost of financing for each amount raised, on a before- and after-tax basis. For example, management raised $50,000 from source A at a cost of 10.2 percent on a before-tax basis. Assuming that the company is in a 50 percent tax bracket, the after-tax cost of borrowing from source A would be half, that is, 5.1 percent. The same arithmetic is done for calculating all other short- and long-term loans.

However, the cost of raising funds from shareholders is 15 percent before and after-tax, because dividends are paid to shareholders with after-tax income. The last two columns in **Table 5.1** present the *weighted cost of financing*. As shown, based on that particular financing structure, it would cost the company 11.53 percent before-tax to raise funds from different sources, and 8.57 percent after tax.

The weighted cost of financing, however, is somewhat irrelevant unless it is compared to the return that the company earns on its assets. **Table 5.2** gives us this comparison. As shown in the table on the left side of the balance sheet, the company earns 14.2 percent (return) on its assets on a before-tax basis, and 7.1 percent after-tax. The before-tax return is based on the assumption that the company generated $170,400 in income before taxes on total assets worth $1,200,000.

The after-tax return is also based on the assumption that the company is in a 50 percent tax bracket (14.2 percent ÷ 2 = 7.1 percent). As shown in the table, the spread is *positive* using the before-tax calculation because the company's assets are generating more than the cost of borrowed funds (14.2 percent versus 11.53 percent). However, the spread is *negative* on an after-tax basis (7.1 percent versus 8.57 percent). After-tax comparison is the common approach used for comparing cost of financing to return on assets.

Let's push this analysis a little further and calculate how much the company is earning on borrowed funds. This is what the lower portion of **Table 5.2** presents. The company borrowed $750,000 ($250,000 from short-term lenders and

TABLE 5.1   Calculating the Cost of Financing

	Amounts	Proportion	Cost of financing Before tax	Cost of financing After tax	Weighted cost of financing Before tax	Weighted cost of financing After tax
Current liabilities						
Source A	$ 50,000	4.2	10.2%	5.1%	.43%	.21%
Source B	100,000	8.3	11.2	5.6	.93	.46
Source C	100,000	8.3	9.6	4.8	.80	.40
Long-term debts						
Mortgage	200,000	16.6	9.2	4.6	1.54	.77
Bond	300,000	25.0	8.8	4.4	2.20	1.10
Equity						
Common shares	150,000	12.6	15.0	15.0	1.88	1.88
Retained earnings	300,000	25.0	15.0	15.0	3.75	3.75
Total sources	$1,200,000	100.0				
Weighted cost of financing					11.53%	8.57%

[
TABLE 5.2   Comparing Cost of Financing to ROA
]

Balance Sheet

Assets			Liabilities		Before Tax	After Tax
Current	$ 400,000		Current	$ 250,000	@ 2.2%	1.1%
Fixed	800,000		Long-term	500,000	@ 3.7%	1.9%
			Equity	450,000	@ 5.6%	5.6%
Total	$1,200,000		Total	$1,200,000	11.5%	8.6%

	ROA	Cost
Before tax	14.2%	11.5%
After tax	7.1%	8.6%

Before tax

Debt $750,000	×	14.2%	=	$106,500
Debt $750,000	×	9.4%	=	70,500
Financial leverage				$ 36,000

After tax

Debt financing	4.71% × .624	=	2.93%
Equity financing	15.68% × .376	=	4.17
Total			7.10%

$500,000 from long-term lenders) and earned 14.2 percent (ROA) or $106,500. As shown below, the weighted cost to borrow the funds from both short- and long-term sources is 9.42 percent. These amounts are drawn from different sources of financing that appear in **Table 5.1**.

Sources	Amounts	Proportion		Before tax cost		Weighted cost
Source A	$ 50,000	6.67	×	10.2%	=	0.68%
Source B	100,000	13.33	×	11.2	=	1.49
Source C	100,000	13.33	×	9.6	=	1.28
Mortgage	200,000	26.67	×	9.2	=	2.45
Bond	300,000	40.00	×	8.8	=	3.52
Total	$750,000	100.00				9.42%

This means that there is 4.8 percent spread (14.2 percent and 9.4 percent) on a before-tax basis between the cost of debt financing and the ROA. As shown in **Table 5.2**, the company's financial leverage—that is, the amount of money the owners earn by using *other people's money*—is $36,000.

The lower portion of **Table 5.2** shows how the shareholders' return can be amplified as a result of the company's profit performance and financial structure.

Since the cost of debt financing is 9.42 percent on a before-tax basis, the after-tax cost of financing (assuming the company is in a 50 percent tax bracket) would be 4.71 percent. Also, the proportion of the $1,200,000 raised from debt is $750,000, or 62.5 percent, and the balance, $450,000 or 37.5 percent, was obtained from shareholders' equity. As shown, instead of earning a 15.0 percent return, the shareholders are actually getting slightly more, 15.68 percent.

Here is how this number is calculated. Debt financing is constant; that is, irrespective of what happens, the company has to pay the interest—here, 4.71 percent, which represents 2.93 percent of the total cost of financing. As shown in the table, the company earns a 7.1 percent after-tax return on assets. By subtracting the 2.93 percent portion of the debt financing from the total cost, we get 4.17 percent. In this particular situation, the shareholders are actually earning 15.68 percent ($.376 \times 4.17$) by using other people's money.

Economic Value Added

A new term that has gained prominence in the business community to measure after-tax net operating profit results to cost of capital is the **economic value added (EVA)**. Each year, *Fortune* magazine lists in one of its November issues under the title, "America's Wealth Creators" companies with the highest EVAs. Basically, this financial tool measures the *wealth* a company has created for its investors. EVA is a performance measure. Specifically, it is an attempt to measure how profitable a company *truly* is. Here is how EVA is calculated. The calculation begins with the company's sales, and then it subtracts the expenses incurred in running the business, and that leads to net operating profits after taxes (NOPAT). Then it subtracts one more expense—the cost of all the capital employed to produce the NOPAT. Capital includes elements such as buildings, heavy equipment, computers, and vehicles as well as working capital.

In effect, EVA charges the company for the use of those assets at a rate that compensates the lenders and the shareholders, for providing those funds. What is left is EVA and it measures profits after all costs are covered—including the cost of using assets shown on the balance sheet.

EVA has become the financial tool of choice at leading companies such as Coca-Cola, AT&T, Wal-Mart Stores, Eli Lilly and Quaker Oats. At Eli Lilly, for example, EVA was linked to the company's bonus plan pay system.

The reasons for the increasing popularity of this performance measurement are:

◆   It more closely reflects the wealth created for shareholders.
◆   It promotes management accountability.
◆   It helps to make better decisions.

Table 5.3 shows an example of how EVA is calculated. As shown, the company's net operating profit before-tax (NOPBT) is $1.0 million. On an after-tax basis, the net operating profit after-tax (NOPAT) is $650,000. It is assumed

TABLE 5.3   Calculating the Economic Value Added (EVA)

	Net Operating Profit	Minus	Cost of Capital	Equals	EVA
NOPBT	$1,000,000	Weighted cost	10.9%		
Minus taxes	450,000	of capital	×		
		Total capital	$4,500,000		
NOPAT	$ 650,000	*MINUS*	$ 490,500	*EQUALS*	$159,500

here that the company is in a 45 percent income tax bracket. The company's cost of capital of 10.9 percent (after-tax) to finance the $4,500,000 worth of capital funds (accounts payable is excluded from this calculation because suppliers do not charge interest) produces $490,500 in financing charges. The difference between the NOPAT and the cost of capital gives a $159,500 positive EVA.

These calculations show the importance of comparing the cost of debt financing to return on assets. If the return on assets is less than the cost of capital, management would have to either increase the return on its assets or to restructure its financing package differently in order to improve the economic value added or the wealth to its shareholders.

Cost of Capital and the Leverage Concept

The rest of this chapter deals with decisions related to raising *new capital*. Here, we are looking at the relationship between the cost of raising new permanent funds (and the most suitable capital mix), and comparing it to the return expected on the investment in new capital assets. Two important concepts that influence the choice and mix of one source of capital financing over another are *cost of capital* and *leverage*.

Cost of Capital for Privately Owned Companies

Cost of capital is a critical element in financing decisions. It is defined as the average rate of return shareholders and lenders expect to earn on the money they invested in their business. To calculate the *weighted cost of capital*, the costs of individual financing sources must be brought together. Finding the weighted cost of capital is an important calculation since it is used in determining the "hurdle rate"—that is, the level of return a project should generate before management will approve it in the capital budgeting process.

Here is how the concept works. Let's assume that Zylox (a privately owned company) has the opportunity to invest $100,000 in a risk-free project that will generate a 14 percent return, or $14,000. If the company has $50,000 of its own money and wishes to raise another $50,000 from external sources, the cost of raising the new capital dollars will determine, to a large extent, whether Zylox will proceed with the project. As shown below, let's assume that the owners are able to raise $20,000 from source A at 9 percent, $20,000 from source B at 8 percent, and $10,000 from source C at 9.5 percent. They also expect to earn at least 12 percent on their own money (equity), since this is what they would expect to earn had they invested the $50,000 in other ways (sometimes referred to as **"opportunity cost"**). Should the company go ahead with this project? To answer this question, we have to calculate the weighted cost of capital and determine whether the risk is worth taking. The following is a simplified way of calculating the cost of capital.

Source of Capital	Amount	Percent of Total		Cost of Capital		Proportion of Cost
Personal	$ 50,000	0.50	×	12.0%	=	6.00%
Source A	20,000	0.20	×	9.0	=	1.80
Source B	20,000	0.20	×	8.0	=	1.60
Source C	10,000	0.10	×	9.5	=	0.95
	$100,000	1.00				10.35%

In this case, the weighted cost of capital is 10.35 percent. This project is expected to generate 14 percent (equivalent to ROA) or $14,000 in profit, while the total cost of borrowing is estimated at 10.35 percent, or $10,350. After looking at these figures, management at Zylox would be inclined to proceed with the project. If the project is considered risk-free, the chances of making a $3,650 net profit before taxes ($14,000 less $10,350) are virtually assured.

Leverage

Leverage is the percentage of debt a firm uses to finance the purchase of assets. For instance, the $100,000 asset referred to in the Zylox example is financed by a $50,000 debt, which means that the company has a 50 percent leverage factor.

A manager can enhance profits and value by using leverage effectively. For example, with a 50 percent leverage factor, Zylox made a profit of $3,650. Profitability can be increased (or amplified) substantially if all funds are obtained from source B, at a cost of only 8 percent. If Zylox was able to raise all funds from that single source, the profit generated would increase to $6,000, since the cost of financing would be only $8,000 and the return on the investment would remain at $14,000. The higher leverage would therefore produce an incremental $2,350 in profit ($6,000 less $3,650).

Interdependence of the Major Areas of Finance

There is an important relationship between the major areas of finance, namely capital structure, cost of capital, and capital budgeting.

As shown in **Figure 5.2**, one of the first steps in planning capital projects (or capital budgeting) is to determine how much funds should be borrowed, from

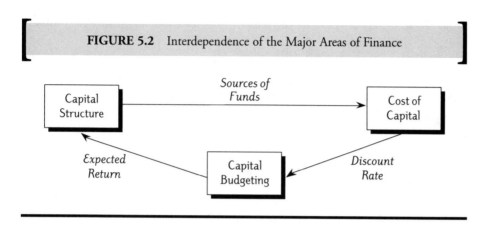

FIGURE 5.2   Interdependence of the Major Areas of Finance

whom, and at what cost. If the treasurer is asked to raise, say, $1 million, the cost of raising the new funds will first have to be calculated. The *capital structure* largely determines the *cost of capital*. As shown below, since raising capital from lenders costs less than from equity, it would be more attractive to obtain capital funds from lenders than from shareholders.

Different capital structures may influence the decision to go ahead with a capital project or not. To illustrate, let's assume that a company has a $1 million capital investment (*capital budget*) which produces a 10 percent ROA. As shown below, raising capital funds through option A gives an 11.5 percent weighted cost of capital, while option B gives only 8.0 percent. With a 10 percent ROA, management would not proceed with this particular project with the option A financing structure, since the company would be losing 1.5 percent. With option B, the company would be earning 2 percent, and management would (depending on the project's risk) probably approve the project.

Option A

	Debt	Equity	Total
Amount	$300,000	$700,000	$1,000,000
After-tax cost	5.0%	15.0%	
Proportion	.30	.70	1.00
Cost of capital	1.50%	10.5%	**11.50%**

Option B

	Debt	Equity	Total
Amount	$700,000	$300,000	$300,000
After-tax cost	5.0%	15.0%	
Proportion	.70	.30	1.00
Cost of capital	3.5%	4.5%	**8.0%**

The more it costs a business to raise funds, the more difficult it is for the business to go forward with its capital projects—unless, of course, the capital projects are exceptionally viable. As we will see in Chapter 7, the cost of capital is often used as the discount rate to compare the present value of a project's future cash inflows to the initial cash outflow.

Cost of Capital (for Publicly Owned Companies)

Up to this point, much of the discussion related to raising funds has focused on privately owned businesses. Let's now turn to raising funds for publicly owned businesses.

The cost of capital (from external sources) incurred by publicly owned companies is set out in contractual agreements made between a borrowing company and the different stakeholders. The key issues that will be focused on are: (1) the amount of interest it will pay to lenders, (2) the dividends it will pay to preferred shareholders, and (3) the dividends and growth potential expected by the common shareholders.

In this chapter, we will calculate the cost of capital for a hypothetical publicly owned company called Wildwood Inc. Let's assume that Wildwood's management wants to raise $20 million to invest in different capital projects. We will calculate the cost of capital of four financing sources, namely:

  a. long-term debt,
  b. preferred shares,
  c. common shares, and
  d. retained earnings.

After, we will define the meaning of marginal cost of capital. But first, let's examine the characteristics of each of these major sources of financing.

Characteristics of Long-Term Capital Sources

Debt, preferred share, and common share financing have one important common characteristic: they are all obtained from external sources. Retained earnings (that is, profit generated by a business) is the only internal financing source. **Table 5.4** summarizes the basic characteristics of these major sources of long-term financing as seen from an issuing company's point of view.

These major long-term financing sources are examined in terms of payout, risk, voting rights or control, cost of capital, tax cost, and cost of a new issue.

Payout means the money that a business must pay to its stakeholders in exchange for funds. Payout ranges from compulsory payment (debt) of principal and interest to non-obligatory payments, such as dividends on common shares.

Risk refers to the impact each source of financing has on a business if it is not able to meet its contractual agreement. Debt financing is the riskiest choice, particularly when economic or business conditions are difficult to predict, since bondholders may demand that interest be paid as per agreement and, if it is not, force the business into receivership.

Voting rights refer to the control that different stakeholders have over a business. Those who have the ultimate control of a company are the common shareholders. The issue of a new bond or preferred shares does not take away the rights of existing shareholders, but the issue of new common shares dilutes common shareholders' voting control. Also, additional shareholders can force a company to spread earnings more widely and thinly (see the figures in **Table 5.5** for the spread of income to new and existing shareholders).

Cost of capital includes factors associated with the borrowing of money, such as payment of interest on debt, dividends for common or preferred shares, underwriting and distribution costs, and taxes. All these elements must be weighted to determine the costs associated with each source of financing. Costs related to debt and preferred shares are more easily determinable and relatively more certain than common share financing.

Tax cost plays an important part in deciding whether to go the route of debt or equity financing. Common or preferred share dividends are not deductible as an expense for calculating a business's income tax; interest on bonds is. Taxes are a real cost that must be examined carefully. **Table 5.5** gives an example of the impact taxes have on debt and equity financing, at a certain level of income. As shown in the table, alternative A (debt financing) is the least attractive form of financing because the income after taxes is $225,000, compared to $250,000 for alternatives B and C. However, alternative A is the most lucrative for the existing shareholders, since they earn $112,500 more than common share financing offers, and $35,000 over preferred share financing.

Cost of issue includes charges associated with the underwriting and distribution of a new issue. Costs of issuing common shares are usually higher because the investigation is more detailed than debt and preferred share financing. A company that wants to raise funds will examine all the advantages and disadvantages of each source of financing and select the one that best meets its specific needs at the time of the issue.

The main factors that are taken into consideration when raising funds are:

- The nature of a company's cash flow.
- The company's annual burden of payments (existing debts).
- The cost of financing each type of capital.
- The control factor.
- The expectations of the existing common shareholders.
- The flexibility of future financing decisions.
- The pattern of the capital structure in the industry.
- The stability of the company's earnings.
- The desire to use financial leverage.
- The market conditions that can easily dictate the use of one form of capital source over another.

TABLE 5.4   Characteristics of the Major Sources of Long-Term Financing

	Debt	**Preferred Shares**	**Common Shares**	**Retained Earnings**
Payout	Interest and principal must be paid as per contractual agreement. Bondholders do not participate in superior earnings.	Same as debt, amount is specified by agreement, but no legal requirement to pay. Dividends may be accumulated from year to year.	Common share dividends are paid after debt and preferred dividends. Company is not forced to make payment.	Reduced payment of dividends puts more funds into a business; may be unfavorable in the short term but favorable in the long term.
Risk	If lenders are not paid according to agreement, they can force a business into receivership. Have a maturity date and may be callable.	Are usually callable. Have prior claim over common shareholders for receiving dividends, and other assets if company is liquidated.	Do not carry fixed maturity date.	Increases value and worth of a business.
Voting Rights (Control)	Have no say in business unless bond goes into default.	Have limited voting privileges; if they do, it is for minority representation on board of directors.	New issue creates change in ownership structure (extends voting rights). Legal right to make major decisions (elect board of directors).	When earnings are retained in a business, existing owners do not lose ownership right.
Cost of Capital	Easy to calculate and determinable since interest rate is stipulated.	Easy to calculate since it has a stated dividend rate and price of a share.	Rate is more difficult to ascertain since external factors and growth potential of a business form part of the cost.	Not easily determinable because of unpredictable growth trends.
Tax cost	Interest charges are tax deductible.	Preferred dividends are not tax deductible.	Common dividends are not tax deductible.	Taxed before payment is made to shareholders.
Cost of Issue	Underwriting cost is less expensive than other alternatives.	Flotation cost is expensive.	Underwriting and distribution costs are usually higher than preferred share and debt financing.	Avoids cost of issue.

TABLE 5.5   Impact of Debt and Share Financing on Income

	A Debt	B Common share	C Preferred share
Before tax income	$500,000	$500,000	$500,000
Interest on debt	50,000	0	0
Taxable income	450,000	500,000	500,000
Taxes (at 50%)	225,000	250,000	250,000
Income after taxes	225,000	250,000	250,000
Preferred dividends	0	0	60,000
Income to common shareholders	225,000	250,000	190,000
Income to new shareholders	—	$112,500	—
Income to existing shareholders	$225,000	112,500	$190,000

Financing assumptions:
A. *Debt financing* of $500,000 raised from lenders with interest rate of 10%.
B. *Common share financing* of $500,000 raised from new shareholders in exchange for 50% of the company's shares.
C. *Preferred share financing* of $500,000 raised from investors with a dividend rate of 12%.

Calculating the Cost of Long-Term Capital Sources

Let's now calculate the cost of long-term capital sources, namely, debt, preferred shares, common shares, and retained earnings.

Debt. **Cost of debt** financing is relatively easy to calculate. For example, if a company borrows $100,000 for one year at 10 percent, the lenders would receive $10,000 in interest. Ignoring income tax for the moment, the cost of capital for that particular source would be 10 percent.

Debt financing considers two fundamental questions. First, how should the cost be calculated when there are several different types of bonds? Second, since interest is a tax-deductible item, how does income tax affect the cost of debt?

First, if there are several bonds with different interest rates, we have to calculate the average rate of interest for that particular financing source. For example, let's assume that Wildwood Inc. decides to issue two bonds, a senior bond (like a first mortgage on a house) for $5 million at 10 percent, and a $2 million subordinated bond (like a second mortgage; it is paid only if the senior bonds are paid) at 12 percent. The average interest rate is calculated as follows:

$$\text{Average cost of bonds} \quad = \quad \frac{(\$5 \times 10\%) + (\$2 \times 12\%)}{\$7} \quad = \quad 10.57\%$$

Second, we must deal with the impact of income taxes on the cost of debt. Since interest is tax-deductible, we must find the income tax rate in order to calculate the effective cost of debt. The higher the income tax rate, the lower the effective cost of debt will be. For example, if a company has a 50 percent income tax rate, the effective cost of borrowing the aforementioned $7 million in bonds is 5.28 percent [10.57 percent $\times$ (1 $-$ .50)] or $369,600. If the income tax rate is 25 percent, the effective cost of borrowing would be 7.9 percent [10.57 percent $\times$ (1.0 $-$ .25)] or $553,000. If no taxes are paid, the effective cost of debt would be 10.57 percent or $739,900 annually.

The formula used for calculating the after-tax cost of debt is:

$$\text{Effective cost of debt} = (\text{before-tax cost}) \times (1.0 - \text{tax rate})$$

By applying this formula to the $7 million bond issue, and assuming that Wildwood Inc.'s tax rate is 50 percent, the effective cost of the debt would be 5.28 percent, calculated as follows:

$$\text{Effective cost of debt} = 10.57\% \times (1.0 - .50) = 5.28\%$$

Preferred Shares. Preferred shares are a hybrid of debt and common shares. Like debt, preferred shares carry a fixed contractual commitment for a company to pay—in this case, the dividends due to the preferred shareholders. In the event of liquidation, preferred shareholders take precedence over common shareholders. Also, dividends are paid to preferred shareholders before the common dividends are paid.

Calculating the **cost of preferred shares** is just as easy as calculating the debt cost, since preferred shares have a stated dividend rate and a current price. For example, if Wildwood Inc. issues preferred shares with a value of $1 million bearing 12 percent, the cost of this issue to the company would be $120,000 annually. If, one year from now, the preferred shares are sold in the market for 90 percent of their value, say $900,000, the interest rate to be earned by the new preferred shareholders would be 13.33 percent (12% ÷ 90%). The factors that may influence a decline in the market value of such shares are:

- The general rise of the interest rate, which forces the price of the shares to drop.
- A renewed fear of rampant inflation.
- A decline in the general value of the business as an investment opportunity.

Also, Wildwood Inc. would have to pay a commission to the investment dealers, and such flotation costs would be incorporated in the calculation.

Assuming that Wildwood Inc. sells 10,000 preferred shares at $100 each, bearing a 12 percent dividend rate, and the investment dealers charge a selling and distribution commission of $4 a share, Wildwood Inc. would net $96 a share. The formula used for calculating the cost of preferred shares is as follows:

$$\text{Cost of preferred shares} \quad = \quad \frac{\text{Dividend on preferred shares}}{\text{Market value of shares} - \text{Flotation costs}}$$

Wildwood Inc.'s cost of the preferred share issue would be 12.5 percent or $125,000. The calculation is as follows:

$$\text{Cost of preferred shares} \quad = \quad \frac{\$12}{\$100 - \$4} = \quad 12.5\%$$

So far, we have calculated the cost of raising $8 million out of the $20 million that Wildwood Inc. wants to raise. The remaining $12 million would have to come from common shares and retained earnings. If we assume that the company expects to reinvest $2 million in earnings into the business, Wildwood would have to raise $10 million from a common share issue.

Common Shares. As seen in the previous paragraphs, both debt and preferred share costs are easily calculated, quite determinable, and certain. They are contractual agreements signed by the company and the bondholders or preferred shareholders.

Finding the **cost of common shares** is more complicated. The common shareholders know what they want, but it is difficult for the treasurer of a company to estimate the future expected values of the business in terms of growth, retained earnings, etc., all of which are incorporated in the calculation. There are two different approaches used for calculating the cost of common shares.

The first approach is based on past performance. By looking at trends related to common share prices and dividend payments, the treasurer can put a price tag on a new issue. For instance, if, during the past five years, the selling price of common shares has been $25, and dividends paid were in the $2.50 range, the average investor's rate of return is therefore 10 percent ($2.50 divided by $25). If there are no significant changes in shareholders' expectations and no changes in the interest rates or investors' attitudes toward risk, the treasurer can assume that the future cost of common shares will be 10 percent.

The second approach is based on forecasts. Here, the treasurer takes into consideration three factors: (1) annual dividends to be paid, (2) price of the common shares, and (3) expected growth in earnings and dividends. The formula to calculate the cost of common shares is as follows:

$$\text{Cost of common shares} \quad = \quad \frac{\text{Dividend yield}}{\substack{\text{Market price of the} \\ \text{share} - \text{Issue costs}}} \quad + \quad \text{Growth rate}$$

Let us refer to Wildwood Inc.'s financing package. The company intends to raise $10 million from common shares. Also, the common share market price is $100 and the company's current annual dividend payout is 10 percent or $10 per share. Historically, the company's growth performance in earnings, dividends, and share price have been growing at 4 percent a year, which is a growth that is assumed to continue during the next few years. Using the above formula, Wildwood Inc.'s cost of common shares would be 14 percent.

$$\text{Cost of common shares} \quad = \quad \frac{\$10}{\$100} \quad + \quad 4\% \quad = \quad 14\%$$

The other factor taken into account is the flotation cost or the cost of selling a new issue. If Wildwood Inc.'s flotation costs are 10 percent on a $100 common share issue, the company would net $90. If we take this factor into consideration, the cost of the new shares would be 15.11 percent.

$$\text{Cost of common shares} \quad = \quad \frac{\$10}{\$100\,(1-.10)} \quad + \quad 4\% \quad = \quad 15.11\%$$

The company is showing growth because a portion of the retained earnings are plowed back into investment opportunities. These investments would generate additional earnings and produce a favorable effect on the growth potential of the company. For example, if Wildwood Inc. earns 20 percent on its investments, and half of each dollar earned is paid in dividends and the other half retained in the business, this means that each new reinvested dollar produces ten cents ($0.50 × 20%). Instead of reinvesting half of the earnings into the business, management decides to pay all its earnings in dividends; this may force a company to bring its growth to a halt. In this case, the market price of the share may remain at $100, since the investors would still receive a 14 percent return. Here is how this rate is calculated:

$$\text{Cost of common shares} \quad = \quad \frac{\$14}{\$100} \quad + \quad 0 \quad = \quad 14\%$$

Retained Earnings. The remaining $2 million is expected to be generated by Wildwood Inc. through its earnings. Calculating the **cost of retained earnings** is similar to the common share calculation, except that issue costs are not incurred. If the company expects to earn $20 a share and pay $10 in dividends during the coming year, and the growth pattern is also 4 percent, the company's cost of retained earnings will be 14 percent.

Weighted Cost of Capital

We have now calculated the individual cost of capital for debt, preferred shares, common shares, and retained earnings. With this information, we can calculate Wildwood Inc.'s **weighted cost of capital**; the arithmetic is simple. All that is required is to: (1) compute the proportion of each source of capital relative to the total capital structure and (2) multiply this number by the appropriate cost of that specific source of capital. As shown in **Table 5.6**, Wildwood Inc.'s weighted cost of capital is 11.428 percent. This rate would be the approximate value that would be used as the hurdle rate when reviewing potential capital investment projects.

Marginal Cost of Capital

Let's assume that, during the year, Wildwood Inc. wants to raise an extra $2 million in order to invest in more capital projects. It also wants to keep its capital structure in the same proportion. For the purpose of this exercise, let's assume that debt and preferred shares are raised at the same cost, while the cost for raising common shares is higher. By using the common share dividend yield, say 12 percent, a 10 percent flotation charge, and a 4 percent growth rate, the new cost of common share issue would be 17.33 percent.

The calculation is as follows:

$$\text{Cost of common shares} \quad = \quad \frac{12\%}{.90} \quad + \quad 4\% \quad = \quad 17.33\%$$

As shown in **Table 5.7**, the calculation of Wildwood Inc.'s new cost of capital is 12.961 percent. The additional dollars raised above the $20 million figure mean that Wildwood Inc. would have a new average cost of capital of 12.96 percent; this is referred to as the **marginal cost of capital (MCC)**. This means that Wildwood Inc.'s MCC, which was 11.4 percent to raise the $20 million, is now increased to 13 percent to raise $22 million (an extra $2 million).

Figure 5.3 shows graphically the relationship between the original $20 million capital structure and that of the new $22 million. The graph shows that the cost curve is flat up to the point where it reaches $22 million; at that point, it moves up gradually and continues to rise. The reason for the rise is that Wildwood Inc. may find it difficult to raise new securities within a short time-span. If it finds

TABLE 5.6   Calculating the Weighted Average Cost of Capital

Source of capital	Amount of capital	% of total	After-tax cost of capital	Proportion of cost
Debt	$ 7,000,000	35	5.28%	1.848%
Preferred shares	1,000,000	5	12.50	.625
Common shares	10,000,000	50	15.11	7.555
Retained earnings	2,000,000	10	14.00	1.400
	$20,000,000	100		11.428%

TABLE 5.7   Calculating the New Weighted Average Cost of Capital

Source of capital	Amount of capital	% of total	After-tax cost of capital	Proportion of cost
Debt	$ 7,000,000	31.8	5.28%	1.679%
Preferred shares	1,000,000	4.5	12.50	0.563
Common shares	12,000,000	54.5	17.33	9.445
Retained earnings	2,000,000	9.1	14.00	1.274
	$22,000,000	100.0*		12.961%

*Rounded

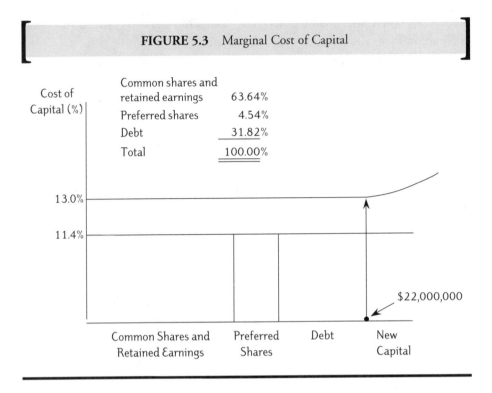

FIGURE 5.3   Marginal Cost of Capital

new sources of capital, they will be more expensive because of the higher risk to be borne by the stakeholders and the corresponding higher return they will demand from the company.

Using the MCC in Capital Budgeting Decisions

The purpose of calculating the marginal cost of capital is to ensure that the cost of borrowing does not exceed the return that will be earned from capital projects. For example, if it costs 15.0 percent to borrow capital dollars from different sources, the company will have to be assured that the aggregate return of all projects is at least equal to 15.0 percent; if it is less, the company would be in a negative return position. Let us examine how this works.

Once the marginal cost of capital is calculated, the next step is to relate it to capital projects. Using the Wildwood Inc. example, if the company intends to invest $20 million in capital projects giving an 11.4 percent return, all projects would be accepted. However, if managers submit capital projects that exceed the $20 million level, management would then have to examine all investment opportunities and accept a mix of projects that will maximize the overall value of the business. The procedure is as follows.

The first step is to find the marginal cost of capital, such as the one shown in **Figure 5.4.**

Second, projects are evaluated and the rate of return of each project is determined. The capital budgeting technique used to assess the economic attractiveness of capital projects is called **internal rate of return (IRR)**. This technique will be explained in Chapter 7. Using the IRR technique, the aggregate cash flow of all projects is discounted. The idea is to find the net present value of all projects that will give a zero figure. This happens when the total cash inflows of all projects equal their total cash outflows. In Wildwood Inc.'s case, management can approve a mix of projects that, when discounted by a rate of 11.4 percent, results in $20 million. If the company's aggregate IRR does not equal the cost of capital, we have to proceed to the next step.

In this step, the discounted present values of the cash flows of all projects are calculated at varying discount rates (say 35 percent down to 5 percent) and the result is plotted on a graph (see **Figure 5.4**). If the company raises $20 million at a cost of 11.4 percent, it will approve $20 million worth of capital projects. If more projects are approved, the aggregate IRR will fall below the 11.4 percent point, and Wildwood Inc. would be in a negative return position.

FIGURE 5.4   Marginal Cost of Capital and Internal Rate of Return

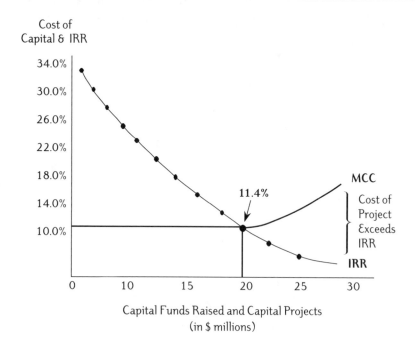

Leverage Analysis

Leverage analysis is used to determine the financing package or cost structure that will optimize the worth of a business. The purpose of leverage analysis is to answer one fundamental question: What is the best financing mix or capital structure to use to finance our assets? An example will illustrate how leverage analysis works. Let us assume that a firm borrows $400,000 at 12 percent (or 6 percent after tax) to finance projects that cost $500,000 and earn 16 percent (after-tax). Here, the owners earn $56,000 (after-tax profit of $80,000 less interest cost of $24,000) on their $100,000 investment, a return on equity of 56 percent. This compares favorably to the project's return of only 16 percent. Under these circumstances, where there is a wide spread between the rate of return and the rate of interest, management would use debt rather than equity funds. As mentioned before, debt is less expensive than equity financing.

Although this example is relatively easy, it is usually more difficult to figure out the leverage factor that produces the most lucrative financial benefits. To understand the mechanics of leverage, we have to examine the behavior of sales revenue, fixed and variable operating costs, earnings before taxes and interest, debt charges, and earnings per share. As shown in **Figure 5.5**, there are three types of leverage: operating leverage, financial leverage, and total or combined leverage.

Operating Leverage

Operating leverage deals with the behavior of costs at the operating level (e.g., company or plant); it does not take financing charges into consideration. This approach determines the most suitable cost (fixed versus variable costs) that will most amplify profit before interest or dividend charges. Leverage is important

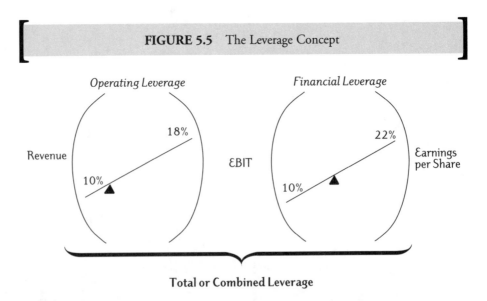

FIGURE 5.5   The Leverage Concept

because operating costs have a direct impact on total corporate charges which, in turn, affect financial leverage.

Operating leverage is based on the break-even analysis concept, which was examined in Chapter 4. It involves the relationship between three elements: sales revenue, fixed costs, and variable costs. The idea is to select the most appropriate cost mix that will maximize profits under a set of economic or industry considerations. A favorable operating leverage is achieved when a change in revenue generates a larger change in earnings before interest and taxes (EBIT). The element that amplifies the earnings is the relationship between fixed costs and total operating costs.

Here is an example of how operating leverage works. Let's assume that management contemplates modernizing a manufacturing plant that will require a $700,000 capital expenditure. To decide whether to modernize or not, management will have to identify the level of sales volume and sales revenue that will be achieved in the future, and the impact that the new technology will have on the company's fixed and variable cost structure.

As shown in **Table 5.8**, the new technology will bring about changes to the company's operating cost structure. Under the present cost structure, the company's fixed costs amount to $200,000 and it also earns a $5.00 contribution. If the company decides to modernize, the cost structure would change and the new fixed costs would be increased to $300,000 (an increment of $100,000 over existing operations). However, the unit variable costs will be reduced to $8.00 (from $10.00) because of the decreased variable costs due to higher productivity. The new contribution margin would be increased to $7.00. In other words, the company would earn an extra $2.00 in contribution to pay for the $100,000 fixed

TABLE 5.8   Operating Leverage

	Present production methods			Proposed production methods		
Fixed costs	$200,000			$300,000		
Selling price	$15.00			$15.00		
Variable costs	10.00			8.00		
Contribution	$ 5.00			$ 7.00		
(in $000s)	High	Expected	Low	High	Expected	Low
No. of units	100,000	70,000	40,000	100,000	70,000	40,000
Revenue	$1,500	$1,050	$ 600	$1,500	$1,050	$ 600
Variable costs	1,000	700	400	800	560	320
Fixed costs	200	200	200	300	300	300
Total costs	1,200	900	600	1,100	860	620
Profit	$ 300	$ 150	$ 0	$ 400	$ 190	−$ 20

cost increment. The question is this: Is the expansion worth the investment? To answer the question, the company would have to estimate the sales volume that it expects to achieve in the next year or two. **Table 5.8** shows that if the level of sales is at 40,000 units, the company would break even with the existing facility, but, if management modernizes its plant, the company would incur a $20,000 loss. However, if the company expects to sell 100,000 units, this new sales level would certainly justify the investment because it would generate a $400,000 profit instead of $300,000 for the present production methods.

Essentially, operating leverage measures how much the operating cost structure amplifies profit performance before interest and taxes. As shown in **Table 5.9**, a 10 percent increase in sales revenue (at the proposed production methods) generates a 17.5 percent increase in profit before interest and taxes (EBIT) or a leverage of 1.75.

Financial Leverage

Financial leverage is used to choose the most favorable capital structure—the one that will generate the greatest financial benefits to the shareholders. It is reasonable to assume that shareholders will favor projects with return rates exceeding the cost of borrowed funds. Since debt is the least costly source of funds, shareholders will prefer to borrow the maximum amount possible from this particular source (provided that the projects can generate enough cash to pay off the debt).

Financial leverage can be gauged by looking at only one alternative and changing its capital structure mix to determine how much the leverage can enhance the earnings per share position for each option. **Table 5.10** shows that a 10 percent increase in EBIT produces a 16 percent increase in income before taxes (or after tax since we are dealing with a 50 percent income tax rate). Here, the financial leverage is 1.6.

TABLE 5.9   Calculating the Operating Leverage

For the proposed production methods (high)

Sales revenue	$1,500,000	$1,650,000	10.0%
Variable costs	800,000	880,000	10.0
Contribution margin	700,000	770,000	10.0
Fixed costs	300,000	300,000	—
Profit (EBIT)	$ 400,000	$ 470,000	17.5

$$\frac{\text{Contribution margin}}{\text{Contribution margin} - \text{Fixed costs}} = \frac{\$700,000}{\$400,000} = 1.75$$

Combined Leverage

Combined leverage simply calculates both the operating and financial leverage. As shown in **Table 5.11**, when sales increase by 10 percent, income after taxes shows a 28 percent increase or a leverage of 2.8.

Decision-Making in Action

Management of National Electronics Ltd. is in the process of reviewing its upcoming operating plans and capital budgets. Prior to making important decisions, members of the management committee wanted some information about

TABLE 5.10   Calculating the Financial Leverage

For the proposed production methods (high)

EBIT	$400,000	$440,000	10.0%
Interest	150,000	150,000	—
Income before taxes	$ 250,000	$ 290,000	16.0

$$\frac{EBIT}{EBIT - Interest} = \frac{\$400,000}{\$250,000} = 1.6$$

TABLE 5.11   Calculating the Combined Leverage

For the proposed production methods (high)

Sales revenue	$1,500,000	$1,650,000	10.0%
Variable costs	800,000	880,000	10.0
Contribution margin	700,000	770,000	10.0
Fixed costs	300,000	300,000	—
Profit (EBIT)	400,000	470,000	17.5
Interest	150,000	150,000	—
Income before taxes	250,000	320,000	28.0
Income taxes	125,000	160,000	28.0
Income after taxes	$ 125,000	$ 160,000	28.0

$$\frac{Contribution\ margin}{EBIT - Interest} = \frac{\$700,000}{\$250,000} = 2.8$$
$$or$$
$$1.75 \times 1.6 = 2.8$$

meaningful numbers to determine whether they should approve or reject some of the capital expenditure projects.

National Electronics Ltd.'s income statement and balance sheet are shown below.

National Electronics Ltd.
Income Statement
For the year ending December 31, 2000

Sales revenue	$5,000,000
Cost of goods sold	2,900,000
Gross margin	2,100,000
Operating expenses	800,000
Operating profit	1,300,000
Interest charges	100,000
Income before taxes	1,200,000
Taxes	600,000
Income after taxes	$ 600,000

National Electronics Ltd.
Balance Sheet
December 31, 2000

Current assets		Current liabilities	
Accounts receivable	$1,000,000	Accounts payable	$500,000
Inventory	1,000,000	Working capital loan	500,000
Total current assets	2,000,000	Total current liabilities	$1,000,000
		Long-term debts	
Capital assets	3,000,000	Mortgage	$1,500,000
		Bonds	500,000
		Total long-term debts	2,000,000
		Shareholders' equity	
		Retained earnings	1,000,000
		Capital shares	1,000,000
		Total shareholders' equity	2,000,000
Total assets	$5,000,000	Total liabilities and equity	$5,000,000

The treasurer indicates to the members of the committee that the before-tax costs of financing the working capital loan, mortgage, and bonds were 13 percent, 10 percent, and 12 percent, respectively. He also pointed out that the shareholders were expecting to earn 15 percent on their equity.

The company's total capital budget was estimated at $2.0 million. The treasurer said that the financing of the total capital budget would come from debt in the amount of $1.2 million and equity for $800,000. The cost of financing the debt would be 12 percent and equity, 15 percent.

One important project that the committee was considering was the modernization of a small manufacturing plant. At the meeting, the plant manager indicated that the project would cost $200,000 and earn an 18 percent internal rate of return. The plant manager indicated that the $200,000 modernization program would make significant changes in the operating cost structure. As he pointed out, currently, the plant produces $450,000 in sales revenue with variable costs estimated at 80 percent of sales revenue and $100,000 in fixed costs. He stated that the modernization program would reduce the variable costs to 75 percent of sales revenue but increase the fixed costs to $115,000. The sales manager indicated that he expected sales revenue to reach $500,000 by the end of the current year and attain the $600,000 objective by the end of the following year.

The treasurer also indicated that the interest charges that were to be allocated to finance the plant's modernization program would be $8,000.

The CEO asked the following questions.

a. What is National Electronics' Ltd. cost of financing?
b. What is National Electronics' cost of capital for modernizing the plant. Should the committee approve the modernization program? Why?
c. What is National Electronics Ltd.'s economic value added?
d. Should the modernization program be approved? Why? To answer this question, the controller has to produce a profit and loss statement for the plant's three levels of sales revenue ($450,000, $500,000, and $600,000), for both current operations and the modernization program.
e. If the modernization program is approved, what is the plant's operating leverage using the $600,000 sales revenue objective?
f. What is the plant's financial leverage using the $600,000 objective in sales revenue if the modernization program is approved?
g. What is the plant's combined leverage?

As evidenced by the discussion at the management committee, several managers are involved in the decision-making process. Input comes from sources such as the treasurer, controller, plant manager, and sales manager. **Table 5.12** shows the calculations to answer the questions raised by the CEO.

Question 1: What is National Electronics' Ltd. cost of financing?
As shown in the table, the first thing that the controller has to do is determine the cost before- and after-tax for each source of financing including their proportion. The company is in a 50 percent tax bracket which is evidenced by the amount of tax that the company pays ($600,000 in taxes deducted from the $1,200,000 income before taxes). As shown in the table, the cost of financing National Electronics Ltd. as an on-going entity is 8.75 percent. The only account that does not bear an interest charge is accounts payable, which is the financing provided by suppliers.

Question 2: What is National Electronics' cost of capital for modernizing the plant? Should the committee approve the modernization program? Why?
National Electronics' capital budget shows that $200,000 will be invested in a modernization program for a small manufacturing plant. By using the same

[

TABLE 5.12   Decision-Making in Action

]

Question 1. Cost of Financing

	Source	Cost Before Tax (%)	Cost After Tax (%)	Proportion	Weighted Cost of Financing (%)
Accounts payble	$ 500,000	0.0	0.0	.10	0.00
Working capital loan	500,000	13.0	6.5	.10	0.65
Mortgage	1,500,000	10.0	5.0	.30	1.50
Bond	500,000	12.0	6.0	.10	0.60
Equity	2,000,000	15.0	15.0	.40	6.00
Total	$5,000,000			1.00	8.75

Question 2: Cost of Capital for Financing the Modernization Program

	Source	Cost Before Tax (%)	Cost After Tax (%)	Proportion	Weighted Cost of Capital (%)
Debt	$ 120,000	12.0	6.0	.60	3.60
Equity	80,000	15.0	15.0	.40	6.00
Total	$200,000			1.00	9.60

Question 3: Economic Value Added

Net operating profit before taxes	$1,300,000	Capital	$4,500,000
Income taxes (50%)	650,000	Cost of capital	× 8.75%
Net operating profit after taxes	650,000	Cost of financing	393,750
Cost of financing	393,750		
Economic value added	$ 256,250		

Question 4: The modernized plant's profit and loss statement at the three sales revenue levels.

	Before Modernization			After Modernization		
Sales revenue	$600,000	$500,000	$450,000	$600,000	$500,000	$450,000
Variable costs	480,000	400,000	360,000	450,000	375,000	337,500
Contribution margin	120,000	100,000	90,000	150,000	125,000	112,500
Fixed costs	100,000	100,000	100,000	115,000	115,000	115,000
Profit before taxes	$ 20,000	$ 000	$(10,000)	$ 35,000	$ 10,000	$(2,500)

continued

financing proportion for the entire company (40 percent for equity and 60 percent for debt) as shown in the calculation for the first question, $120,000 will be financed by debt and $80,000 by equity. The cost for equity and debt is 15 percent and 12 percent on a before-tax basis and 15 percent and 6 percent after tax. As shown in the table, the cost of capital for financing the project is 9.6 percent. The

TABLE 5.12   Decision-Making in Action, continued

Question 5: Operating Leverge using the modernization option at $600,000 sales revenue level.

			Increase
Sales revenue	$600,000	$660,000	10.0%
Variable costs	450,000	495,000	10.0
Contribution margin	150,000	165,000	10.0
Fixed costs	115,000	115,000	—
EBIT	$ 35,000	$ 50,000	42.9

$$\frac{\$\,150,000}{\$\,35,000} = 4.29$$

Question 6. Financial Leverage

			Increase
Profit	$ 35,000	$ 38,500	10.0%
Interest	8,000	8,000	—
EBIT	$ 27,000	$ 30,500	13.0

$$\frac{\$\,35,000}{\$\,27,000} = 1.30$$

Question 7. Combined Leverage

			Increase
Sales revenue	$600,000	$660,000	10.0%
Variable costs	450,000	495,000	10.0
Contribution margin	150,000	165,000	10.0
Fixed costs	115,000	115,000	—
EBIT	35,000	50,000	42.9
Interest	8,000	8,000	—
EBIT	$ 27,000	$ 42,000	55.6

4.29 × 1.3 = 5.58

plant manager indicated that the modernization program would earn an 18 percent internal rate of return. This compares favorably to the 9.6% cost of capital (an 8.4 percent positive difference). This is a good result in view of the fact that the modernization program would not be considered a high-risk investment.

Question 3: What is National Electronics Ltd.'s economic value added?
As shown in the income statement, National Electronics Ltd. produces a net operating profit before taxes (NOPBT) in the amount of $1.3 million. On the investor's side of the balance sheet (liabilities and shareholders' equity), the company raised $4.5 million from lenders and shareholders with a weighted cost

of financing of 8.75 percent. By deducting from the NOPBT the 50 percent income tax charge of $650,000 and the $393,750 financing charges, the company is left with an economic value added in the amount of $256,250.

Question 4: Should the modernization program be approved? Why? A profit and loss statement for the plant's three levels of sales revenue ($450,000, $500,000, and, $600,000) for both current operations and the modernization program is as follows.

On the basis of the information provided by the plant manager and the sales manager, the management committee should approve the modernization program. As shown in the table, the modernized plant would generate $35,000 in profit versus $20,000 at the $600,000 sales revenue level. The existing plant shows a ratio of 80 percent in variable cost leaving a 20 percent contribution margin to pay for the $100,000 fixed costs. The modernization program would reduce the variable costs to 75 percent but increase fixed cost by an extra $15,000, that is, up to $115,000. The most determining factor that will influence the management committee to approve (or not approve) the project is the sales estimates provided by the sales manager. Even at the $500,000 sales level, it would be economically attractive for the company to modernize. Nevertheless, the most probable estimate based on the sales manager's input is in the $600,000 range.

Question 5: If the modernization is approved, what is the plant's operating leverage using the $600,000 sales revenue objective?

The operating leverage is very attractive at the $600,000 sales revenue level for the modernization option. As shown in **Table 5.12**, a 10 percent increase in sales revenue would generate a 43 percent increase in earnings before interest and taxes (EBIT). The operating leverage is 4.29. Since National Electronics is in the 50 percent tax bracket, the leverage on an after-tax basis would be the same. The after-tax profit level for a 10 percent increase in sales revenue would also produce a 43 percent increase in earnings after interest and taxes ($17,500 versus $25,000).

Question 6: What is the plant's financial leverage also using the $600,000 objective in sales revenue if the modernization program is approved?

The financial leverage is not as attractive, but still good. A 10 percent increase in earnings before taxes produces a 13.0 percent increase in earnings after taxes. The financial leverage is 1.3. Here, it is estimated that an $8,000 interest charge will be paid to finance the modernization program.

Question 7: What is the plant's combined leverage?

The combined leverage is very positive. A 10 percent increase in sales revenue generates a 55.5 percent increment in earnings before (or after) taxes, or a combined 5.56 (4.28 × 1.3).

Summary

Financing decisions consider not only sources and forms of financing but also, and of equal importance, cost of capital and capital structure. Capital structure represents the permanent forms of financing, such as long-term debt, common shares, preferred shares, and retained earnings.

Cost of capital means the weighted rate of return a business must provide to its investors in exchange for the money they have placed in a business. Cost of capital is a critically important element in the financing decision process, since it is the basis for determining the capital expenditure investment portfolio. To illustrate, if the average cost of capital is 10 percent, management of a company will approve a capital expenditure portfolio that will earn 10 percent or more.

The economic value added (EVA) is a performance measure that attempts to measure how profitable a company truly is. It is calculated by deducting the cost of using the assets (interest charges) from the net operating profit after taxes.

The most important factors to consider when determining a permanent financing scenario are payout, risk, voting rights, cost of capital, tax cost, and cost of issue.

The four major components used to calculate the cost of capital are the cost of long-term debt, the cost of preferred shares, the cost of common shares, and the cost of retained earnings. Once the individual costs for each source are determined, the average cost of capital is calculated. Computing the proportion of each source of capital by the appropriate cost of each specific source of capital gives this number.

The marginal cost of capital is the increased cost to be paid for new funds that are raised.

Leverage analysis is used to determine the financing package or cost structure that will maximize the worth of a business. There are two types of leverage: operating leverage and financial leverage. Operating leverage deals with the cost behavior of an operating unit; it determines the most appropriate cost mix (fixed versus variable) that will maximize profitability under a given set of economic and industry conditions. Financial leverage is used to determine the most favorable capital structure—that is, the one that will generate the greatest financial benefits to the shareholders.

CHAPTER 6

Time Value of Money

*T*he Edwards are currently examining several investment options. Even though they are interested in investing money in CompuTech Inc., they also want to make sure that they will invest enough in retirement plans and educational funds for their two children, Vincent and Takara. To evaluate their needs, the Edwards know that they must become familiar with the banking and investment community language, that is, concepts dealing with compounding and discounting. They realize that if they are to invest money in retirement plans and educational funds today, the element of time will make their investment grow. They therefore need to learn how to use interest tables and financial calculators capable of performing **time value of money** calculations.

The Edwards realize that if they are to communicate knowledgeably with bankers, insurance agents, and financial advisors they have to understand financial concepts. For example, if the Edwards deposit $1,000 in the bank today for one year at 10 percent, time is the factor that will make their investment grow to $1,100. Similarly, if Len Edwards wants a $100,000 life insurance policy, the actuary would determine the amount of premium he would have to pay each year during a certain number of years (depending on the average age expectancy). Financial advisors who want to recommend to clients how much they need to save each year in different investments need a good understanding of these time value of money concepts.

Bankers, insurance agents, and financial advisors use the expression that a *dollar earned tomorrow is worth less tomorrow*. This has to do with the concept of discounting. For example, if the Edwards want to have $60,000 for both children by the time they go to college or university (say in twenty years from now), they know that they have to invest a much smaller amount today. For example, by investing $14,000 today at an 8 percent interest rate, it would grow to about $60,000 by the twentieth year and be sufficient to meet their children's needs.

The Edwards also realize that the time value of money concept is not only important for personal financing, but can also be applied to business decisions. The application, however, focuses almost exclusively on **discounting**. The fact that insurance companies pay the death benefits in the future, the future values of the premium payments will have to be compounded (future value), that is, brought into the future for comparison purposes (death benefit vs. premium payments). Conversely, businesses make a different calculation. Since business investments are made today (purchase of assets, opening of a new retail store or the expansion of an existing one), all cash flows that would be earned in the future would be discounted in order to find their present value and compared to the initial investment.

The Edwards recognize that in order to make wise personal and business decisions, they must learn the time value of money techniques.

This chapter examines the time value of money concept. In particular, if focuses on three key topics:

1.   What is the time value of money and why is it important to businesses?
2.   Using compound and discount interest tables.
3.   Applying the time value of money concepts to business decisions.

Introduction

The next chapter, "Capital Investment Decisions," deals with capital budgeting decisions such as the purchase of equipment or machinery; construction, modernization, or expansion of a plant; and research and development. These kinds of decisions involve *outflows* of money which take place during the year a decision is made and *inflows* of money which are generated years after the initial funds are disbursed. To make effective decisions in capital budgeting, it is important to understand *why* money has a time value.

In this chapter we will focus on:

♦   Understanding why money has a time value and differentiating it from the concepts related to inflation and risk.

♦   Learning how to use compound and discount interest tables.

♦   Getting acquainted with basic capital budgeting terms and concepts such as present value, net present value, and internal rate of return.

The first part of this chapter explains how interest tables can be used both on a personal basis and in business. It touches on the meaning of compounding, discounting, and annuities. The second part of the chapter serves as a brief introduction to the application of interest tables (time value of money) when making business decisions. In particular, investment decision tools such as net present value (NPV) and internal rate of return (IRR) will be explained briefly. Chapter 7 (Capital Investment Decisions) explains in more detail their usefulness and applications. Therefore, the objective of the second part of this chapter makes the link between the time value of money concept and investment decision making.

Why Money Has a Time Value

If a company invests $1,000 this year in a capital asset that will generate a one-time inflow of cash of $1,050 (the original $1,000 plus a $50 profit or 5 percent) next year, we can ask a fundamental question: Should the asset be purchased? These numbers tell us that the asset is totally paid for by the end of the first year, and produces a $50 profit. If money could be obtained from a bank interest-free to finance the capital asset and the company contemplated no other investments, the capital decision would be justified since it earns 5 percent. However, we know that money cannot be obtained interest-free from the banks and that there is always a cost attached to any sort of financing. A business may borrow $1,000 for, say, 12 percent; if this is the case, the $1,000 purchase of the capital asset would not be justified since the cost of borrowing would exceed the 5 percent return generated by the investment. After the cost of financing, the company would have a 7 percent negative return.

The fact that there is a cost (interest) associated with the borrowing of money, whether provided by shareholders or lenders, confirms the fact that money has a **time value**. If you have a choice between receiving $100 today or $110 a year from now, which option would you prefer? If money is worth 10 percent, it does not matter which option you select. You could invest the $100 in a term deposit which would give you 10 percent interest and increase your initial $100 to $110 one year from now. *Time* is the only element here that would have made you earn $10 or 10 percent. Conversely, we can say that the $110 you would receive one year from now equals today's $100.

This illustration shows that a dollar earned today is worth more tomorrow (compounded). Or, a dollar earned tomorrow is worth less today (discounted). In capital budgeting, if a company invests money in a long-term producing asset and wants to calculate the return on the investment of that asset, it must also take into account the fact that money has a time value. The reason is simple. The company invests cash today in exchange for cash that it will earn in future years. In order to respect the time value of money notion, all monies, whether spent today or earned next year or five years from now must be placed on an equal footing. That is why it is important to understand the fundamentals of the mathematics of interest, that is, compounding and discounting.

Sometimes, businesses simply avoid the use of the more sophisticated capital budgeting techniques to calculate the return on capital projects. They feel that mathematics of interest, which is the foundation of time value capital budgeting techniques, is complicated and cumbersome and that they have to understand the derivations of complex mathematical compound and discount formulas. This is not so. All that is required is to know how to read interest tables. Once this is understood, it is easy to use the more effective capital budgeting techniques such as *internal rate of return* and the *net present value* method and assess the economic viability of capital projects in a more meaningful way. Today, spreadsheets and finance software can easily help financial analysts perform quickly, complex financial calculations. Although capital budgeting techniques such as the net present value and internal rate of return will be introduced in this chapter, they will be explained in detail in Chapter 7.

Time Value of Money and Inflation

People often believe that money has a time value because of inflation. This is not the case. However, **inflation** is taken into consideration when capital decisions are considered. For example, if you invest $100 in a term deposit bearing a 10 percent interest rate at a time when inflation is running at 5 percent, the purchasing power of the $110 would be reduced to $105. Time value and inflation should not be confused, particularly in capital investment decisions, since the calculation of inflation is a separate exercise.

Let us examine a capital asset that generates a multi-year funds flow. The revenues and expenses generated by the investment during the entire economic life of the asset include two elements. First there are the revenues that are calculated on the basis of the expected volume increments, and second, the anticipated increase in unit selling price, which should include the element of inflation. Expenses also take into consideration inflation increments in wages and the costs of material, utilities, etc. The difference between the projected revenues and projected expenses gives a net profit level that incorporates the inflationary factor. Once the profit projections are calculated (which includes the built-in factor for inflation), the time value calculation of the future cash flows (compounding or discounting) begins.

Time Value of Money and Risk

People also confuse time value and risk. It is not because risks are inherent in capital projects that money has a time value. Nevertheless, it is important to consider the risk factor when contemplating capital investment decisions. A $1,000 investment in United States Savings Bonds with a 10 percent interest rate bears little **risk**. The chances of recovering the $1,000 amount and the interest are virtually assured. However, if $1,000 is invested in a mining venture, risks may be considerable. Because of the relative inherent risk involved in these types of investment opportunities, the investor would be comfortable with the 10 percent interest rate for the US Savings Bonds but would require a much higher return on the mining investment.

This demonstrates how risk and interest rates are related when an investor requires a certain percentage return on the original investment. Although risk and capital decisions are closely related, it is important to note that they are two distinct concepts. While interest implies *time value*, risk suggests the *level of return* one should expect to earn from a particular investment.

Investment Decisions

As shown in **Figure 6.1**, investment decisions deal with two key concepts: time and cash. *Time* is important because as mentioned earlier, when management invests money in capital assets today, they expect to earn money from these assets over an extended number of years. For example, when a company invests $100,000 to modernize a plant that has a ten-year life span, that initial cash outflow must be compared to all the cash inflows that will be generated through the savings in the future. There is no question that a $100,000 investment that generates $50,000 in savings during a three-year period (for a total of $150,000) instead of $15,000 a year during a ten-year period (also for a total of $150,000), would alter the financial attractiveness of that investment.

The second critical element is *cash*. If a company invests money in equipment, machinery, or research and development, it invests cash. Such an investment is commonly referred to as a **cash outflow** or *cash disbursement*. Management will want to compare cash invested with cash generated by the investment. The cash (not profit) that a project generates is commonly referred to as **cash inflow** or *cash receipts*. The common denominator that ties a project together is cash. Therefore, when preparing a project's pro-forma income statement, the net income figure shown at

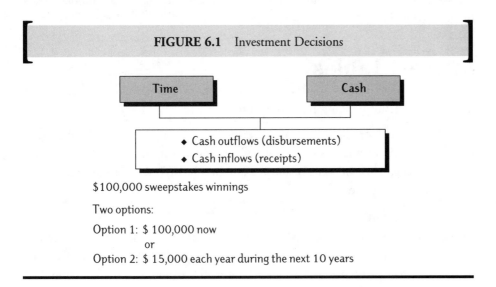

FIGURE 6.1   Investment Decisions

the bottom of the income statement must be converted into cash (e.g., by adding back depreciation) since time value yardsticks use cash, not profit, to calculate a project's viability. The bottom line is this: To make capital budgeting decisions meaningful, one has to compare apples (cash outflows) with apples (cash inflows).

The following illustrates the significance of time and cash in capital budgeting. Assume that you have won a $100,000 sweepstakes and are given the following options:

♦   Option 1: to receive the $100,000 lump-sum amount today
♦   Option 2: to receive $10,000 each year during the next ten years (also for a total of $100,000)

There is no question that you will go for the first option. In both options, we are dealing with cash and with time. It would be absurd to accept the $10,000 despite the fact that the total receipts equal $100,000. The fact that you could invest the $100,000 in term deposits at, say, 10 percent would make option 1 more economically attractive. However, if you were offered $12,000 a year for ten years, which option would you choose? How about $15,000? Or $20,000? How about $25,000 for each of the next six years (for a total $150,000) instead of only $100,000? As you can see, different time factors (here, six or ten years) and varying amounts, call for an analysis to determine the most lucrative option.

The same applies in capital budgeting. If you were to invest $100,000 in a capital asset that has a ten-year life span, how much should that asset generate in cash in order to make it economically attractive?

At the end of this chapter, once you understand the time value of money concept and how interest tables are used, you will calculate exactly how much cash you should agree to receive each year (and for how long) from a sweepstakes. You will also be able to determine how much cash an investment in capital assets should generate each year (and for how long) in order to make a $100,000 investment worthwhile.

Interest Tables

Let's now turn to interest tables and examine how they can be used as capital investment decision-making instruments to calculate:

♦   The future (compounding) and present (discounting) values of a single sum of money received or paid out at a given point in time.
♦   A constant flow of sums of money (an annuity) received or paid out over a given time period.

Algebraic Notations

Algebraic notations are introduced for two reasons. First, to show how the interest tables appearing in Appendix A are calculated, and second to explain the make-up of the various financial equations used in calculating future and present value amounts.

It is not necessary to understand the roots of the various algebraic formulas used to calculate future and present values. It is important, however, to grasp how interest tables are used to calculate the **future value** of a sum received today and the present value of a sum received in the future.

Algebraic formulas are made up of symbols and letters. The symbols that you should be familiar with are:

P   The *principal*, which is the amount available today, or the present value of a single sum. This is expressed in dollars.

F   The *future value* of the principal or a sum. This is also expressed in dollars.

i   The *rate of interest*. This can be expressed on an annual, semi-annual, quarterly, or monthly basis.

n   The *number of periods* over which funds are borrowed. This is expressed in years or months.

R   A *constant stream of funds* to be received or spent over a number of periods. This is commonly referred to as an annuity. This equal flow of funds is expressed in dollars.

B   The *present value of a constant stream of funds* to be received or spent over a number of periods. It is the present value of an annuity. This figure is expressed in dollars.

W   The *future sum of a stream of funds* to be received or spent over a number of periods. It is the future value of an annuity and is expressed in dollars.

Calculating the Future Value of a Single Sum

We said earlier in this chapter that money has a time value because of the existence of interest. This means that if you deposit $1,000 in the bank today at 10 percent, you will collect $1,100 at the same date next year. If you keep your original amount in the bank for an indefinite period of time, interest will continue to accumulate, and your $1,000 will grow year after year.

Interest can be paid in two ways. First, it can be paid by means of simple interest, which is the simplest form. Here, the banker calculates the interest only on the original $1,000 amount. If the original amount is kept in the bank for three years, you would then earn $300 in interest. This is not, however, the conventional way that lenders pay interest. Usually, when money is deposited in a bank, the banker pays interest on the accumulated balance, which increases each succeeding period as a result of the period's interest being added to the existing balance. This form of interest is called **compound interest**.

Let us examine how the compound value of $1,000, deposited in the bank today at 10 percent, would grow at the end of three years. **Table 6.1** shows that, at the end of the first year, the investor earns $100 and the ending amount is $1,100. During the second year, $110 in interest will be earned, which is made up of $100 on the original $1,000 and $10 on the interest earned during the first year.

	Beginning		Interest		Amount of		Beginning		Ending
Year	Amount	×	Rate	=	Interest	+	Amount	=	Amount
1	$1,000		.10		$100		$1,000		$1,100
2	1,100		.10		110		1,100		1,210
3	1,210		.10		121		1,210		1,331

TABLE 6.1   Calculating the Future Value of a Single Sum

The value of the original amount at the end of the second year is $1,210. The same arithmetic is done for calculating the interest earned during the third year; the value of the amount at the end of that period is $1,331.

An investor does not have to go through these calculations to determine the value of the initial investment for a specific period. This would be extremely cumbersome, particularly when one deals with a 10-, 20-, or 25-year time span. That is why interest tables come in handy. Here is how these tables are used. **Table 6.2** shows interest factors for interest rates ranging from 9 percent to 20 percent covering 25 years. By looking at the 10 percent column, you can readily see that the future value of $1,000 at the end of the third year amounts to $1,331 ($1,000 × 1.331), the same amount that was calculated in **Table 6.1**. **Table A** in Appendix A contains factors for interest rates from 1% to 36% for a 25-year period.

The algebraic equation used to calculate the future value of a single sum is as follows:

$$F_n = P (1 + i)^n$$
$$F^3 = \$1,000 (1.10)^3$$
$$F^3 = \$1,000 \times 1.331$$
$$F^3 = \$1,331$$

The Rule of 72. There is a quick and easy way to calculate the approximate number of years it takes for someone's investment to double when compounded annually at a particular rate of interest. It is called the **rule of 72**. To find the answer, all that is needed is to divide 72 by the interest rate related to the invested principal. If you want to know how many years it takes for an investment to double at 10 percent interest compounded annually, as shown below, you divide this figure into 72 and obtain 7.2 years.

$$\frac{72 \text{ (rule)}}{10(\%)} = 7.2 \text{ (approximate number of years)}$$

To verify this answer, look at **Table 6.2**. If we go down the 10 percent interest column, we see that the $1.00 amount reaches $2.00 between year 7 (1.949) and year 8 (2.144).

TABLE 6.2 Compound Interest Factors to Calculate
the Future Value of a Single Sum

N	9%	10%	11%	12%	14%	16%	18%	20%
1	1.090	1.100	1.110	1.120	1.140	1.160	1.180	1.200
2	1.188	1.210	1.232	1.254	1.300	1.346	1.392	1.440
3	1.295	1.331	1.368	1.405	1.482	1.561	1.643	1.728
4	1.412	1.464	1.518	1.574	1.689	1.811	1.939	2.074
5	1.539	1.611	1.685	1.762	1.925	2.100	2.288	2.488
6	1.677	1.772	1.870	1.974	2.195	2.436	2.700	2.986
7	1.828	1.949	2.076	2.211	2.502	2.826	3.185	3.583
8	1.993	2.144	2.305	2.476	2.853	3.278	3.759	4.300
9	2.172	2.358	2.558	2.773	3.252	3.803	4.435	5.160
10	2.367	2.594	2.839	3.106	3.707	4.411	5.234	6.192
11	2.580	2.853	3.152	3.479	4.226	5.117	6.176	7.430
12	2.813	3.138	3.498	3.896	4.818	5.936	7.288	8.916
13	3.066	3.452	3.883	4.363	5.492	6.886	8.599	10.699
14	3.342	3.798	4.310	4.887	6.261	7.988	10.147	12.839
15	3.642	4.177	4.785	5.474	7.138	9.266	11.974	14.407
16	3.970	4.595	5.311	5.130	8.137	10.748	14.129	18.488
17	4.328	5.054	5.895	6.866	9.276	12.468	16.672	22.186
18	4.717	5.560	6.544	7.690	10.575	14.463	19.673	26.623
19	5.142	6.116	7.263	8.613	12.056	16.777	23.214	31.948
20	5.604	6.728	8.062	9.646	13.744	19.461	27.393	38.338
21	6.109	7.400	8.949	10.804	15.668	22.575	32.324	46.005
22	6.659	8.140	9.934	12.100	17.861	26.186	38.142	55.206
23	7.258	8.954	11.026	13.552	20.362	30.376	45.008	66.247
24	7.911	9.850	12.239	15.179	23.212	35.236	53.109	79.497
25	8.623	10.835	13.586	17.000	26.462	40.874	62.669	95.39

Calculating the Present Value of a Single Sum

The opposite of compounding is discounting. Compounding means that when money is invested today, it appreciates in value because compound interest is added. The opposite takes place when money is to be received in the future; in this case, the future amount is worth less today. By referring to our previous example, because of the existence of the 10 percent interest rate, both amounts, $1,000 in year 1 and $1,331 ($1,000 × 1.331) in year 3, have equal values today. This, therefore, supports the argument that the $1,331 to be received three years from now has a $1,000 value today. Since discounting is the opposite of compounding, all we need to do is to reverse the compound algebraic equation as follows:

$$P = F\left[\frac{1}{(1 + i)^n}\right]$$

$$P = \$1{,}000 \times \frac{1}{(1 + .10)^3}$$

$$P = \$1{,}000 \times \frac{1}{1.331}$$

$$P = \$1{,}000 \times .75131$$

$$P = \$751.31$$

This means that the $1,000 to be received three years from now at 10 percent is worth $751.31 today; or, to reverse the process, if you invest $751.31 in the bank today at a 10 percent interest rate, it would appreciate to $1,000 in three years' time ($751.31 × 1.331).

Like the compound interest calculation, calculating the present value of a promised future sum would be time-consuming. To avoid this clerical chore, we can use present value tables. **Table 6.3** shows present value factors for interest rates ranging from 9 percent to 16 percent between 1 and 25 years. Looking at the appropriate interest column (10%) and at year 3, we find factor .75131. This means that by multiplying the promised $1,000 future sum by .75131, we obtain a $751.31 present value. A more complete present value table appears as **Table B** in Appendix A.

We now have two interest factors to keep track of, the compound interest factor and the present value factor. In the former case, factors are used to make a sum grow (compound), while in the latter case, factors are used to depreciate (discount) a sum expected to be received in the future.

Figure 6.2 shows graphically the impact that 10 percent, 20 percent, and 30 percent compound and discount factors have on a $1,000 amount over a 12-year period. For example, on the left side of the figure, a $1,000 investment at 10 percent grows to $3,138 in 12 years, while the same investment grows to $23,298 at 30 percent. The right side of the figure shows that $1,000 received 12 years from now is worth $319 today at 10 percent, and only $43 at 30 percent.

The Meaning of Annuity

Up to this point, we have talked about the growth and discount values of single sums. In capital budgeting, projects have multi-year economic life spans and, as a result, generate a flow of funds over many years. A series of periodic income payments of equal amounts is referred to as an **annuity**. A mortgage repayment, IRAs, whole-life insurance premiums, and even salaries and wages are considered typical annuities. If a company modernizes its plant at a cost of $100,000 and produces a "fixed yearly $25,000 savings," that would also be considered an annuity.

TABLE 6.3   Present Value Factors to Calculate
the Present Value of a Single Future Sum

N	9%	10%	11%	12%	13%	14%	15%	16%
1	0.91743	0.90909	0.90090	0.89286	0.88496	0.87719	0.86957	0.86207
2	.84168	.82645	.81162	.79719	.78315	.76947	.75614	.74316
3	.77218	.75131	.73119	.71178	.69305	.67497	.65752	.64066
4	.70843	.68301	.65873	.63552	.61332	.59208	.57175	.55229
5	.64993	.62092	.59345	.56743	.54276	.51937	.49718	.47611
6	.59627	.56447	.53464	.50663	.48032	.45559	.43233	.41044
7	.54703	.51316	.48166	.45235	.42506	.39964	.37594	.35383
8	.50187	.46651	.43393	.40388	.37616	.35056	.32690	.30503
9	.46043	.42410	.39092	.36061	.33288	.30751	.28426	.26295
10	.42241	.38554	.35218	.32197	.29459	.26974	.24718	.22668
11	.38753	.35049	.31728	.28748	.26070	.23662	.21494	.19542
12	.35553	.31863	.28584	.25667	.23071	.20756	.18691	.16846
13	.32618	.28966	.25751	.22917	.20416	.18207	.16253	.14523
14	.29925	.26333	.23199	.20462	.18068	.15971	.14133	.12520
15	.27454	.23939	.20900	.18270	.15989	.14010	.12289	.10793
16	.25187	.21763	.18829	.16312	.14150	.12289	.10686	.09304
17	.23107	.19784	.16963	.14564	.12522	.10780	.09293	.08021
18	.21199	.17986	.15202	.13004	.11081	.09456	.08080	.06914
19	.19449	.16351	.13768	.11611	.09806	.08295	.07026	.05961
20	.17843	.14864	.12403	.10367	.08678	.07276	.06110	.05139
21	.16370	.13513	.11174	.09256	.07680	.06383	.05313	.04430
22	.15018	.12285	.10067	.08264	.06796	.05599	.04620	.03819
23	.13778	.11168	.09069	.07379	.06014	.04911	.04017	.03292
24	.12640	.10153	.08170	.06588	.05322	.04308	.03493	.02838
25	.11597	.09230	.07361	.05882	.04710	.03779	.03038	.02447

FIGURE 6.2   Graphic View of the Compounding and Discounting Process

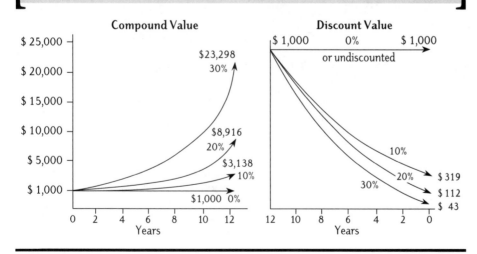

Since capital budgeting deals with multi-year funds flow situations, it is also important to understand how to calculate the future growth and the present value of annuities.

Calculating the Future Value of an Annuity

Let's calculate the future growth of a five-year $1,000 yearly annuity bearing a 10 percent interest factor. There are two ways to do this calculation. First, we can go to the compound interest table in **Table 6.2** and compute the growth of each $1,000 individually. As shown in **Table 6.4**, the sum of all future receipts amounts to $6,105, made up of $5,000 in receipts and $1,105 in interest. The calculation is done as follows. It is assumed that the annuity is paid at the end of each period—that is, on December 31—starting at the end of year 1. In five years, the $1,000 amount will grow to $1,464. Since the fifth payment is received on December 31 of the last year, this receipt does not produce any interest.

This is a very complicated and drawn-out way to calculate the future value of an annuity.

The second approach is to use annuity tables. **Table 6.5** shows annuity factors for interest rates ranging from 9 percent to 20 percent for periods ranging from 1 to 25 years. By going down the 10 percent interest rate column to year 5, we find factor 6.105. If we multiply this factor by the $1,000 amount representing the fixed annuity receipts, we obtain $6,105. This is a much easier way to calculate future values. **Table C** in Appendix A gives annuity factors for interest rates ranging from 1 percent to 32 percent.

The algebraic formula used to calculate the future value of an annuity is as follows:

$$W = R \left[\frac{(1 + i)^n - 1}{i} \right]$$

$$W = \$1,000 \times 6.105$$

$$W = \$6,105$$

TABLE 6.4 Calculation of the Compound Value of an Annuity

Year	Amount Received	×	Interest Factor	=	Interest	+	Amount Received	=	Future Sum
1	$1,000		1.464		$ 464		$1,000		$1,464
2	1,000		1.331		331		1,000		1,331
3	1,000		1.210		210		1,000		1,210
4	1,000		1.100		100		1,000		1,100
5	1,000		0.000		—		1,000		$1,000
Total	$5,000				$1,105		$5,000		$6,105

TABLE 6.5 Compound Interest Factors to Calculate the Future Value of an Annuity

N	9%	10%	11%	12%	14%	16%	18%	20%
1	1.000	1.000	1.000	1.000	1.000	1.000	1.000	1.000
2	2.090	2.100	2.110	2.120	2.140	2.160	2.180	2.200
3	3.278	3.310	3.342	3.374	3.440	3.506	3.572	3.640
4	4.573	4.641	4.710	4.779	4.921	5.066	5.215	5.368
5	5.985	6.105	6.228	6.353	6.610	6.877	7.154	7.442
6	7.523	7.716	7.913	8.115	8.536	8.977	9.442	9.930
7	9.200	9.487	9.783	10.089	10.731	11.414	12.142	12.916
8	11.029	11.436	11.859	12.300	13.233	14.240	15.327	16.499
9	13.021	13.580	14.164	14.776	16.085	17.519	19.086	20.799
10	15.193	15.937	16.722	17.549	19.337	21.322	23.521	25.959
11	17.560	18.531	19.561	20.655	23.045	25.733	28.755	32.150
12	20.141	21.384	22.713	24.133	27.271	30.850	34.931	39.581
13	22.953	24.523	26.212	28.029	32.089	36.786	42.219	48.497
14	26.019	27.975	30.095	32.393	37.581	43.672	50.818	59.196
15	29.361	31.773	34.405	37.280	43.842	51.660	60.965	72.035
16	33.003	35.950	39.190	42.753	50.980	60.925	72.939	87.442
17	36.974	40.545	44.501	48.884	59.118	71.673	87.068	105.931
18	41.301	45.599	50.396	55.750	68.394	84.141	103.740	128.117
19	46.019	51.159	56.940	63.440	78.969	98.603	123.413	154.740
20	51.160	57.275	64.203	72.052	91.025	115.380	146.628	186.688
21	56.765	64.003	72.265	81.699	104.768	134.840	174.021	225.026
22	62.873	71.403	81.214	92.503	120.436	157.415	206.345	271.031
23	69.532	79.543	91.148	104.603	138.297	183.601	244.487	326.237
24	76.790	88.497	102.174	118.155	158.659	213.977	289.494	392.404
25	84.701	98.347	114.413	133.334	181.871	249.214	342.603	471.981

Calculating the Present Value of an Annuity

Calculating the present value of an annuity is the reverse of compounding an annuity. Compounding gives the future growth of a series of fixed receipts or payments; **discounting** gives the present value of a series of receipts or payments. Let us figure out the present value of a $1,000 amount received every year during a five-year period that bears a 10 percent interest factor. This calculation can also be done two ways. First, we can multiply yearly receipts by their respective interest factors. We must therefore refer to **Table 6.3** and compute the present value of each receipt. As shown in **Table 6.6**, the present value of the $1,000 five-year annuity totals $3,790.

There is no reason to go through this long process to calculate the present value of an annuity. By referring to **Table 6.7**, which contains a series of present value factors for annuities for varying interest rates, we can find the answer quickly and easily. Looking at the 10 percent interest column at the line for year 5, we find

TABLE 6.6   Calculating the Present Value of an Annuity

Year	Amount Received	×	Interest Factor	=	Present Value
1	$1,000		.9091		$ 909
2	1,000		.8264		826
3	1,000		.7513		751
4	1,000		.6830		683
5	1,000		.6209		621
Total	$5,000				$3,790

TABLE 6.7   Present Value Factors to Calculate the Present Value of an Annuity

N	9%	10%	11%	12%	13%	14%	15%	16%
1	0.9174	0.9091	0.9009	0.8929	0.8850	0.8772	0.8696	0.8621
2	1.7591	1.7355	1.7125	1.6901	1.6681	1.6467	1.6257	1.6052
3	2.5313	2.4868	2.4437	2.4018	2.3612	2.3216	2.2832	2.2459
4	3.2397	3.1699	3.1024	3.0373	2.9745	2.9137	2.8550	2.7982
5	3.8896	3.7908	3.6959	3.6048	3.5172	3.4331	3.3522	3.2743
6	4.4859	4.3553	4.2305	4.1114	3.9976	3.8887	3.7845	3.6847
7	5.0329	4.8684	4.7122	4.5638	4.4226	4.2883	4.1604	4.0386
8	5.5348	5.3349	5.1461	4.9676	4.7988	4.6389	4.4873	4.3436
9	5.9852	5.7590	5.5370	5.3282	5.1317	4.9464	4.7716	4.6065
10	6.4176	6.1446	5.8892	5.6502	5.4262	5.2161	5.0188	4.8332
11	6.8052	6.4951	6.2065	5.9377	5.6869	5.4527	5.2337	5.0286
12	7.1607	6.8137	6.4924	6.1944	5.9176	5.6603	5.4206	5.1971
13	7.4869	7.1034	6.7499	6.4235	6.1218	5.8424	5.5831	5.3423
14	7.7861	7.3667	6.9819	6.6828	6.3025	6.0021	5.7245	5.4675
15	8.0607	7.6061	7.1909	6.8109	6.4624	6.1422	5.8474	5.5755
16	8.3125	7.8237	7.3792	6.9740	6.6039	6.2651	5.9542	5.6685
17	8.5436	8.0215	7.5488	7.1196	6.7291	6.3729	6.0472	5.7487
18	8.7556	8.2014	7.7016	7.2497	6.8399	6.4674	6.1280	5.8178
19	8.9501	8.3649	7.8393	7.3658	6.9380	6.5504	6.1982	5.8775
20	9.1285	8.5136	7.9633	7.4694	7.0248	6.6231	6.2593	5.9288
21	9.2922	8.6487	8.0751	7.5620	7.1016	6.6870	6.3125	5.9731
22	9.4424	8.7715	8.1757	7.6446	7.1695	6.7429	6.3587	6.0113
23	9.5802	8.8832	8.2664	7.7184	7.2297	6.7921	6.3988	6.0442
24	9.7066	8.9847	8.3481	7.7843	7.2829	6.8351	6.4338	6.0726
25	9.8226	9.0770	8.4217	7.8431	7.3300	6.8729	6.4641	6.0971

factor 3.7908. The more simplified approach is, therefore, to multiply this factor by $1,000; this gives us $3,790. **Table D** in Appendix A gives a more complete set of interest factors for annuities ranging from 1 to 25 years.

The algebraic formula used to calculate the present value of an annuity is as follows:

$$B = R\left[\frac{1 - (1 + i)^{-n}}{i}\right]$$

Using our example,

$$B = \$1,000 \times 3.7908$$
$$B = \$3,790$$

Present Value of an Uneven Series of Receipts

Our definition of an annuity includes the terms "fixed amount." In other words, annuities are made up of *constant* and *equal receipts* or *payments*. But often the receipts from a capital project are sporadic. If this is the case, in order to evaluate the economic desirability of the project (unless you have a financial calculator, spreadsheet or software to calculate the present values of the future receipts), you must calculate each receipt or payment individually.

To illustrate the process of calculating uneven flows of receipts, let us assume that you contemplate investing $1,500, which would produce an inflow of funds of $200 in the first year, $500 in the second, $400 in the third, $600 in the fourth, and $200 in the fifth. The discounted value calculation of the future receipts with an interest rate of 12 percent is shown in **Table 6.8**. In this case, the investment is not desirable because the discounted value of the future receipts, which amounts to $1,356, is less than the $1,500 initial outflow.

Using the same example, but changing the $200 receipt in the fifth year for a $200 annuity received over six years (from year 5 to year 10), would require a slightly different procedure to calculate the present value. As shown in **Table 6.9**, the present value of the receipts for years 1, 2, 3, and 4 are the same as those

---

TABLE 6.8   Calculating the Present Value for Uneven Series

Year	Receipts	×	Discount Factor	=	Present Value
1	$ 200		.8929		$ 178
2	500		.7972		399
3	400		.7118		285
4	600		.6355		381
5	200		.5674		113
Total	$1,900				$1,356

calculated in **Table 6.8**. However, because the last $200 receipt is an annuity, we can use a shortcut. The calculation process is shown in **Table 6.9** and illustrated graphically in **Figure 6.3**. In total, the discounted value of the receipts amounts to $1,765.75, which is more than the original outflow. Therefore, in this case, the investment is desirable because it compares favorably to the initial $1,500 investment.

Using Interest Tables

As illustrated in **Table 6.10**, there are four **interest tables** in Appendix A. It is important to understand their function before using them. **Tables A** and **C** deal with compounding. If you want to find the future value of a single sum, use **Table A**. If you want to calculate the future value of an annuity, use **Table C**.

In capital budgeting, however, financial analysts use discounting tables—that is, **Tables B** and **D**. If you want to calculate the present value of a single sum, use **Table B**. If you want to find the present value of an annuity, use **Table D**.

TABLE 6.9   Calculating Procedures for Uneven Series of Receipts

A.	PV of $ 200 in year 1 (.8929)	= $ 178.58
	PV of $ 500 in year 2 (.7972)	= 398.60
	PV of $ 400 in year 3 (.7118)	= 284.72
	PV of $ 600 in year 4 (.6355)	= 381.30
	PV of $ 200 in years 5 to 10	
B.	Step 1: $ 200 × 4.1114 = $822.28	
	Step 2: $ 822.28 × .6355	= 522.38
C.	PV of total receipts	= $1,765.58

FIGURE 6.3   Graphic Illustration of the Present Value Calculations from Table 6.9

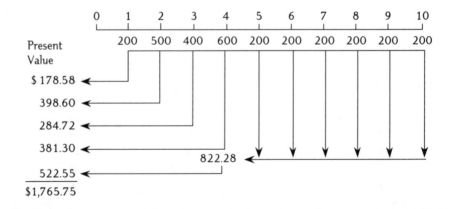

TABLE 6.10   Using Interest Tables

These two tables are used in capital budgeting

	To Compound	To Discount
Single sum	Table A	Table B
Annuity	Table C	Table D

Working Examples

Let us review what we have seen so far in this chapter by working out four simple calculations.

Problem 1:   Suppose you were to deposit $5,000 in your bank account today for a period of five years at an interest rate of 10 percent; to what amount will it have grown at the end of that period?

Answer: By referring to **Table 6.2** or **Table A**, we obtain the following: $5,000 × 1.611 = $8,055.00

Problem 2:   Suppose you were offered the alternatives of either receiving $700 now or $1,000 five years from now. If the current rate of interest is 12 percent, which option should you choose?

Answer: By referring to **Table 6.3** or **Table B**, we obtain the following answers:
Option 1: $1,000 × .56743 = $567.43
Option 2: $700.00
The second option is the more attractive one.

Problem 3:   If you were to deposit $500 a year for the next ten years, what would be the sum of all ten deposits if the interest rate is 12 percent?

Answer: By referring to **Table 6.5** or **Table C**, we obtain the following: $500.00 × 17.549 = $8,774.50

Problem 4:   Suppose you were offered the following choices: a ten-year annuity of $1,000.00 or a $6,000.00 lump-sum payment today. If the current rate of interest is 10 percent, which option would you select?

Answer: By referring to **Table 6.7** or **Table D**, we obtain the following answer:
Option 1: $1,000.00 × 6.1446 = $6,144.60
Option 2: $6,000.00
The first option is the more attractive one.

Using Time Value of Money Concepts in Investment Decisions

Let's now turn to the practical side of decision-making and examine how interest tables can help managers evaluate the economic desirability of capital expenditure projects. The remaining segments of this chapter look at the meaning of time value yardsticks within the context of the following capital budgeting techniques:

◆ Future value
◆ Net future value
◆ Present value
◆ Net present value
◆ Internal rate of return

To describe how these techniques are used, we will turn to the $100,000 sweepstakes winnings example presented earlier in the chapter (**Figure 6.1**) and determine how much the winner should receive each year during a ten-year period in order to make the annuity equal to the lump sum. We will also use the same number in another example by assuming that a manufacturing manager is looking at the possibility of investing $100,000 to improve the efficiency of a plant which would save $15,000 each year.

Future Value and Net Future Value

Question 1: Should the sweepstakes winner accept the $100,000 lump-sum
payment or $15,000 a year over the next 10 years?
Question 2: Should the manufacturing manager invest $100,000 in order to
save $15,000 a year during the next 10 years?

Assuming that money is worth 10 percent, here are the answers.

If the sweepstakes winner is given the option of receiving a $100,000 lump-sum amount now or $15,000 a year during the next ten years, the future value of both amounts is calculated as follows:

$100,000 × 2.594 (**Table A**) =	$259,400
$15,000 × 15.937 (**Table C**) =	239,055
Net future value	$ 20,345

Unquestionably, if the $100,000 was invested now in the bank at 10 percent over the next ten years, this amount would grow (because of time) more ($259,400) than if the $15,000 amount was put in the bank each year ($239,055). As shown, by the tenth year, the lump-sum payment would give an extra $20,345. Individually, both amounts are referred to as the *future value* and the difference between both future amounts is referred to as the **net future value**.

Present Value and Net Present Value

On the other hand, if you want to justify which option to choose by comparing the discounted amounts, you would get a difference of $7,831 in favor of the lump-sum payment. Here is how the arithmetic works.

$$
\begin{array}{lll}
 & -\$100,000 & \\
\textit{Present value} & 92,169 & = \quad \text{or } \$15,000 \times 6.1446 \text{ (\textbf{Table D})} \\
 & \underline{-\$ \quad 7,831} & = \quad \textit{Net present value}
\end{array}
$$

As you can see, whether you take both sums into the future (tenth year) or bring them to the present, the decision is the same—choose the $100,000 lump-sum payment.

If the manufacturing manager wants to invest $100,000 (cash outflow) to modernize the plant in order to save $15,000 (cash inflow) a year, the calculations do not justify the investment. As shown above, the discounted $15,000 (or $150,000 over the ten-year period) gives a **present value (PV)** of only $92,169. At the 10 percent discount rate, the *difference* between the outflow and the inflow results in a negative $7,831 difference, which is referred to as the **net present value (NPV)**. Whenever there is a negative NPV, the return on the investment is less than the rate used to discount the future cash receipts, which in this case happens to be less than 10 percent. When the NPV is positive, the return on the investment is more than the rate used to discount the future receipts.

Internal Rate of Return

Now, if both amounts were to have the same value, the sweepstakes winner would have to receive $16,275 each year for the next ten years. This $16,275 amount is calculated by dividing the $100,000 amount by the factor found in **Table D** under 10% column, 10 years (6.1446). As shown, both numbers are the same; that is, the lump-sum amount is equal to the present value of the $16,275 annual receipts—the NPV is 0.

$$
\begin{array}{lll}
 & -\$100,000 & \\
\textit{Present value} & + \; 100,000 & = \quad \$16,275 \times 6.1446 \text{ (\textbf{Table D})} \\
 & \underline{\$ \qquad 0} & \quad \textit{Net present value}
\end{array}
$$

Now, if the plant manager wants to make a 10 percent return on the $100,000, plant efficiencies would also have to generate $16,275 each year. If the saving is more than this, the plant would generate more than 10 percent; if it is less, the return would be less. The bottom line is this: When the interest rate makes the discounted future receipts ($100,000) *equal* the original investment ($100,000), it is referred to as the **internal rate of return**. In this particular case, since 10 percent makes the future savings equal to $100,000 or that the net present value equals 0, the internal rate of return on this particular investment is 10 percent. If the savings are more than $16,275, then the plant generated a higher return. For example, if the plant were to generate $18,429 savings per year during the next ten years, the internal rate of return would be 13 percent, because it is this rate that makes the NPV equal to zero.

$$
\begin{array}{lll}
 & -\$100,000 & \\
\textit{Present value} & + \; 100,000 & = \quad \$18,429 \times 5.4262 \text{ (\textbf{Table D})} \\
 & \underline{\$ \qquad 0} & \quad \textit{Net present value}
\end{array}
$$

On the opposite side, if the annual receipts were less than $16,275, then the internal rate of return would be less. In the case of the manufacturing plant, the annual savings are $15,000. This means that the IRR would be less than 10 percent; to be exact, 8.1 percent. Here's the proof. This number is arrived at by looking at **Table D**, under the column 8% at 10 years, where we find the factor 6.7101.

$$
\begin{array}{lll}
 & -\$100,000 & \\
\textit{Present value} & +\ \ 100,651 & =\quad \$15,000 \times 6.7101\ (\textbf{Table D}) \\
 & \underline{+\$\qquad 651} & \qquad \textit{Net present value}
\end{array}
$$

As shown, the 8 percent figure gives a positive $650 net present value, which means that the project generates 8 percent plus $651. If we were to convert this number on a percentage basis, the answer would be 0.144 percent. If **Table D** had a factor of 8.144, then the present value would have been exactly $100,000 and the NPV would be zero.

Food for Thought. As shown in **Table 6.11**, using traditional accounting methods to calculate the return on this project, one would divide the $15,000 amount by the $100,000 asset and obtain a 15 percent return (ROA). If a time value of money yardstick was used, such as the IRR, the investment would give only 8.1 percent. In this case, the company would be losing 1.9 percent (after financing) each year during the next ten years instead of making a net 5.0 percent.

This simple illustration proves that using accounting rates of return in capital budgeting decisions could be misleading. As we will discover in the next chapter, there are different ways of calculating the accounting rates of return, and they are not the most reliable capital budgeting yardsticks. As shown in **Table 6.11**, time value yardsticks are more suitable for measuring the desirability of capital projects and can be compared more accurately to the cost of capital.

How Interest Tables Came About

The concepts of compounding and discounting have been known for hundreds of years. Interest tables, however, have been around for only 70 years. These tables

---

TABLE 6.11   Accounting Rate of Returns versus the IRR

Calculating the accounting rate of return method (ROA)

$$
\frac{\text{Receipts}}{\text{Assets}} \quad \frac{\$15,000}{\$100,000} \quad = \quad 15\%
$$

The Balance Sheet

ROA	15.0%	Cost of Capital	10%
IRR	8.1		

were not conceived by bankers or accountants, but by actuaries working for insurance companies. Here is how they used these tables. As shown in the upper portion of **Table 6.12**, if someone wished to buy a $50,000, 20-year insurance policy, that person could have been asked to pay $1,000 a year during his or her expected life span, which in this case happened to be 20 years. The insurance companies would have invested these $1,000 receipts at, say, 10 percent and, over the 20-year period, these sums would have a future value of $57,275. In 20 years, when the $50,000 amount was paid out (cash outflow), the company would have made a surplus of $7,275 (net future value).

In the 1950s, the industrial community decided to use the time value of money idea as a capital budgeting decision-making instrument. Industrial managers said that if the time value of money was good for the insurance companies, it would also be good for the industrial companies, as both have cash outflows and cash inflows. However, there is one major difference: the time of making the cash disbursement or payment. In the case of insurance companies, the cash outflow (payment) is made in 20 years. In the case of industrial companies, the cash outflow is made at the beginning, and it is for this reason that cash receipts have to be discounted (in order to compare them to the initial investment) instead of bringing them into the future.

TABLE 6.12   Insurance Versus Industrial Companies

Compounding

Insurance companies

Years 1 ──────────→ to ──────────→ 20

Yearly premiums (cash inflows) $1,000	$ +57,275
Money is worth 10% ($1,000 × 57.275)	
Death benefit (cash outflow)	−50,000
Net cash flow or NFV	$ +7,275

Discounting

Industrial companies

Years 0 ──────────→ to ──────────→ 20

The company invests $150,000 (cash outflow) to modernize a plant. As a result, the company's sales increase by $20,000 (cash inflows) each year.

$−150,000 cash outflow

+170,272 present value of the savings if money is worth 10%
($20,000 × 8.5136)

$ +20,272 net cash flow or net present value (NPV)

As shown in the lower portion of **Table 6.12**, the $150,000 asset which earns $20,000 a year over the next 20 years gives a $170,272 present value when using a 10 percent discount rate. As shown, at 10 percent, the net present value gives a surplus of $20,272, which means that the company would earn more than 10 percent. If, by interpolation, we use a discount factor of 11.9 percent, the present value of the $20,000 receipts would be equal to $150,000 and make the outflow equal to the inflows. In this particular case, the IRR would be 11.9 percent.

Using Interest Tables in Capital Budgeting

To calculate the financial returns by using time value of money yardsticks, you need four elements:

- Investment (cash outflow or disbursement)
- Annual cash inflows (receipts)
- Expected life-span of the project
- Cost of money (or the return that management wants to make on the investment)

Let's use one more example to calculate the NPV and the IRR of a capital project by applying interest tables. As shown on the left side of **Table 6.13**, the company invests $25,000 in a new capital asset and obtains $1,000 in savings each year during the next 25 years. If management wants to make 10 percent, the present value of the $1,000 receipts gives $9,077. Here, the NPV is a negative $15,923. This means that the IRR is negative.

TABLE 6.13 Investing in a New Asset

1. You invest $25,000 in an asset.			How much must you save each year if you want to make 10% on your asset?	
2. It generates $1,000 in savings each year.				
3. The expected life of the asset is 25 years.				
4. Cost of capital is 10%.				
1. Investment	−$25,000		−$25,000	Investment
2. Annual savings: $1,000				Savings per year: $2,754
3. Total savings: $25,000				Total savings: $68,850
4. Present value of savings (9.0770 × $1,000)	+$ 9,077		+$25,000	Present value of the savings (9.0770 × $2.754)
Net present value	−$15,923		0	Net present value

- ◆ Sylvia, $58,000
- ◆ Phil, $55,000
- ◆ Michael, $48,000

Steve and Lucy indicated that they were interested in making a contribution each year for their three children. Andrew recommended funds that would earn 12 percent a year over the life of the fund.

On the basis of the above information, calculate:

- ◆ How much Steve and Lucy will have in their IRA the year they retire.
- ◆ How much Steve and Lucy will have to save each in order to have enough money for their children's education by the time they each reach their eighteenth birthday.

The following calculations are made on yearly installments. These figures would be different if Steve and Lucy were to invest their money in these funds on a monthly or quarterly basis. Also, assume that all tax benefits are excluded from these calculations.

1. Steve and Lucy will have accumulated $245,867 if they invest a combined $2,500 a year in their IRA plan.

   Calculation
   Yearly $2,500 contribution for 25 years at a 10% annual compounded growth rate.
   $2,500 × 98.347 (**Table C**) = $245,868

2.   An annual amount of $1,040.36 will have to be invested in Sylvia's education account.

Calculation

Steve and Lucy want a $58,000 amount in 2018 that is in 18 years from now bearing a 12 percent interest rate.

$58,000 ÷ 55.750 (**Table C**) = $1,040.36.

3.   An annual amount of $1,125.11 will have to be invested in Phil's education account.

Calculation

Steve and Lucy want a $55,000 amount in 2017 that is in 17 years from now bearing a 12 percent interest rate.

$55,000 ÷ 48.884 (**Table C**) = $1,125.11.

4.   An annual amount of $1,712.51 will have to be invested in Michael's education account.

Calculation

Steve and Lucy want a $48,000 amount in 2013 that is in 13 years from now bearing a 12 percent interest rate.

$48,000 ÷ 28.029 (**Table C**) = $1,712.51.

Steve and Lucy would therefore have to invest a total of $5,377.98 each year or $448.17 each month.

Steve and Lucy's IRAs	$2,500.00
Sylvia's education fund	1,040.36
Phil's education fund	1,125.11
Michael's education fund	1,712.51
Total	$5,377.98

Summary

A knowledge of compound and discount value concepts is essential for understanding many different topics in finance and for improving the quality of capital budgeting decisions. It is important to know how to use compound and discount tables.

Tables A and **C** deal with compounding. If you want to find the future value of a single sum, use **Table A**. If you want to calculate the future value of an annuity, use **Table C**.

In capital budgeting, analysts use discounting tables, that is **Tables B** and **D**. If you want to calculate the present value of a single sum, use **Table B**. If you want to find the present value of an annuity, use **Table D**.

CHAPTER 7

Capital Investment Decisions

By the end of 2002, the Edwards were looking at several investment possibilities in order to expand their retail operations. The most viable and interesting option, one that was in line with their longer-term objective, was opening a new retail outlet. Now that they had several years of experience in the retail business and had accumulated enough cash, they were ready to move ahead with their plans.

The Edwards estimated that it would cost around $350,000 to open their new retail store. Since they intended to lease a building for a ten-year period, the investment would be mainly in leasehold assets and the purchase of office equipment.

During the first year of operations, the Edwards expected to invest an additional $100,000 in working capital, mostly in inventory and a smaller amount in accounts receivable. During the second year, they expected to invest an additional $75,000 in working capital for a net investment amounting to $175,000.

The following summarizes the Edwards' investment plan for their new retail store:

Year 0	Capital assets		$350,000
Year 1	Working capital	$100,000	
Year 2	Working capital	75,000	175,000
Total capital employed			$525,000

At the end of the lease, the Edwards would have the option of either expanding the store to cope with the growth, or moving to a larger building. Also, instead of making these changes, if they were to sell the store, they estimate that they would be able to get $900,000 in cash from a potential buyer.

CompuTech's after-tax cost of capital amounts to 11.0% (to be exact, 10.93%). This is based on funds that could be raised from lenders (short term and long term) and from shareholders.

The Edwards hired a market research firm to determine the level of sales revenue that could be generated by the new store. On the basis of that information, they prepared the new store's pro-forma financial statements, to be included in the investment proposal presented to potential investors. The cash flow generated by the new store is estimated to be as follows:

Year	Cash inflow
1	$ 75,000
2	80,000
3	100,000
4	125,000
5	140,000
6–10	150,000

As shown above, the new store's cash flow during the first year is estimated at $75,000 with gradual increments between years 1 to 6. Starting the sixth year, the Edwards estimate that the cash flow will remain constant until the tenth year.

This chapter examines different time value of money yardsticks that could be used by the Edwards to determine the level of viability and return of their new store. In particular, the chapter focuses on three key topics:

1. The more important elements that should be taken into account when gauging the economic desirability of capital projects.
2. The time value of money techniques such as net present value (NPV), the payback period and the internal rate of return (IRR) used to measure the return on investment of capital projects.
3. Capital budgeting techniques used to assess the factor of risk inherent in capital projects.

Introduction

Capital budgeting is the process of planning, evaluating, and choosing capital expenditure projects that generate benefits (returns, profits, savings) over an extended number of years. Capital decisions are critical to the financial destiny of a company because they are irreversible, usually require a significant amount of financial resources, and can alter the future success of a business for many years. Capital projects may call for the development of a new product, a major expansion of an existing product line, the launching of a new product line, the construction of a new facility, or a significant change in direction geared to take advantage of foreseeable opportunities.

A **capital investment** (expenditure or cash disbursement) may be defined as a project that requires extensive financial resources (outflows) in return for expected flow of financial benefits (inflows) to be earned over a period of many years. A capital investment differs from an **expense investment** in that the latter generates benefits for a short period (less than one year). For example, a capital investment may represent the construction of a new plant costing $30 million (cash outflow) with an economic or physical life span of 25 years and generating a $3 million profit (cash inflow) each year. An expense investment may consist of a $20,000 advertising cost that produces favorable effects on the profit performance during the current operating year. **Table 7.1** compares capital investments and expense investments.

Why Capital Projects Are Critical

Capital investments are critical for a number of reasons. First, since new funds may need to be raised, the capital structure of a business can be altered significantly. Second, long-term return on a company's assets and shareholders' yield can be highly influenced by the mix of projects undertaken. It only takes one ill-conceived capital decision to reduce a firm's return (often for many years) and with it, management's credibility. Third, the future cash position of a company can be affected significantly, a vital consideration for a firm that is committed to meeting fixed debt obligations, paying dividends, and growing (which usually means undertaking more capital investments). Fourth, once committed, a project often cannot be revised, or, if it can, only at a substantial cost.

The Capital Investment Portfolio

Companies invest in capital projects for many reasons. A firm wishing to improve its financial performance could invest in cost reduction programs or research and development, expand a manufacturing operation, replace obsolete equipment, install computer equipment, build a warehouse, or even buy an on-going business.

TABLE 7.1 Capital Investments and Expense Investments

	Capital Investments	Expense Investments
Size of cash outlay	Large	Small
Nature of commitment	Durable	Impermanent
Accounting treatment	Capitalized	Expensed
Cash turnover	Recurrent and spread over many years	One-time and immediate
Financial impact of commitment	Significant	Minimal
Effect on financial structure	Minimal to sizeable	None

Each project varies significantly with respect to cash outlay, risk, profit levels, and time horizon. Capital projects can fall into several major categories:

- Necessary investments to reduce operating costs.
- Replacement investments to supplant worn-out equipment.
- Market investments to improve the distribution network.
- Expansion investments to increase sales volume (and profit) in existing product lines.
- Research and development investments to develop new products and new manufacturing or processing technologies.
- Product improvement investments to sustain the life cycle of a product.
- Strategic investments to alter a business' mainstream activity.

These types of capital projects can be grouped into two main categories: *compulsory investments*, which are essential to sustain the life of a business, and *opportunity investments*, which are discretionary and made only if management wants its firm to prosper over the long term. **Table 7.2** compares these two types of capital investments.

Compulsory Investments

Generally, **compulsory investments** are made for three reasons: contingency, legislative, and cosmetic. Those in the first category respond to a *need*. For example, a manufacturing department may have to increase its operating capacity to meet an expanded market need. Or a production manager may request that certain producing assets be replaced in order to eliminate substandard operations and maintain an acceptable level of operating efficiencies. In short, these types of investments prevent a company's rate of return from deteriorating. The second type of compulsory investment is dictated by *legislation*. For instance, the govern-

TABLE 7.2   Compulsory and Opportunity Investments

	Compulsory Investments	Opportunity Investments
Effects	Maintain operating efficiencies	Increase momentum of the firm
Response	To a need	To an opportunity
Benefits	Immediate	Long-term
Risk	Negligible	High
Management involvement	Low-level	Top-level
Implications	Legislative, employee safety and satisfaction	Economic returns, share of market
Analytical techniques	Simple calculation	Mathematical models

ment may force businesses to invest in pollution abatement machinery, in equipment that will meet regulatory quality control standards, or in assets affecting the safety of their employees. The third type of investments are made for *cosmetic* reasons; these include expenditures for office furniture, for protecting existing company assets (e.g., fences, warehouses) from fire, pilferage, and so on, for improving the company's image, and for making employees more comfortable (e.g., cafeteria, sports facilities).

These types of capital expenditures do not require in-depth analytical studies. Since the investments have to be made for one reason or another, all that has to be done is to include the required capital amounts in the company's annual budget and to register them when the funds are disbursed. The major requirement in this process is to ensure that the firm obtains the best possible assets for the best possible price. The impact from such investments on profit position (minor expansion or modernization programs) can be measured with relative accuracy.

Opportunity Investments

Opportunity investments, however, are far more complex and require sophisticated analysis, state-of-the art decision-making tools, and sound managerial judgment. Examples of these investments are launching a new product line, constructing a new plant, or substantially increasing manufacturing output to capture new markets. These capital projects are usually considerable and have far-reaching financial implications. The risk factor is enormous: If the venture is not successful, management's reputation suffers and there will likely be a heavy cash drain from existing operations—or, even worse, bankruptcy may result. These types of investments, however, can improve a company's competitive capability and profitability beyond current levels of performance.

Before the company commits to such investments, the first step is to appraise the investment's chances of success as accurately as possible. Since the investment's financial return is dependent on internal and external environmental forces, the investment appraisal demands an incisive analysis of all aspects of the capital venture.

Figure 7.1 illustrates the impact investment decisions can have on a company's future. The vertical axis shows the return on investment; the horizontal axis represents the improvement profile of the return position against that of the industry over an extended number of years.

The ultimate reason for injecting funds into capital assets is to improve the return on investment—either to close the "return gap" with that of industry or to improve further the company's financial position. For example, as shown in the figure, the company's return may be at 13 percent compared to the industry's 14 percent. If nothing is done (e.g., improving the productivity of its existing capital assets, injecting funds into new equipment, or doing research and development on new product lines), over the long term, the company's return will drop to 10 percent, while the industry's climbs to 16 percent; the gap widens from 1 percent to 6 percent. If the company plows funds into compulsory investments, it can hold

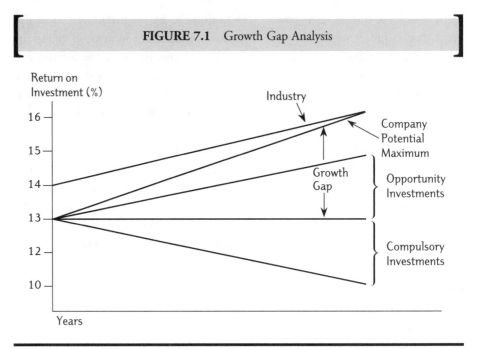

FIGURE 7.1   Growth Gap Analysis

its position at 13 percent and the gap with industry will only be 3 percent. With additional financial resources, the firm may make opportunity investments, thus reducing the gap further. But, because of resource constraints, the firm may not still match the industry's growth. If, however, the firm is not financially bound, it could grow to a 16 percent level and reach both its full potential and industry's growth.

The Capital Budgeting Process

As shown in **Figure 7.2**, several steps are involved in capital budgeting. The first step is to establish strategic and operating objectives, within the framework of the external general and industry environments (opportunities and threats) and internal environment (strengths and weaknesses). The future can never be predicted with certainty, but with the level of information available and modern risk analysis techniques, it is possible to deal with the uncertainty factor in a relatively proficient manner. It is within this framework that the company mission's statement, strategic objectives, and plans are formulated.

The second step is to formulate the capital expenditure portfolio. Capital projects affect a business in different ways such as improving operating efficiencies or increasing market share. Management must therefore identify, select, and implement the most lucrative projects, those that will best help the business achieve its strategic objectives.

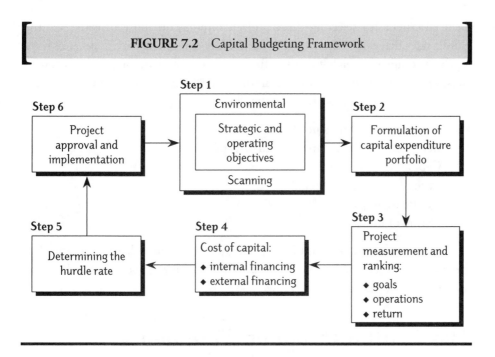

FIGURE 7.2 Capital Budgeting Framework

The third step is to measure and rank projects on the basis of the following:

- *Goals.* Most companies have a hierarchy of goals, and projects should be ranked according to how they will meet these overall strategic objectives. (Are they to increase market share, improve manufacturing efficiencies, or diversify operations?)
- *Operations.* Capital projects must also be ranked within their respective operations (e.g., marketing, research, manufacturing, distribution).
- *Return.* Since a healthy return is probably the ultimate objective of any business, the economic acceptability of a capital portfolio should be judged largely on this basis.

The fourth step is to explore fully the cost of alternate sources of capital. Funds are obtained from two sources: internally (e.g., through depreciation and retained earnings) and externally (e.g., from shareholders and lenders). If internal funds are to be used, management must decide what types of projects it intends to launch, several years before the funds are committed, so that the necessary cash can be set aside. External funds are generally obtained by issuing new long-term debt or shares. As discussed in Chapter 5, while the right-hand side of a balance sheet can be structured in a number of ways, it is critical to find the optimum financial structure, the one that combines the lowest cost with the least amount of risk.

The fifth step is to determine the hurdle rate, that is, the level of return that each project should generate in order to be accepted. Since the capital needed to finance an investment portfolio usually exceeds the funds available, a firm needs financial criteria for selecting those projects offering the most attractive returns. Hurdle rates that can be used for that purpose are determined in a number of ways, such as a company's weighted cost of financing new projects, long-term borrowing rates, on-going internal rate of return, or even a figure chosen arbitrarily by top management. Hurdle rates are influenced by:

- Level of capital funds needed.
- Reputation of the company or management.
- Capital structure.
- Type of issues to be offered.
- Nature of projects.
- Nature of industry.

Once the hurdle rate has been agreed upon and projects have been ranked on the basis of objectives, operations, and return, all that remains is the last step, selecting and implementing the projects.

The Capital Budgeting Elements

A few basic capital budgeting concepts should be understood before examining the techniques used for gauging the economic desirability of capital projects. This section reviews the elements that serve as major input for capital project evaluation. They include cash outflows, cash inflows, economic or physical life span, and sunk costs.

Cash Outflows

When management decides to invest funds in a capital project, the decision entails an outflow of cash in terms of the initial cash outflow, working capital, and normal capital additions.

Initial Cash Outflow. When a decision is made to proceed with a capital project, such as the purchase of equipment, an initial cash outflow is registered only once. **Cash outflows** could also take place over a period of several years. For instance, a new plant could be constructed over a three-year period with cash outflows taking place over that same time span. Irrespective of the accounting treatment, all initial cash disbursements must be considered cash outflows. For example, a firm may invest $10 million to modernize a plant; from an accounting perspective, part of that amount, say $200,000, could be expensed the year the outflow takes place, while the remaining $9.8 million is capitalized and depreciated over a ten-year period. However, for capital budgeting evaluation purposes, all outflows must be shown as disbursements the year the money is spent.

Another point to consider about the initial cash outflow is that the financing of a project need not be taken into account. A company may receive say 50 percent financing on the $10 million capital outlay. Irrespective of the amount of funds to be received from external sources, the project should be evaluated on the premise that the company uses its "own" cash or its equivalent for the entire project.

Interest charges should *not* be considered an expense and thus should *not* be included in the pro-forma income statements. The intent of capital budgeting is to (1) gauge the economic returns of individual capital projects, (2) compare each competing project with the others, and (3) compare the return (i.e., IRR) to the cost of capital (see the lower portion of **Figure 5.1** in Chapter 5).

Working Capital. Another cash outflow to consider is working capital. Some projects, such as modernization, replacement of obsolete equipment, or installation of anti-pollution equipment may not require additional working capital. However, other projects such as the construction of a new plant or the expansion of an existing facility, may cause revenues and working capital to increase. The working capital spending usually takes place at the time the project comes on stream, usually the first and second year of operation. Incremental net working capital can take place several years after the launching of the new plant. These additions to working capital should therefore be included as cash outflows in the evaluation of the project.

Normal Capital Additions. Some capital projects may require additional capital expenditures for repairs and parts after the initial capital investment. If this is the case, these expenditures should be included as cash outflows when evaluating the capital project.

Cash Inflows

A capital project usually generates **cash inflows** during its entire physical life. This inflow of cash originates from several sources: net income, noncash expenses, and residual value.

Net Income. A new project will generate additional cash because of increased sales (see **Table 7.3**) or produce savings resulting from more efficient operations.

Noncash Expenses. Since depreciation and amortization are not cash outflows but used solely for income tax relief purposes, the net income (or profit) figure does not reflect the true cash inflow. The calculation of net income and cash flow is shown in **Table 7.3**. As shown, since capital projects deal with cash flows and not net income, the amount incorporated in the project evaluation is $75,000 (cash) and not $25,000 (income).

Residual Value. Since money has a time value, it is important to anticipate not only the future cash inflows of a project generated by additional sales revenue or savings, but also, the **residual value** of the assets at the end of the life of the project. Estimating the residual value of an asset can be done in a number of ways:

◆ Engineers can examine similar facilities and, based on historical experience, estimate the future residual value of the asset.

◆ Accountants can calculate the undepreciated book value of the assets and determine the residual value of the newly acquired assets by using several assumptions.

	Net Income
TABLE 7.3 Net Income versus Cash Outflow	

	Net Income
Gross profit (after expenses)	$100,000*
Depreciation expense	50,000
Income before taxes	50,000
Income taxes (50%)	25,000
Income after taxes	25,000
Add back depreciation	50,000
Cash flow	$ 75,000

*Could include incremental profit resulting from increased sales.

♦ Suppliers of equipment and machinery can also provide valuable assistance in estimating residual values.

Residual values can have a significant impact on the return calculation. The impact of the present value of residual assets is examined in the next section.

Economic or Physical Life of a Project

A capital investment (cash outflows) is made in exchange for future income (cash inflows). Since the **economic life** span of a project plays a key role in determining the financial return of a project, this aspect of the analysis should be done with prudence. In one instance, engineers, suppliers, or accountants may determine that a piece of equipment will last 5 years; in another instance, they may estimate 25 years. The longer the physical life of the project, the longer the cash inflows will be generated, and the more beneficial the financial return of the project will be. For example, if we refer to Chapter 6, the present value of a 5-year $10,000 annuity bearing a 10 percent interest rate amounts to $37,908 ($10,000 × 3.7908), while the present value of a 25-year $10,000 annuity bearing the same interest rate amounts to $90,770 ($10,000 × 9.0770).

Also, the physical life span of a project is important in order to calculate the present value of the residual value of the asset. The time span and the interest rate also have an impact on the financial return of a project. **Table 7.4** shows the present values of an asset that has a residual value of $10,000 with varying discount rates and economic lives.

Sunk Costs

Sunk costs are funds that have already been spent on a project prior to making the decision to proceed with it. For instance, a firm may hire engineers to study the feasibility of investing huge sums of money in a project; the engineering costs may amount to $300,000. The recommendation may be to proceed or not to proceed with the capital project. The engineering fees are considered "sunk costs," meaning that these costs should not be taken into consideration when calculating the finan-

| TABLE 7.4 | Present Values of $10,000 Residual Value |

Interest Rate (%)	Economic Life (Years)				
	5	10	15	20	25
5	783	614	481	377	295
10	621	385	239	149	92
15	497	247	122	61	30
20	402	161	65	26	10
25	328	107	35	11	4
30	269	72	19	5	1

cial return of the project. The fact that management wants to make a decision on the project means that they have discretion (go or no go); sunk costs, on the other hand, offer no discretion. Whether the decision is positive or negative, the $300,000 amount will still have been disbursed.

Evaluating Capital Expenditure Projects

The main purpose of capital budgeting is to make decisions that will maximize a company's investments. Capital budgeting compels management to answer two basic questions: First, which of the many projects proposed by various departments should be approved? Second, how many projects, in total, should be approved?

In short, capital budgeting provides a methodology that helps management rank a multitude of investment proposals in order of priorities, strategic and economic importance, and return on investment.

Rate of return is probably the most widely used guide for helping managers make decisions related to the commitment of capital investments. The purchase of securities, acquisition of new assets, investment in product development, modernization, expansion, or construction of a new plant, all have one common trait—they generate income in return for funds disbursed. The rate of return can, therefore, be regarded as the relationship between funds committed and funds generated. This relationship is expressed in terms of a ratio or percentage. The arithmetic itself is relatively simple, but the fact that there is a choice in selecting the numerator and the denominator when calculating the return suggests that the results can vary substantially. The denominator, for example, can be expressed in terms of the original investment, depreciated investment, average investment, or capital employed. The numerator, where profit is shown, also varies depending on the selected year of income. The formula for calculating accounting returns also varies. The countless variables and formulas used for calculating return on investment have generated a good deal of bewilderment.

This section reviews different types of capital budgeting methods available and the arguments for and against each technique. Five capital budgeting methods used for gauging and ranking capital project proposals will be discussed. They are:

- Accounting methods
- Payback period
- Net present value (NPV)
- Internal rate of return (IRR) or discounted cash flow (DCF)
- Profitability index (PI index)

Each of these capital budgeting methods will be discussed in terms of (1) what it is, (2) what it does, (3) how it works, and (4) the arguments for and against it. After reviewing these capital budgeting techniques, sensitivity analysis and risk analysis will be discussed.

The Accounting Methods

What it is. The **accounting methods** (also referred to as the traditional yardsticks, the financial statement methods, the accountant's methods, and the book value rate of return) make use of data presented on financial statements to express the economic results of a capital investment.

What it does. It gives a rate of return of a capital project at a particular point in time (year) based on a book profit and a book investment.

How it works. The rate of return calculation based on this yardstick is relatively simple. Profit is divided by an appropriate investment base. It can be calculated in one of the following ways: (1) the annual return on original investment, (2) the annual return on average investment, (3) the average book return on investment, and (4) the average return on average investment. By using the following assumptions, let us examine how each is calculated:

- Original investment $200,000
- Residual value   N/A
- Life of the project   5 years
- Method of depreciation $40,000 (straight-line)
- After-tax income or profit $60,000

1. The *annual return on original investment* is calculated as follows:

$$\frac{\text{Annual income}}{\text{Original investment}} \times 100 = \frac{\$60,000}{\$200,000} \times 100 = 30\%$$

2. The *annual return on average investment* is calculated as follows:

$$\frac{\text{Annual income}}{\dfrac{\text{Original investment}}{2}} \times 100 = \frac{\$60,000}{\dfrac{\$200,000}{2}} \times 100 = 60\%$$

Note that instead of using the original or depreciated investment in the calculation, half of the investment, or the mid-point of the life of the assets (2.5 years) is used.

3.   The *average book return on investment* is calculated as follows:

$$\frac{\text{Total Income} - \text{Original investment}}{\text{Weighted average investment}} \times 100$$

$$\frac{\$300,000 - \$200,000}{\$600,000} \times 100 = 16.7\%$$

The calculation of the *average investment* is as follows:

Year	Original Investment	−	Accumulated Depreciation	=	Book Value
0	$200,000		—		$200,000
1	200,000		$ 40,000		160,000
2	200,000		80,000		120,000
3	200,000		120,000		80,000
4	200,000		160,000		40,000
5	200,000		200,000		—
Average investment					$600,000

4.   The *average return on average investment* is calculated as follows:

$$\frac{\text{Total Income} - \text{Original investment}}{\dfrac{\text{Original investment}}{2} \times \dfrac{\text{Life}}{\text{of assets}}} \times 100 = \frac{\$300,000 - \$200,000}{\dfrac{\$200,000}{2} \times 5} \times 100 = 20.0\%$$

The following summarizes the different rates of return obtained by using various accounting methods:

Methods of calculation	*Rate of return*
◆ Annual return on original investment	30.0%
◆ Annual return on average investment	60.0%
◆ Average book return on investment	16.7%
◆ Average return on average investment	20.0%

There are numerous ways of calculating the return on investment by using the accounting methods. For the same project, there are four returns ranging from 16.7 percent to 60.0 percent. If this project had generated uneven flows of income (say, year 1, $25,000; year 2, $70,000; year 3, $80,000; year 4, $90,000; and year 5, $100,000), this would compound the combinations for calculating the different rates of return. We could obtain different returns for each year reflecting the profit level for one particular year. When using these accounting methods for capital budgeting purposes, it is important that strict guidelines be written to ensure that all departments are consistent in their return calculations.

Arguments for accounting methods:
- They are simple to use and easy to calculate.
- The audit is simple because the information relates to accounting data.
- Emphasis is on income or profit rather than cash flow.

Arguments against accounting methods:
- They do not take into account that money has a time value.
- They do not provide a "true" rate of return, which is essentially the exact earning rate of the dollars in use. The average book return method usually understates the rate of return, while the annual return method overstates it.
- The returns focus only on one specific year, while a project usually has a longer physical life span.
- It is meaningless to compare an accounting rate of return to other rates offered on bonds, loans, or any other figures quoted on the financial markets.
- It assumes that a capital project will last for the depreciable life, when in fact this is generally not true.
- Since the time pattern of income varies from project to project, it is difficult to make effective comparisons between them.

The Payback Method

What it is. This method measures the period of time it takes for the cash outflow of a project to be totally recovered by the anticipated cash inflows; in other words, it measures how soon the initial funds disbursed are recovered by the project. The **payback method** is also known as the cash recovery period, the payoff method, or the payout method.

What it does. This technique measures "time risk" and not "risk conditions." It is helpful in the project selection process and also gives a valid measure of the expected project risk. The longer it takes for the initial investment to be recovered, the greater the risk. This is critical for a company engaged in an industry where product obsolescence is a factor, and where there are abrupt technological changes. A firm engaged in a relatively stable industry will be more likely to accept projects with longer payback periods. Payback can be considered an indicator of profitability. Projects that have a short payback period should have higher earnings in the short run. However, since this method favors immediate cash inflows, it may sacrifice future cash growth.

How it works. There are different ways of calculating the payback. It is true that the arithmetic process required to do the payback calculation is simple. For example, a business that invests $1.5 million in a venture that generates an annual cash inflow of $500,000 during its physical life will have a three-year payback period. The formula is:

$$P \quad = \quad I/NCF$$

where the original investment (I) is divided by the net cash inflows (NCF). It should be noted that this formula works only when cash inflows are equally distributed annually, or the irregular annual cash inflows are averaged out. The application of this formula to the above example is as follows:

$$\text{Payback} = \frac{\$1,500,000}{\$500,000} = 3.0 \text{ years}$$

The traditional payback method, the payback reciprocal, and the discounted payback are three methods used for calculating the economic desirability of a project.

The traditional payback method. When cash inflows are irregular, the calculation of the traditional payback period is done in the following way:

Years	Annual Net Cash Flows	Cumulative Cash Flows	
0	$(200,000)	$(200,000)	
1	25,000	(175,000)	
2	70,000	(105,000)	
3	80,000	(25,000)	← Payback
4	90,000	65,000	
5	100,000	165,000	
Total cash inflows	$ 365,000		

The illustration shows that the payback period takes place between years 3 and 4, since cash flow turns positive during the fourth year. In most cases, cumulative cash flows will not equal zero at specific given years, but instead, in fractions of a year or months. If this is the case, interpolation will have to be calculated in the following way.

Dividing the remaining cumulative net cash negative flow for the third year, amounting to $25,000, by the positive net cash flows for the fourth year of $65,000. This gives a fraction of a year of 0.385. The payback period therefore is 3.385 years.

The payback reciprocal. Another way of calculating the payback is by finding the reciprocal, which gives a very rough estimate of the return on investment. The calculation of the reciprocal is done in two steps. First, the average net cash inflow generated by the project must be calculated. In this case, the project generates an average net cash inflow of $73,000. The calculation is as follows:

$$\frac{\text{Total net cash inflow}}{\text{Number of years}} = \frac{\$365,000}{5} = \$73,000$$

Second, the average net cash inflow is divided by the initial cash outflow.

$$P = \frac{\$73,000}{\$200,000} = 36.5\%$$

The discounted payback method. A company concerned about the element of time value will go beyond the traditional way of calculating the payback period. During the early 1980s, because of high interest rates, more businesses were taking into account the time value of money when calculating the payback period. Therefore, they calculated the present value of future cash inflows to find the number of years it takes for the initial cash outflow to be totally recovered. Using a discount factor of 15 percent to calculate the present value of the future stream of funds, the discounted payback period is 4.75 years. The calculation is as follows:

Years	Annual Net Cash Flows	Discount Factors	Present Values	Cumulative Present Values
0	$(200,000)	1.00000	$(200,000)	$(200,000)
1	25,000	.86957	21,739	(178,261)
2	70,000	.75614	52,930	(125,331)
3	80,000	.65752	52,602	(72,729)
4	90,000	.57175	51,457	(21,272) ← Payback
5	100,000	.49718	49,718	28,446

Arguments for the payback method:

♦   Because it is simple to use, it may be employed as a crude screening device. Before the company embarks on extensive, complicated, and costly feasibility studies, a quick calculation can easily distinguish between profitable projects and those that will produce marginal financial results. In short, the payback can quickly separate the desirables from the undesirables.

♦   A firm that thrives on technological innovations would be inclined to use this method. In this type of business, management would want to be reasonably assured that the total cost of a venture could be recovered before better products or manufacturing processes are introduced. Here, management may have no alternative but to embark on capital projects that generate high initial cash inflows and recover their costs within a short time frame.

♦   A growth business that relies heavily on internal cash may find payback a useful method. Management of businesses in desperate need of cash may wish to trade off longer-term yield for short-term cash. A rapidly growing firm that opts for "dynamic projects" would find this method appropriate.

♦   Payback focuses on factors that are more visible. Even under dynamic environmental conditions, a firm equipped with good intelligence reports and forecasting techniques can, within reasonable limits, determine a project's potential initial cash outlay and the cash inflow, at least up to the payback point. Time value yardsticks, such as the internal rate of return (to be discussed later in this chapter), must incorporate into the calculation the more distant and unpredictable cash inflows (total physical life of the assets) which, in many circumstances, are merely guesses.

Arguments against the payback method:

♦   This technique fails to measure the "true economic worth" of a capital expenditure project because it focuses only on cash flows earned before the payback point, and it ignores the project's total physical life span. The payback period techniques place emphasis on liquidity and not return. The issue is this: should a firm invest for the purpose of recovering its cash as quickly as possible, or should the decision be based on return? In other words, should management inject funds into a project that offers a short payback at the expense of lucrative profits earned beyond the payback point?

♦   The adversaries of this method say that it does not adequately compare the relative economic worth of projects, since it can encourage the deployment of capital funds toward less efficient projects rather than highly efficient ones. For example, a capital-intensive project with high initial cash outflow and start-up expenses and a 20-year physical life may show a long payback period. On the other hand, a labor-intensive project with a minimal initial cash outlay but substantially higher labor and operating costs over its physical life may show a shorter payback and probably a shorter physical life span. Because of a shorter payback, the less efficient (or labor-intensive) project may be accepted instead of the capital-intensive project that could very well be more efficient.

♦   It does not take into consideration the time of the flow of funds even before the payback point. Although the payback method is geared to gauge liquidity, it fails even to do this job properly. Consider the following hypothetical example. Two projects with initial cash outflows of $1.6 million may show a four-year payback period.

	Cash Flow in $000's		
Years	Project A	Project B	Cash Flow Difference
0	$(1,600)	$(1,600)	—
1	400	200	$200
2	400	200	200
3	400	600	(200)
4	400	600	(200)
Net cash flow	0	0	
Payback period	4 years	4 years	

Project A shows a superior cash flow profile because it produces $400,000 more by the end of the second year. These funds can be reinvested in lucrative endeavors. Also, if both projects cease to operate at the end of the second year, the firm would recoup 50 percent of the original outlay in project A and only 25 percent in project B. (This method is called the bailout payback period).

The Net Present Value Method

What it is. The **net present value** technique measures the difference between the sum of all cash inflows and the cash outflows discounted at a predetermined interest rate which sometimes reflects the company's weighted cost of capital.

What it does. This method helps to establish whether or not the use of borrowed funds for a specific undertaking has greater financial merits than the cost itself. The rationale is relatively straightforward. If the net present value of a project, discounted at the company's cost of capital rate, is positive, the project may be classified as acceptable. If, on the other hand, the resulting net amount is negative, it would be economically unattractive and therefore rejected. This method is also useful for making realistic comparisons between projects. Since a common denominator (interest rate) is used in the calculation, it is easy to identify those projects that generate the most favorable results.

How it works. There are several steps in calculating the net present value of a project: (1) determine the projected cash flows, (2) determine the expected weighted cost of capital, then (3) compute the net present value itself. Referring to the example used in the payback calculation in the section titled "The Payback Method," the present value of the $200,000 investment with a 15 percent discount rate gives a total of $222,845 in discounted cash inflows for a net present value of $22,845.

Years	Net Cash Flows	Discount Factors	Net Present Value
0	$(200,000)	1.00000	$(200,000)
1	25,000	.86957	21,739
2	70,000	.75614	52,930
3	80,000	.65752	52,602
4	90,000	.57175	51,457
5	100,000	.49718	49,718
Net present value			$ 22,845

Arguments for net present value:
- This method is easy to use since no trial-and-error calculations are required (unlike the internal rate of return method, which will be discussed next).
- It examines the total physical life of the assets.
- It facilitates the choice between different projects.

Arguments against net present value:
- The time value of money concept is more difficult to grasp than the accounting methods such as return on assets.
- It is difficult to determine which cost of capital should be used to find the present value: Short-term or long-term? Current weighted cost of capital or next year's? Current rate of return or the short- or medium-term rate?
- The net present value method does not measure the level of risk of a project. It is difficult to determine whether or not a project offers sufficient benefits in relation to its potential hazards. A statement like "This project shows a $22,845 net present value when discounted at 15%" is meaningless in the context of evaluating the risk of a capital project.

The Internal Rate of Return

What it is. The **internal rate of return**, also known as the DCF (Discounted Cash Flow) rate of return, the true yield, or the investors' method, can be described as the specific interest rate used to discount all future cash inflows, so that their present value equals the initial cash outflows. The financial community has used the discounting mechanism for many decades to calculate insurance premiums and bond yields. Later, the industrial community adopted it to measure capital projects.

What it does. It shows the economic merits of several projects and compares their returns to other financial indicators, such as the weighted cost of capital and the company's aggregate rate of return.

How it works. The internal rate of return is found by trial and error (if a financial calculator or a spreadsheet is not available). Once the total annual cash flows are estimated, the net present value of the cash inflows and outflows is computed using an arbitrary interest rate. The totals are then compared. If the present value of the cash inflows is lower than the cash outflows, the procedure is repeated, this time using a lower interest rate. If, however, the present value of the cash inflows is higher than the cash outflows, a higher interest rate is called for. The process continues until the total net cash flows equal zero. The required calculation for our earlier example is illustrated as follows.

Years	Net Cash Flows	At 18%		At 20%		At 22%	
		Factors	PV	Factors	PV	Factors	PV
0	$(200,000)	1.00000	$(200,000)	1.00000	$(200,000)	1.00000	$(200,000)
1	25,000	.84746	21,186	.83333	20,833	.81967	20,492
2	70,000	.71818	50,273	.69444	48,611	.67186	47,030
3	80,000	.60863	48,690	.57870	46,296	.55071	44,057
4	90,000	.51579	46,421	.48225	43,402	.45140	40,626
5	100,000	.43711	43,711	.40188	40,188	.37000	37,000
	NPV		$ 10,281		$(670)		$(10,795)

The calculation shows that it is the 20 percent interest rate that equalizes (near enough) the cash flows. (By using a financial calculator or a spreadsheet, we get exactly 19.87 percent.) The internal rate of return on this investment is therefore 20 percent. Trial and error calculations would have to be done if the net difference is more significant.

If the cash outflows take place at year 0 and all cash inflows are constant each year of the project, it is quite easy to figure out the internal rate of return. For example, a $200,000 initial cash outflow and a $70,000 annual cash inflow gives a 22 percent internal rate of return. This is how it works. First, you divide the $200,000 by the $70,000, which gives you a factor of 2.8571. By referring to the present value of an annuity of $1, we can obtain the internal rate of return by finding the 2.8571 present value factor in the row opposite five years. The present value factor of 2.8571 lies between 22 percent (2.8636) and 23 percent (2.8035).

Arguments for internal rate of return:
- It focuses attention on the entire economic life of an investment. It concerns itself with cash flows and ignores book allocations.
- It considers the fact that money has a time value.
- It permits a company to compare the return of one project to the cost of capital (see **Figure 5.1** in Chapter 5).
- It facilitates comparisons between two or more projects.

Arguments against internal rate of return:

- This method covers activities which take place during the entire life span of a project. While this may be considered a strong point, it could also be a drawback. How can one predict internal and external environmental conditions 10, 15, and 20 years ahead?

- It ignores potential "cash throwoffs"—that is, should a company assess the financial desirability of a project in a vacuum, or should it include the added income produced by the incremental cash that is generated by the project? For example, when a project generates, say, $25,000 during the first year of operation, should the interest earned on this money be taken into account when calculating the return of the project in question?

- The technique is relatively difficult to grasp. Operating managers understand ratios, such as the division of profit by the project investment; however, the internal rate of return calculation contains more than simple arithmetic. Concepts such as cash flow, time span, discounting, and present value—all essential components of the internal rate of return calculation— are introduced.

- This method poses some difficulty for determining the "true" financial benefits of a project. Since the investment return is expressed in terms of a percentage or a ratio, this method poses an element of delusion. For instance, a company's capital expenditure budget may contain several projects in the amount of $100,000, with internal rates of return in the 25 percent range. Other important projects in the $1 million range with a 20 percent internal rate of return may be weeded out, due to the comparative low factor yield. The absolute present value sums are not evident. Put simply, you can invest $100 at 30 percent and $10,000 at 25 percent for a one-year period and, although the return on the first project is highly attractive, the absolute dollars earned are only $30. In the second case, the yield is lower; however, the dollars earned are $2,500. This cash throw-off can be reinvested in other projects generating additional revenue.

- It assumes that the cash flows can be reinvested at the calculated rate of return.

The Profitability Index

What it is. The **profitability index**, also known as the present value index, or benefit-cost ratio, shows the ratio of the present value of cash inflows to the present value of the cash outflows, discounted at a predetermined rate of interest.

What it does. This method helps to rank capital projects by the ratio of the net present value for each dollar to the cash outflow, and to select the projects with the highest index until the budget is depleted.

How it works. Refer to the earlier example, where the initial cash outlay is $200,000, the cost of capital is 15 percent, the life of the project is five years, and the cash inflows are as follows:

Years	Cash inflows	PV using discount rate of 15%
1	$ 25,000	$ 21,739
2	70,000	52,930
3	80,000	52,602
4	90,000	51,457
5	100,000	49,718
PV		$222,845

The present value of the future cash inflows is $222,845. The PI is calculated as follows:

$$\frac{\$222,845}{\$200,000} = 1.142$$

If the index is greater than 1.0, it means that the flow of cash discounted at a predetermined discount factor (i.e., cost of capital) is "more" than the cash disbursement. If it is less than 1.0, it means that the incoming cash flows of the project give "less" than the discounted factor. For example, if 15 percent was used to calculate the PI of all projects shown in **Table 7.5**, it means that projects A to E generate more than 15 percent, and projects F to K, less.

This method helps to rank capital projects in a logical way because it looks at projects both in relation to budget constraints and in terms of which ones offer the highest total net present value. **Table 7.5** illustrates this methodology. Let us say that a company has a maximum of $1.7 million to invest. As shown in the table, the company has 11 projects under review (A to K), each having specific cash outflows with corresponding net present values and profitability indexes. The company will give the green light to projects A to E for a total cash outlay of $1.7 million. This means that projects F to K will be deferred until the following year. The aggregate PI for all approved projects is 1.36.

TABLE 7.5   Capital Rationing and the Profitability Index

Projects	Cash Outflows	PV of Cash Inflows	PI	Aggregate PI
A		$510,000	1.7	
B		320,000	1.6	
C	$1,700,000	840,000	1.4	1.36
D		440,000	1.1	
E		200,000	1.0	
F		160,000	0.8	
G		175,000	.7	
H		60,000	.4	
I		27,000	.3	
J		60,000	.2	
K		0	0	

(Cash Outflows by project: A $300,000; B 200,000; C 600,000; D 400,000; E 200,000; F 200,000; G 250,000; H 150,000; I 90,000; J 300,000; K 200,000)

Arguments for and against the profitability index:

The arguments for and against the profitability index are the same as those for and against the net present value method, with one exception: The NPV expresses all dollars in absolute terms, while the PI method expresses the results in relative terms, that is, an index.

Capital Budgeting Techniques That Cope with Risk

It was mentioned earlier that time value yardstick results are based on a project's total physical life span. This implies the need to deal with the future, to use a series of underlying assumptions as benchmarks, for computing the "best possible estimates." There is one overriding weakness in this approach: It is vulnerable to the element of change. No one can predict, with any certainty, future environmental conditions, such as those related to economic, political, social, and technological factors, and, more specifically, elements affecting the industry, such as prices, competitors' aggressiveness, level of investment intentions by competitors, research and development, and labor costs. So the internal rate of return is based on the assumption that all estimates will materialize, that the price over the next five years will be x, that the cost of materials and wages will be y and z, etc. Thus, there are many chances for estimates to be off target. For example, a 15.6 percent internal rate of return can be increased or decreased by one change or several changes in the estimates.

More sophisticated capital budgeting techniques have been developed to help decision-makers deal with probabilities or possibilities. These yardsticks can identify a range of results based on patterns of variations, rather than using one single set of factors to generate the "best possible result" such as the one used to calculate the internal rate of return.

Two techniques used for dealing with "range of results" are sensitivity analysis and risk analysis.

Sensitivity Analysis

Sensitivity analysis involves the identification of profitability variations as a result of one or more changes in the base case related to certain key elements of a project. These could include:

◆   The purchase of land, buildings and equipment.
◆   Changes in sales volume, selling price, or cost of material or labor.
◆   Physical life of the assets.
◆   Change in the tax rate.

To illustrate, the internal rate of return of the project mentioned earlier in the section titled "Internal Rate of Return" was 20 percent based on one set of estimates. If selling prices vary by 10 percent, construction costs by 5 percent, and sales volume by 10 percent, the effect of these changes (individually) on the base case would be as follows:

Factors	% Variation in Factor	Internal Rate of Return
Base case	—	20.0%
Selling price	−10%	16.3
Cost of construction	+ 5	18.8
Sales volume	−10	7.5

These factors may vary either individually or in combination. It is important to note that sensitivity checks do not contain the element of probability related to individual factors. This method simply illustrates the degree of change in the base internal rate of return as a result of one or more changes related to a project.

Risk Analysis

Risk analysis is the process of attaching probabilities to individual estimates in the base case. It was stated earlier that the process of appraising investment proposals has one weakness—the element of uncertainty. Those preparing the estimates to be included in the return calculation must know the degree of uncertainty related to their respective estimates.

Past experience alerts managers to the possible degree of error in their estimates. Therefore, management's knowledge should be used extensively to obtain the best quality decision-making. The risk analysis method will produce a full spectrum of return outcomes, from the most pessimistic to the most optimistic. Weighing the uncertainty factor, therefore, becomes an integral part of the project evaluation process. In this way, the sales manager, the production manager, the financial executive, the plant engineer, the cost accountant, the purchasing agent, and others can all provide their calculated guesses regarding the likelihood of possible outcomes in the selling price, cost of labor, cost of machinery, cost of raw material, and so on. Their input can be illustrated as follows:

Sales volume (000s of units)	100	200	300	400
probabilities (%)	.05	.15	.65	.15
Selling price ($)	1.50	1.70	1.90	2.10
probabilities (%)	.05	.15	.70	.10
Cost of labor ($)	.75	.80	.85	.90
probabilities (%)	.10	.15	.60	.15
Project cost ($000s)	200	250	300	350
probabilities (%)	.05	.10	.75	.10
Life of project (years)	10	11	12	13
probabilities (%)	.05	.10	.80	.05

As mentioned earlier, the probabilities indicated under each variable (volume, price, etc.) are provided by managers based on their experience or calculated guesses.

The results of the risk analysis calculations could read as follows:

IRR Range (%)	Occurrences (%)	% of Total	% Cumulative
5–8	4	.4	.4
8–11	30	3.0	3.4
11–14	133	13.3	16.7
14–17	323	32.3	49.0
17–20	283	28.3	77.3
20–23	167	16.7	94.0
23–26	43	4.3	98.3
26–29	17	1.7	100.0
Total	1,000	100.0	

The above means that there are 4 chances out of 100 that the project's internal rate of return would fall between 5 percent and 8 percent, 30 chances out of 100 that it will fall between 8 percent and 11 percent, etc. The report could also indicate the following:

Minimum rate of return	5.3%
Maximum rate of return	29.3%
Mean	18.1%

Probability
68.3% that the return will fall between 15.6% and 22.0%
95.5% that the return will fall between 9.0% and 23.9%
99.7% that the return will fall between 5.9% and 29.0%

This example indicates that of the 1,000 internal rates of return outcomes (an arbitrary number chosen by the financial analysts) under the most pessimistic circumstances, the financial return is 5.3 percent, while the most optimistic calculated guesses would predict a 29.3 percent return. Within these two extremes lies a full range of outcomes to help judge the risk factors inherent in a project.

Capital Constraints

Two reasons can prevent a business from proceeding with a large number of capital projects: cash insufficiency and hurdle rate (which determine in a large measure the extent to which projects are satisfactory or viable).

Cash Insufficiency. Before overloading a business with too much debt (a cheaper source than equity), management will calculate the appropriate debt to total capitalization ratio. The risk factor largely determines this optimum capital mix. If a firm adds too much debt to its capital structure, future fixed charges will increase, affecting the firm's cash position. The question to answer is: Will the capital projects generate sufficient cash to meet proposed fixed commitments?

Hurdle Rate. As mentioned earlier, **hurdle rate** is used to rank the financial desirability of capital projects according to their cost of capital. Essentially, capital budgeting is the process of finding the break-even point between the yield of a capital project and the weighted cost of capital. Obviously, the wider the spread between the aggregate yield or IRR of the projects and the cost of capital, the better it is for the shareholders.

To find this break-even point, the aggregate IRR must, of course, be known. It is also essential to pinpoint the sources and cost of the capital needed to finance all capital projects (i.e., internal financing, such as retained earnings, and external financing, such as bond or share issues).

The capital project selection system is often referred to as the rationing process, meaning that only the most viable projects—that is, those that exceed the hurdle rate—are approved. **Figure 7.3** presents this process. As shown in the figure, the company's total capital projects requested amount to $7 million, made up of ten individual projects (A to J) and several other minor projects grouped under K. The aggregate or cumulative internal rate of return for all projects is 17.0 percent. Based on the company's cost of capital, management decides to set the project's hurdle rate (or cut-off rate) at 15.0 percent. (This rate does not necessarily reflect the cost of capital; instead, it shows the minimum acceptable rate of return.) As indicated, if the company invests beyond $5 million (dotted line), it may have to obtain an extra $2 million at a higher interest rate.

FIGURE 7.3   Capital Rationing Process

Projects	Project Costs		IRR	
	Each Project	Cumulative Costs	Each Project	Cumu-lative
A	1.5	1.5	25.0	25.0
B	.5	2.0	22.5	24.4
C-D-E	2.5	4.5	17.5	20.7
F	.5	5.0	15.0	20.1
G-H	1.0	6.0	10.0	18.4
I	.5	6.5	2.5	17.5
J	.3	6.8	1.3	17.3
K	.2	7.0	—	17.0

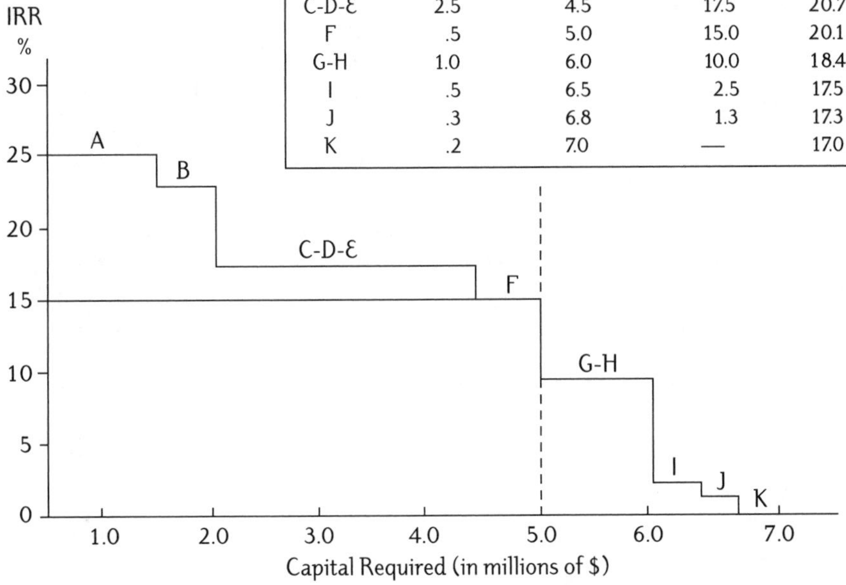

Decision-Making in Action

Let's now turn to analyzing capital expenditure projects to see how these various capital budgeting techniques are used. Three projects will be analyzed:

◆ Modernization
◆ Launching a new product
◆ Constructing a new plant (New-Tech Inc.)

Modernization

Suppose a business contemplates investing $1.5 million to modernize a plant. On the basis of the following information, it is possible to determine whether a capital expenditure is worth the investment.

◆ The economic life of the project is estimated at ten years.
◆ The savings (or net cash inflows) are estimated at $300,000 per year.
◆ The cost of capital is 14 percent.

This information is sufficient for assessing whether or not the project has some economic merits. By referring to the discount tables, we can calculate the present value of the future savings by using the 14 percent discount factors. If the sum of the future savings, discounted to today's value, exceeds the $1.5 million initial capital outlay, it means that the project is economically attractive. If, however, the sum of the inflows is negative, it means that the project should not go forward. As shown in **Table 7.6**, since the difference between the initial cash outflows and the future cash inflows is positive by $64,830, the project could very well be approved.

TABLE 7.6   Cash Flow Forecast for Modernizing a Project

Year	Outflow	Inflows	Discount Factors @ 14%	Present Value
0	$1,500,000	—	—	($1,500,000)
1	—	$300,000	0.87719	263,157
2	—	300,000	0.76947	230,841
3	—	300,000	0.67497	202,491
4	—	300,000	0.59208	177,624
5	—	300,000	0.51937	155,810
6	—	300,000	0.45559	136,676
7	—	300,000	0.39964	119,891
8	—	300,000	0.35056	105,167
9	—	300,000	0.30751	92,252
10	—	300,000	0.26974	80,921
	Total Inflows			+ $1,564,830
	Net Difference			+ $ 64,830

Figure 7.4 graphically displays the results of the present value calculations for individual years. The shaded squares show the present values of each $300,000 receipts, while the white portion of each square shows the loss in value because of time.

However, since we are dealing with an annuity situation, instead of using **Table B** (present value of a single sum), we can use **Table D** and look under column 14 percent (cost of capital) for 10 years. By multiplying the $300,000 expected savings by the 5.2161 discount factor, we get the same number: $1,564,830 for a positive $64,830 NPV. If we used a 15 percent discount factor, the NPV would be $5,510. In this case the IRR is 15.1%.

The following factors may reinforce or reverse our decision:

- A change in the economic life of the project.
- A change in the income tax bracket.
- A change in the initial cash outflow.
- A change in the cash inflows.
- A change in the cost of capital.
- A change in the expected return on the capital assets.
- The economic attractiveness of other projects considered by the company.
- The shortage in the amount of funds available.
- The nature of other projects. (Other projects may generate a lesser return but may be required by law—for example, anti-pollution equipment.)

FIGURE 7.4 Graphic Illustration of the Yearly Cash Inflows and Outflows

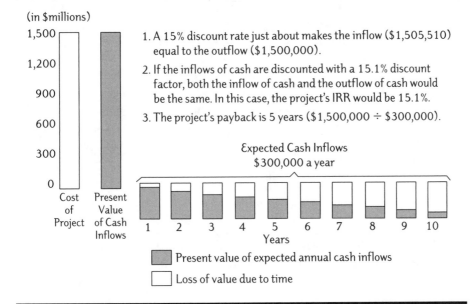

1. A 15% discount rate just about makes the inflow ($1,505,510) equal to the outflow ($1,500,000).
2. If the inflows of cash are discounted with a 15.1% discount factor, both the inflow of cash and the outflow of cash would be the same. In this case, the project's IRR would be 15.1%.
3. The project's payback is 5 years ($1,500,000 ÷ $300,000).

Launching a New Product

Let's look now at the launching of a new product. **Table 7.7** gives detailed information about the project and is divided into four parts:

◆   Part A shows the various elements related to the $2.0 million cost or cash outflow of the project.

◆   Part B gives the project's pro-forma income after taxes for five years.

◆   Part C shows the project's pro-forma income statement and cash flow.

◆   Part D gives the overview of the project's cash flow forecast, that is, the cash inflows and cash outflows for each year.

Here are the assumptions related to the project. As shown in Part A, management invests $2.0 million in the project; $1.5 million in research and development (R & D), equipment and machinery, and other assets; and $500,000 in working capital. The investment in working capital consists of the following:

Accounts receivable	$600,000	cash outflow
Inventory	+ 300,000	cash outflow
Total	900,000	
Accounts payable	− 400,000	cash inflow
Net working capital	$500,000	net cash outflow

Part B gives the five-year pro-forma income statement. If management wants to calculate the return outcomes of the project by using the accounting methods, it could compute the following yearly returns:

	Yearly return on	
	Capital employed	Capital assets
Year 1	2.5%	3.3%
Year 2	10.0	13.3
Year 3	18.7	25.0
Year 4	25.5	34.0
Year 5	34.5	46.0
Average return	18.2	24.3

	Return on average investment		Return on depreciated assets	
	Capital Employed	Capital Assets	Capital Employed	Capital Assets
Year 1	4.0%	6.7%	2.9%	4.2%
Year 2	16.0	26.7	14.3	22.2
Year 3	30.0	50.0	34.0	66.6
Year 4	41.0	68.0	63.7	170.0
Year 5	55.2	92.0	138.0	1,000.0

Part C of **Table 7.7** gives a more detailed forecast of management's pro-forma income statement and statement of cash flows. The most difficult part of a project analysis is not to calculate the payback or the internal rate of return, but making the forecast related to the project itself. For example, the marketing department

TABLE 7.7   Evaluating a Capital Expenditure Project

A. The project

Assets	
R&D	$ 150,000
Equipment/machinery	850,000
Other assets	500,000
Net working capital	500,000
Total capital employed	$2,000,000

B. The pro-forma income statement

Years	Income After Taxes
1	$ 50,000
2	200,000
3	375,000
4	510,000
5	690,000

C. Pro-forma income statement and cash flow (in thousands)

Years	1	2	3	4	5
Sales revenue	$1,300	$1,700	$2,415	$3,000	$3,700
Cost of goods sold	600	700	990	1,240	1,560
Gross margin	700	1,000	1,425	1,760	2,140
Selling & administrative expenses	350	400	500	600	650
Income before depreciation	350	600	925	1,160	1,490
Depreciation	250	200	175	140	110
Income before taxes	100	4000	750	1,020	1,380
Taxes (50%)	50	200	375	510	690
Income after taxes	50	200	375	510	690
Add back depreciation	250	200	175	140	110
Cash flow	$ 300	$ 400	$ 550	$ 650	$ 800

D. Pro-forma cash flow (in thousands)

Years	0	1	2	3	4	5
Assets	$(1,500)	—	—	—	—	—
Working capital	—	$(250)	$(250)	—	—	—
Pro-forma cash flow	—	300.0	400	550	650	800
Sale of assets	—	—	—	—	—	300
Recovery of working capital	—	—	—	—	—	500
Total cash flow	$(1,500)	$ 50	$ 150	$550	$650	$1,600

would have to estimate the company's sales revenue, which includes both the number of units sold (or service) and the unit selling price, adjusted for inflation.

The manufacturing department would have to forecast the cost of goods sold, which includes the cost of raw materials, freight in, and the transformation of the raw materials into finished products. This forecast also includes anticipated inflation increments over the life of the project.

Similar cost forecasts would also have to be prepared by other organizational units that are expected to be part of the project. As indicated, this forecast takes into account depreciation to calculate the income taxes to be paid each year over the life of the project. In order to determine the yearly cash flows generated by the project, since depreciation is not a cash outflow (but a tax-deductible expense), it is added back to the income after taxes.

Part D of **Table 7.7** gives the actual disbursements (cash outflows) and receipts (cash inflows) of the project. There are two distinct cash disbursements: the $1.5 million related to R & D, purchase of the machinery and equipment, and other assets made during year 0; and the $500,000 disbursements related to working capital, which in this case are spread equally over years 1 and 2. The third line is the pro-forma cash inflow generated by the project. This line is drawn from Part C of the table. Other assumptions related to the project are that the assets have a five-year life span and that, at the end, the assets (equipment/machinery and other assets) will be sold for $300,000 and the $500,000 in working capital will be totally recovered.

Based on the above cash flows, the project's payback period, NPV, and IRR are as follows:

A.   Payback period is 4.1 years.

	Annual Net Cash Flows	Cumulative Cash Flows
Year 0	($1,500,000)	($1,500,000)
Year 1	50,000	(1,450,000)
Year 2	150,000	(1,300,000)
Year 3	550,000	(750,000)
Year 4	650,000	(100,000)
Year 5	1,600,000	1,500,000 ← Payback

B.   Net present value (NPV) based on a 10% cost of capital.

	Annual Net Cash Flows	Discount Factors	Present Values
Year 0	($1,500,000)	1.000	($1,500.0)
Year 1	50,000	0.909	45.4
Year 2	150,000	0.826	123.9
Year 3	550,000	0.751	413.1
Year 4	650,000	0.683	444.0
Year 5	1,600,000	0.621	993.6
Present value			2,020.0
Net present value (NPV)			**+ $520.0**

C. Internal rate of return (IRR) is 18.4%.

Annual Net Cash Flows		Present Values		
		17%	18%	19%
Year 0	($1,500,000)	($1,500.0)	($1,500.0)	($1,500.0)
Year 1	50,000	42.7	42.4	42.0
Year 2	150,000	109.6	107.7	105.9
Year 3	550,000	343.4	334.7	326.4
Year 4	650,000	346.8	385.3	324.1
Year 5	1,600,000	729.8	699.4	670.4
Net present value (NPV)		+ $72.3	+ $19.5	− $31.2

IRR 18.4%

Someone who does not have a financial calculator or a spreadsheet has to find the internal rate of return on a trial-and-error basis, by using the 17, 18, and 19 percent discount rates until the NPV moves from a positive to a negative. As shown above, the calculation indicates that the internal rate of return is between 18 percent (NPV of +$19.5 thousand) and 19 percent (NPV of −$31.2 thousand).

Constructing a New Plant (New-Tech Inc.)

Let's look now at the third capital expenditure project. New-Tech Inc. is contemplating opening a new plant to manufacture pocket calculators. The cost of the project is as follows:

Land	$ 50,000	
Buildings	200,000	
Equipment/Machinery	100,000	
Trucks	150,000	
Total capital assets		$500,000
Net working capital		150,000
Total capital employed		$650,000

The company expects to realize $2.0 million in sales revenue during the first year of operation, which would be maintained during the life of the plant. The company's pro-forma income statement is as follows:

Sales revenue		$2,000,000
Cost of goods sold		1,700,000
Gross margin		300,000
Depreciation	$ 25,000	
Interest	40,000	
Other operating expenses	143,000	
Total operating expenses		200,000
Income before taxes		100,000
Income taxes (50%)		50,000
Income after taxes		$ 50,000

The company engineer indicates that the life span of the plant is 15 years. According to the company's real estate division manager, in 15 years, the market value of the land will have increased to $150,000, and the residual value of the buildings, equipment, and trucks will be in the order of $150,000. Working capital is expected to be totally recovered at the end of the project.

The company will borrow from different sources to finance the project, and the cost of capital, according to the company's treasurer, will be 11 percent. Management would like to obtain at least 25 percent on the project (hurdle rate). If you were a member of the management committee, would you go along with this proposal?

Table 7.8 gives the payback period, the NPV, and the IRR. As shown below, the first thing that needs to be done is to calculate the annual cash flow from operations. This is done by rearranging the income statement and converting the $50,000 after-tax income into cash flows; as shown, the calculation gives an amount of $95,000. Here are some of the assumptions and the arithmetic:

Gross margin		$300,000
Less: Depreciation	$25,000	
Other expenses	135,000	160,000
Income before taxes		140,000
Income taxes (50%)		70,000
Income after taxes		70,000
Add back depreciation		25,000
Cash flow from operations		$ 95,000

It is assumed that the $300,000 gross margin is all cash inflow. The two other expense items deducted from the gross margin are depreciation, and other operating expenses. Assuming the company pays 50 percent in income taxes (from the projected income statement, $50,000 ÷ $100,000), the project itself will be taxed for $70,000. Interest expenses are excluded from the calculation because one of the objectives of finding the "internally generated return" (IRR) is to compare it with the cost of the capital—that is, funds obtained from external sources. Depreciation is simply used as a tax shield; it is added back to the profit after taxes, which gives a net yearly cash inflow from operations in the amount of $95,000. As shown in **Table 7.8**, using the cost of capital (11%) as the discount rate gives the project a positive NPV of $142,051. On the basis of this discount rate, company management would be tempted to approve the project. However, because of the risk factor, management has established a 25 percent hurdle rate. Using 25 percent as the discount rate gives the project a $237,535 negative NPV, which is far less than expected. As shown in the table, using 15 percent as the discount rate gives the project a negative NPV of $19,632. With a financial calculator or a spreadsheet, we obtain exactly 14.42 percent. The bottom line is this: The project generates a 14.4 percent IRR, and after the cost of capital of 11 percent (or paying the external cost of financing the project), the company would be left with only 3.4 percent.

This is much less than the 10.6 percent spread (25.0% − 14.4%) that management was hoping to realize to offset the risk associated with the project.

TABLE 7.8   New-Tech Inc.

Year	Cash Flow	25% Factors	Cash Flow	11% Factors	Cash Flow	15% Factors	Cash Flow
0	$(500,000)	1.00000	$(500,000)	1.0000	$(500,000)	1.0000	$(500,000)
1	(150,000)	.80000	(120,000)	.9009	(135,135)	.8696	(130,435)
1	95,000						
		3.85930	366,634	7.1909	683,136	5.8474	555,503
15	95,000						
15	450,000	.03518	15,831	.03518	94,050	.1229	55,300
Net present value:			$ (237,535)		$ 142,051		$ (19,632)

Payback period: 6–7 years
Internal rate of return: 14.4%

Summary

Capital budgeting is the process of planning and evaluating capital projects and deciding which ones will generate the best returns over an extended period. Capital projects are critical because they can alter the financial destiny of a business. Capital projects fall into two groups: compulsory investments, which should be done in order to sustain the life of a business, and opportunity investments, which can be done if management wants the business to grow.

The capital budgeting process includes six key steps: establishing strategic objectives; formulation of a capital expenditure portfolio; project measurement and ranking, by using capital budgeting methods; calculating the cost of capital; determining the hurdle rate; and project selection and implementation. Capital budgeting elements include cash outflows, such as the initial cash outlays, net working capital, and normal capital additions; cash inflows, which include net income; noncash expenses, such as depreciation and the residual value; the establishment of the economic life of a project; and sunk costs.

Many different techniques are used for evaluating and ranking capital projects. There are the accounting methods, the payback method, the net present value method, the internal rate of return, and the profitability index. More seasoned methods are used to evaluate the element of risk; they are the sensitivity analysis and the risk analysis. There are arguments for and against using each of these methods.

Two reasons will cause a business to refrain from going forward with all proposed capital projects: lack of cash and the hurdle rate.

CHAPTER 8

Budgeting, Financial Planning and Controling

After spending several months going over the economics involved in opening a new retail store, the Edwards were now preparing their investment proposal to be presented to several investors. In year 2002, CompuTech was able to reduce its debt and purchase all assets from internally generated funds. The Edwards were also pleased with their financial results in terms of managing their liquidity and debt structure. The financial statements also revealed that they had the ability to manage their assets (productivity) well and to generate a reasonable return on the company's assets (profitability). Those financial statements and financial ratios that were presented and calculated in Exercise 44 of Chapter 3 would be presented to investors.

CompuTech's break-even point that was calculated in Exercise 43(a) of Chapter 4 also shows positive results only two years after the company started. Furthermore, Exercise 53(a) of Chapter 7 reveals that the new retail outlet would be a viable venture, in fact, it shows an excellent internal rate of return. Even the financing package that the Edwards were considering appeared reasonable. As mentioned in the opening case in Chapter 5, of the $449,000 that they required for the new retail store ($350,000 in capital assets and $99,000 in working capital), 35 percent would be financed from internal operations and 15 percent from shareholders. The business and shareholders would therefore provide 50 percent of the funds. The Edwards would be seeking 50 percent of the funding requirements from lenders ($150,000 from long-term lenders and $74,500 from short-term lenders).

Everything looked positive. However, the Edwards realized that they had to present to the lenders and to potential shareholders their projected financial statements about the company for the next several years and a detailed cash budget for 2003. The Edwards also had to prove that they had an efficient system in place to help them manage their monthly cash budget and to pay their bills as they came due. They also realized that the banks would not require looking at the company's detailed cost structure. Still, the Edwards planned to show them that they knew, through their cost accounting system, how they made informed business decisions and that they had in place an effective control system to reveal, in a precise and timely way, good or bad operating and financial results.

As part of their investment plan, the Edwards were to include the following financial reports:

- Last two years' financial statements
- Personal financial statements
- Projected income statements (3 years)
- Projected balance sheets (3 years)
- Projected statement of cash flows (3 years)
- Projected working capital requirements (1 year)
- Monthly cash budget (1 year)
- Detailed sources and uses of funds (1 year)
- Credit references
- Loan repayment schedule

In addition to the above information, the Edwards were prepared to demonstrate that CompuTech would have the ability to manage its 90 percent growth in sales revenue in year 2003 and that they were going to more than double their income after taxes (sustainable growth). They also wanted to show that the company's overall financial health position is excellent (Z-score).

The Edwards wanted to prepare a business plan that satisfied not only investors' needs, but more importantly their own needs. They realized that planning and budgeting were prerequisites to the success of any business and were prepared to take the time to go about their planning activity in an accomplished and professional way.

This chapter examines in detail three key topics:

1. How a business should go about preparing different types of budgets.
2. How to prepare projected financial statements.
3. How managers should monitor their business activities through effective control systems.

Introduction

This chapter deals with three major themes: budgeting, financial planning, and controling. Of these, *budgeting* is probably the most crucial. Setting corporate objectives and priorities, determining departmental and unit goals, formulating programs and policies, developing market/product strategies, and writing detailed operational plans and procedures are all essential steps in arriving at a perfectly orchestrated planning effort. Individually, these steps can accomplish very little; they become meaningful only as part of an integrated whole—that is, when in keeping with a company's financial capabilities. The way these planning efforts are translated into the common language of business—dollars—is budgeting.

Financial planning involves putting together all individual operating budgets (sales, manufacturing, administration, R & D, etc.) into pro-forma or projected financial statements such as the income statement, the balance sheet, and the statement of cash flows, and making sure that the business grows without depleting its physical, human, and financial resources.

Controling is the feedback system designed to compare actual performance to predetermined standards in order to identify deviations, measure their significance, take any action required to assure that all corporate resources are being used in the most effective and efficient way possible for achieving corporate objectives.

Budgeting

Budgeting is the process by which management allocates corporate resources, evaluates the financial outcome of its decisions, and establishes the financial and operational profile against which future results will be measured. If managers regard budgeting simply as a mechanical exercise or a yearly ritual performed by planning groups or accountants, they will not really grasp how the company can improve its economic performance and operating efficiencies. This section looks at budgeting by exploring the following questions:

♦   What part does budgeting play in planning as a whole?
♦   What can budgeting contribute to the decision-making process?
♦   What types of budgets are available?
♦   What information should be considered when formulating a budget?
♦   What are the pitfalls to avoid if budgeting is to be done effectively?

Before discussing these questions, let's examine the underlying purpose of budgeting and the importance of the responsibility-center concept.

Reasons for Budgeting

Essentially, budgeting translates corporate intentions into specific tasks and identifies the resources needed by managers to accomplish these tasks. To do this well requires effective communication, sound coordination, and a detailed search, by all managers, to find new ways of improving economic performance and efficiencies at the operating level. Budgeting also establishes specific financial and operational boundaries (standards, targets, and ratios) for controling purposes.

Let's explore the key elements of this brief description and relate them to the role of budgeting within the organization as a whole.

Communication. Budgeting enforces communication in two directions. Front-line managers must *communicate vertically* to justify the resources they need to achieve their goals. For example, they will have to explain, in considerable detail, how their tasks will be performed, as well as the scope and volume of their activities. This process is repeated at every level in the organization. Thus, budgeting activates communication between superiors and subordinates, and helps reaffirm their mutual commitment to the firm's goals.

Horizontal communication between organizational units (receivers and providers of services) is also necessary. For example, computer or administrative services must obtain confirmation from, say, the marketing or manufacturing departments about service needs and the resources required for implementing specific projects.

Coordination. Hundreds of different tasks are performed by an organization's various divisions. To realize the corporate profit goals, these tasks must be synchronized. Unquestionably, budgeting is essential to the creation of a unified whole. For example, budgeting helps to link the number and types of units to be marketed to elements such as number of units that should be manufactured and distributed, the funds needed for credit purposes, and the purchase of new equipment and raw materials.

Decision-Making. No other part of the business plan requires more decisions than a budget. What is the most effective way of performing this task? Is this particular activity really needed? If yes, how extensive should the service be? How can we best measure the efficiency of this operation? How relevant is this task to the rest of the organization? What resources are needed to do this job, project, or program? How does this activity relate to the overall objectives of the company? All these questions and many more must be scrutinized and resolved before management can arrive at a perfectly balanced profit plan.

Monitoring. As indicated earlier, budgeting involves setting standards (i.e., financial and operational performance indicators) that are central to management accountability. When resources are allocated to a manager, they should be accompanied by standards that stipulate, in *precise terms*, how efficiently they should be deployed. Standards facilitate reporting, and a well-designed reporting system helps management to keep up-to-date on the following issues:

- Are we on target? If not, why?
- Who is responsible for the unfavorable profit performances?
- What impact will an increase in material or labor costs have on profits?

- If we are to maintain or increase profits, should certain costs be trimmed? Should prices be changed?
- What are the causes of the variances in each organizational unit?

Performance Evaluation and Accountability. Budgeting is a key instrument in the evaluation of a manager's performance and accountability. In the light of a fixed budget, managers can be evaluated from two angles: as planners or decision-makers and as implementers or doers. Those who exceed or underspend their budgets are not necessarily bad or good managers. Nevertheless, budgeting establishes the targets that help gauge managerial performance and accountability, something that cannot be done by intuition and personal judgment alone.

Responsibility Centers

An important task of the budgeting function is to establish a planning and controling system that enables managers to gauge an organization's operational and financial performance. The management tool that facilitates pinpointing managerial responsibility and accountability for attaining objectives and realizing plans has to do with the concept of the **responsibility center**. If a manager is to be responsible and accountable for objectives, plans, and resources, there must be a mechanism that helps to fulfill this mandate.

The responsibility center concept establishes control systems that are used to gauge managerial performance. These controls include costs, revenues, and investment of funds. A responsibility center manager may be responsible for one or all three.

The responsibility center concept has led to *responsibility accounting* (also called profitability accounting and activity accounting), which is a system of collecting and reporting revenue and cost information by responsibility centers.

Responsibility accounting:

- facilitates the delegation of decision making.
- promotes the concept of management by objectives, in which managers agree on a set of goals.
- helps use the management by exception tool.

The structure of a company's management control system should be tied closely to the company's responsibility centers. According to the responsibility concept, all tasks, duties, or objectives should be assigned to a specific individual in an organization and he or she should be held accountable for achieving the intended results. Any organizational chart comprises a hierarchical organization structure in which each unit is headed by a responsibility center manager.

As shown in **Figure 8.1**, the manager reporting to the director is responsible for specific objectives. For example, a marketing manager may be responsible for introducing a new program by October 30 at an estimated cost of $100,000 to generate 150,000 units and $4 million in sales revenue. When a manager *accepts*

FIGURE 8.1   Responsibility and Accountability Process

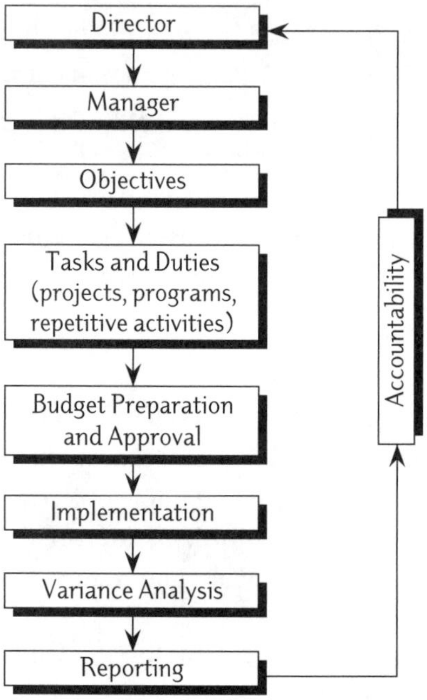

```
        Director ◄─────────┐
           │               │
        Manager            │
           │               │
       Objectives          │
           │               │
     Tasks and Duties      │
    (projects, programs,   │
    repetitive activities) │
           │          Accountability
   Budget Preparation      │
     and Approval          │
           │               │
     Implementation        │
           │               │
    Variance Analysis      │
           │               │
       Reporting ──────────┘
```

---

the funds to launch a program, that person is *accountable* for performing the tasks and for realizing the objectives. Here, the manager is responsible for reporting to his or her superior (the director) about the attainment of the objective, the realization of the plans, and the manner in which the resources were used to realize the objective.

Responsibility centers help to establish effective managerial controls which help to measure organizational units in terms of:

- Costs or expenses (on-going operating costs or capital costs).
- Outputs (units produced or revenues).
- Inputs (resources consumed to produce the outputs).
- Efficiency (relationship between the outputs and the resources used to produce them).
- Effectiveness (degree of success in attaining the objectives).
- Ratios to gauge the operational and financial performance.

Responsibility centers can be grouped under four categories: revenue centers, cost centers, profit centers, and investment centers.

The revenue center is measured in terms of sales revenue generated by what it sells. There is no need here to relate inputs to outputs. These responsibility centers are found in sales organizations responsible for product lines. For example, a sales manager may be responsible for a region, a district, or a territory. A revenue center usually has few costs (e.g., salaries, rent, lease). Revenue center managers are responsible for sales volume, selling price, and sales revenue. In service organizations, this manager would be responsible for billing rates, billable time, and cost per hour of employee time.

The cost center, also called an expense center, measures an organizational unit's resource inputs—that is, the costs used to make a product or to provide a service. It is called "cost" because the responsibility center manager's performance is measured in terms of the funds spent to make a product or provide a service. This type of unit is usually the smallest segment of activity for which costs are spent. These managers have no control over sales or marketing functions. It is difficult to measure profit performance for cost centers because of the problem of allocating revenue to these units.

This type of performance-measurement system is concerned only with *direct costs* and meeting *production budgets* and quotas. Under the cost center, the manager is measured in terms of standard (budgeted) costs to actual costs. Variances are analyzed and corrective measures are implemented (if necessary) in order to make the units more efficient. Activities often associated with cost centers are departments such as accounting, MIS, maintenance units in a manufacturing company, legal services, human resources, and public relations.

Non-profit organizations such as hospitals, schools, universities, and government agencies are often structured on the basis of cost centers. Although cost centers are usually small, they can be large if the managers are responsible for the administrative activities of an entire plant.

There are two categories of cost centers. The first is the *engineered-cost center* or standard-cost center, where it is possible to make a rough estimate of the expenses that a center will incur in order to provide a specific service. For example, the average cost for testing samples in a laboratory may be established at $17.45, while the annual per-square-foot maintenance and cleaning costs of a building may be $5.85.

In other cases, it is not possible to make even a rough estimate of the resources required to produce a service. Here, inputs cannot be related to outputs scientifically, and the operating efficiencies cannot be measured quantitatively. These expense centers are referred to as *discretionary cost centers*.

The profit center combines both revenues (outputs) and expenses (inputs). When expenses are deducted from revenues, we obtain a standard called *profit* that can also be measured in terms of contribution margin, gross margin, controllable profit, and incremental profit. For profit centers, both the inputs and the outputs can be measured in dollar terms. These centers sell services or goods to customers (this may represent the major portion of a center's revenue) or internally, to other units within a company. Examples of profit centers are auto repair centers in a department store and an appliance department in a retail store. An important advantage of a profit center is that it enhances the delegation of authority and encourages managers to make more enlightened decisions.

The investment center is identical to the profit center except that investments are considered when measuring performance. Here, profits are compared to investments, and this relationship is an overall economic goal called *return on investment* (ROI). Here, management is not only interested in looking at profit levels (outputs), but also at comparing it to investments (inputs). Investment centers are widely used in large decentralized organizations.

Budgeting Process in Terms of Planning as a Whole

Creating a budget is not the same as creating a plan. A budget is a component of a plan; therefore, the plan must be created first. Strategic and operational objectives must be established, along with strategic plans to accomplish them; then, priorities must be set.

Figure 8.2 shows how planning and budgeting are linked to one another. The process is as follows. Top-level managers analyze the company's (1) external environment in terms of opportunities and threats and (2) existing resources (financial, human, materials) in terms of strengths and weaknesses. A document is prepared and subsequently reviewed by the management committee (corporate review, which is step 1 of the corporate-level responsibility). Simultaneously, the responsibility centers (or divisions) review past and current operating performances (step A of the division responsibility) and develop the division and sales budget (step B). These plans are reviewed and tested against the planning assumptions (steps 2 and C). If the division plans show compatibility, the next steps involve the development of the corporate strategies to assess the impact the plans may have on existing operations. The strategic plans, division plans, and sales budget are reviewed by the management committee (steps 4 and 5). If the strategies, division plans, and budgets are approved, the responsibility center managers are given the go-ahead (step 6). The divisions then prepare the variable and overhead budgets (step D). All budgets are then consolidated into a master budget and financial plan (step E), which are reviewed by the management committee (step 7). The information contained in these plans is used as input for the following year's planning and budgeting cycle (step 8). The plans are implemented and results are reviewed for monitoring purposes and for making changes (if necessary) to the plans and budgets (step F).

Companies do not necessarily follow these steps in the order presented, but they usually go through each one. If one step is missed, the appropriate amount of budget dollars may fail to be allocated to the correct responsibility centers, priorities, and plans.

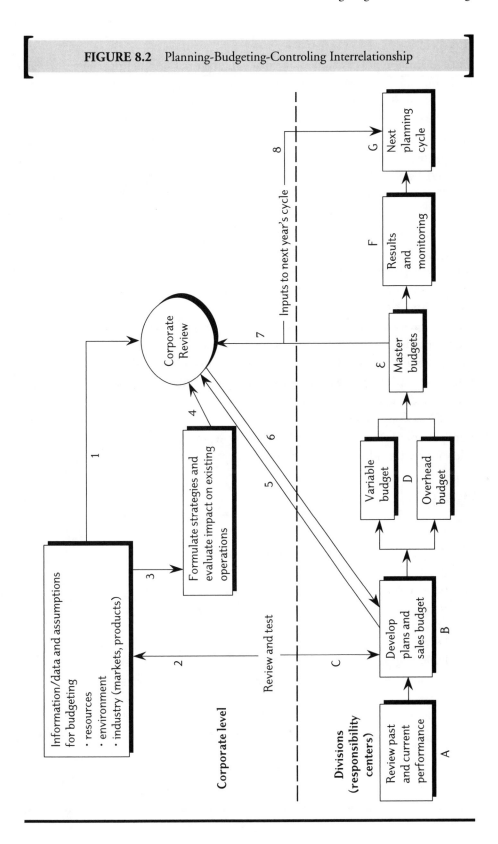

FIGURE 8.2 Planning-Budgeting-Controling Interrelationship

Types of Budgets

Since different types of decisions are made in organizations, managers use different budgeting methodologies. **Table 8.1** shows the different types of budgets prepared by organizations and the reasons why they are prepared.

These budgets can be grouped under four headings: (1) operating budgets, (2) complementary budgets, (3) comprehensive budgets, and (4) capital budgets. Let's examine the meaning of each of these budgets.

Operating Budgets. As shown in **Figure 8.3**, three types of budgets are used to formulate a *master budget* or projected income statement. These are the sales budgets, manufacturing budgets, and staff or overhead budgets. At the start of a budget year, the master budget serves as a plan or standard. At the end, it is used as a control device to help managers gauge their performance against plans. Today, with the help of spreadsheets and customized software packages, budgeting can be used as an effective tool for evaluating "what-if" scenarios through sensitivity analysis and simulations. By incorporating different assumptions in the master budget, managers can quickly find the best courses of action to follow to optimize their financial performance. Among the variety of budgets used in organizations, the sales budget is used by marketing departments, the flexible or variable budget is used by manufacturing departments, and incremental or zero-based budgeting is used by indirect or overhead units.

Sales budgets are prepared by the sales organization and are critical because they provide the basis for formulating other segments of the master budget. The sales budget includes the number of units expected to be sold and the unit selling

TABLE 8.1 Types of Budgets and Their Purposes

	Type of Budget	Purpose
1.	Manufacturing budget (operations budget)	Production requirement (materials, labor, energy, etc.)
2.	Marketing budget	Sales and advertising plans
3.	Branch, division, or regional budget	Responsibility centers
4.	Product budget	ROI on specific products
5.	Executive staff budget	Specialized budget (compensation and personnel requirements)
6.	Cash budget	To meet current obligations and obtain line of credit
7.	R & D budget	Strategies upon which future sales and revenue depend
8.	Capital expenditure budget	New plans, expansions, modernizations, R & D
9.	Pro-forma income statement	Profit forecast
10.	Pro-forma balance sheet	Financial structure forecast

FIGURE 8.3 Pro-Forma Profit Plan (Master Budget)

Sales	$1,000,000 }	Sales budgets
Less:		
Manufacturing expenses: variable and direct expenses such as labor and materials	600,000 }	Flexible budgets
Contribution margin	400,000	
Fixed expenses such as depreciation, insurance, and plant maintenance	100,000 }	Absorption costing
Profit margin on manufacturing operations	300,000	
Overhead expenses: Indirect and overhead expenses such as service organizations, support functions, projects, and overhead units for:		
(1) operating units (tooling, quality control, scheduling)	50,000	Incremental budgeting or
(2) corporate units (finance, human resources, engineering)	100,000	zero-based budgeting
Total overhead expenses	150,000	
Profit	$ 150,000	

---

price which translates into the sales revenue forecast. The sales budget is often broken down on a quarterly or monthly basis.

Flexible or variable budgets are used by plant or production departments where costs of production (standard costs) are used as *benchmarks* for comparing actual results to identify price and quantity variances. The intent here is not to only verify if a production unit is living within its budget, but more important, whether it is operating within pre-determined engineered standards.

Other costs, such as utilities, depreciation, or insurance, are fixed. They are, however, chargeable, or absorbed by individual products or divisions. Therefore, to determine net margin on manufacturing for each product line, these fixed costs are included in appropriate units through a variable-costing mechanism. For example, under the absorption costing mechanism, if a plant produces six different products (or services) and incurs a $50,000 overhead expense such as insurance, utilities, and general maintenance, this amount will be absorbed (or charged) by each product, depending on the numbers of units produced or the amount of time it takes for each product to be manufactured. The accounting system used to allocate overhead costs will be discussed in the next section of this chapter called "Cost Accounting."

In *incremental budgeting*, or traditional budgeting, projected new expenses for the coming year are added to the previous year's total expenses and are expressed as percentages of the previous year's total. Such a budget might look like this:

		% Increase
Last year's expenses	$350,000	
Inflation	7,000	2.0%
New activities	10,500	3.0%
Increase due to volume	14,000	4.0%
Next year's budget	$381,500	9.0%

The incremental budgeting approach has the following flaws:

♦ It is difficult to relate the budget to specific objectives and plans.

♦ Past activities may be approved without being put to the test and really justified.

♦ Corporate priorities may get lost in the shuffle.

♦ The previous year's figures could have been inflated by one-time special expenses.

Zero-based budgets (similar to activity-based budgets) are based on the premise that every budget dollar requires justification. Unlike the traditional budgeting approach in which expenditures of the previous years are automatically incorporated into the new budget proposal and only increments are scrutinized and subjected to debate, zero-based budgeting places all dollars, including last year's authorized expenditures and new requests, on an *equal footing*. It assumes that a responsibility center manager has had no previous expenditures. It is much like the reengineering process, in which managers ask the question "If we were recreating this organizational unit or company today given what we know and given current technology, what would it look like?"

In the zero-based budgeting process, responsibility center managers prepare budget proposals called *decision packages*. These budget proposals are subsequently ranked against each other to compete for scarce corporate resources. Zero-based budgeting is a priority form of budgeting process in which all budget proposals are ranked in order of importance. It is an effective tool used to analyze programs, proposals, or projects for the purpose of optimizing the use of a company's resources.

Zero-based budgeting focuses on input-output relationships. It is a process that can be used by overhead organizational units such as in purchasing, marketing, administration, engineering, human resources, legal services, and operations research.

The three steps involved in zero-based budgeting are:

1. Identifying the *decision units* (responsibility centers) in terms of their mission, activities, outputs, and measurement indicators.

2. Preparing the *decision packages* (budget proposals) that contain a description of the objectives, activities, programs, projects, outputs, efficiency and effectiveness standards, resource requirements (person-years, physical, budgets), risk, and time requirements.

3. Ranking the decision packages based on corporate priorities and strategies.

Complementary Budgets. **Complementary budgets** are the offspring of operating budgets and present operating budget data differently. They too can be classified into separate groups: product budgets, program budgets, item-of-expenditure budgets, and cash budgets.

Product budgets are used by marketing organizations to identify the profit performance of different products. For example, the budgets for three products may be prepared in the following way:

| | **Products** | | |
	A	B	C
Sales revenue	$500,000	$770,000	$1,300,000
Cost of goods sold	250,000	300,000	600,000
Gross margin	250,000	470,000	700,000
Marketing budget			
Distribution	50,000	75,000	100,000
Advertising	25,000	40,000	70,000
Salaries and commissions	100,000	150,000	250,000
After-sales service	50,000	40,000	100,000
Total marketing budget	225,000	305,000	520,000
Net product margin	$ 25,000	$165,000	$ 180,000

From this budget, it is possible to find out how much money will be spent by each department and on each product. This budget therefore gives an idea of the profitability level of each product. A business may also calculate the return on investment of each product by identifying, for each, the capital investments and the profit level (after allocating the company's overhead).

Program budgets are used mostly by nonprofit organizations, including federal, state, and municipal governments. Program budgeting has been called the planning-programming-budgeting system (PPBS). Five basic steps are involved in this budgeting process:

♦ The objectives of the major activities or programs are identified.

♦ The benefits (or results) to be generated by each activity or program are analyzed.

♦ The initial outlay and the future costs for each program are estimated.

♦ The alternatives are examined.

♦ The budget is prepared on the basis of the first four steps.

Item-of-expenditure budgets are the most popular format of budget preparation. Here, resources are classified in an entirely different way. For example, expenses might break down into salaries, supplies, equipment, travel, and utilities. A typical item-of-expenditure budget follows:

Items	Amounts
Salaries and wages	$200,000
Transportation and communication	25,000
Information	12,550
Professional services	35,500
Maintenance	10,000
Purchases, repairs and upkeep	5,000
Utilities, materials, and supplies	32,000
Other expenditures	20,000
Total	$340,050

Cash budgets are used for cash planning and control. They are also used for negotiating a line of credit with commercial banks. These budgets trace, on a monthly basis, the funds that will be (1) available and (2) required prior to their occurrence. In short, cash budgets ensure adequate monthly cash balances and avoid unnecessary idle cash and possible cash shortages. The cash budget is usually broken down into four sections:

1. The cash receipt section
2. The cash disbursement section
3. The cash surplus or deficit section
4. The financing section

The cash budget is prepared in two steps as shown in **Table 8.2**. The first step requires that all future receipts from cash sales and collections are identified for each month. The second step requires that all cash disbursements for individual expense items be pinpointed. The difference between the receipts and the disbursements gives either a net cash gain or loss.

Several departments must participate in the preparation of the cash budget, and it requires a certain degree of judgment. For example, the sales department provides the sales revenue figures, while the credit manager provides a breakdown of the approximate percentage of sales revenue that will be made on a cash basis, on credit, or paid within 30, 60, or 90 days. Various departmental heads also provide information on operating expenses.

The financial officer then determines the amount of cash that should be:

1. Kept in the bank at all times (cash at start of month).
2. Invested in short-term securities (surplus cash).
3. Required from the bank in the form of a line of credit (outstanding loans).

The cash budget is a tool that allows for deliberate planning for the efficient acquisition of funds and for short-term investments.

Comprehensive Budgets. When the controller has received all revenue forecasts and budgets from the operating managers, the accountants consolidate and

TABLE 8.2 The Cash Budget

	January	February	March	April	May	June	July
Sales	$ 225,000	$ 285,000	$ 290,000	$ 300,000	$ 400,000	$ 500,000	$600,000
Collections							
Cash (10%)	22,500	28,500	29,000	30,000	40,000	50,000	60,000
Current month (40%)	80,000	90,000	114,000	116,000	120,000	160,000	200,000
Last month (50%)	142,500	100,000	112,500	142,500	145,000	150,000	200,000
Total collections	245,000	218,500	255,500	288,500	305,000	360,000	460,000
Cost of goods sold	115,000	125,000	100,000	150,000	200,000	250,000	300,000
Payments							
Cash (30%)	34,500	37,500	30,000	45,000	60,000	75,000	90,000
30 days (70%)	70,000	80,500	87,500	70,000	105,000	140,000	175,000
Total payments	104,500	118,000	117,500	115,000	165,000	215,000	265,000
Collections	245,000	218,500	255,500	288,500	305,000	360,000	460,000
Payments	104,500	118,000	117,500	115,000	165,000	215,000	265,000
Sales and							
administration	52,300	50,300	50,060	50,500	38,000	56,000	55,000
Disbursements	108,000	82,000	111,500	85,860	88,000	84,000	71,000
Total expenses	264,800	250,300	279,060	251,360	291,000	355,000	391,000
Gain(loss)/month	(19,800)	(31,800)	(23,560)	$37,140	14,000	5,000	69,000
Gain(loss)/cumulative	(67,600)	(99,400)	(122,960)	(85,820)	(71,820)	(66,820)	2,180
Beginning bank balance	$ 27,200	$ 7,400	$ (24,400)	$ (47,960)	$ (10,820)	$ 3,180	$ 8,180
Receipts	245,000	218,500	255,500	288,500	305,000	360,000	460,000
Expenses	264,800	250,300	279,060	251,360	291,000	355,000	391,000
Ending bank balance	$ 7,400	$ (24,400)	$ (47,960)	$ (10,820)	$ 3,180	$ 8,180	$ 77,180

prepare the pro-forma financial statements. The various projected financial statements will be discussed later in this chapter under the heading "Financial Planning."

Capital Budgets. **Capital budgets** reveal how much is required to invest in capital assets. This budget breaks down the capital assets by major category, how much funding is needed and when it is required, the location of the assets, and reasons for spending. These budgets include investments such as cost reduction programs or research and development projects, expansion of a manufacturing operation, replacement of obsolete equipment, installation of computer equipment, construction of a warehouse, or even the purchase of an on-going business. Capital projects or capital assets generate benefits (returns, profits, savings) over an extended number of years. Projects that are included in capital budgets are critical since they usually require a significant amount of financial resources. The capital budgeting process and the evaluation methods were examined in Chapter 7.

Rules for Sound Budgeting

Table 8.3 summarizes the most important rules to follow when preparing budgets, especially operating budgets. The first five rules are prerequisites for effective budgeting, and violation of any of them can easily jeopardize the entire budgeting process. Ignoring the remaining five rules may not necessarily make budgeting a pointless exercise, but applying them makes decision-making, communication, and coordination more meaningful.

How to Make the Budgeting Exercise Effective

If a new or revised budgeting process is to be implemented in an organization, senior management should ask the following questions if they want the system to be effective and meaningful.

*   What should budgeting do for this organization?
*   What type of budgets and budgeting process should we have?
*   How much of a new budgeting system can the organization absorb during the first year of implementation? During the second year? (It may take years to get managers technically and mentally involved in a new planning and budgeting system.)
*   How should the information flow? How should our various organizational units communicate?
*   What authority should be delegated to the various levels of the organization? Where should decisions be made?
*   How much time and money are we prepared to spend to get the budgeting system off to a good start?
*   Who should be in charge of implementing the new planning and budgeting program?

When these questions have been answered and top-level managers are committed to making budgeting work within the context of the overall planning framework, the next steps are: (a) to design the new planning and budgeting system, (b) to fix responsibilities, and (c) then to implement the program.

Design a Permanent Budget Program. Budgeting should be regarded as a permanent process. If there are difficulties with a new budgeting system during the initial years, it should not be completely abandoned. Too many changes confuse people, so it is better to meet new organizational needs by making gradual adjustments.

Fix Responsibilities. Usually a firm's planning group or controller is responsible for designing and coordinating the budget. But it is not, and should not be, the controller's responsibility to prepare the operating managers' budgets. These people should be responsible for preparing their own budgets for funds and fully

TABLE 8.3   Ten Rules for Sound Budgeting

Rule 1: Pinpoint authority
Make sure that reporting responsibilities are clear and managerial authority is well defined.

Rule 2: Integrate all planning activities
To be effective, budgeting must be linked in a systematic way to other planning activities, such as setting objectives, identifying corporate priorities and strategies, and establishing guidelines and management objectives.

Rule 3: Insist on sufficient and accurate information
Information is essential to decision-making, the prime purpose of budgeting. All budget aspects, from cost-benefit analyses to the establishment of performance standards, depend upon the availability of current and accurate data.

Rule 4: Encourage participation
Essentially, accountability is measuring achievement against objectives. Participation in goal-setting encourages enthusiastic efforts. Few people like to be held accountable for hitting or missing someone else's targets.

Rule 5: Link budgeting to monitoring
Budgeting is meaningless if it is not linked to monitoring. What is the point of spending endless hours formulating plans and budgets, if management does not follow up by comparing actual performance with standards?

Rule 6: Tailor budgeting to the organization's needs
How information is presented, consolidated, and reviewed is a highly individualized matter. A system that works well for one organization will not necessarily produce the same results for another. Because management style, information needs, and corporate structures differ, each must create a budgeting system that meets its own special requirements.

Rule 7: Communicate budget guidelines
To ensure economy of time and effort, remove confusion in an organization, and prevent the budgeting system from faltering, it is essential to establish and communicate premises, guidelines, and assumptions.

Rule 8: Relate costs to benefits
It is essential to appraise every unit in terms of its contribution to the organization, the benefits expected from the services it provides, and the funds it needs to perform its tasks.

Rule 9: Establish standards for all units
One reason for preparing budgets is to make sure resources are spent efficiently and effectively. To determine this, it is important to establish performance standards. Although it may be easy to establish performance standards at the production level, it is harder with overhead units (e.g., administration, research groups, or accounting operations). Nevertheless, every effort should be made to set performance goals.

Rule 10: Be flexible
Managers should be able to respond easily to changing circumstances. On the manufacturing side, budget levels change with the level of production; managers responsible for production operations will clearly not be limited to their budget ceilings if sales levels are exceeded by 10 or 20%. They will respond to marketing needs. With overhead units, however, because of the absence of engineering standards, budgets often become permanently fixed. Yet it is only common sense that, during the operating year, managers responsible for overhead units should be allowed to increase or reduce their activities, and in turn their budgets to meet new requests or priorities.

comply with all guidelines and procedures. It may take a fair amount of time for some managers to accept these responsibilities and to become familiar with the system, but in the long run their participation will have favorable effects on organizational productivity and morale.

Implementation. Once the budgeting procedures have been carefully thought out and budgeting responsibilities are understood by all, the next step is implementation and monitoring.

How to Avoid Budgeting Pitfalls

Putting a budgeting system in operation is one thing; maintaining it as a purposeful management instrument is another. If these four rules are followed, many budgeting problems can be avoided.

Keep the paperwork to a reasonable level. If managers get entangled in procedures and waste their time filling out pointless reports and compiling endless columns of numbers, the results will be a budgeting system that is being served by managers rather than helping them make better decisions.

Keep budgeting subservient to objective setting. Budgeting is not an end in itself. It is a tool that helps managers determine how best they should deploy their resources to achieve the organization's objectives and priorities.

Do not take past activities for granted. Since objectives and priorities change from year to year, the budgeting exercise should be flexible enough to adapt to current priorities and demands, regardless of the way things were done in the past. Each year, when managers prepare their budgets, they should justify their requests and outline how they are going to spend the budgeted funds in order to realize their objectives and implement their plans.

Make budgeting a top-management practice. Budgeting is the responsibility of every manager in an organization, and all (including top-level managers) must be involved in the process. If top management abdicates its budgeting responsibility, this may have adverse effects on the organization. Lower-level managers may lose interest in budgeting, and it may be regarded as an exercise done by accountants. On the other hand, strong support by top-level managers promotes a view of budgeting as a meaningful process.

Cost Accounting

Cost accounting is a key component of accounting. Usually, large organizations have a staff of cost accountants that devote all of their time collecting and analyzing costs for the purpose of improving managerial decisions regarding future production and product strategies. Cost accounting is the process of collecting information for reporting the costs incurred related to the acquisition or production of products or services. It provides managers with information on the costs associated with buying or selling a product because the cost of each unit must be known to help determine how much it should be sold in order to make a reasonable profit. If a company is not able to sell a product at a price greater than its costs, it would be risky to be in that business.

The cost accounting process involves the allocation of all cost data related to manufacturing, purchasing, and selling. The process of properly documenting variable costs and equitably allocating fixed costs helps an organization to control its costs more thoroughly and to increase the transparency of managerial accountability. This next section deals with three headings: activity-based costing, cost accounting systems, and variance reporting.

Activity-Based Costing

One important branch of cost accounting that emerged during the late 1980s is **activity-based costing (ABC)**. This system focuses on the analysis of overhead costs to determine whether they can be directly related to specific activities.

Organizational activities usually include two types of costs: direct and indirect. **Direct costs** generally consist of direct labor and direct materials that are directly incurred when making a product or providing a service. These costs increase proportionately with volume of production. **Indirect costs** are those that cannot be identified clearly to a single product or service. Employees working on the production line are considered direct costs for that particular department while the cost for heating a building is regarded as an indirect cost and would have to be allocated among different departments in the building.

Activity-based costing helps managers avoid allocating indirect costs on an arbitrary basis. Activity-based costing is the process that allocates these indirect costs to products and services, not necessarily proportionately to the products that caused them to be incurred. The activity-based costing mechanism process provides managers with better information for costing and pricing decisions. The focus of activity-based costing is therefore to pinpoint the various *drivers* of the indirect costs to determine whether they can be related to an activity, a product, or a service that can be measured.

Cost Accounting Systems

To obtain the real benefits of activity-based costing, the system should provide information about costs to managers to help them make informed decisions. The two basic cost accounting systems that can help managers analyze costs are job order costing and process costing.

Basically, job order costing focuses on how much it costs to produce a specific product, service, contract, or order. Process costing, on the other hand, gathers information by production departments (or cost center) related to a continuous stream of identical products and costs are averaged out to all the production output that takes place in the department. For example, a textile plant may produce shirts with different colors and sizes. The cotton used in the production runs will be assigned to all shirts at the same cost per yard used. Irrespective of the size and color of the shirts produced, the selling price itself does not change the cost of the cotton even if the packaging and marketing costs vary with each category of shirts. The production of similar products manufactured on a continuous basis through a series of uniform production steps is known as *processes*. **Table 8.4** summarizes the basic differences between these two costing accounting systems.

Let's examine this in more detail by giving some examples of how job order costing and process costing work.

Job Order Costing. With a **job order costing** system, material, direct labor, and manufacturing overhead are charged to a specific job, shop, or customer order. These costs are directly related to producing a good or providing a service. For example, if a company produces a pen made up of plastic, ink, and felt, the costs of these materials would be identified and be part of the direct cost related to making the pens. This costing system is best suited in situations in which products are manufactured in identifiable lots or batches or when the products are manufactured to customer specifications. This system is widely used by custom manufacturers such as printing shops, aircraft manufacturers, and construction companies. In the service sector, organizations such as auto repair shops and professional services also use this job costing accounting system.

Here is a simplified example of how the costs of a particular job can be calculated.

Direct materials		Direct labor	
June 14	$2,000	Week of June 14	210 hours @ $11.40
June 22	1,800	Week of June 21	130 hours @ $9.30
June 28	2,400		
Total	$6,200		

Let's assume that the factory overhead rate is set at $5.50 per direct labor hour. With this information, here is how the costs and the selling price of a specific job including a mark-up of 35 percent of costs would be calculated:

TABLE 8.4 Job Order Costing Versus Process Costing

	Job Order Costing	Process Costing
Who uses it	Custom manufacturing	Processing industries
Nature of the work	Jobs, contracts, and orders	Physical units
Type of information recorded	Job cost sheets	Cost of production reports
The way costs are accumulated	By work orders	By departments
What the system calculates	◆ Inventory costing ◆ Profit and loss of each job	Unit cost used to calculate cost of goods completed and work-in-process

a.   *Cost of the job*

Direct materials		$ 6,200
Direct labor:		
210 hours @ $11.50	$2,415	
130 hours @ $9.30	1,209	3,624
Manufacturing overhead:		
340 hours @ $5.50		1,870
Cost of job		$11,694

b.   *Selling price of the job*

$11,694 + 35\% (\$11,694) = \$11,694.00 + \$ 4,092.90 = \underline{\$15,786.90}$

Process Costing. **Process costing** focuses on the accumulation of costs by departments or production processes. As shown in the following example, these costs are accumulated under two distinct categories: direct materials and conversion costs (sum of direct labor and departmental overhead). The unit cost is calculated by dividing the total costs charged to a responsibility center by the number of outputs generated by that particular responsibility center or department. Process costing is used by organizations where products or services are based on a continuous process and can be found in manufacturing organizations such as petroleum, oil refinery, textiles, chemicals, and food processing, and service-oriented institutions such as hospitals, schools and banks.

The following gives a simplified example of how the costs for a food processing plant would be calculated. There are two departments (X and Y) involved in the processing of the food during the month of September.

Actual production costs:

Direct materials used: 22,000 gallons costing $39,600

Direct labor and departmental overhead (conversion cost): $26,040

Actual production:

Completed and transferred to department Y: 10,000 gallons

Ending work-in-process: 12,000 gallons and 20% complete as to conversion

(a) The accounting process starts with the calculation of the flow of physical units (gallons) on which the work was done during the period (September). As shown, all inputs (gallons) must equal all outputs (gallons).

To be accounted for:

Added in September	22,000 gallons

Accounted for as follows:

Completed in September	10,000 gallons
In process, end of September	12,000
Total	22,000 gallons

(b) This next step in the cost accounting process involves the calculation of output in terms of *equivalent units*. The total amount of work done during the month is calculated in order to determine the unit cost of production. The partially finished units are measured on an "equivalent whole-unit" basis for process costing purposes. For example, if 200 units are 50 percent completed, this will be considered the equivalent of 100 completed units.

	Materials Gallons	Conversion Cost
Units completed	10,000	10,000
Ending working-in-process (12,000 gallons)		
100% of materials	12,000	
20% of conversion cost		2,400
Equivalent units produced	22,000	12,400

(c) This next step involves the identification of all costs assigned to the department during the period (in this case, September) and from this, the unit cost per equivalent unit is calculated. This is arrived at by dividing the total costs by the equivalent units of production during the period. The unit costs are then applied to work-in-process and finished goods units.

	Total Cost	Equivalent Production (gallons)	Unit Cost
Materials	$39,600	22,000	$1.80
Conversion cost	26,040	12,400	2.10
To be accounted for	$65,640		$3.90
Ending work-in-process			
Materials	$21,600	12,000	$1.80
Conversion cost	5,040	2,400	2.10
Total work-in-process	$26,640		
Completed and transferred	39,000	10,000	$3.90
Total accounted for	$65,640		

Variance Reporting

Variance analysis compares standards to actual performance. A *standard* is the predetermined cost of manufacturing, servicing, or marketing a product during a specific time period. It is based on current and projected future operating conditions and is dependent on quantitative and qualitative measurements. These standards may be based on engineering studies involved in time and motion studies. *Actual performance* is the actual cost experienced by a department for processing quantity of outputs during a period in question.

Organizations that have managers responsible for responsibility centers such as a division, a department, a program, a product, or a territory will find the variance analysis system useful for performance evaluation and making accountability more transparent. Variance analysis can be done on a daily, monthly, quarterly or yearly basis depending on the importance of highlighting problems quickly.

Under the variance analysis reporting environment, the responsibility center manager analyzes how much it will cost to produce a product (or provide a service) for every unit of output. This is subsequently compared to standard costs used as *benchmarks* and useful for gauging efficiencies. For example, if the standard cost to produce a widget is $6.37 and the actual cost is $6.68, the factors causing the *variation* will be identified in order to take the necessary remedial actions. The $0.31 difference between the actual costs and the standard costs is referred to as a *variance*. Variances are caused by three factors: materials, labor, and departmental overhead. Let's examine how each of these variances is calculated.

Material Variance. Actual material costs may vary from standard costs for two reasons: price and quantity. For instance, if a department forecasts an output of 30,000 units, the actual material cost compared to the standard would be calculated as follows:

Standard:	30,000 units @ $3.00	$90,000
Actual:	30,400 units @ $3.20	$97,280

Material Cost Variance

		In $ Amount	Variance
Quantity Variance			
Actual:	30,400 units @ standard price of $3.00	$91,200	
Standard:	30,000 units @ standard price of $3.00	90,000	
Variance (unfavorable)			$1,200
Price Variance			
Actual:	30,400 units @ actual price of $3.20	97,280	
Standard:	30,400 units @ standard price of $3.00	91,200	
Variance (unfavorable)			6,080
Total material variance (unfavorable)			$7,280

The actual costs of the material compared to the standard costs for making the units varied by $7,280. Total material used exceeded the standard by 400 units while the unit price exceeded standard by $0.20 per unit.

The mix making up the $7,280 variance shows what types of information should be reported to the appropriate responsibility center managers. The quantity variance will be brought to the attention of the processing manager while the price variance will be reported to the purchasing department.

Labor Variance. **Labor variance** is also made up of two components, time and rate. If the actual time taken to produce x number of units varies from the standard, this is referred to as *time variance*. If the actual salaries or wages paid to process a number of units vary from standard, this is referred to as *rate variance*. To illustrate, lets assume that an organization processes x number of units, the actual labor cost compared to the standard would be presented in the following way:

Standard:	10,000 hours @ $4.10	$41,000
Actual:	9,800 hours @ $4.21	41,258

The difference between the standard and actual is $258. Part of this difference is due to time variance and part is due to rate variance. The $258 variance can be explained in the following way:

Labor Cost Variance

		In $	
		Amount	Variance
Time			
Standard:	10,000 hours × standard rate @ $4.10	$41,000	
Actual:	9,800 hours × standard rate @ $4.10	40,180	
Variance (favorable)			$ 820
Rate			
Actual:	9,800 hours × actual rate of $4.21	$41,258	
Actual:	9,800 hours × standard rate of $4.10	40,180	
Variance (unfavorable)			1,078
Labor variance (unfavorable)			$ 258

Just like in the case of material variance, the labor variance would be reported to the appropriate responsibility managers.

Plant Overhead Variance. Plant overhead standard rate is calculated by dividing the expected plant overhead costs by the standard quantity of outputs. Included in these overhead costs are items such as purchases of indirect materials, indirect departmental wages, and maintenance. Such costs usually change with varying production output levels. Other costs including depreciation, taxes, and insurance are fixed and remain constant irrespective of the level of output.

In view of possible changes in total overhead costs as a result of varying output levels, it is preferable to prepare various budgets showing the costs incurred at varying production levels. It is most common to show the costs at production levels that vary above and below capacity. Here is how this departmental overhead budget would be presented.

Departmental Overhead Budget
In $

	% of capacity			
	80%	90%	100%	110%
Direct labor (hours)	8,000	9,000	10,000	11,000
Units (standard)	24,000	27,000	30,000	33,000

Budgeted Departmental Overhead

Variable costs

Utilities, power and heat	$ 5,040	$ 5,670	$ 6,300	$ 6,930
Indirect materials	2,480	2,790	3,100	3,410
Maintenance and repairs	2,000	2,250	2,500	2,750
Indirect plant wages	9,120	10,260	11,400	12,540
Total variable costs	$18,640	$20,970	$23,300	$25,630

Fixed costs

Departmental supervision	$ 3,250	$ 3,250	$ 3,250	$ 3,250
Depreciation				
Machinery	1,750	1,750	1,750	1,750
Equipment	800	800	800	800
Insurance and taxes	1,400	1,400	1,400	1,400
Total fixed costs	7,200	7,200	7,200	7,200
Total plant overhead	$25,840	$28,170	$30,500	$32,830

Variable cost:	($23,300 ÷ 10,000 hours)	=	$2.33
Fixed overhead:	($ 7,200 ÷ 10,000 hours)	=	0.72
Departmental overhead hourly rate:			$3.05

As shown, the standard departmental overhead hourly rate is $3.05 ($30,500 ÷ 10,000 hours). If the department's actual production is 27,000 units (90% of capacity), the variance would be calculated as follows:

Standard:	9,000 hours at $3.05		$27,450
Actual:	Variable departmental overhead	$23,300	
	Fixed departmental overhead	7,200	30,500
Variance (unfavorable)			$ 3,050

The $3,050 variance can be explained in the following way:

Departmental Overhead Variance
In $

Controllable costs		
Actual departmental overhead	$30,500	
Budgeted departmental overhead for standard units produced (90% of capacity)	28,170	
Variance (unfavorable)		$2,330
Volume		
Normal capacity hours	10,000	
Standard hours for actual units produced	9,000	
Normal capacity hours not used	1,000	
Fixed overhead rate	× 0.72	
Variance overhead (unfavorable)		720
Total departmental overhead variance (unfavorable)		$3,050

As shown, the controllable cost variance of $2,330 would be referred to as the departmental manager's responsibility.

Financial Planning

As shown in **Figure 8.4**, operating budgets are ultimately integrated into projected financial statements also known as **pro-forma financial statements**. The most important financial statements that managers, owners, lenders, and other interest groups examine to gauge the overall financial performance of a business are the income statement, the balance sheet, and the statement of cash flows.

Pro-Forma Income Statement

Table 8.5 presents Eastman Technologies Inc.'s pro-forma income statement. The statement shows the company's future sales revenue, costs, and profit performance.

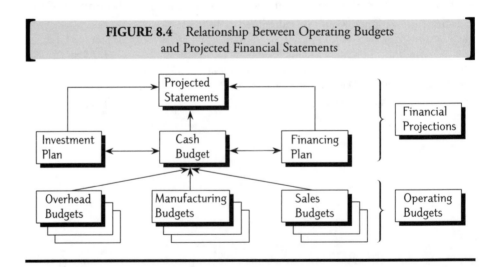

FIGURE 8.4   Relationship Between Operating Budgets and Projected Financial Statements

To examine the company's expected financial performance, managers can refer to the ratios that were examined in Chapter 3 and also use the common size statement analysis (see **Tables 3.3** and **3.4**) and horizontal analysis (see **Tables 3.5** and **3.6**). Eastman's 2000 year-end forecast and 2001 budget year operating performance are summarized below.

| | As % of sales | |
	2001 Estimated	2000 Budget
Sales	1.00	1.00
Cost of goods sold	0.67	0.76
Gross margin	0.33	0.24
Selling expenses	0.06	0.06
Administrative expenses	0.09	0.09
Income after taxes	0.09	0.04

TABLE 8.5   Pro-Forma Income Statement

Eastman Technologies Inc.
Income Statement for the Years Ended December 31

	2001	2000	Planning Assumptions
Net sales	$3,050,000	$2,500,000	(22% increase)
Cost of goods sold	2,050,000	1,900,000	(67% of sales from 76%)
Gross margin	1,000,000	600,000	(67% increase)
Operating expenses			
Selling expenses:			
Sales salaries	153,000	140,000	(5% of sales from 6%)
Advertising expenses	34,000	20,000	
Total selling expenses	187,000	160,000	
Administrative expenses:			
Office salaries	183,000	170,000	(6% of sales from 7%)
Rent	29,000	20,000	
Depreciation	48,000	40,000	
Total administration expenses	260,000	230,000	
Total operating expenses	447,000	390,000	(15% of sales from 16%)
Operating income	553,000	210,000	
Other income	23,000	20,000	
Other expenses (interest)	41,000	35,000	
	18,000	15,000	
Income before taxes	535,000	195,000	
Income taxes	267,500	97,500	
Income after taxes	**$267,500**	**$ 97,500**	(9% of sales from 4%)

The pro-forma income statement summarizes the various components of sales revenue and expense projections for a specific budgeting period. However, for controling purposes, the pro-forma income statement should be done on a quarterly or even monthly basis.

As shown in the table, there were significant improvements in the cost of goods sold, which has a favorable effect on the gross margin and income after taxes.

The horizontal analysis (increments between two consecutive income statements) shows the following:

	% Increase
Sales	22.0
Cost of goods sold	7.9
Gross margin	66.7
Selling expenses	5.9
Administrative expenses	13.0
Income after taxes	174.4

Table 8.6 shows Eastman's 2001 pro-forma statement of retained earnings. The company will pay $50,000 in dividends and retain $217,500 in the business. Retained earnings at the end of the year will be $472,500.

TABLE 8.6 Pro-Forma Statement of Retained Earnings

Eastman Technologies Inc.
Retained Earnings Statement
For the Year Ended December 31, 2001

Retained earnings (beginning balance)		$255,000
Earnings	$267,500	
Dividends	50,000	217,500
Retained earnings (ending balance)		$472,500

Pro-Forma Balance Sheet

A similar analysis can be done for the balance sheet. As shown in **Table 8.7**, Eastman Technologies Inc.'s pro-forma balance sheet presents the financial structure in terms of current assets, capital assets, current liabilities, long-term debt, and owners' equity, and how these elements are distributed during 2000 and 2001. As shown in the table, Eastman Technologies Inc.'s total assets increased by $280,000—that is, from $1,800,000 to $2,080,000.

The pro-forma balance sheet is formulated by starting with the balance sheet for the year just ended and adjusting it, using all activities that are expected to take place during the budgeting period. The more important reasons for preparing a pro-forma balance sheet are:

◆ To disclose some unfavorable financial conditions that management might want to avoid.

◆ To serve as a final check on the mathematical accuracy of all the other schedules.

◆ To help managers perform a variety of financial ratios.

◆ To highlight future resources and obligations.

To determine where these increments are registered, we have to examine the key elements of the assets such as accounts receivable, inventories, and capital

---

TABLE 8.7 Pro-Forma Balance Sheet

Eastman Technologies Inc.
Balance Sheets
December 31, 2000 and 2001

	2001	2000	
Assets			
Current Assets			
Cash	$ 46,000	$ 22,000	(Cash to sales to 1.5% from 0.9%)
Prepaid expenses	67,000	60,000	
Accounts receivable	325,000	300,000	(5 day improvement)
Inventory	230,000	218,000	(0.2 time improvement)
Total current assets	668,000	600,000	
Capital assets (at cost)	1,600,000	1,340,000	(see capital budget for details)
Accumulated depreciation	188,000	140,000	
Capital assets (net)	1,412,000	1,200,000	
Total Assets	$2,080,000	$1,800,000	
Liabilities			
Current liabilities			
Accounts payable	$ 205,000	$ 195,000	(10% of COGS)
Notes payable	140,000	150,000	
Accrued expenses	32,500	20,000	
Taxes payable	90,000	80,000	
Total current liabilities	467,500	445,000	
Long-term debt	840,000	800,000	
Common shares	300,000	300,000	(no change)
Retained earnings	472,500	255,000	(see income statement and statement of retained earnings for details)
Owners' equity	772,500	555,000	
Total liabilities and equity	$2,080,000	$1,800,000	

assets as a percentage of total assets. The vertical analysis of the key components of Eastman's balance sheet is as follows:

| | As % of Total Assets | |
	2001 Projected	2000 Budget
Current assets	0.32	0.33
Capital assets	0.68	0.67
Total assets	1.00	1.00
Current liabilities	0.23	0.25
Long-term debts	0.40	0.44
Total debt	0.63	0.69
Owners' equity	0.37	0.31
Total assets	1.00	1.00

As shown, there is little change in the ratio of total assets compared to capital assets. However, when looking at the mixture of the liability and equity accounts, debt is reduced from 69 percent, as a percentage of total liabilities and owners' equity, to 63 percent.

Pro-Forma Statement of Cash Flows

Table 8.8 presents Eastman's pro-forma statement of cash flows. Essentially, it shows how cash will be provided and used during 2001. As shown in the investing activities portion of the statement, $260,000 will be invested in capital assets. Operating activities will generate $294,000 and will be used to buy the assets and to pay the dividends to the shareholders.

Now that management has produced the operating budgets and the pro-forma financial statements, the next two key questions are:

- Is the company growing within its operating and financial capabilities?
- How healthy is the business? Will its financial health improve or deteriorate?

Managing Growth

Most people equate growth with success, and managers often see growth as something to be maximized. Their view is simple: If the company grows, the firm's market share and profits should also increase. However, growing too fast (if growth is not properly managed), may create problems. In some instances, growth outstrips a company's human, production, and financial resources. When that happens, the quality of decision making tends to deteriorate under constant pressure, product quality suffers, and financial reserves often disappear. The bottom line is this: If growth is not managed, a business can literally grow broke.

There is no question that there are limits to how fast a company should grow. Preoccupation with growth at any cost can overextend a company administratively and financially. Results can be lower profit, cash shortages, and, ironically, slower

[**TABLE 8.8** Pro-Forma Statement of Cash Flows]

Eastman Technologies Inc.
For the Year Ended December 31, 2001

Cash Flow from Operating Activities

Income after taxes	$ 267,500	
Add: Depreciation	48,000	
Increase in accounts payable	10,000	
Increase in accrued expenses	12,500	
Increase in taxes payable	10,000	
	348,000	
Deduct: Increase in prepaid expenses	(7,000)	
Increase in accounts receivable	(25,000)	
Increase in inventory	(12,000)	
Decrease in notes payable	(10,000)	
	(54,000)	
Cash provided by operating activities		$ 294,000

Cash Flow from Investing Activities

Purchase of capital assets	260,000	
Cash used by investing activities		(260,000)

Cash Flow from Financing Activities

Payment of dividend	(50,000)	
Long-term debt	40,000	
Cash used by financing activities		(10,000)

Cash Balance

Increase (decrease) in cash		24,000
Cash at beginning of year		22,000
Cash at end of year		$ 46,000

growth ultimately as managers pause to regroup and repair the damage. Some signs of trouble associated with growing too fast are substantial increases in receivables and inventories relative to sales, declining cash flow from operations, and escalating interest-bearing debt.

In order to understand growth management, we must first define a company's **sustainable growth rate**. It is defined as the maximum rate at which a company's sales can increase without depleting financial resources. Managers must therefore look at different options when they target the company's sustainable growth rate. In many instances, management should limit growth in order to conserve financial strength.

If a company wants to grow, it has several options:

- Increase its profit margin on sales.
- Reduce the payout of dividends in order to retain earnings.
- Sell new equity.
- Increase leverage (more debt versus equity).
- Increase the productivity of its assets.

It is possible to develop a sustainable growth equation that shows a company's optimum growth rate. The formula that can help determine the optimum growth rate is:

$$\text{Growth} = \frac{(M)\,(R)\,(1 + D/E)}{(A) - (M)\,(R)\,(1 + D/E)}$$

where:

M	=	Ratio of net income to sales
R	=	Ratio of reinvested income to income before dividends
D/E	=	Ratio of total liabilities to net worth
A	=	Ratio of assets to sales

Eastman's 2000 and 2001 sustainable growth rates are 10.1 percent and 40.5 percent respectively. The ratios used to arrive at these growth potentials are:

			2000	2001
M	=	Ratio of net income to sales	0.04	0.09
R	=	Ratio of reinvested income to income before dividends	0.51	0.81
D/E	=	Ratio of total liabilities to net worth	2.24	1.69
A	=	Ratio of assets to sales	0.72	0.68

The reason Eastman can grow faster in 2001 than in 2000 is that important favorable changes are expected. As shown, there is a significant change in the ratio of net income to sales. In 2000, the company had only $0.04 in profit for every dollar's worth of sales to invest in growth such as investments in capital assets or research and development. This ratio jumped to $0.09 in 2001.

The ratio of reinvested income to income before dividends also increased. In 2000, the company's ratio was only 0.51 (with income after taxes of $97,500 and payment of $47,500 in dividends), compared to 0.81 for 2001 (with profit after taxes of $267,500 and payment of only $50,000 in dividends). This means that the company will have more cash to reinvest in the business for growth purposes.

A similar improvement is taking place in the ratio of total liabilities to net worth. In 2000, 68 percent of the company's total assets were financed by debt which is expected to drop to 63 percent in 2001. The ratio of total liabilities to net worth will also improve from 2.24 to 1.69. This improved performance gives the company more flexibility to borrow in the future.

The fourth ratio used in the formula is the total amount of assets needed to support every dollar's worth of sales. As shown, in 2000, the company required $0.72 worth of assets to produce $1.00 in sales; in 2001, the company required only $0.68. This is another improvement.

Because it has shown improvements in these four ratios, the company will be able to improve its sustainable growth to 40.5 percent which compares favorably to the company's expected sales revenue growth in 2001 which is 22 percent. This means that the company is well within its organizational and financial capabilities.

The Financial Health Zone

Let's turn now to measuring Eastman's financial health. In 1962, Edward Altman developed a mathematical model to help financial analysts predict the financial performance of businesses. Altman utilized a combination of traditional ratios and a sophisticated statistical technique known as *discriminant analysis* to construct a financial model for assessing the likelihood that a firm would go bankrupt. The model combined five financial measures utilizing both reported accounting and stock/variables to arrive at an objective overall measure of corporate health called the *Z-score*. For example, if the five ratios give a Z-score of 3.0 or higher, the company is in a healthy financial position, or in a safe zone. If the score falls between 1.8 and 3.0, the company would be in the grey zone and could go either way. If the score is less than 1.8, the company would be in danger of bankruptcy.

Table 8.9 shows Altman's Z-score formula and Eastman's five financial ratios for the years 2000 and 2001. As shown, Eastman scored 2.34 in 2000 (grey zone) and 3.11 in 2001 (safe zone). This indicates that the company was able to take positive financial steps to make the company more viable. Here is a brief explanation for each of these ratios.

- Ratio (a): There was no change in the ratio of total assets to net working capital between the two accounting periods.
- Ratio (b): The relationship between total assets and retained earnings increased substantially in 2001 over 2000 (from 0.14 to 0.23). This change is a result of an 84 percent increase in the retained earnings account shown on the balance sheet. This reflects a strong profit performance ($0.09 income after taxes for every dollar's worth of sales in 2001 compared to $0.04 in 2000) with a small increase in dividend payments.
- Ratio (c): The ratio of total assets to earnings before interest and taxes also increased substantially. This reflects a strong profit performance in 2001 compared to 2000.
- Ratio (d): The debt-to-equity ratio also improved in 2001 (0.59 compared to 0.45).
- Ratio (e): The total assets to sales ratio also improved in 2001 (1.39 to 1.47).

TABLE 8.9   Altman's Z-Score

**Measuring the financial health zone of
Eastman Technologies Inc. for 2000 and 2001**

Safe zone	3.0 and over
Grey zone	1.8 to 3.0
Bankrupt zone	0 to 1.8

$$Z = 1.2(a) + 1.4(b) + 3.3(c) + 0.6(d) + 1.0(e)$$

		2000	2001
$a = \dfrac{\text{Working capital}}{\text{Total assets}}$		0.09	0.09
$b = \dfrac{\text{Retained earnings}}{\text{Total assets}}$		0.14	0.23
$c = \dfrac{\text{Earnings before interest and taxes}}{\text{Total assets}}$		0.12	0.26
$d = \dfrac{\text{Equity}}{\text{Total liabilities}}$		0.45	0.59
$e = \dfrac{\text{Sales}}{\text{Total assets}}$		1.39	1.47
Z-score		2.34	3.11

Controling

Controling is a function of the management process that closes the management loop. What is the point of planning and budgeting if managers are not informed of the results of their efforts? We sometimes hear people say "We have things under control;" that means that all activities involved in realizing a project are well coordinated. On the other hand, if someone says that an activity is "out of control," it means that it is at the mercy of events. Establishing strategic and operational control points is crucial to ensuring that objectives and plans are realized.

The Control System

As shown in **Figure 8.5**, establishing an effective control system involves six steps:

Step 1: Design the subsystem.
Step 2: Establish performance indicators.
Step 3: Determine performance standards.
Step 4: Measure performance.

Step 5: Analyze variations.

Step 6: Take corrective action to resolve unfavorable situations that may arise.

Design the Subsystem. The first step in establishing a control system is to determine the type of subsystem within the overall management system that would be most effective. The control subsystem should fit the culture of the organization and be one that will benefit managers and employees at all levels. Managers in bureaucratic organizations may prefer a bureaucratic control system, while democratic organizations may opt for decentralized controls. Managers should also ask questions such as: How do we want the system to help us? Should the control system be more future-oriented (solve the problem before it appears) or reactive (give us information after an event takes place)? Or should we have both systems?

The system should be designed on the basis of what specific inputs (quantity and quality) are required by managers and when they need the information for analyzing their activities and making decisions. Managers will also prefer that the information output be presented in a certain way (e.g., reports or computer printouts).

Establish Performance Indicators. As shown in **Figure 8.5**, the entire control process is closely linked to the planning activity. Establishing operational and financial objectives during the planning phase allows managers to figure out the type of indicators they should use for measuring accomplishments. The control process allows managers to determine how organizational units should be measured. Here, we are talking about two elements. First, determine the key elements or characteristics of the organizational units in terms of costs and benefits. Second,

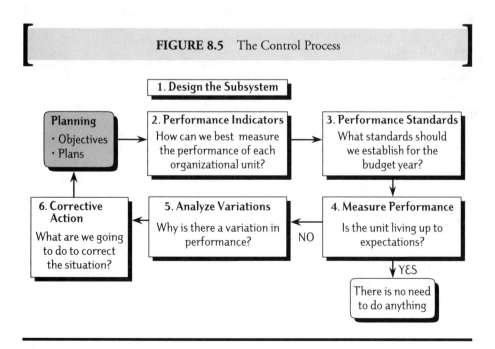

FIGURE 8.5 The Control Process

determine which of these elements need to be measured. We are referring here to the principle of selectivity (also known as Pareto's Law), which states that often only a small number of vital activities account for the largest number of outputs. If the appropriate indicators are not identified, it may be difficult for managers to measure the real organizational performance. For example, return on investment is an appropriate indicator for assessing the global company performance; cost per unit is suitable for gauging manufacturing operations; and share of market is excellent for measuring marketing performance. **Table 8.10** gives examples of performance indicators (operating and financial) suitable for gauging objectives for different organizational units.

Indicators can also be used to measure the performance of specific activities within a department such as marketing and production, or units such as sales and quality control. Indicators can also help to measure employee performance.

Determine Performance Standards. Once performance indicators are selected, the next step is to pinpoint the standards applicable for a particular time period (day, week, month, or year). These standards are established during the planning phase and serve as benchmarks for comparing results. Standards can fall under four broad categories: time, output, cost, and quality.

Time standards determine the length of time required to perform a specific task. For example, the length of time it takes to serve a customer at a bank or the length of time between a customer complaint and the response to it determines the quality of service offered and, thus, customer satisfaction.

TABLE 8.10   Performance Indicators and Standards

Organizational Units	Performance Indicators	Standards	Performance	Variations
Company-wide	Return on investment (%)	17.5	17.7	0.2
Departments				
◆ Marketing	Share of market (%)	12.7	12.4	(0.3)
◆ Production	Cost per unit ($)	2.07	2.05	0.02
Units				
◆ Sales	Number of units sold	200,000	210,000	10,000
◆ Quality control	Number of tests per day per technician	6	6	—
Employees				
◆ Marketing	Number of customers visited per day per sales representative	3	2.5	(0.5)
◆ Production	Number of units produced per hour	35	38	3

Output standards measure the number of units that should be produced by individuals or groups. Managers of ticket agents for an airline company know the number of calls they can respond to on an hourly basis or the number of minutes it takes on average to provide information to their clients. For a telephone company, management knows the number of service calls technicians can respond to each day. At a university, student advisors know how many students they can meet daily.

Cost standards measure the resources required to produce goods or services. Holiday Inns or Westin Hotels know how much it costs to clean their rooms each day; Bic knows how much it costs to make a pen, and Gillette knows how much it costs to produce a can of shaving foam.

Quality standards pinpoint the level of quality needed to meet customer expectations. The "total quality management" concept focuses on quality standards that signal whether customers are receiving the expected quality products or services. For example, the services expected by guests at Holiday Inns or Journey's End may be different from those expected from the Westin Hotels or Four Seasons, and the customer expectations for a Rolex watch would be different than for a Timex. Although these organizations sell products of different qualities, the critical point is to gauge the quality standards anticipated by the customers and to carefully respond to their needs. **Table 8.10** also gives examples of performance standards.

Measure Performance. Performance could be measured daily, weekly, monthly, or annually. To measure performance, managers need information that can be obtained from four sources: written reports, computer printouts, oral presentations, and personal observations.

Written reports are used widely, particularly in large organizations. They are costly because of the time it takes to write the reports and for others to read them. To be effective tools, written reports should be brief (one page), in outline rather than narrative form, and structured to highlight the most critical information. *Computer printouts* can quickly provide all types of operating and financial information. Today, spreadsheet programs allow managers to enter data which the computer calculates and presents numerically or graphically. From these printouts, managers can readily extract specific information. *Oral presentations* are effective since there is an immediate exchange of ideas during staff meetings between subordinates and supervisors. Individuals communicating information at such meetings can use simple visual displays (e.g., simple line graphs, milestone charts) which are considered effective media for explaining performance and remedial action plans. To be effective, however, such meetings should be planned and selective reports should be established prior to the meeting.

To compare results to standards, managers must analyze information. **Table 8.10** also shows how results are compared to standards. For example, the company established a target of 17.5 percent return on investment and achieved 17.7 percent, a superior performance.

Analyze Variations. Variations between standards and results must be analyzed to determine the reasons for "off-performance" situations. Unfavorable variations do not necessarily mean mediocre performance. For example, is $10,000 over budget in manufacturing expenses unfavorable? A close analysis may reveal that the manufacturing department produced more units to meet marketing needs, and thus increased corporate profits. If the advertising department spent $100,000 less than was budgeted, does this represent a favorable situation? Perhaps at first glance it may. However, after scrutiny, the manager may find that corporate revenues are $800,000 less than expected and profits $125,000 less than budgeted due to not having spent the $100,000 advertising budget. Overall, the company profit performance is down by $125,000.

Let's take another example to show the importance of properly analyzing variations. The credit department may have exceeded its salary budget by $14,000, but if credit clerks worked overtime to recover the accounts receivable more rapidly and succeeded in reducing the average collection period from 50 to 45 days, the benefits could have exceeded the $14,000 overtime cost.

It is not enough just to look at the column showing variations and judge quickly the performance of an organizational unit. Managers should investigate the reasons for the variations and determine whether they have favorable or unfavorable effects on the overall company performance.

Take Corrective Action. When variations have been identified and the exact causes are known, managers then take the necessary steps to solve the problems. Managers have three options. First, there is the status quo. If a manager is on target or the variation is only minimal, he or she may decide not to do anything. Second, a manager may wish to correct a situation. This is a likely option if the manager sees serious operating problems and wants to bring operations back in line. Third, the manager may want to change the standard. This may be appropriate if the original standard was set too high or if uncontrollable circumstances have changed the environment dramatically.

Types of Controls

Most control systems are one of three types: preventive controls, screening controls, or feedback controls (see **Figure 8.6**).

Preventive Controls. **Preventive controls** (also known as feedforward controls, preliminary controls, steering controls, or proactive controls) take place when one wants to guide actions toward intended results. A recipe for making a cake is a classic example. The recipe will guide the cook to help him or her realize the intended results (the cake). This control system emphasizes the future; a manager knows what she or he wants, and puts in place the necessary mechanism to ensure that the intended results are achieved. Let's take two business situations to illustrate how preventive controls work. Before hiring bank tellers, the human resources department will identify the required qualifications to ensure that the manager hires efficient and effective tellers, and maintains the employee turnover at a low level. The job description *prevents* staffing officers from hiring unsuitable job applicants; that is why this system is called preventive control. Similarly, in a manufacturing operation that makes products such as soft drinks, coffee, pens, chocolate bars, or hamburgers, management will specify the quality level and the ingredients *before* production actually begins.

Screening Controls. **Screening controls**, also known as concurrent controls, take place during the implementation phase or as the process takes place. Some screening controls take the "yes–no" form. This means that the process can either be continued or stopped in order to take corrective actions. For example, when buying a house, a potential homeowner will say yes or no during each step of the purchase process (visit the house, negotiate the price or other terms, agree with the terms of the mortgage loan) before signing the final purchase agreement.

Screening controls can also be done by using what is called the "steering" mechanism. This means that as the process evolves, the degree of deviation is gradually brought back into line without actually stopping the process. In an automobile manufacturing plant, for example, control points are established at every critical step of the assembly line. As a car moves along the line, periodic control checks are executed to see that each job is performed according to standard before the car moves to subsequent assembly points. Steering controls reduce unnecessary manufacturing costs (e.g., having to remove the dashboard if the electrical wiring system is improperly installed).

FIGURE 8.6   Types of Control Systems

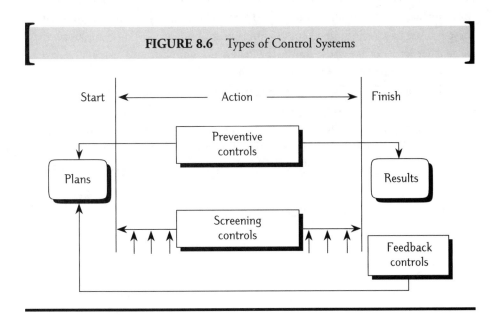

Feedback Controls. **Feedback controls**, also known as corrective controls or post performance controls, are like thermostats. They place emphasis on past performance and the manager takes corrective action only when comparisons are made and the variations detected. Managers are reacting to a given situation; for example, if your bank statement shows an overdraft, you will immediately take action by rushing to the bank to make a deposit. In organizations, daily, weekly, and monthly reports work the same way: They inform managers about performance so they can take the necessary actions to correct unfavorable situations. Typical post action controls are report cards, budget reports, and audit reports.

The objective of these three types of control systems is the same—to assist managers to gauge performance and take corrective action to reach stated objectives.

Summary

Budgeting is a vital element of the management planning and control process. Budgeting is the process that translates corporate intentions into specific tasks and identifies the resources needed by each manager to carry them out. In the process, budgeting enhances communication and coordination of different organizational units, facilitates decision-making, and provides a framework for monitoring and performance evaluation.

Budgeting is only a part of the planning and control framework. For a budgeting process to be effective, it must be preceded by objectives and priorities set by senior management, as well as objectives set at the operating level. Budgeting must also be followed by a control mechanism. Managers should follow basic rules when they prepare their operating budgets. To avoid budgeting problems, remember these points: paper should be kept at a minimum; budgeting should be subservient to goal-setting; no activities should be taken for granted; and top management should be committed to participate actively in the budgeting process.

The aim of *cost accounting* is to provide managers with information on the costs associated with buying or selling a product or providing a service. *Activity-based costing* focuses on the analysis of overhead costs to determine whether they can be directly related to specific activities. There are two types of cost accounting systems that help managers make effective decisions: job order costing and process costing.

All managers are responsible for preparing a budget. Since specific departments play important roles in improving various components of the balance sheet and the income statement, it is critical that they prepare their budgets in a responsible way.

An organization may have different types of budgets which can be grouped under three categories: operating budgets (flexible and overhead budgets), complementary budgets (product budgets, program budgets, item-of-expenditure budgets, and cash flow budgets), and comprehensive budgets (pro-forma financial statements and capital expenditure budgets).

Flexible budgets are employed at the plant level, where costs of production are used as checkpoints for comparing actual results and to ascertain price and quantity variances. A production budget will vary with the number of units produced. Zero-based budgeting is used by administrative or overhead units. Here, the manager of each unit reviews all activities—past, present, and projected—and evaluates them in terms of productivity versus costs.

Financial planning is the activity that integrates all budgets into pro-forma financial statements to determine whether the company is improving its financial performance. There are three pro-forma financial statements: the pro forma income statement; the pro-forma balance sheet, and the pro-forma statement of cash flows. Management should also be able to manage the company's growth. This is important if the company is not to deplete its human and financial resources. The sustainable growth formula is a tool that identifies how fast a company should grow in order to conserve financial strength. The Z-score formula, which combines five ratios, is used to assess the financial health of a business.

Controling is the management activity that helps managers determine whether they have realized their plans and objectives. Establishing a control system involves six steps: design the subsystem, establish performance indicators, determine performance standards, measure performance, analyze variations, and take corrective action to resolve unfavorable situations that may arise. Control systems can be grouped into three major categories: preventive controls, screening controls, and feedback controls.

CHAPTER 9

Sources and Forms of Financing

*N*ow that the Edwards' have identified their financial needs and financing requirements (shown below) and have completed their investment proposal, they are ready to approach investors (short- and long-term lenders and shareholders) for the purpose of raising funds.

	Financial Needs	Financing Requirements
Working capital		
Cash	$ 4,000	
Prepaid expenses	5,000	
Accounts receivable	45,000	
Inventory	45,000	
Capital assets	350,000	
Internal sources		
Income after taxes	$ 77,000	
Depreciation	80,000	
Total internal sources		$157,000
Working capital financing		
Accounts payable	27,000	
Term loan	20,000	
Working capital loan	25,000	
Total working capital financing		72,000
External sources		
Capital shares	70,000	
Long-term debts	150,000	
Total external sources		220,000
Total	$449,000	$449,000

As shown on the previous page, CompuTech needs $449,000 to finance its existing retail store (primarily working capital) and to open the new one. As shown, $99,000 will be needed to finance the working capital (cash, prepaid expenses, accounts receivable, and inventory) and $350,000 to open the new store.

Based on the Edwards' financial projections for the year 2003, 35 percent or $157,000 will be provided by internally generated funds (income after taxes and depreciation) and 16 percent or $72,000 will be obtained from suppliers and short-term lenders. The Edwards will approach banks to obtain $45,000 that is half of the $90,000 required to finance accounts receivable ($45,000) and inventory ($45,000). To finance the $350,000 capital assets, the Edwards will be contacting various investors and will try to obtain $70,000 from shareholders (i.e., friends, family members, private investors) and $150,000 from long-term lenders.

Although the Edwards have identified their financing requirements, they are not sure whether these various sources are the most adequate and best mix to finance the $449,000 financial needs. They were analyzing various sources of financing and raised questions about the ways to raise the funds. Should they obtain funds from:

♦ Lenders or shareholders?
♦ Short-term lenders or suppliers?
♦ Leasing or owning?
♦ Friends or private investors?
♦ Banks or government institutions?

They were also questioning themselves about the best forms of financing. For example, should they seek:

♦ Term loans or conditional sales contracts?
♦ A line of credit or a revolving loan?
♦ Secured loans or unsecured loans?
♦ Seasonal loans or factoring receivables?

This chapter explores typical financing issues that businesses often consider. It focuses on three key topics:

1. How can financial needs and financing requirements be identified?
2. What are the various sources and forms of financing?
3. How are the economics of leasing versus owning an asset calculated?

Introduction

Financing is one of senior management's most constant preoccupations. There are many ways a chief financial officer (CFO) can finance the purchase of assets and funds can be obtained from a variety of sources and in different forms. Selecting the right source and form of financing can improve the long-term financial structure and profitability of a business.

Chapter 5, "Cost of Capital and Capital Structure" focused on how financing decisions could help optimize the use of funds provided by investors (shareholders and lenders). This chapter focuses on the sources and forms of financing, that is, where, why, and how funds can be obtained, and the different types of financing instruments available to businesses.

The considerations to take into account when choosing the right form and source of financing are the:

- Firm's annual debt commitments or obligations
- Cost of financing
- Risk factor arising from a slowdown (or acceleration) in economic or market conditions
- Control factor (related to existing shareholders)
- Flexibility to respond to future financing decisions
- Pattern of the capital structure in the industry
- Stability of the company's earnings
- Common shareholders' expectations

Financial Needs and Financing Requirements

The first thing that a CFO has to do before approaching investors is to identify *what* is to be financed. These are the **financial needs**. Financial needs have to do with *what* needs to be financed and the *amount* needed. A few examples of financial needs are:

1. Purchase of capital assets.
2. Additional working capital (inventory and accounts receivable).
3. More investments in research and development.
4. The launching of a new product requiring large expenditures in promotional and advertising activities.

Once the financial needs have been identified, the next step is to pinpoint where the financing will come from and the amounts required from different sources. Both the nature of the financial needs and the amount required will determine, to a large extent, the financing requirements in terms of sources and forms.

Figure 9.1 on page 353 shows how the financial needs and financing requirements are related to one another. The left side of the figure shows that the company will require $1.0 million to finance the expansion of its business activities. This could be in the form of the purchase of capital assets that will appear on the balance sheet, and operating expense items such as advertising, promotion, and salaries for research and development that will appear on the income statement. The composition of this $1.0 million dollar financial need could be made up as follows:

1. Working capital		$ 200,000
2. Capital assets		600,000
3. Marketing costs		100,000
4. Research and development		100,000
Total		$1,000,000

Before approaching lenders and shareholders, the CFO has to be very careful and precise when calculating the financial needs. Lenders want to be assured that the amounts that will be financed are backed up by reasonable and consistent assumptions. Here are a few examples of planning assumptions:

◆   Are the sales revenue estimates reasonable relative to the expected market growth?

◆   Are the level of accounts receivable and inventory in line with the company's sales growth?

◆   Will the investment in capital assets produce the estimated number of units and sales revenue?

◆   Will the company be able to service its debt with the projected sales growth?

◆   Are the company expenses incurred in cost of goods sold and selling and administrative expenses reasonable and in line with industry standards?

The right side of the figure (debt and equity) shows the **financing requirements**, that is, the amount of cash needed, and where it will come from to finance the $1.0 million expansion. This is what this chapter covers. As shown below, the $1.0 million financial needs identified in **Figure 9.1** will be financed in the following way:

A.	Internal sources		$ 200,000
B.	External sources		
1.	Short term debt		
	◆ Conventional	100,000	
	◆ Risk capital	25,000	$125,000
2.	Long-term debt		
	◆ Conventional	400,000	
	◆ Risk capital	25,000	425,000
3.	Equity		
	◆ Shareholders	200,000	
	◆ Risk capital	50,000	250,000
	Total external sources		800,000
	Total financing requirements		$1,000,000

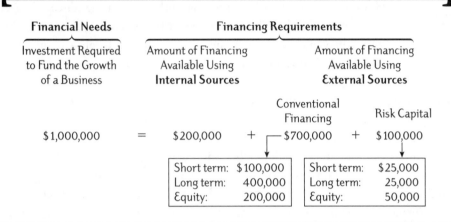

FIGURE 9.1   Financial Needs and Financing Requirements

Internal Versus External Financing

As explained in the previous section, businesses can obtain financing from two principal sources: internal and external. **Internal financing** is funds generated by the business itself. The principal sources of internal financing include income from operations, sale of capital assets, sale of investments, and a decrease in working capital accounts. **External financing** comprises funds obtained from outside sources. The two principal sources of external financing are shareholders (equity) and lenders (loans). As indicated earlier, equity financing can be obtained from conventional shareholders and risk capital lenders. Similarly, debt financing can also be obtained from conventional lenders such as banks, suppliers, and insurance companies and risk capital investments such as factoring receivables and subordinated debts. This chapter deals primarily with external financing. But first, let's examine how a business can generate its own funds internally.

Income from operations is the most common source of internal funding. To calculate the amount of funds generated by a business, we have to refer to the income statement and the statement of retained earnings. By examining Eastman Technologies Inc.'s income statement and statement of retained earnings, shown in Chapter 2, **Tables 2.3** and **2.4** respectively, we obtain the following:

Net income from operations	$ 97,500
Add: depreciation (non-cash expense)	40,000
Total cash generated by the business	137,500
Less: dividends paid to shareholders	47,500
Funds retained in the business	$ 90,000

In this case, after paying taxes and dividends, an amount of $90,000 will be reinvested into the business. These funds can be used to purchase capital assets or to help finance working capital accounts.

Working capital is also an important source of financing. Working capital accounts, such as accounts receivable and inventory, usually increase when a business grows. However, if a business is in financial difficulty, it can reduce the level of its net working capital and could generate extra funds. During the late 1970s and early 1980s, when interest rates reached unprecedented heights, many businesses had to reduce their inventory and accounts receivable.

Let's examine how a business can generate funds from its accounts receivable and inventory accounts. To illustrate the calculation, let's refer to Eastman Technologies Inc.'s income statement and balance sheet, shown in Chapter 2, **Tables 2.3** and **2.5** respectively.

In 2000, Eastman Technologies has $300,000 in accounts receivable and an average collection period of 44 days. If management wants to reduce this figure to 30 days, it will have to squeeze more funds from this account without placing sales performance in jeopardy; therefore, management may implement a more aggressive credit policy. With an average daily sales performance of $6,849 and a collection period target of 30 days, accounts receivable could be reduced to $205,470 ($6,849 × 30) from $300,000. This would produce an additional one-time source of funds of $94,530.

Also, the balance sheet shows inventory at $218,000 and the turnover is 8.7 times. If management sets an inventory target of 10 times, it can achieve this by introducing more efficient purchasing practices and better inventory management control systems. The 10-time ratio reduces inventory to $190,000 ($1,900,000 which is the cost of goods sold, divided by 10) thus generating an additional one-time amount of $28,000.

Financing Options

Once the CFO has identified the company's financial needs, working capital ($200,000), capital assets ($600,000), marketing costs ($100,000), research and development ($100,000), and the financial requirements also identified earlier, the next step is to pinpoint the instruments (or forms) that could be used to finance the expansion program. To do so, the CFO will have to focus on the following questions:

1. What will be required to finance the temporary working capital, permanent working capital, and capital assets (financial requirements)?
2. What are the financing options (or instruments) available to meet our needs? Financing instruments include conventional financing instruments and risk capital financing instruments.

When selecting a specific financing source, it is important to understand that each source bears different costs. Risk is the key to determining how much it costs to finance a business. There is a direct relationship between risk and return. Risk (the rate of return generated by the investment opportunity or the business) and return (what investors expect to earn) go hand in hand. As the risk of a project or business venture increases, the return (or cost of capital) that investors expect to earn on their investment to compensate for the risk will also increase.

Before examining the various forms and sources of financing, let's define the three different types of risks that businesses encounter. They are business risk, financial risk, and instrument risk.

Business risk is intrinsic in a firm's operations. It has to do with the uncertainty inherent in projecting the future operating income or earnings before interest and taxes (EBIT). The industry and economic environment in which a firm operates imposes business risk. A high-tech firm, for example, may face a great deal more business risk than a food processing company. Expected future demand and product life cycle for food are less difficult to predict than the future demand for most high-technology products. General economic cycles and changing industry conditions cause business variations. This is the single most important determinant that will influence a firm's capital structure (debt versus equity).

Financial risk has to do with financial leverage, that is, a firm's capital structure. In general, the more debt a firm takes on, the greater the risk of insolvency and hence the riskier it is to finance the business. Essentially, financial risk is an additional burden of risk placed on common shareholders as a result of management's decision to use more debt. Highly leveraged firms may not have the financial strength to ride out a prolonged sales decline or an economic recession. The bottom line is this: financial risk can magnify business risk since there is a greater reliance on fixed-cost (interest) or the amount of cash required to pay for the loans.

Instrument risk has to do with the quality of the security available to satisfy investors (i.e., secured versus unsecured loans). For example, a first mortgage loan is less risky (because of the guarantees) than a second mortgage. Also, a conditional sales contract is less risky than financing accounts receivable through factoring.

It is also important for management to take into account the interplay between business risk and financial risk and to maintain an appropriate balance between the two. For instance, a firm facing a relatively low level of business risk can be much more aggressive in using debt financing than a business operating in a relatively high level of business risk.

Also, when risks are high, the financing instruments (common shares versus risk capital) must offer a corresponding high rate of return to attract investors. **Figure 9.2** shows the risk curve, that is, the relationship between risk and return for different financing instruments. As shown in the figure, financing instruments, based on their specific characteristics (security, claim on cash flow, liquidity/marketability, and pricing) can be placed at different points on the risk curve.

Although equity appears to command a high return, for a growing business, it is often the most stable and appropriate source of capital. Conventional financing, which is generally provided by commercial banks, credit unions and trust companies, tends to accept a lower return since the risk related to the investment is low because of the collateral used to guarantee these loans. In contrast,

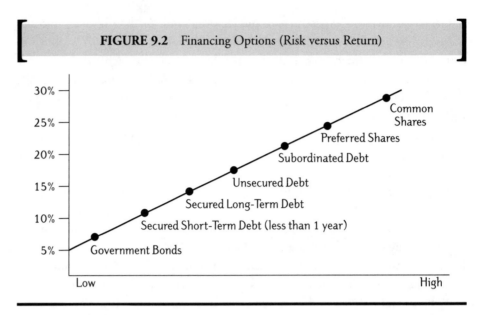

FIGURE 9.2   Financing Options (Risk versus Return)

high-risk investors tend to invest in projects with higher levels of risk and, for this reason, will demand a higher rate of return.

The rest of this chapter deals with external forms and sources of financing. The features, including the advantages and disadvantages of each source of financing, will be examined.

External Forms and Sources of Financing

As mentioned earlier, a business can obtain money from a wide range of sources and in different forms. **Sources** are institutions which provide funds and include commercial banks, investment bankers, equipment vendors, government agencies, private venture capital investors, suppliers, trust companies, life insurance companies, mortgage companies, individuals (angels), institutional investors, and shareholders. **Forms** are the financing instruments used to buy assets or to finance the growth of a business. They include short-term loans (secured or unsecured), term or installment loans, revolving loans, lease financing, mortgage, bonds, preferred and common shares, risk capital.

Table 9.1 shows different forms and sources of external financing broken down into four categories: short-term debt, intermediate debt, long-term debt, and equity financing. But, before looking at the various forms and sources of short-term financing, let's examine the meaning of the matching principle, the criteria used by investors to rate borrowers, and how a business can make itself creditworthy.

TABLE 9.1 Forms and Sources of Financing

Reasons for financing:	Forms	Sources
Short-term financing		
1. Flexible current assets Cash	Line of credit Seasonal loan Revolving credit Notes payable Single loan Trade credit	Commercial banks Suppliers

Accounts receivable
Inventory
	Accounts receivable financing
	Inventory financing
	  (general lien, floor planning,
	  warehouse financing)
	Consignment
		Factoring companies
		Confirming institutions
		
		Suppliers

2. Durable current assets:		
Accounts receivable and inventory	Working capital loans	Commercial banks Trust companies Government agencies
Intermediate financing		
3. Machinery and equipment	Term loans Conditional sales contracts Service leases Sale and leaseback Financial leases	Commercial banks Trust companies Finance companies Leasing companies
Long-term debt financing		

4. Fixed assets:
Land, buildings, and
heavy equipment
	Leases (as above)
	Bonds
	Mortgage
	  (secured and unsecured)
		Leasing companies
		Investment dealers
		Pension, insurance and
		  trust companies,
		  commercial banks
		Government agencies

Equity financing		
	Retained earnings Shares (common and preferred) Grants	Reinvested earnings Ownership investment Government agencies

The Matching Principle

The basic idea of the **matching principle** is to match the maturity of the financial needs to the period of time the funds are required (financing requirements). This principle takes into consideration two factors: cost and risk.

As shown in **Figure 9.3**, funds are needed to finance capital assets, durable (permanent) current assets, and flexible (or variable) current assets. The matching principle stipulates that capital assets and current assets should be financed by the appropriate sources of financing: capital assets by long-term debt and current assets by short-term credit. As shown in the figure, the flexible component of the current assets fluctuates depending on the financing needs of a business. Durable current

FIGURE 9.3   Strategies for Financing Working Capital

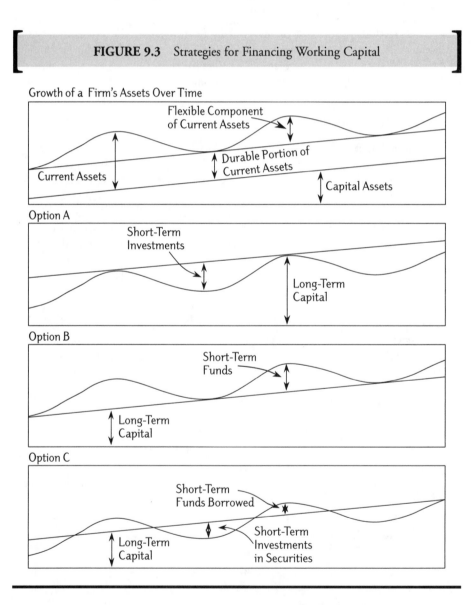

assets are necessary in order to operate a business and the flexible current assets fluctuate with changing business conditions.

Three basic strategies can be used to finance current asset (or working capital) accounts. In the first strategy (option A), all current assets are financed by long-term debt. This is considered the most conservative strategy, but is also the most costly. It is not risky because the business always has the required financing to meet its current needs. However, it is costly because if there is excess cash, it is invested in short-term securities. The return earned from the short-term investments (say, 4 percent) is far less than the cost of a loan (say, 10 percent).

In the second strategy (option B), all current assets are financed by short-term credit. This option is risky because interest rates may rise when it is time to renew a loan, and the lender may refuse to renew the loan if there is a tight money supply.

The third strategy (option C) is a compromise between the first option (conservative and more costly) and the second (risky and less expensive). In this option, the business uses a small amount of short-term credit to meet peak seasonal working capital requirements. However, during the off season, excess cash or liquidity is stored in marketable securities. The crests above the line represent short-term financing; the troughs below the line represent holdings in short-term securities.

Criteria Used by Investors to Rate Borrowers

Investors require certain information before investing funds in a business. Some of the information will be provided by the business and the investors will obtain the rest through their own files and networking. Investors look at potential borrowers using different criteria commonly referred to as the **"Cs" of credit**: character, collateral, capacity, capital, circumstances (or conditions), and coverage.

Character means two things to an investor (lender or shareholder). First, it means that the borrower should have the required skills and abilities to manage his or her business professionally and be serious, dependable, and accountable. Second, investors look for persons who are true to their words, those who appear to feel morally obligated to pay their debt, dividends, or principal according to their promise. What investors are really looking for is reputation and honesty. Credit is derived from the Latin word *credere*, meaning "to believe" or "to trust," and it implies a promise to pay. There is no question that investors are concerned with borrowers' integrity and willingness in meeting their financial commitments.

Collateral is the pledge offered by a business (particularly to lenders) in exchange for a loan. It is like a form of insurance on physical assets, which will be rightly owned by the lender if a business stops operating or is liquidated. This is vital to lenders, since the absence of such security increases their risk. Businesses which have a high credit rating may obtain a loan on an unsecured basis, that is, on faith and trust; others, however, are obliged to back their borrowings with collateral.

Capacity means two things to investors. First, it means the ability of a business to generate enough cash to meet its obligations—that is, repayment of the principal and interest or dividends. A close examination of a business's cash flow forecast or cash budget can indicate a business's capacity to meet its financial commitments. Second, it means how capable the management team is in managing a new project or an expanded operation—essentially, managerial skills or technical ability in the areas of production, marketing, manufacturing, distribution, finance, and competence in making a business expansion or a new operation a real success.

Capital refers to a business's financial structure—the mix between the shareholders' equity and the funds provided by lenders. The more money shareholders have invested in their business, the more confidence the lenders will have about providing a loan.

Circumstances, or *conditions*, refer to the environment governing a business's performance, specifically the status of the industry in terms of trends in demand, prices, competition, profitability, and government regulations.

Coverage refers primarily to insurance coverage. Most businesses are subject to losses arising from different sources: death of a principal owner or manager; damage to the business property resulting from fire, explosion, or any violent cause; embezzlement, theft, or any dishonest acts committed by a shareholder, officer, or employee; and public liability suits. Investors feel less vulnerable when businesses to which they have lent money are adequately covered by insurance.

The information regarding the "Cs" of credit is usually required by investors. If appropriate information is not provided, they will seek it elsewhere, such as from business contacts or other investors.

Making a Company Creditworthy

Making a business creditworthy is the first step for obtaining funds quickly and at a more attractive rate. The reasons for investors to turn down loans or capital shares are numerous, ranging from objective to subjective.

Potential borrowers should analyze their business situation from an investor's perspective when deciding to seek funds. This is important since fund-raisers should anticipate investors' questions and give careful consideration to the way that they should be answered. Although specific and detailed questions vary according to a particular situation, investors may reject applications for many reasons such as:

Factors related to creditworthiness:

- poor earnings record
- questionable management ability
- collateral of insufficient quality or quantity
- slow and past due in trade or loan payments
- poor accounting system

- new firm with no established earnings record
- poor moral risk (character)

Factors related to an investor's own policies:

- not enough equity
- requested maturity of the loan too long
- applicant has no established relationship with the investor (i.e., no deposit relationship with the bank)
- type of loan not handled by the bank or investment company
- line of business not handled by the investor
- loan portfolio for the type of loan already full

Let's now turn to the different types of forms and sources of short-term, intermediate, and long-term financing.

Sources of Short-Term Financing

Short-term financing can be obtained from suppliers (trade credit or accounts payable), trust companies, and specialized lenders who finance current assets such as accounts receivable (factoring companies) and inventory (confirming institutions) on a secured basis.

Suppliers

Supplier credit is also known as trade financing. Almost all businesses use trade credit. When a firm (purchaser) buys goods or services from another firm (supplier), the former does not have to pay for the goods or services immediately. When this takes place, a debt becomes outstanding to the supplier. Invoices for materials, supplies, and services provided by suppliers are not received until some days after the materials are delivered or services performed.

This type of debt is shown on the balance sheet as *accounts payable*. This is a very attractive form of financing since, in most instances, buyers do not have to pay for the goods or services for a period of 30 days, or sometimes 60 days; furthermore, it is interest-free. As a business grows, supplier credit also grows. The volume orders increase, resulting in increased credit. Trade credit is offered to buyers who usually have a good credit rating. Nevertheless, it may be dangerous for a business that does not know how to use this credit instrument. In some cases, businesses abuse their credit limit and have difficulty reimbursing their suppliers. This situation can easily damage a business's reputation.

Table 9.2 lists the advantages and disadvantages of supplier credit.

Banks and Trust Companies

The second most important source of short-term financing is banks and trust companies. Banks make short-term loans that usually appear on the borrowing firm's balance sheet as seasonal loans, operating loans, or working capital loans.

TABLE 9.2 Advantages and Disadvantages of Supplier Credit	
Advantages	**Disadvantages**
• Inexpensive source	• Usually not sufficient to fully cover the timing difference between paying for supplies and receiving cash from sales
• Limited documentation required	
• Easy access	• Very short term in nature
• No costs	• If company does not pay on time, the supplier might cut off future supplies, which could have adverse effects on the business.
• No controls	
• No security	
• Discount for early payment	

These loans can fluctuate as often as daily to cover expected cash shortfalls. These credit instruments are designed to finance fluctuating current assets.

Short-term loans do not come spontaneously. Borrowers must specifically request them. They are, of course, more flexible than trade credit, since the money can be spent on a wider range of business needs. Bank loans can be either unsecured or secured by some form of collateral that the bank can foreclose on if the borrower cannot pay back the loan as agreed. Unsecured loans usually have a higher cost.

As a firm's financing needs increase, it usually asks its banker to increase its line of credit. If the bank refuses, the firm may be forced to forgo attractive growth opportunities. Most firms try to choose a bank that is willing to provide service, advice, and counsel, assume some risks, and show some loyalty to its customers. A business owner therefore expects to develop a long-term relationship with its banker. When an owner looks for financing, it is preferable to select a commercial bank that will be an asset, not a liability, to the business. Here are some of the more important attributes to look for when selecting a bank.

Financial counseling. It is a banker's job to stay abreast of financial developments, so one of the most valuable functions that a commercial loan officer can perform for a business is that of external financial expert. Management or owners should look for a bank where the commercial loan officers specialize in businesses of their size and type and should develop a strong relationship with the person handling the loan.

Loyalty. The loyalty of a commercial bank to its customers is very important. Certain banks, when times get a little rough, may quickly shut the window on applications for increases in their line of credit (especially for smaller businesses). Other banks will work with a business as much as possible to help ride the storm.

Degree of loan specialization. It is important that lending arrangements be serviced by the department in the bank that specializes in the business's particular type of loan such as working capital loan or revolving loan.

Understanding the nature of the industry. A banker who has adequate knowledge of the industry and its particular financing requirements can be an invaluable resource. The banker will not have to get familiar with the business; taking the required time to find such a banker can help business owners receive the financial counseling they need to solve their problems.

Full range of services. Management should choose a bank that offers a full range of banking services.

Reputation. The reputation of the bank or branch in terms of counseling services and providing loans to businesses is also important. Bank loans exhibit much greater variability than other sources of business funds.

Most bank loans are short-term and self-liquidating. That is, money is lent for a business purpose such as the purchase of inventory and repaid from the proceeds of the sale of the inventory. Since firms need to buy inventory before they can sell it, they need to borrow frequently to cover seasonal shortfalls in cash flow (e.g., the pre-holiday sales season for retailers). Then, at the end of the sales season, they can pay off the loans.

A bank loan might have a maturity of only 90 days. When it is repaid, the bank can lend the money to other firms that have different cash flow patterns. Most of the fixed maturity loans (i.e., 90 days) are made at what is called discount interest, which means that the interest is deducted in advance.

A large percentage of the outstanding loans of banks are classified as operating loans and used by businesses to finance inventories and accounts receivable. These loans are frequently renewed year after year and basically amount to quasi-permanent working capital financing. Most of the operating loans are not made on a basis of fixed maturity, but instead, on a demand basis. This means that the bank can request payment at any time. Demand loans are risky because if the bank suddenly demands repayment, the company would have no choice but to negotiate another loan with another financial institution. Also, the interest rate of this type of loan is usually not fixed, but floating. The floating rate is usually specified as prime rate plus some premium for risk. The cost of bank loans varies for different borrowers at any given time because of differences in the risk to the lender. The cost of bank loans also varies over time as economic conditions change and interest rates fluctuate. The base interest rate is the one established by the Federal Reserve Board. This is the rate a bank would have to pay if it borrowed from a Federal Reserve bank. Commercial banks must therefore charge a higher rate to their customers. The lowest rate for any given bank is the prime rate, which is the rate the banks charge their best (least risky) customers. Other borrowers pay more, depending on the risk of the loan. A typical operating loan might have a cost stated as prime plus two, meaning that if the prime rate were 6 percent, the borrower would pay 8 percent. As the prime goes up or down, the loan rate also changes if it is floating. Usually interest is calculated each month and is deducted from the firm's bank account.

Banks offer different forms of credit to their clients. First, there is the **line of credit**, which is a formal or written agreement between a banker and a borrower regarding the maximum amount of loan that will be extended to a business during a given year. For instance, a business may estimate that it will require a $20,000 loan during a four-month period to produce goods and to sell them on credit. Although the business may have a high credit rating and may be able to obtain as much as $50,000, the business owner will have to indicate to the loan officer the exact amount required, when it will be needed, and the amount of interest to be paid. The agreement is confirmed when the business owner signs a promissory note for the agreed amount. This formal agreement confirms that the funds to be provided will be available in the form of a temporary loan and will not be of a permanent nature.

Table 9.3 lists the advantages and disadvantages of a bank line of credit.

Second, seasonal or **self-liquidating** loans are used by businesses primarily to finance temporary or fluctuating variations in accounts receivable and inventory, that is, the working capital accounts that are flexible. For instance, a business that sells ski equipment may have a specific seasonal borrowing pattern. It may need some financing in July, as inventory begins to accumulate. Once it is shipped to the retailer in September and October, buyers start to make their payments. These loans can be secured or unsecured and interest rates can fluctuate over time. Like a demand loan, the bank can call such loans at any time. In most cases, these loans are repaid on an installment basis (amortized over the life of the loan), but they may also be repaid in a lump sum.

Third, there is **revolving credit**, which is similar to a line of credit. In this case, the bank signs an agreement with the borrower (business) to extend credit up to a maximum amount. This type of financing costs a little more because addi-

TABLE 9.3 Advantages and Disadvantages of a Bank Line of Credit	
Advantages	**Disadvantages**
• Easy and fairly quick to access	• Increases the financial risk since cash servicing is required
• Relatively inexpensive	• Amount available is limited by the ceiling
• Flexible	• If the company experiences problems, lender is in a position to demand/cancel the line, and go for the option of realizing on the security
• Loan revolves up and down and maximizes the use of cash	
• Suitable for short-term temporary needs	• Not suitable for long-term requirements where the company expects return over a long-term
• Usually, reporting requests are minimal	• The company may not have suitable security of financial risk may be too high
• Interest/fees are tax deductible	

tional fees can be levied by the bank. For instance, if the bank offers a credit limit of $300,000 and the borrower uses only $200,000, the unused portion of the borrowing may be liable to a stand-by fee, say 0.5 percent, which is charged to compensate the bank for committing itself to the loan.

Finally, there is **interim financing**, also called bridge financing, which is a loan made available to businesses to help them finance the construction of a new plant or the expansion of an existing one until regular financing, such as a first mortgage loan, is received. This financing is called interim because it is used to bridge the time gap between the date construction begins and the time that construction is completed and can serve as security for a mortgage.

Secured Loans. Firms that are not able to obtain unsecured credit, such as a line of credit, a seasonal loan, or revolving credit, because of low credit standing (or because they want a lower interest rate) will have to pledge some of their assets as security in order to obtain a loan. In this case, the borrower puts up some assets such as marketable securities, equipment, machinery, buildings, land, accounts receivable, and inventory, as collateral to be claimed by the lender if the borrower does not respect the loan agreement or if the business is liquidated. Since most of the capital assets are financed by long-term loans (mortgages), short-term lenders will use accounts receivable and inventory as collateral to secure short-term loans.

An instrument frequently used by banks is *commercial paper*, or *corporate paper*. For larger firms, commercial paper is an alternative to bank loans. The maturity of commercial paper is generally very short but may go as long as one year. When the maturity date arrives, the borrower must pay; extensions are usually out of the question. Failure to pay on time will cause irreparable damage to a firm's reputation, perhaps preventing it from borrowing in the future.

Asset-Based Financing

Asset-based lending is a form of short-term risk capital financing. Just like a bank line of credit, an asset-based loan is subject to a ceiling amount based on accounts receivable and inventory margins. It also involves a security pledge on accounts receivable and inventories. However, pure asset-based loans differ from bank loans because they rely on collateral coverage rather than being linked directly to financial forecasts. Therefore, business and financial risk are less of an issue with asset-based lenders compared to conventional short-term lenders. However, pricing is higher, and interest charges may range from the prime rate plus 2 to 5 percent annually.

Short-term risk capital financing is offered by factoring companies and confirming institutions.

Factoring Companies. Under **factoring,** the business makes an outright sale of its accounts receivable to finance a business. The customer is told that the invoice has been sold and is asked to make payments directly to the finance company (the factor). This arrangement clearly increases the lender's risk. To reduce the risk, the factor virtually takes over the work of the borrower's credit department. All orders received from customers are sent to the finance company, which does a credit check. Factoring is fairly costly for businesses. Factoring involves a continuing agreement under which the factor purchases accounts receivable as they take place. The factor assumes the risk of accounts becoming uncollectible and is responsible for collections. The factor may also perform credit checks on customers. There are two general types of factoring arrangements.

First, there is *maturity factoring*. Here, the business and the factor agree on an average collection period such as 30 days. Regardless of whether the customer has paid the account at 30 days, the factor pays the business. For example, at the end of 30 days, the customer pays $500 but owes $500 more. The factor pays the business $1,000 less a commission (typically, 0.5% to 1.5% of total face amount). The factor may charge the business interest on the outstanding portion of the invoice.

Second, there is *old-line factoring*. Here, the factor performs a lending function. It will advance funds to the company based on 70 percent to 90 percent of the value of an invoice. The factor may charge interest at prime rate plus 1 percent to 1.5 percent per annum, as long as the invoice is outstanding. In this case, the company receives cash almost immediately after the sale is made.

Confirming Institutions. Inventory is an asset that can serve as excellent security for short-term loans. The major factor that is taken into account by lenders before extending inventory financing is the marketability of the inventory. Work-in-process inventory, for example, is poor collateral. Raw materials may be more secured, since they can be sold to other manufacturers; finished goods, ready to be shipped to retailers, may not be as good a collateral as raw materials. The level of financing obtained on inventory depends largely on the nature of the goods.

Inventory can be financed in a number of ways. First, it can be financed by having a *blanket coverage* or a general lien put on it, such as the one used for accounts receivable. Then the lender can claim as collateral a percentage of the business's inventory. This type of arrangement is easy to set up, but the lender takes a risk in that it does not have absolute control over the quality and quantity of the goods held in stock.

Second, there is *floor planning*. This type of financing is used primarily in the durable goods industry to finance automobile, farm, and industrial equipment dealers. In this case, each product is identified by a serial number and, when the good is sold, a portion of the proceeds is forwarded to the lender for repayment of the loan. Each time goods are replenished, the borrower must sign a new agreement which specifies the terms and conditions. Sometimes, the lender will make a spot check to certify the quantity and quality of the physical assets.

Third, there is *warehouse financing*. This type of financing involves an independent third party that controls access to the goods as security for the lender. There are two basic types of warehousing arrangements. First, there is *field warehousing*. Here, the inventory is located in a specified area on the borrower's property and the warehousing agent exercises very strict control. Second, there are *public warehousing* arrangements. Here, the merchandise is located away from the borrowers' premises, probably in a public warehouse under the control of the warehouse agent.

Fourth, there is *consignment*. This means that although a seller delivers goods to a buyer, the seller remains the owner until the goods are sold to the public. Since the buyer does not purchase the goods, the seller must obtain short-term loans to finance the product. In this case, the buyer takes no risk, the profit margin on consigned goods is normally smaller than that on similar non-consigned items.

Table 9.4 lists the advantages and disadvantages of asset-based financing.

TABLE 9.4   Advantages and Disadvantages of Asset-Based Financing

Advantages	Disadvantages
◆ Ideal for growing, highly leveraged, and turn-around situations, because of the higher level of risk assumed by the lender.	◆ Not suitable for all industries; needs high levels of accounts receivable and inventories.
◆ No complicated financial covenants, which require monitoring and compliance. This results in less chance of default under a loan agreement.	◆ Increases the financial risk, due to interest servicing.
◆ Given the heavy reliance on the value of the collateral, it increases the opportunity for leverage.	◆ More expensive than conventional short-term financing.
◆ Lowers the need to raise equity, avoiding equity dilution.	◆ Onerous inventory and accounts receivable monitoring requirements, sometimes as often as daily.
◆ Interest is tax deductible.	

Sources of Medium- and Long-Term Debt Financing

At the risk of oversimplification, we will differentiate intermediate financing from long-term debt financing by the length of time funds are borrowed. Intermediate financing refers to a two- to five-year loan, while long-term financing refers to five years or longer.

The next several sections deal with loans that are provided to businesses for a long term in order to finance the purchase of capital assets.

Conventional Long-Term Financing

Medium- and **long-term loans** usually finance capital (or fixed) assets. These may be straightforward term loans, usually secured by the physical asset itself. Banks, life insurance companies, pension funds, and federal and state government agencies provide longer financing on capital assets.

Term loans are a principal form of medium- and long-term financing used for the purchase of capital assets (usually three to seven years). However, in certain circumstances, the maturity may be as long as 15 years. A term loan involves an agreement whereby the borrower agrees to make a series of interest and principal payments on specific dates to a lender. This differs from a bank line of credit, whereby repayment is at any time (demand) or at a specified time, in one lump sum. The key characteristics of a term loan are the following:

- Terms of the loan are tailored to suit the needs of the borrower.
- Security is usually in the form of a mortgage on equipment or machinery.
- In addition to collateral, the lender places specific restrictions on the operations of the business such as no additional borrowings or no increase in salaries to the officers of the company without prior approval of the lender.
- The loan is retired by systematic repayments over the life of the loan.

A **conditional sales contract** is a written agreement between a buyer and a seller regarding the purchase of production equipment or other physical assets on a time-payment basis. Under this arrangement, the seller of the capital asset accepts a partial payment of the value of the asset as a down payment, which is usually a minimum of one-third; the rest is paid on a monthly installment basis. Legal ownership of the property is retained by the seller until the buyer has made all the required payments according to the term of the agreement, which usually runs from 12 to 36 months.

Table 9.5 lists the advantages and disadvantages of terms loans and conditional sales contract.

Bonds are long-term contracts, typically for 20 or 30 years, under which a borrowing firm agrees to make payments of interest and principal, usually semi-annually, to the holder of the bond contract. The investor buys an annuity with regular payments until the maturity date, when the principal amount is repaid. An

TABLE 9.5   Advantages and Disadvantages of
Term Loans and Conditional Sales Contracts

Advantages	Disadvantages
• Longer term repayment terms	• Ties up asset
• Easy access	• Increases financial risk given the cash payments of interest and principal
• Flexibility	
• Tax deductibility of interest	• Commits the business since it is subject to penalties
• Suitable for long-term needs: permanent current assets and capital assets	• Often includes restrictive covenants
• Low cost relative to other long-term sources of financing	• Business may not have suitable security to offer since the business/financial risk may be too high
• Commits the lender for a long term	
• Does not dilute equity	

indenture is a legal document that spells out the rights of both the bondholders and the issuing firm. A *trustee*, usually a trust company, represents the bondholders and makes sure that the firm lives up to its obligations. The firm pays the total interest payment to the trustee as scheduled, and the trustee then pays the bondholders.

Bonds may be secured or unsecured. *Secured bonds* are essentially long-term promissory notes. Holders of secured bonds have contractual claims to the assets and earnings (similar to first or second mortgages). *Unsecured bonds* are called debentures. Only the earning power of the firm backs them up. Bonds may also be convertible into shares of stock of the issuing company, or redeemable before the stated maturity date, at the request of either the bondholder or the firm. The firm does not know who buys the bonds. Thus the issuance of bonds is a very impersonal and inflexible financing method, not suitable for all firms. These unsecured bondholders are similar to general creditors; they have a claim on the residual value of all assets after all secured creditors have been paid.

Mortgages are a pledge of a specific real property, such as land or buildings. Mortgages are long-term financing (e.g., 30 years). The amount of the mortgage is calculated based on the market value of the property. For example, 80 percent of the market value is a common mortgage amount. The repayment schedule is usually based on equal blended payments of interest and principal. Usually the interest rate is fixed for a specific term and it depends on the going market rate, the length of the term, and availability. This type of financing is most commonly provided by banks, mortgage companies, and investment companies.

Table 9.6 lists the advantages and disadvantages of mortgage financing.

TABLE 9.6 Advantages and Disadvantages of Mortgage Financing

Advantages	Disadvantages
• Long-term commitment, without equity dilution	• Fairly rigid financing instrument
• Maturity matches the long life of the asset.	• Increases financial risk due to fixed stream of interest and principal repayments.
• Interest is tax deductible.	• If company fails to make payment, it could be subject to penalties.
• Relatively inexpensive source of long-term financing	
• Easy to access	
• Considers the value of the asset, more than the value of the business.	
• Standard documentation requirements. Restrictive covenants will be basic.	

Risk Capital Long-Term Financing

Risk capital investors invest funds in equity shares and equity-related debt in relatively small or untried enterprises thereby absorbing much of the risk that commercial lenders are unwilling to shoulder. These investors prefer dealing with companies whose products are already selling and are proven successes but which lack funds to exploit their markets.

Subordinated debts are term debts in which investors accept a higher level of risk compared to conventional sources. These instruments require a rate of interest that typically ranges from 8 percent to 12 percent. However, the overall rate of return to the investor will be higher. Participation features that give investors the right to share some corporate profits could increase the rate of return and make the expected return range between 15 percent to 25 percent per year. This type of financing is good only if a business has exhausted secured financing options. Subordinated debts are best suited to rapidly growing companies, expansion programs, and management and leveraged buyouts and acquisitions.

Effectively, under such lending arrangements, investors structure the instrument to share in the expected success of the company. Here are a few examples of participation features:

- Royalties (percentage of net cash flow generated from operation).
- Participation fees.
- Normal cost of commons shares.
- Warrants or options to purchase shares.
- Rights to convert debt into common shares.

Subordinated debt repayments can be tailored to the characteristics of individual businesses. Therefore, the risk of the borrower defaulting is less compared to conventional long-term sources of financing. Sources of subordinated debts include private sector venture capital firms, institutional investors, labor-union funds, and government-sponsored corporations.

Table 9.7 lists the advantages and disadvantages of subordinated debts.

Equity Financing

Equity is the interest an owner holds in a business. If a business is *privately-owned*, the owners can also obtain funds directly from banks or trust companies that specialize in small- and medium-sized business loans and mortgages. In this case, owners of the privately-owned business will prepare an *investment plan* or business plan and will go directly to specific individuals or investors and ask them to become shareholders or lenders of the business.

For *publicly-owned* businesses, the process is more complicated. The owners have to prepare a prospectus and approach an investment dealer in order to raise funds from the general public through a *public issue* known as an initial purchase

TABLE 9.7   Advantages and Disadvantages of Subordinated Debts

Advantages	Disadvantages
• Flexible and can be tailored	• Takes time to access
• Less expensive than equity	• Expensive relative to other sources of short-term and long-term financing
• Fills a financing gap and high leverage is available	• Some cash flow servicing requirements
• Not as much dilution as straight equity	• Investors will take a more active role in the company than other lender
• Available to a variety of industries	• High set-up costs
	• Restrictive covenants often apply
	• Does not provide the stability of equity

offer (IPO). A public issue raises funds from the general public. The investment dealer buys the securities from the firm at a set price, marks it up, and then sells them to the general public.

Let's turn now to the role of the investment dealer and the cost of raising funds from the general public. As mentioned earlier, long-term financing can be obtained from two distinct sources: *lenders*, when money is provided in the form of a loan, such as bonds or mortgages and *shareholders*, when funds are raised from shareholders by issuing shares. Investment dealers (or investment bankers) facilitate the financing of business by buying securities (bonds or shares) at wholesale and reselling them at retail to their clients. Investment dealers borrow the money they need to finance the issue. Usually, they get it from banks on a very short-term basis and repay their lenders when the issue sells out. This process may take a week or two, or it may all be completed in one day.

The cost of public issues of either bonds or shares is high because there are many legal details and requirements. The process is lengthy, requiring approval of the securities and exchange commission (SEC). Thus, this source of funds can be used only at infrequent intervals and for large amounts of money. New firms are usually either too small to use investment dealers or find their services, which may cost as much as 10 percent to 25 percent of the funds raised, too expensive. **Table 9.8** summarizes the steps involved for making a public issue.

Let's now turn to the major sources of equity funds: shareholders, risk capital investors and government institutions.

Shareholders

Funds can be provided by shareholders in the form of common shares and preferred shares. The owners (shareholders) of a business provide *common share* financing. The collective and specific rights of the shareholders related to common shares are listed in **Table 9.9**.

TABLE 9.8   Steps Involved for Making a Public Issue

Step 1: The firm decides to list (or not to list) its issue on an exchange (such as New York Stock Exchange or NASDAQ).

Step 2: The firm selects one or more investment dealers who will take the responsibility for buying and selling the issue (the underwriter(s)).

Step 3: A preliminary conference takes place between the issuing company and the underwriter(s) to discuss the amount of capital to be raised, the type of security to be issued, and the general terms of the issue.

Step 4: A preliminary prospectus is prepared. The preliminary prospectus discloses important aspects of the issue and forms the basis of the agreement among all parties.

Step 5: A public accounting firm makes an audit of the company's financial situation and prepares the required financial statements to be included in the preliminary prospectus.

Step 6: After it is signed, the preliminary prospectus is filed with the SEC. This is followed by a waiting period (usually around 15 business days) during which the staff of the SEC goes over the prospectus to evaluate the accuracy of the data and content, and to ensure that there are no deficiencies or misrepresentations in the document.

Step 7: After clearance is given by the SEC, the final prospectus is prepared and final clearance is given. At this point, the underwriting agreement is signed between the issuing company and the underwriter(s). Here, an agreement is reached about the date of the issue, the actual price that the underwriter(s) will pay, and the commission for the underwriter(s).

TABLE 9.9   Shareholders' Collective and Specific Rights

Collective Rights
+ Amend articles of incorporation
+ Adopt and amend bylaws
+ Elect the directors of the corporation
+ Authorize the sale of fixed assets
+ Authorize mergers and divestitures
+ Change the amount of authorized common and preferred shares
+ Alter the rights and restrictions attached to the common shares
+ Create a right of exchange of other shares into common shares

Specific Rights
+ Vote in the manner prescribed by the corporate charter
+ Sell their share certificates to other interested parties
+ Inspect corporate books (practical limitations)
+ Share in residual assets of the corporation (last among the claimants)

To a company, the most attractive feature of issuing common shares is that they do not entail fixed charges. Unlike a mortgage payment, dividends do not have to be paid. Common shares do not have fixed maturity dates and can be sold more easily than debt.

Preferred share financing has some characteristics of common share and debt financing. The preferred share appears in the equity section of the balance sheet. Although this type of financing is considered equity, preferred shareholders do not have the same rights as common shareholders.

Table 9.10 lists the advantages and disadvantages of equity financing.

The payout of income, control, and risk factors related to common share financing, preferred share financing, and long-term debts are listed in **Table 9.11**.

Risk Capital Investors

Risk capital investors provide equity financing to small or untried enterprises thereby absorbing much of the risk that commercial lenders are unwilling to shoulder. These investors are rarely interested in inventions requiring further research, development, and engineering. They have certain preferences about the companies they want to back. These preferences are usually based on the type, history, and status of the company and the amount of financing needed.

Risk capital investors prefer dealing with companies whose products are already selling and are proven successes but that lack the capital to exploit their markets and generally provide equity financing or both equity and long-term debt financing.

Risk capital investments are unique in the following ways:

- They are used mostly by fast-growth businesses.
- Usually, several years are required before the risk capital investors can liquidate their investments or make an exit.

TABLE 9.10   Advantages and Disadvantages of Equity Financing

Advantages	Disadvantages
• Low risk	• Extends voting rights or control to additional shareholders.
• Dividends are paid when income is generated	
• No restrictive covenants that could cause default	• Gives the right to more owners to share in income thus diluting the equity interest.
• Provides stability and permanency	
• Common shares do not have fixed maturity dates	• Takes time to access.
• Shares can be sold more easily and investors realize a return on their equity in the market place at no cost to the company.	• Underwriting costs are expensive.
	• Dividends are not tax deductible.

[**TABLE 9.11**   Determining the Choice of Long Term Financing]

	Payout of Income	**Control**	**Risk**
Common shares	Paid after interest and preferred share dividends; by decision of the board of directors, all or a portion of the remaining funds may be retained by the business or distributed in the form of dividends.	Common shareholders have the legal right to make all major decisions and to elect the board of directors. They have the ultimate control of the corporation.	Since they have the last priority of claims in the event of liquidation, they bear the highest risk for the claimants.
Preferred shares	Dividends are paid before common dividends and are cumulative if they are not paid during a specific year.	Preferred shareholders sometimes have a right to elect some of the directors on the board of directors (minority).	They have priority over the common shareholders regarding the assets (in the event of liquidation) and earnings for payment of dividends.
Long-term debts	There is a fixed payment of interest which is made in the form of a sinking fund.	Usually, long-term creditors do not have the right to vote. However, if the bond goes into default, the bondholders may be able to take control of the company. Since they have the last priority of claims in the event of liquidation, they bear the highest risk for the claimants.	Bondholders have the first claim (secured) over the assets of a company (in the event of liquidation) and earnings.

- In many instances, during the early years there is usually no organized secondary markets.
- The new firm faces a high risk of failure.
- Several infusions of capital are frequently necessary before the new enterprise becomes a "going concern."

Risk capital investments can be categorized as embryonic, start-up, development, expansion, turn-around, or buyout. *Embryonic investments* are made in firms intending to develop a new product or process up to the point where it is possible to make a prototype. *Start-up investments* are made in new firms just getting started with a new product or service in an established market. *Development investments* are made in small firms that are already in production and just about to realize profits but do not have sufficient cash flow to continue operations. *Expansion investments* are made in smaller firms in need of additional productive capacity, but without sufficient funds of their own. *Turn-around investments* are made in firms that are currently experiencing financial difficulties, but which have great potential for profitability with more capital and better management. *Buyout investments* are made in firms that are already established and have a proven and good track record, but whose owners are seeking to sell out and retire.

Here is a profile of the general types of risk capital investors.

Angel investors are professional investors, retired executives with business experience and money to invest, or high net worth individuals simply looking for investment opportunities. Angels will usually invest between $25,000 to $300,000 in a venture. Many angels are sophisticated investors and will go through the formal due diligence review.

Private investors and **venture capital firms** are individuals or groups of professionals with a vast amount of experience, contacts, and business skills that can help a business become more profitable. The size of their investment can range from $25,000 to millions of dollars. Investors in this category have particular preferences, strategies, and investment criteria. While some private firms will be more interested in investing in the development stage, many will be interested in companies involved in the expansion, acquisition, and management/leveraged buyout stages.

Institutional investors provide equity and subordinated risk capital investment to small and medium-sized businesses. Institutional investors include subsidiaries of banks, investment companies, certain life insurance companies, and pension funds. These companies fund investments from a few hundred thousand to millions of dollars.

Corporate strategic investors differ from traditional venture capital companies in that their motivation extends beyond financial reasons. Their business agreements are referred to as strategic alliances or corporate partnerships. A strategic investor may have a broad range of objectives that include enhancing innovation, gaining exposure to new markets and technologies, identifying and accessing acquisition candidates, assuring sources of supply, assisting a client, initiating new ventures internally, and spinning off businesses that are not appropriate for in-house purposes.

Government Institutions

Government financing is a direct or indirect form of financial assistance to businesses offered by municipal, state, or federal agencies to help businesses carry out capital expenditure projects or expand their activities which, without such assistance, would be delayed or even abandoned completely. Government financing (or programs) can be grouped into two broad categories: allowances for income tax purposes and direct and indirect incentives. Federal financing aid can come from nonrefundable grants, refundable incentives, conditionally refundable incentives, direct loans, guarantee of loans, remission of tariff, export financing, cost sharing, training grants, and small business loans. State financing aid can come from forgivable loans, direct loans (mortgage, small business loans), working capital loans, training grants, guarantee of loans, inventory financing, leasebacks, and venture capital. Municipal financing aid can come through free land, deferred property taxes, and infrastructure improvements.

The primary federal government agency providing financing for small businesses is the *Small Business Administration (SBA)*. Much of the financing from the SBA is in the form of loan guarantees. For example, the 7(a) Loan Guaranty Program helps businesses obtain financing that would otherwise not be available. Often businesses have insufficient equity or collateral to meet the borrowing requirements of commercial banks. With an SBA loan guarantee, the lender will make the loan because the SBA assumes much of the risk. A loan guarantee means that if a business is unable to repay part of the loan, the SBA will make the repayment. The loan guarantee also makes the interest rate more affordable to business. SBA loans and loan guarantees have interest rates set at the prime rate plus two to two and one-half points.

Funds guaranteed by the SBA can be used for many purposes including purchases of capital assets, financing working capital, making lines of credit available, and financing business expansion. The SBA 504 program combines loan guarantees with the funding of certified development corporations. The program is specifically designed to help businesses expand their long-term fixed assets. The loan guarantee portion is similar to the 7(a) Loan Guaranty Program. For the other portion, the SBA funds nonprofit certified development corporations (CDCs) that are set up to assist the economic development in a community. Many CDCs have been set up to assist businesses in communities that have lost jobs as a result of NAFTA. The funds from the CDCs are grants that may amount to 40 percent of the fixed assets purchase price. Even though the funds are provided for fixed asset purchases, the goal is to create and retain jobs.

The SBA assists businesses with short-term working-capital needs through CAPLines. Five types of CAPLines are available:

- Seasonal lines are designed to even out the peaks and valleys that many businesses experience each year. Businesses borrow against anticipated inventories or accounts receivable.
- Contract lines are used by manufacturing businesses for materials and direct labor involved in making products under contract. The contract serves as the collateral.
- Builders lines are available to building contractors to finance direct labor and materials during construction or renovation. The building project provides the collateral.
- Standard asset-based lines use assets as collateral for revolving lines of credit. These lines are used for short-term needs.
- Small asset-based lines are similar to standard asset-based lines. The amounts are smaller and the primary condition of maintaining this revolving line is consistent repayment from the normal cash flow of the business.

The Small Business Administration also provides assistance to businesses engaged in international trade. The primary programs are the International Trade Loan Program and the Export Working Capital Program. These programs assist businesses preparing to enter the export market and businesses that have been hurt by competition from imports.

Other government agencies provide assistance to certain markets or for specific types of business activities. The *Farmers Home Administration* offers loan guarantees, loans, and grants to agricultural businesses. The *National Marine Fisheries Services*, part of the Department of Commerce, offers various forms of financing for fishing and cargo vessels. Both the Department of Defense and the Department of Health and Human Services participate in the SBIR and STTR programs that offer grants to small research and development enterprises for the development of new technologies and products that advance the technology used by these government agencies.

Lease Financing

Almost any physical asset can be purchased or leased. We are all familiar with residential apartment leasing, whereby a lessee (the renter) acquires the right from the lessor (owner) to inhabit the apartment in return for monthly rental payments.

Leasing is an alternative to more traditional financing for many assets, but especially for equipment that has a useful life of three to ten years. The **lessee** or user gets the full use of the assets without the bother of owning them, and frequently this can be accomplished with little or no down payment. The **lessor** is the one who lends the asset to the lessee. The three most popular forms of leases are operating leases, financial leases, and sale and leaseback.

Operating Leases. **Operating leases** provide not only financing but also maintenance of the asset, so they are popular for office equipment and cars as well as highly technical types of equipment, such as computers. The operating lease is an agreement between a lessee and a lessor which can be canceled by either party upon due notice. Usually, the lease price includes services and repairs. Operating leases are not always fully amortized during the original contract period; the lessor expects to recover the rest of its costs by either leasing the asset again or selling it. If the original lessee believes that the equipment has become obsolete, it is usually possible to cancel the contract at little or no penalty cost prior to the normal expiration date of the lease period.

Financial Leases. A **financial lease** is a mutually agreed upon commitment by the lessor and lessee under which the latter agrees to lease a specific asset over a specified period of time. It does not provide for maintenance, is usually fully amortized, and does not normally include a cancellation clause. Financial leases are commonly used for such assets as airplanes, office equipment, movable offshore oil drilling rigs, medical equipment, railroad cars, and construction equipment.

Lessors generally borrow 80 percent of the cost of the asset from a third party (or parties) on a non-recourse basis. The loan is secured only by the lease payments and is not a general obligation of the lessor. Lease periods as long as 15 or 20 years are common. The lessor records on its balance sheet only the net investment (20 percent) but can deduct both interest on its debt financing and depreciation on the asset; therefore income for tax purposes is usually negative in the early years of the lease. The lessee may get lower lease payments than would otherwise be the case, and all of its lease payments are usually tax-deductible. Virtually all financial institutions are involved in leasing, either directly or through subsidiaries.

In a financial lease, three parties are involved: the lessee, the lessor, and a lender. Here is how a typical financial lease works. The company (lessee) decides on the equipment or machinery it wants to use. The company approaches a leasing company and specifies the asset it wants and the length of time for which it will be needed. The leasing company then (1) borrows money from a lender (if necessary), (2) buys the asset from a manufacturer, and (3) leases it to the company (lessee). Usually, the lease period lasts throughout the useful life of the asset so that the leasing company does not find itself in the position of having to lease it to another company. In this lease agreement, the leasing company does not even take physical possession of the asset.

Sale and Leaseback. A **sale and leaseback** arrangement can be used only once, since it requires the firm to sell an asset, then lease it back. Thus, it still gets to use the asset while increasing the funds available within a particular time period. Lease payments in such arrangements are similar to mortgage payments or payments on a long-term loan. For example, a firm could sell its factory building and land to a financial institution, then lease it back. The selling firm in this case receives the full purchase price of the property, which it can use for any purpose. It is committed to making periodic payments to the financial institution, which is equivalent to paying rent.

Lease or Buy Analysis

Medium- and long-term financing methods are generally used to acquire capital assets, such as buildings, machinery, and equipment. As long as the assets do the job, managers are not concerned about how assets are financed. Their main concern is to see that the assets do the job at the lowest possible cost. To financial managers, however, the choice between owning or leasing has significant financial implications. Their job is to ensure not only that assets are obtained at the lowest possible cost and on the most favorable terms, but also that they produce the greatest financial benefits to the owners. Although leasing has far-reaching legal and accounting implications, we will deal here only with the cost factors in comparing the choice between leasing or owning an asset. **Table 9.12** on page 380 presents a cost comparison between owning and leasing $1 million worth of assets. The assumptions underlying this comparative cost analysis are:

- Life of the assets is ten years.
- Duration of the lease is ten years with annual installments of $162,745 (before tax). (It is based on a 10 percent compounded interest charge.)
- Debt agreement is 100 percent of assets; a ten-year repayment schedule with a 10 percent compounded interest charge. (Assets are rarely financed at 100 percent of value; however, this assumption is made only to illustrate the true economic comparison between the two options.)
- Depreciation for tax purposes is 15 percent.
- Income tax is 50 percent.
- There is no residual value of the asset.

As shown in column 1, the annual cost of the lease is $81,373, or $162,745 × 50% (income tax rate). The second column shows the annual payment for the $1,000,000 loan. The $162,745 figure is obtained by dividing $1,000,000 by the factor 6.1446 (from **Table D** at the end of the book, column 10 percent and line 10 years). Columns 3 and 4 show how much will be paid each year for interest and principal. In the first year, with a $1,000,000 loan at a 10 percent interest rate, the interest charge will be $100,000 (column 3) and the principal repayment will be $62,745. Column 5 shows the annual depreciation for tax purposes for the $1,000,000 capital assets. Year 1 shows $75,000 ($1,000,000 × 15%) and the remaining yearly figures are calculated on a declining basis. Column 6 shows the total tax-deductible amount made up of the interest charges (column 3) and depreciation (column 5). Column 7 shows the yearly tax shield. Using a 50 percent income tax rate, the company will benefit from a $125,000 (column 6 ÷ 2) tax shield. Column 8 shows the net cost of owning the asset, which is the annual payment of the loan (column 2) less the annual tax shield. Column 9 (net advantage or disadvantage versus lease) shows the net difference between the after-tax lease payment and net cost of owning. As indicated, it is preferable to lease the asset. During the 10-year period, the total cost of owning is $912,363 versus $813,720 for leasing, for a net difference of $98,643. In the early years, there is a distinct cash flow advantage to owning the asset; in the fifth year, however, cash flow favors leasing.

At this point, it appears that the lease option is better. However, because of the existence of interest, both alternatives should be discounted to arrive at a more meaningful and realistic comparison. As shown in column 10 of the table, using a 10 percent discount factor, in this particular case, owning is the better option by $8,040.

Factors That Influence Lease or Buy Decisions

This example of comparative cost analysis does not consider all the cost factors affecting the economics of each option. Many other reasons may also have to be considered. The most common include interest rate, residual value, obsolescence,

TABLE 9.12   Comparison of Cost of Owning versus Cost of Leasing

Computing Net Cost of Owning

Year	1 Lease Payment After Tax at 50%	2 Total Payment (3 + 4)	3 Interest	4 Principal	5 Deprec. for Tax Purposes	6 Income Tax-Deductible Expenses (3 + 5)	7 Tax Shield 50% (6 ÷ 2)	8 Net Cost of Owning (2 − 7)	9 Net Advantage (Disadvantage) vs Lease (1 − 8)	10 Present Value at 10%
1	$ 81,372	$ 162,745	$100,000	$ 62,745	$150,000	$ 250,000	$125,000	$37,745	$ 43,627	$ 39,657*
2	81,372	162,745	93,725	69,020	127,500	221,225	110,612	52,133	29,239	24,151*
3	81,372	162,745	86,823	75,922	108,375	195,198	97,599	65,146	16,226	12,186*
4	81,372	162,745	79,230	83,515	82,119	171,349	85,674	77,071	4,301	2,937*
5	81,372	162,745	70,880	91,865	78,300	149,180	74,590	88,156	(6,783)	(4,212)
6	81,372	162,745	61,587	101,052	66,556	128,249	64,125	98,620	(17,248)	(9,728)
7	81,372	162,745	51,587	111,158	56,573	108,100	54,080	108,866	(27,494)	(14,104)
8	81,372	162,745	40,472	122,273	48,086	88,558	44,279	118,466	(37,094)	(17,286)
9	81,372	162,745	28,245	134,500	40,874	69,119	34,560	128,185	(46,813)	(19,849)
10	81,372	162,745	14,795	147,950	34,743	49,538	24,789	137,976	(56,604)	(21,792)
	$813,720	$1,627,450	$ 627,450	$1,000,000	$ 803,126	$1,430,576	$ 715,288	$912,363	$(98,643)	$ 8,040*

*Favors owning   ( ) Favors leasing

risk factors, increase of financial leverage, related costs, depreciation rate, tax rate, and discount rate.

Interest Rate. Although the example in **Table 9.12** assumes the same interest rate for both leasing and owning, this may not always be the case. It is important to compare the lessor's interest rate with prevailing lending interest rates. Some leasing firms offer specialized services, and their costs will be included in the leasing charges, thus complicating the comparison.

Residual Value. Most assets have a residual value at the end of a lease period. If a firm owns an asset and sells it at the end of a similar period, the resulting cash inflow would be a reason to favor owning.

Obsolescence. The type of equipment also influences owning versus leasing. If a piece of equipment will soon become obsolete, leasing may be the best option. Why purchase a piece of equipment with a ten-year life span when it will become obsolete to the company after four? Some will argue that the higher the obsolescence factor, the higher the cost of the lease. This is not always true, since lessors can often find other users for their equipment; not all users have the same obsolescence rate.

Risk Factor. Leasing a piece of equipment with a high rate of obsolescence passes the element of risk to the lessors.

Increase of Financial Leverage. Leasing is often claimed to have a double effect on financial leverage. First, more money is usually available to finance assets through a lease than its alternate source, a loan. Assets can be leased at 100 percent, but property mortgage or conditional sales contracts can be obtained at only 50 percent or 75 percent. Second, financing part of a capital asset through leasing leaves room for future financing, if an expansion is contemplated right after start-up. However, while leasing may seem to hold out the promise of greater leverage, less risk of obsolescence, and lower cost, care should be used in considering this financing option. Lenders are wise to the financial obligations of "off balance sheet" financing and take them into account when assessing creditworthiness.

Related Costs. Certain costs, such as legal fees, are not as high for leasing as for debt financing; these should also be considered in the cost comparison.

Depreciation for Tax Purposes. A change in the depreciation rate may alter the decision. For example, if the depreciation rate increases from 15 percent to 25 percent, this would favor the purchase option.

Discount Rate. The same discount rate is used in **Table 9.12** to find the present value of owning and leasing. Since discounting reflects a risk factor, and owning may be riskier than leasing, a higher interest factor would be used to discount the owning option than leasing; this would favor the lease option.

Decision-Making in Action

The owner of Microplus Inc., Ted Bentley is very encouraged about his company's expansion program and its capability for producing power modules. He feels that the market is growing rapidly and that power modules would provide Microplus Inc. with higher margins that would help improve his company's financial performance. He points out that the key to Microplus's future growth and success is to market new highly profitable power modules.

Before meeting investors, the first thing that the company's controller did was to formulate financial projections based on the company's objectives and plans. After several months of discussions with the key members of the management team, the controller was able to prepare three-year projections for the company's income statements, balance sheets, and cash flow statements. The expansion program is expected to cost $1.1 million and is broken down as follows:

Financial Needs

Capital assets		$ 600,000
Working capital requirements		
Accounts receivable	$200,000	
Inventory	200,000	
Subtotal	400,000	
Accounts payable	100,000	300,000
Marketing costs		200,000
Total		$1,100,000*

*Note: This $1.1 million financial need is netted out after supplier financing (accounts payable). Excluding supplier financing, Microplus would have to raise $1.2 million.

On the financing side, Microplus's bank will lend a very small amount to the company on its accounts receivable (30 percent) and inventories (40 percent). The bank is also prepared to finance part of the capital assets in the amount of $200,000 with annual payments bearing an annual 10 percent interest charge. The controller informed Ted Bentley that on the basis of the pro-forma financial statements, particularly the cash flow statement, an amount of $200,000 would be available to finance the expansion. Shareholders are also prepared to invest an extra $100,000 into the business to finance the expansion.

Ted Bentley realizes that he will be short by $460,000 in financing to meet his $1.1 million investment need. After some discussion with several financial experts, they suggest that he should approach non-conventional investors who would be prepared to provide risk capital financing. This suggestion is based on the nature of the business (high tech) and the fast growth that is expected to take place in the industry and particularly by Microplus. Ted decided to meet two risk-capital investors.

The first was the *Small Business Administration* who indicated that they would provide a subordinated debt in the amount of $200,000 with collateral on the capital assets. He also met a risk capital lender who was also interested in investing equity funds in Microplus. Ted Bentley was aware that although the cost of equity would be high, it would not have to be paid by Microplus on an annual basis. The high return expected by the risk capital investor would be earned at exit through a buyout situation probably in the fourth or fifth year after the expansion.

On the basis of the above information, the following presents how Microplus's financial needs will be financed. **Table 9.13** summarizes both, the company's financial needs and financing requirements.

Financial Needs (Uses)		Financing Requirements (Sources)	
Capital assets	$ 600,000	Bank	$ 200,000
Accounts receivable	200,000	Bank (30%)	60,000
Inventory	200,000	Bank (40%)	80,000
Marketing costs	200,000	Suppliers	100,000
		Internal sources	200,000
		Shareholders	100,000
		SBA	200,000
		Risk capital firm	260,000
Total	$1,200,000	Total	$1,200,000

Financial requirements can be analyzed from different angles. First, on the basis of internal sources versus external sources showing the percentages provided by short-term lenders and long-term investors. As shown below, 16.7 percent of the financing will come from internal sources while total external funding represents 83.3 percent with short-term representing 20 percent and long-term, 63.3 percent of the funding requirements.

	Amount		Percentage
Internal		$ 200,000	16.7%
External			
Short-term	$240,000		20.0%
Long-term	760,000		63.3
Subtotal		1,000,000	83.3
Total		$1,200,000	100.0%

Another way to analyze Microplus's financing requirements is to differentiate between the amount of funds generated from debt versus equity (capital structure or financial leverage) after internal sources have been provided. As shown below, lenders (debt) provide 53.3 percent of the total financing package.

	Amount		Percentage
Internal		$ 200,000	16.7%
External			
Debt	$640,000		53.3%
Equity	360,000		30.0
Subtotal		1,000,000	83.3
Total		$1,200,000	100.0%

As shown below, risk capital financing accounts for 38.3 percent of the total financing package and the remaining is split between internal sources (16.7 percent) and conventional sources (45 percent).

		Amount	Percentage
Internal		$ 200,000	16.7%
External			
Conventional	$540,000		45.0%
Risk	460,000		38.3
Subtotal		1,000,000	83.3
Total		$1,200,000	100.0%

TABLE 9.13 Microplus's Financing Requirements

	Internal Sources	External Sources				
	Cash Flow From Operations	Conven-tional	Risk	Conven-tional	Risk	Total
Internal						
From Operations	$200,000					$ 200,000
External						
Conventional financing						
Short-term						
♦ Suppliers		$ 100,000				100,000
♦ Accounts receivable						
(30%) – Bank		60,000				60,000
♦ Inventory (40%) – Bank		80,000				80,000
Intermediate and long-term debt financing						
1. Conventional financing – Bank		200,000				200,000
2. Risk financing Subordinated debt – (SBA)			$200,000			200,000
Equity financing						
1. Conventional shareholders				$100,000		100,000
2. Risk capital Institutional investors					$260,000	260,000
Total financing requirements	$200,000	$440,000	$200,000	$100,000	$260,000	$1,200,000

Summary

The first thing that a company must do before approaching investors is to identify its financial needs which could be in the form of working capital, capital assets, marketing costs, and research and development.

Financing can be obtained from two sources. First, *internally*, by using income from operations and by managing the current assets more effectively; second, *externally* that is, from shareholders (through purchase of common or preferred shares) and short-term and long-term lenders.

External financing can be obtained from different sources and comes in different forms. Each is used to finance a specific asset, different venture, or business undertaking. A business faces three types of risks. *Business risk* has to do with the uncertainty inherent in projecting future earnings of a business. *Financial risk* deals with a company's financial structure. *Instrument risk* focuses on the type of instrument that should be used to finance a business.

When considering financing, businesses should attempt to match, as closely as possible, the maturity of the source of funds to the period of time for which the funds are needed. To do this, both cost and risk should be taken into consideration. Investors use different criteria for assessing the worthiness of prospective clients. These "Cs" of credit are character, collateral, capacity, capital, circumstances (or conditions), and coverage.

The most popular sources of *short-term financing* are suppliers (for trade credit) and banks that offer line of credit, seasonal or self-liquidating loans, revolving credit, and interim financing. Other financing institutions also offer secured loans on accounts receivable and inventory. Lenders can offer asset-based loans. These include factoring on accounts receivable and general lien, floor planning, warehousing agreements, and consignment to finance inventory.

Medium- and long-term debts are obtained from conventional institutions and include terms loans, conditional sales contracts, bonds, and mortgages. Risk capital funds can also be obtained on a subordinated debt basis whereby investors accept a higher level of risk.

Equity financing can be secured from shareholders and risk capital firms. These types of funds can be obtained from private or public sources. If public offerings are made, investment dealers must be used to process the issue. When considering common share, long-term debt, and preferred share financing, different factors must be taken into account: the payout of income, control, risk, and the advantages and disadvantages of each.

Risk capital firms provide financing for smaller, high-risk firms. They generally provide equity financing or both equity and long-term financing. Risk capital investments can be categorized as embryonic, start-up, development, expansion, turn-around, or buyout. They include angel investors, private investors, institutional investors and government-backed corporations.

Government financing is a direct or indirect form of financial assistance to businesses offered by municipal, state, or federal agencies to help them carry out capital expenditure projects or expand their activities.

Lease financing is another popular way of acquiring assets. The three major types of leases are operating leases, financial leases, and sale and leaseback. Before deciding on buying or leasing assets, the cost of each option should be evaluated. The factors that will determine the choice are interest rate, residual value, obsolescence factor, risk factor, financial leverage, depreciation rate, tax rate, and discount rate.

Working Capital Management

*D*uring the third year of operation, the Edwards were spending more time on the management of their working capital accounts. This is quite understandable because during the early years of any business, only a small amount of funds are invested in a business. As a business grows, more funds are invested in working capital. The following shows the evolution of CompuTech's current assets, net working capital, and total assets between the years 2001 to 2003.

In 000's of $	2001	2002	2003
Current assets	105	136	235
Current liabilities	52	60	132
Net working capital	53	76	103
Total assets	237	268	637

As shown, the Edwards' current assets and net working capital increased by 124 percent and 94 percent between 2001 and 2003 while current liabilities show a 154 percent growth. In order to improve their profit and financial performance, the Edwards realize that they have to be very cautious as to how they manage their working capital accounts.

Len and Joan are beginning to realize that managing working capital accounts is more complex and time-consuming than managing capital assets. In the case of capital assets such as investing in a new store, they have to go through a detailed capital budgeting using time value yardstick analysis in order to make their decision. However, once that decision is made, nothing much can be done. They have to live with the consequences, good or bad. On the other hand, managing working capital accounts such as accounts receivable and inventory is a daily chore and has to be done in a meticulous and knowledgeable way.

The Edwards know that they have to sell goods and services on credit and maintain adequate inventory in their store. These working capital accounts represent *essential investments* and must be made in order to generate sales. However, they realize that they have to be wise in the way that they spend their cash in these unproductive but necessary accounts. As Len pointed out: "Too great an investment in accounts receivable and inventory is considered a drain on CompuTech's cash flow position and can even blemish the return on our investment. The more that we have to invest in these accounts, the more we will have to borrow from short-term lenders. And of course, the larger the loan, the more interest charges CompuTech has to pay which ultimately reduces profitability." As shown on the previous page, part of the 154 percent increase in current liabilities is loans obtained from bankers.

The Edwards must therefore ensure that *just enough* funds are invested in working capital accounts to meet their day-to-day operations and maximize profitability, and not so much that such unproductive assets represent a cash drain on CompuTech. For this reason, they have to manage each current asset and current liability on a continual basis to make sure that they know exactly how much cash is needed (current assets) and how much cash is required (current liabilities).

This chapter explores the importance of managing working capital accounts. In particular, it focuses on three key topics:

1. What is the goal of managing working capital and why is it important to accelerate the cash conversion cycle?
2. How can current asset accounts such as cash, accounts receivable, and inventory be managed?
3. How can current liability accounts such as accounts payable, accruals, and working capital loans be managed?

Introduction

In Chapter 1, **"working capital"** (or operating capital) referred to all accounts appearing in the current accounts of the balance sheet, that is, current assets and current liabilities. In the early years of financial management, working capital included only current asset accounts such as cash, marketable securities, accounts receivable, and inventory. These assets are essential for operating a business. Having money in the bank to pay on-going bills, holding money in marketable securities such as short-term investments, and maintaining accounts receivable and inventory are surely not productive assets. However, if a company is to produce goods and sell its products, a certain amount of money must be tied up in these types of accounts. What is important for a business, however, is to ensure that a minimum amount of funds is tied up in these current asset accounts, *just enough* to ensure that it can meet its day-to-day operations and maximize profitability, and not so much that such unproductive assets represent a cash drain on the business. Managing current assets is a critical factor since it represents a major portion (in many cases, about half) of a company's total assets.

Today, working capital is defined more broadly. It includes current liabilities, such as accounts payable, notes payable, other accruals, or all loans that are due within a 12-month period (see **Table 10.1** for a typical list of working capital accounts). A current liability, such as accounts payable, is interest-free. Therefore, it is worthwhile for a business to take advantage of this type of short-term liability to finance its business activities. However, a business should be careful not to jeopardize its position by not being able to meet its short-term obligations.

Net working capital is defined as the difference between current assets and current liabilities. As shown in **Table 10.1**, for instance, if a company's current assets total $1,420,000 and its current liabilities are $720,000, the net working capital is $700,000.

Working capital management refers to all aspects of the management of individual current asset and current liability accounts to ensure proper interrelationships among all current asset accounts, all current liability accounts, and other balance sheet accounts such as capital assets and long-term debts.

Working capital accounts require more time than capital assets such as land, buildings, machinery, and equipment. The level of investment in each of the working capital accounts usually changes on a day-to-day basis, and, in order to effectively manage the business, managers must always know how much money is required in each of these accounts. Mismanagement of current accounts can be costly; excess current assets means a drain on profits and can be a source of undue risk. Not enough current assets, on the other hand, may entail a loss of revenue since a shortage of inventory, for example, may mean that goods wanted by customers are not readily available.

This chapter deals with how current asset and current liability accounts should be managed in order to maximize an organization's profitability. The accounts that will be examined in this chapter are the current assets cash, marketable securities, accounts receivable, prepaid expenses (accruals), and inventory and the current liabilities accounts payable, accruals (wages and taxes), and working capital loans.

TABLE 10.1   The Meaning of Working Capital

Working Capital Accounts

Current Assets		Current Liabilities	
Cash	$ 25,000	Accounts payable	$400,000
Marketable securities	100,000	Accrued wages	50,000
Accounts receivable	500,000	Taxes payable	20,000
Prepaid expenses	40,000	Notes payable	50,000
Inventory	755,000	Bank loan	200,000
Total current assets	$1,420,000	Total current liabilities	$ 720,000

Net working capital = $1,420,000 − $720,000 = $700,000.

The Goal of Working Capital Management

The goal of managing working capital is to accelerate the cash flow cycle in a business after sales have been made. The faster the cash circulates, the more profitable it is to the business, because it means that a company has less cash tied up in unproductive (but necessary) assets. Let's use **Table 10.1** as an example. If accounts receivable and inventories were reduced by $75,000 and $100,000 respectively, the company would be able to deposit $175,000 in investment securities, say at 10 percent, and earn $17,500 in interest annually. Instead, management would probably want to invest this excess cash in more productive assets such as plant modernization or new equipment, which would generate a 20 percent return on the assets each year, as long as the inventories and accounts receivable are kept at the new level.

There are two broad approaches for measuring the productivity of cash within a business: days of working capital (DWC) and cash conversion efficiency (CCE). The objective of the **days of working capital ratio** is to calculate the amount of days in working capital a business holds in order to meet its average daily sales requirements. The lower the number of days, the more efficient a business is in managing its cash. Consider, for example, Eastman Technologies Inc. that was introduced in Chapter 2. In this case, the company shows 47.2 days of working capital. This ratio is calculated as follows:

$$\frac{(\text{Accounts receivable} + \text{Inventory}) - \text{Accounts payable}}{\text{Net sales}/365} = \text{Days of working capital}$$

The information used to calculate Eastman's DWC is drawn from the income statement (**Table 2.3**) and the balance sheet (**Table 2.5**).

$$\frac{(\$300,000 + \$218,000) - \$195,000}{\$2,500,000/365} = \frac{\$323,000}{\$6,849} = 47.2 \text{ days}$$

The **cash conversion efficiency ratio** measures the efficiency with which a business converts sales revenue to cash flow within its operations. The financial data used for calculating Eastman's CCE ratio is drawn from **Table 2.7** (Statement of Cash Flows) and **Table 2.3** (Income Statement).

$$\frac{\text{Cash flow from operations}}{\text{Net sales}} = \frac{\$126,500}{\$2,500,000} = 5.1\%$$

Eastman Technologies cash performance ratios do not mean much unless they are compared to previous years' data and to industry standards. The first working capital survey prepared by *CFO Magazine* appeared in the July 1998 issue. The survey lists the cash conversion efficiency ratio (CCE) and the days of working capital ratios (DWC) for many companies and industries. The average for all industries included in the survey was 10.0 percent for the CCE, and 64.2 days for the DWC. The following gives the results of the 1998 *Working Capital Survey* for 10 industries[1].

	CCE	DWC
Apparel	4.3%	101.0 days
Beverage	12.5	15.9
Building materials	5.4	90.3
Computer	10.1	72.9
Electronics	8.3	86.3
Food	8.4	49.5
Food services	9.9	−3.5
Furniture	8.0	65.7
Metal products	7.2	85.0
Motor vehicles	7.5	68.1
Pharmaceuticals	15.1	90.7

The company that ranked first for the CCE was Vastar Resources, a petroleum company located in Houston, Texas with 61.1 percent and for DWC, it was Paging Network, also a Houston-based company in telecommunications at 42.7 days.

Managing working capital accounts means reducing costs related to working capital accounts, investing short-term excess cash, and keeping receivables and inventory as low as possible while increasing payables. All this allows a business to do more business. Increasing sales is not the only answer to improving profitability; all accounts that are affected as a result of incremental sales must be managed efficiently and effectively.

An important criterion for measuring financial performance is return on investment (ROI). The accounts appearing under current assets are in the denominator of the ROI equation; consequently, if working capital accounts are minimized, ROI is improved.

An important concept related to the management of working capital accounts is the **cash conversion cycle**, depicted in **Figure 10.1**. As shown, working capital accounts can be displayed on a wheel, and the faster the wheel turns the faster and more effectively management can use the cash generated from sales. The goal is to identify the number of days it takes to perform each activity shown on the wheel. For example, if it takes 12 days for customers to make their purchase decisions, 6 days for the credit manager to approve a new customer, 19 days to process goods in the plant, and 9 days to bill customers, the objective would be to reduce the number of days for each of these activities. If, overall, it takes 95 days for cash to circulate in a business once a sale is made, the objective would be to reduce this to, say, 80 days. In Chapter 1, under the heading "Investment Decisions," we examined how the use of financial ratios to gauge the management of working capital accounts can help improve cash flow.

The shaded portion of **Table 10.2** shows the difference between *profit* and *cash flow* and how improvement in working capital accounts can accelerate cash

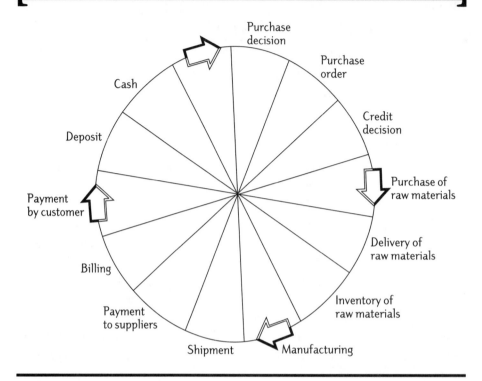

FIGURE 10.1   The Cash Conversion Cycle

flow. The upper portion of the table shows the amount of profit generated each month. The middle section (Current Performance) shows the amount of cash generated by the business by collecting 10 percent of sales within the first month, 50 percent in the second month, and 40 percent in the third month. Disbursements for purchases are paid in the same month that goods are purchased. The lower portion of the table (Targeted Performance) shows how cash flow is improved by collecting the accounts receivable faster and by paying the suppliers more slowly.

The following summarizes the cash balance at the end of each month as a result of managing these two working capital accounts more efficiently.

	January	February	March	April
Current performance	$30,000	—	$(65,000)	$(20,000)
Targeted performance	30,000	$17,500	—	60,000
Cash flow improvement	—	$17,500	$ 65,000	$ 80,000

By improving the management of only two working capital accounts (accounts receivable and accounts payable), the business was able to improve its cash position by $17,500 in February, $65,000 in March, and $80,000 in April.

Let's now examine how individual working capital accounts can be managed.

TABLE 10.2   Profit Versus Cash Flow

	Profit Forecast			
	January	February	March	April
Sales	$ 200,000	$ 250,000	$ 300,000	$ 200,000
Cost of goods sold (70% of sales)	(140,000)	(175,000)	(210,000)	(140,000)
Operating expenses	(55,000)	(60,000)	(65,000)	(55,000)
Total expenses	(195,000)	(235,000)	(275,000)	(195,000)
Profit	$ 5,000	$ 15,000	$ 25,000	$ 5,000 ←
	Cash Flow Forecast (Current Performance)			
Beginning cash balance	$ 20,000	$ 30,000	—	$(65,000)
Collections*				
10% of 1st month sales	20,000	20,000	25,000	30,000
50% of 2nd month sales	100,000	100,000	100,000	125,000
40% of 3rd month sales	80,000	80,000	80,000	80,000
Total cash available	220,000	230,000	205,000	170,000
Disbursements				
Purchases	(140,000)	(175,000)	(210,000)	(140,000)
Operating expenses**	(50,000)	(55,000)	(60,000)	(50,000)
Total disbursements	(190,000)	(230,000)	(270,000)	(190,000)
Ending cash balance	$ 30,000	—	$ (65,000)	$ (20,000) ←
	Cash Flow Forecast (Targeted Performance)			
Beginning cash balance	$ 20,000	$ 30,000	$ 17,500	—
Collections*				
70% of 1st month sales	140,000	140,000	175,000	$210,000
30% of 2nd month sales	60,000	60,000	60,000	75,000
Total cash available	220,000	230,000	252,500	285,000
Disbursements Purchases***				
50% of 1st month	(70,000)	(87,500)	(105,000)	(70,000)
50% of 2nd month	(70,000)	(70,000)	(87,500)	(105,000)
Operating expenses**	(50,000)	(55,000)	(60,000)	(50,000)
Total disbursements	(190,000)	(212,500)	(252,500)	(225,000)
Ending cash balance	$ 30,000	$17,500	—	$60,000 ←

*Assumes sales at $200,000 per month for October, November, and December.
** Excludes $5,000 for depreciation expense.
***Assumes cost of goods sold of $140,000 in November and December.

Managing Cash Flow

Cash consists of cash on hand and short-term deposits. Paying for ongoing obligations, such as the purchase of raw materials and the payment of salaries and current bills, is a constant drain on a company's cash reservoir. However, this reservoir is constantly being replenished by cash sales of inventory and the collection of accounts receivable. Let's examine how cash flows in a business.

The Flow of Cash

Cash management is usually assigned to a high-level manager in a business—usually the chief financial officer (CFO) or the treasurer. The goal is to ensure that cash flows into a business as fast as possible and is used wisely. **Figure 10.2** gives a visual presentation of how cash flows in and out of a business. At the center of the system lies the cash pool (or cash reservoir). The cash is used to pay operating expenses and lenders, suppliers, dividends, taxes, for buying capital assets, and for maintaining inventory and accounts receivable.

Why Maintain an Adequate Cash Pool?

The cash pool must be maintained at an appropriate level and specific amounts must be designated for specific purposes such as inventory, marketable securities, and accounts receivable. Maintaining a balanced cash pool is important for four reasons. First, it enables a business to conduct its ordinary operating transactions, such as paying current bills and to partially finance its inventories and accounts receivable. Second, balanced cash pool serves in emergencies because of the diffi-

FIGURE 10.2   Cash Flow

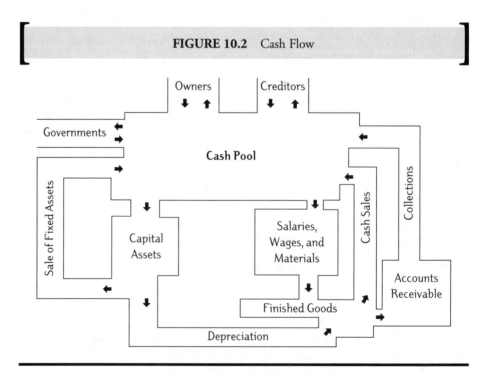

culty in forecasting accurately the matching of cash receipts and cash disbursements. It can also be used as leverage for borrowing additional cash on a short-term basis. Third, it can be used for taking advantage of opportunities, such as cash discounts if bills are paid within a specified number of days. Finally, it can be used as an instrument for maintaining a credit standing with short-term lenders and suppliers.

Making Cash a Productive Asset

The main objective of cash management is to maintain a reasonable amount of cash so that profitability is not affected and payment of short-term commitments is possible. One way to increase profitability is to reduce the time-lag between the date money is mailed by customers and the date it is deposited in the company's bank account to produce a return. For example, if a business can make 12 percent on short-term securities, and an amount of $30,000 tied up in the mail arrives 20 days late, the company misses the opportunity of making $197.26. The calculation is as follows:

$$\$30,000 \times 12\% \times \frac{20\text{-day delay}}{365\text{ days}} = \$197.26$$

If a company has hundreds or thousands of such checks arriving late, it can easily miss the opportunity of making thousands of dollars each year in interest alone.

Establishing a Minimum Cash Balance

One of the activities of cash management is to determine exactly how much cash is needed on hand to conduct the on-going operations of a business. In order to manage cash effectively, a firm must synchronize its cash inflows with its cash outflows on a monthly basis. *Cash planning* is done through the cash budget (see **Table 8.2** of Chapter 8 for an example of a monthly cash budget). The cash budget allows a firm to ascertain the:

1. Flow of the monthly cash receipts.
2. Flow of the monthly cash disbursements.
3. Surplus or shortages of cash at the end of each month.
4. Amount of cash that should be invested in short-term securities (surplus) or that will be required from the bank in terms of a loan (shortage).

The objective of cash management is to set a minimum level of cash to satisfy business needs under normal operating conditions in order to increase organizational profitability, but without lessening business activities or exposing a firm to undue risk in meeting its financial obligations. Cash reserves including marketable securities should be sufficient to satisfy daily cash expenditures. What a business needs is:

◆   A practical minimum cash balance to operate with.
◆   An amount necessary to absorb any unforeseen expenditures.

◆ Some money to take advantage of profitable business opportunities (e.g., cash or special discounts on purchases, anticipation of an increase in the price of raw materials, an attractive price on a specialized piece of equipment).

Cash needs can be estimated using the following two steps:

Step 1:   Determine the average daily cash expenditures over recent months.

Step 2:   After recognizing the special characteristics of the business, estimate the appropriate cash reserves as a specific number of days' average cash outflow.

For example, if a business spends $300,000 in cash each month, the average daily cash outflow is $10,000 ($300,000 ÷ 30). Here, the treasurer might determine that six days of cash are required to meet the average expenditures under normal business operations. If this is the case, management would need a cash balance of no more than $60,000 ($10,000 × 6 days).

Ways to Improve the Collection of Cash

There are different ways a firm can speed up cash receipts in order to make that asset productive.

Facilitate the Customer's Decisions to Purchase. A customer's decision to purchase goods or services initiates the cash conversion period. Introducing the most rapid communication process to encourage a customer to place an order as quickly as possible is the first step in the cash conversion cycle. A purchase order serves as the medium of communication. Customers should be able to transmit their orders to the company as quickly as possible.

Reduce the Negative Float. **Float** is defined as the time lag between the day a check is *mailed* to the firm and the time the funds are *received* by the firm. There are three ways to improve a negative float, that is, eliminate idle cash.

The first is the *electronic communications.* The wire transfer process and the Internet are effective means of collecting payments from customers for large purchases. Because wire transfer eliminates delays caused by the postal system, the administrative structure of a business, or the check clearing process, it allows a business to use the collected funds more rapidly. This process transfers money from the sender or customer's bank account into the receiver or firm's bank account in a matter of hours.

Under the electronic system, money is wired directly from a customer's bank account to a business's bank account. This system allows accounts to be debited and credited daily. At the end of each day, excess cash is invested in short-term deposits in order to generate additional earnings. Unfortunately, many businesses look only at personnel and equipment costs involved in these alternatives and overlook the one- to seven-day reduction in their cash conversion period that results from eliminating mail delays.

The electronic communication of purchase orders is generally suitable when a business has an on-going relationship with a customer. Repeat customers usually make up the bulk of the sales; so using electronic communication for them helps a business improve its service and accelerate cash flow.

The second process involves **regional banks**. Under this process, customers pay their accounts to banks and the payment can be transferred to the company's account more quickly than by mail delivery. Collection accounts are established at a series of commercial banks strategically located around the country, and customers are encouraged to pay their bills in their region rather than sending the payments to a central location.

The third strategy is to establish a **lockbox** in an area where the firm has many customers. The lockbox system is a procedure whereby a firm rents post office boxes in different cities and entrusts their management to banks, which monitor the lockboxes periodically. The firm instructs customers in a particular region to mail their checks to regional post office box numbers rather than directly to the firm. As soon as checks from customers arrive, they are microfilmed, checked for completeness, and deposited in the firm's account. Although this system can be an effective means of improving the collection of cash, a business must weigh the bank's fees against the benefits that accrue from a shorter cash conversion period. Often, the profit potential of a more rapid cash flow can make the cost of the lockbox service insignificant.

The following compares the traditional payment system and the lockbox system.

Traditional Payment System	The Lockbox System
1. Invoice is sent to the customer.	**1.** Invoice is sent to the customer.
2. Invoice and payment are sent to the company lockbox.	**2.** Invoice and check are sent to the company's post office box.
3. Company processes payment and credits customers' account.	**3.** Bank processes payment and credits the customer's bank account.
4. Company deposits the check at the bank.	**4.** Bank advises the company of payment information.
5. Bank processes the check and forwards it to the customer's bank.	**5.** Bank forwards check to the customer's bank.
6. Customer's bank debits customer's account and returns the cancelled check with the next bank statement.	**6.** Customer's bank debits customer's account and returns the cancelled check with the next bank statement.

Such a system can help reduce the time lag by three to four days.

Managing Marketable Securities

One of the responsibilities of the CFO is to adjust the company's cash balance on an on-going basis, either by investing excess cash in temporary short-term securities or by securing extra cash through short-term bank borrowings.

It is more profitable for a business to invest cash in marketable securities, even if it is only for several days, than to leave it dormant in a bank account that does not generate interest. The main objective of managing marketable securities is to invest the temporary excess cash in order to increase profitability.

Funds are held in short-term marketable securities or temporary investments for three reasons:

1. To finance seasonal or cyclical operations (temporary working capital).
2. To finance known financial requirements, such as purchase of equipment or machinery.
3. To invest funds received from the sale of long-term securities (shares or bonds).

Different types of marketable securities can be held by businesses, and the attributes of each one should be examined carefully before investing. Four main attributes should be considered. First, there is *maturity,* the length of time by which the principal amount of a marketable security must be paid back to the investor. Second, there is the *denomination,* the unit of transaction for buying or selling a short-term security. Third, there is *marketability,* or the ability of an investor to sell a marketable security. Finally, there is the *yield determination,* which is the method of earning a return on the investment.

There are different types of **investment securities**, such as U.S. Treasury bills, bank deposits, commercial paper, finance company paper, U.S. government bonds, Fed funds, and corporate bonds with different maturity dates and yields. Depending on the length of time a treasurer wants to place funds, he or she will have to find the most suitable type of security, that is, the one that responds most favorably to the business's needs.

Strategies for Managing Marketable Securities

Managing marketable securities for a small business is relatively easy. The only requirement is the need to match the short-term investments with the excess cash shown in the monthly cash budget. A large business, on the other hand, must determine investment strategies that will optimize the return on investment. In many cases, businesses have millions of dollars tied up in cash or near-cash accounts. It is therefore important for such businesses to determine effective investment strategies in short-term marketable securities. There are six approaches.

First, there is the *do nothing option.* In this case, the company simply lets the excess funds accumulate in its bank account. Here, funds are not invested in short-term securities; therefore profitability is sacrificed.

Second, there is the investment of funds on an *ad hoc basis*. This approach is accomplished when investment securities are synchronized with projected cash disbursements. This method is used by firms that, because of a shortage of resources or a lack of expertise within the company, do not want to devote much time and energy to this activity.

Third, there is the *riding the yield approach*. Here, the treasurer examines the investment portfolio and invests in the securities that will offer the highest interest rate. For example, he or she may sell off a long-term security before maturity and purchase a short-term security simply to obtain a higher yield.

Fourth, *guidelines* can be developed. This is particularly useful if many people are involved in investing in short-term securities such as in insurance companies and trust companies. Such guidelines give the securities analysts procedures to be followed systematically in order to reflect senior management's viewpoint and take into consideration both return and risk.

Fifth, *control limits* are established and the system allows the analysts to take action only when the cash balance reaches an upper or lower control limit. This approach does not specify which marketable securities should be bought or sold, but when action should be taken.

The sixth option is the *portfolio approach*. Here, individual marketable securities are not examined as isolated investment opportunities, but as part of a group of investments. In this case, both risk and returns are taken into consideration from a broader viewpoint—the portfolio perspective. There may be hundreds of different investment options, and each option is evaluated on the basis of a *total investment strategy* that is consistent with the financial objectives of the firm. Some securities may offer low return and low risk; others, high risk and high return.

Managing Accounts Receivable

Since most firms sell on credit, and for most of them credit accounts for the bulk of their sales, it is important to manage the accounts receivable effectively. The level of accounts receivable is determined in two ways: first, by the volume of sales made on credit; and second, by the time it takes for customers to pay off their accounts.

The mission of the credit manager is to:

1. Set credit terms
2. Grant credit to customers
3. Bill the customers
4. Monitor payments made by customers
5. Collect accounts receivable
6. Ensure adequate credit insurance

Set Credit Terms

It is the responsibility of the credit manager to decide what **credit terms** a firm should adopt. These terms are greatly influenced by the industry of which the firm is part. A basic element of credit terms to businesses is the length of time given to customers to pay their accounts.

Trade discounts can help a company's cash flow at the expense of earnings and may very well be a good trade-off. For example, a business may allow a 2 percent discount off the original sales price of goods if a customer pays an invoice within 10 days of shipment, and charge the full amount for payment within 30 days (i.e., 2/10, n/30). However, before deciding to offer trade discounts, the credit manager estimates the costs and benefits that will result. Should a firm offer its customers a policy of 2/10, n/30, 1/10, n/30, or 2/10, n/45? To answer this question, the credit manager must explore the following points.

First, the manager measures the benefits. When a customer pays in accordance with the discount terms, it shortens a company's average collection period and accelerates cash flow. At the same time, the investment in receivables is reduced, as are the costs associated with carrying that investment. Cash discounts presumably benefit both parties in the transaction: The customers reduce their purchase costs when taking the discount, and the firm enjoys a better cash flow and a lower investment in accounts receivable.

Second, the credit manager calculates the effective price when offering a purchase discount. The bottom line is this: Before introducing discounts into credit terms, the credit manager recognizes how such allowances affect a company's earnings.

Before changing the policy, the credit manager must go through a detailed calculation. To illustrate, let's assume that a company sells products with an average unit-selling price of $400.00. The cost of manufacturing or buying materials from suppliers is $250.00. Furthermore, in that particular industry, customers have the habit of paying 60 days after purchase. As shown below, if the cost of money is 10 percent, it would be more advantageous for the firm to offer the 2/10, n/60, since the profit generated when customers pay in 10 days is $146.65, compared to $145.90 if they pay in 60 days. If the customer benefits from the 2 percent discount, line 1 shows that the company would receive $392.00 ($400.00 × 98%) instead of $400.00. Whether the company offers a 2 percent discount or not, line 2 indicates that the company would have to pay $250.00 to manufacture the product or to buy it from a supplier. Line 3 shows the credit costs for both options. The company would have to pay a $0.68 ($250.00 × 10% × 10/365) credit cost to finance the $250.00 purchase if payment is received in 10 days, and $4.11 ($250.00 × 10% x 60/365) if payment is received in 60 days. Line 4 shows that the company would make $5.37 ($392.00 × 10% × 50/365) if the $392.00 is deposited in the bank for the 50-day period and earns 10 percent. Based on this calculation, line 5 shows that there is an economic advantage to offering the 2 percent discount.

Line		10-Day Payment	60-Day Payment
1.	Effective price	$392.00	$400.00
2.	Purchase (or manufacturing) cost	−250.00	−250.00
3.	Credit cost (10 and 60 days)	−0.68	−4.11
4.	Interest on money (50 days)	+5.37	—
5.	Net profit	$146.69	$145.89

The above calculation does not take into consideration the $250.00 payment made to the suppliers or for manufacturing the goods, since such a payment would be incurred by the company whether the customer takes advantage of the 2 percent discount or not.

Grant Credit to Customers

The second activity of the credit manager is the granting of credit. Two questions must be asked in the context of credit analysis: Should credit be granted to a customer? If yes, how much? The criteria used by firms to rate borrowers can be summarized as the six "Cs" introduced in Chapter 9: character, collateral, capacity, capital, circumstances, and coverage.

In order to shorten the cash conversion cycle, the credit decision should be made as soon as a purchase order is received. Therefore, it is important to approve lines of credit for major customers in advance. In other words, the credit manager should anticipate customers' needs before they exceed their credit limits.

Little is lost if a customer does not use the full credit line. However, customers who do increase their purchases will find their orders delivered more promptly. Indeed, pre-approved credit facilitates the completion of a sale and improves a firm's service capability. A faster response inevitably offers a competitive advantage.

The same approach can be used for new customers. It is preferable to check the creditworthiness of a new account in advance, before receiving a larger order. Obtaining the information for a credit check—bank checks, supplier checks—can take several days and thus lengthen the cash conversion period. Moreover, if the delay is too long, the business may risk losing the sale to a competitor with a more efficient credit-decision process.

However, reliable credit analysis should not be sacrificed for the sake of speedy approval. Even a modest increase in bad-debt losses (if some customers do not pay their bills) can offset the benefits from a lower cash-conversion period. At the same time, any element in the administrative process that delays the completion of a sale hampers the smooth flow of cash into a business.

Let's review the types of credit analysis that businesses go through when granting credit to consumers and businesses.

Consumer Credit. Credit-scoring systems are often used to analyze the creditworthiness of potential customers. Under a **credit-scoring system**, the credit clerks are given specific guidelines for rating a potential customer as a low or high risk. This system is used by businesses offering credit cards to thousands of consumers. **Table 10.3** shows a typical credit-scoring system. As shown, several variables are examined and each is given a weight. This weight has been determined by taking a sample of existing customers and finding the factors that distinguish those who pay their accounts promptly from those who are slow payers. In this case, the variables include age, marital status, occupation, time on last job, annual income, residence, home ownership, and telephone; and, the credit score totals 117.6. The credit clerk will then decide, using the predetermined guidelines, what steps should be taken with each consumer. For example, the guidelines may stipulate that if the score is less than 60 points, credit will be denied; if it is between 60 and 80, the customer will be investigated further; and if it is greater than 80, credit is granted. Under these guidelines, the consumer in our example would be granted credit.

Business Credit. Granting credit to commercial enterprises involves a different type of analysis. Here, the firm may want to go through an analysis of the potential customer and obtain information regarding its credit standing. In certain cases, the firm will ask for a credit report, such as the one provided by Dun & Bradstreet. Typical information provided by credit institutions is summarized in **Table 10.4**.

On the basis of the information obtained, the firm will specify the type of account that should be granted (open account or other arrangement), the credit period (when payment is due), the size of the discount, and the discount period.

Impact of Alternative Credit Policies. Decisions about the extent of credit to be provided to customers are determined by a firm's **credit policy**. If a business has a restrictive credit policy, it will most likely sell less, have less invested in accounts receivable and inventory, and have lower bad debts. Conversely, as a firm

TABLE 10.3   A Credit-Scoring System

Variable	Measurement	Value	Weight	Weighted value
Age	In years as reported	36	0.4	14.4
Marital status	Coded 1 (yes) or 0 (no)	1	20.0	20.0
Occupation	Coded 1 to 5 for different professions	4	4.3	17.2
Time on last job	In years as reported	6	0.9	5.4
Annual income	In thousands of dollars as reported	45.0	0.6	27.0
Residence	Coded 1 to 5 for different postal zones	3	4.6	13.8
Home ownership	Number of years owned as reported	4	1.2	4.8
Telephone	Coded 1 (yes) or 0 (no)	1	15.0	15.0
Total credit score				117.6

[**TABLE 10.4**   Information Shown on Business Credit Reports]

Summary	Classification code for line of business, year business started, rating, principal executives (owners)
Report information	Payments, sales worth, number of employees, trends
Payments	How business pays its bill (i.e., amounts owing, amounts past due terms of sales, manner of payment, and supplier comments)
Finance	Financial conditions and trend of business (balance sheet and income statement)
History	Names, birthdates, and past business experience of the principals or owners, affiliations, ownership, outside interests of the principal owners
Operations	Nature of the premises, neighborhood, size of floor space, production facilities

relaxes its credit terms, it sells more goods to a wider range of customers that include poorer credit risks; this in turn increases bad debts.

An integrated management analysis should precede any change in a firm's credit terms or policies. There is a close connection between selling and credit. Since most firms do not really have a choice of selling on credit or for cash, the most important decision for a business is when to change the credit policy of the firm over time. An ROI framework is appropriate for comparing credit alternatives because it focuses on the investment a firm makes in accounts receivable. It also allows a business to systematically consider potential sales and profits, alternative credit terms including cash discount, and bad debt expenses. Changing credit terms therefore requires the analysis of certain links or relationships that should not be ignored when evaluating alternative credit terms and policies. The decision to extend credit consideration and carry the resulting investment in accounts receivable focuses on a trade-off between (1) the cost of carrying the investment in accounts receivable, and (2) the benefits of a larger sales volume.

The most important links are between

- Credit terms and policy and your firm's total marketing effort.
- Credit policy and the inventory level.
- Credit policy and production capacity.
- Credit policy and the efficiency of your firm's operations.

To establish an appropriate credit policy, the credit manager must examine the changes in the level of profit generated as a result of a relaxed credit policy, and the extra investment in accounts receivable and inventory. **Table 10.5** shows how to calculate changes in profit and investment resulting from a change in credit terms. In this case, if the firm's cost of capital is 12 percent, it will not go ahead with the proposed credit policy.

[
TABLE 10.5 Establishing a Credit Policy
]

	Existing terms	Proposed terms
Expected volume (units)	500,000	550,000
Expected sales revenue ($10.00 per unit)	$5,000,000	$5,500,000
Expected profit before bad debts (10% of revenue)	500,000	550,000
Expected bad debt expense*	25,000	55,000
Expected profit (after bad debts)	475,000	495,000
Incremental profit	—	20,000
Expected collection period (days)	31	38
Average accounts receivable	425,000	575,000
Inventory	850,000	900,000
Incremental investment	—	200,000

*A 0.5% factor is used for calculating bad debts for existing credit terms, and a 1.0% factor is used for the proposed terms.

$$\text{Return on investment} = \frac{\$20,000}{\$200,000} = 10\%$$

As shown in the table, the levels of accounts receivable and inventory are affected by the proposed change in the credit policy. It is important to calculate the effect each change in credit policy has on working capital accounts.

Bill the Customers

The invoice identifies the merchandise sold, the shipment date, and the amount due from the purchaser. Prompt completion and transmission of an invoice are important elements of the cash cycle for two reasons. First, few purchasers will pay for merchandise prior to the receipt of the invoice. Indeed, in most businesses, the invoice typically serves as the trigger for the payment process in the accounting system. Second, the invoice date usually initiates the payment period defined by a firm's selling terms.

Prompt completion and transmission of the invoice increases cash availability and earnings. A firm should not render a monthly statement of account to trigger customer payment. Rendering statements is a costly, time-consuming, and self-defeating administrative process. Also, allowing customers to pay in response to monthly statements, rather than to purchase invoices, adds from one to 30 days to the cash conversion cycle, as customers ignore the invoices and wait for the monthly statement. Issuing the invoice that completes a sale is the final step in the administrative process.

Monitor Payments Made by Customers

Irrespective of how a credit policy is determined, once it is adopted, collection must be monitored continually to gauge the effectiveness of the policy and how well it is applied. Several approaches can be used to gauge the effectiveness of a credit policy, to monitor the payment behavior of customers over a period of time, and to take corrective action on delinquent accounts. The most common are (1) average collection period (in days), and (2) the aging of accounts receivable.

Average Collection Period. The **average collection period** is the average time it takes for customers to pay their accounts after credit sales have been made. Let us examine how this works. Assume that a business sold $3.0 million last year and the same amount this year. However, the accounts receivable increased from last year's $450,000 to this year's $500,000. This is an indication that customers paid their accounts more slowly over the last 12 months. The calculation is done as follows:

$$\text{Last year's average collection period} = \frac{\$450,000}{\$3,000,000} \times 365 = 54.7 \text{ days}$$

$$\text{This year's average collection period} = \frac{\$500,000}{\$3,000,000} \times 365 = 60.8 \text{ days}$$

The company shows a 6.1-day deterioration in the average collection period.

Aging of Accounts Receivable. While 6.1 days may seem like a small increase, the credit manager may want to examine in more detail the aging of its accounts receivable. The credit manager may want to spot changes in customer paying behavior by preparing an aging schedule showing the percentage of each month's sales still outstanding at the end of successive months. The schedule gives a picture of any recent change in the make-up of the receivables. This type of information is presented in **Table 10.6**. As shown, **aging of accounts receivable** groups accounts by age category and by what percentage of receivables outstanding fall in each age category.

TABLE 10.6   Aging of Accounts Receivable

As a percentage of total receivables

% of receivables	Last year	This year
under 30 days old	60.4	54.2
between 31 and 60 days	24.4	23.8
between 61 and 90 days	7.2	10.4
between 91 and 120 days	6.5	8.3
over 121 days	1.5	3.3

Examining the aging process is an essential element of the accounts receivable analysis; it identifies specific groupings of accounts within the total component that make up an overall investment. The aging schedule also shows how long accounts receivable have been outstanding at a given point in time.

Collect Accounts Receivable

The collection of accounts was discussed earlier in this chapter under the heading "Managing Cash Flow." Effective credit collection begins by mailing invoices promptly. Once the invoice is mailed, the credit manager must examine, on a regular basis, the average collection period and take remedial action if targets are not realized. Several steps can be adopted to accelerate the collection of accounts from delinquent customers. First, there is the "dunning" approach, mailing a duplicate copy of the original invoice. Second, the credit manager can make a personal telephone call, which can serve as a routine, but stronger, reminder. Third, the credit manager can call on customers and initiate constructive counseling. Fourth, registered letters can be sent to delinquent accounts as notices that if payment is not received by a certain date, the firm will involve a third party such as a collection agency in the collection process. Finally, the most expensive way is to resort to formal legal charges.

Credit Insurance

Credit insurance provides protection against the cash drain caused by uncollectible accounts receivable. Just as a vehicle theft or a warehouse fire can disrupt a business, the inability to collect a large receivable can cut off its cash flow. Not only can credit insurance prevent a cash flow crisis, it can also lead to higher earnings. Insurance protection on accounts receivable can be secured in three ways:

The **indemnification policy** is insurance a business takes against the catastrophic loss in cash that might occur when a large receivable becomes uncollectible because of debtor bankruptcy, debtor composition (reorganization of debt by creditors), or any other proceedings that reflect a debtor's insolvency.

The **credit insurance policy** provides coverage for losses suffered from any of a firm's accounts receivable that become uncollectible. The coverage is subject to two practical limits. First, the insurance company can apply a deductible amount to each loss. Second, the insurance company can limit the maximum coverage for each debtor. Typically, those limits are tied to ratings established by national credit agencies such as Dun & Bradstreet. While premiums vary, the coverage may cost 0.25 percent to 0.5 percent of annual sales which could be a small price to pay for survival.

With this type of insurance, a company can be more liberal in granting credit to high risk customers. If they don't pay, the insurance company would compensate the company. Would someone have more confidence in driving a car knowing that in the event of an accident, the insurance company would pay for the damages. How would one feel driving your car without insurance? The same applies with this type of policy. Here, instead of dealing with car insurance or house insurance, we are dealing with credit insurance.

Managing Inventory

The objective of inventory management is to replenish inventory or stocks in such a way that associated order and holding costs are kept to a minimum in order to enhance profitability.

Turning inventory more rapidly improves cash flow, earnings, and ROI. One more way for a firm to analyze its management effort is by calculating the annual inventory turnover rate, or the number of times a business sells, or turns, its investment in inventory in the course of a year. It is an activity indicator that relates an investment in inventory directly to sales volume for a retail or wholesale business or cost of goods sold for a manufacturer.

The turnover rate calculation is significant because of its direct relationship to cash flow and profits. Thus, the faster the inventory turns over, the lower the investment in inventory. Most managers understand that moving merchandise more rapidly is the key to profitability.

To calculate the inventory turnover rate, the annual cost of goods sold or sales revenue must be divided by the average investment in inventory.

Maintaining the right level of inventory can be compared to maintaining an appropriate level of water in a bathtub. If water flows out of the tub more rapidly than into it, the tub will soon be empty. However, if more water is let in than out, the tub will overflow. The same principle applies in inventory management. On one side, inventory is used continuously to produce manufactured goods and, on the other, raw materials keep flowing into the storage area. The idea is to determine two things: (1) the proper level of investment that should be kept in inventory, and (2) how much inventory should be purchased, and at what interval, to maintain an appropriate level of stock.

A delay in shipment lengthens the cash conversion period and hinders cash flow. To avoid delays in shipment, a firm should have a well-organized shipping department that is well-coordinated with the administrative process.

An inventory control system should answer two essential needs:

◆   It should maintain a current record of the amount of each inventory item held in stock.
◆   It should be able to locate that stock.

Neither element should be left to chance or memory. Accountants refer to this system as perpetual inventory. The sale and purchase of each item in inventory is logged on a computerized stock sheet. Then, at any time, the sheets specify the total inventory of each item held in stock; the sheet should also identify the exact location of the items. This prevents shipping delays, as employees do not have to search for stock in the warehouse. The perpetual inventory system also helps to determine the reorder points for each item on the stock ledger sheets when the economic ordering quantity system (to be discussed later) is applied.

A periodic count of every item in stock is the first, fundamental principle of sound inventory management. The physical count serves two primary objectives:

1. It enables a business to verify the accuracy of its accounting procedures that keep track of the investment in inventory. As the exact amount of each item in stock is verified, it confirms the value of the investment.

2. The physical count provides the basic data necessary to perform an item analysis of the inventory.

Item analysis enables a firm to control its investment in inventory. This analysis measures the amount of investment in each item in stock against the amount actually required, based on the firm's recent sales experience. It identifies the specific source of any excess investment in inventory.

Types of Inventory

Before examining the techniques used to make inventory decisions, let us look at the different things that are inventoried. These include (1) office supplies such as pencils, paper, and pens and (2) spare parts, which are used by the manufacturing operations in the event of breakdowns. However, the three most important types of inventory for most manufacturing operations are raw materials, work-in-process, and finished goods.

Raw material inventories consist of goods purchased for the purpose of manufacturing goods. This type of inventory is influenced by the level of production, the reliability of sources of supply, and the efficiency of scheduling purchases and production operations.

Work-in-process inventories consist of partially assembled or incomplete goods in the production cycle. Such inventories are not ready for sale.

Finished goods inventories consist of products that are ready to be sold and shipped to customers.

Inventory Decision Models

Inventory management means determining the optimal level of inventory that should be kept in stock at all times. Three models will be discussed here: material requirements planning, just-in-time inventory management, and economic ordering quantity.

Material Requirements Planning. **Material requirements planning (MRP)** is excellent for developing a production schedule to help coordinate and execute resources (materials, people, and equipment) more effectively. The greater breadth and variety of product lines, together with increasingly expensive inventory, spurred management to adopt computers and use them to manage the huge amounts of production-related information in an entirely new way. By using MRP, it is possible to link individual departments in the production flow from a planning and scheduling point of view.

The MRP system that is based on anticipated shipments of finished goods uses that finished unit schedule to derive subassembly schedules and component schedules. To develop these schedules for individual departments requires a thorough understanding of how components feed into subassemblies, and how subassemblies in turn feed into the finished products. This information is referred to as a bill of materials for a finished end item.

When planning material requirements, it is also necessary to know the timing relationships between various departments and the production cycle times within each department. Knowing the bill of materials for that final assembled item and those timing relationships can help managers use the schedule for final assembly. They can also derive the schedules by which subassemblies would have to be produced in preceding time periods, and by which components would have to be produced in even earlier time periods. In addition, it helps to ensure that the components and subassemblies would come together according to the final assembly schedule.

Just-in-Time Inventory Management. Using the **just-in-time inventory** process helps to reduce inventory, speed up the cash conversion cycle, and increase profitability. In the last decade, the Japanese supply system called just-in-time (JIT) or *kanban* has received a great deal of attention. It includes frequent (even daily) deliveries of parts or supplies, which help to reduce working inventories. This system places responsibility on the supplier for "no defects," as well as responsibility for scheduled delivery of exactly the right quantity with "no excuses." Thus, safety stock and production-line float can be eliminated.

To make near-perfect coordination feasible, suppliers are encouraged or even required to locate plants very close to the customer's production line. These and other coordination activities in planning and production dramatically reduce raw materials inventory, improve product quality, reduce need for inspection, and increase salable output per day.

Economic Ordering Quantity. Another commonly used approach for determining optimal levels of inventory is the **economic ordering quantity (EOQ)** model. The main purpose of this technique is to minimize total inventory costs, consisting of ordering costs and carrying costs. Inventory decisions are influenced by the reorder point, which is the level of inventory that is held at the time a new order is placed, and the reorder quantity, which is the quantity ordered each time. Before examining the EOQ model, let's look at the different types of costs associated with inventory management. Inventory costs fall into two groups: ordering costs and holding costs.

Ordering costs. Costs associated with ordering include:

◆   The actual cost of the merchandise acquired.

◆   The administrative costs of scheduling, entering, and receiving an order.

- The labor costs for receiving, inspecting, and shelving each order.
- The cost of accounting and paying for the order.

Since inventory acquisition costs rise as a business places more orders, the frequency of acquisitions should be kept to a minimum. Everyone recognizes the direct costs of acquiring inventory: the purchase price of the merchandise. However, many overlook other acquisition costs, which increase the actual cost of any particular order, and the inverse relationship they have to the size of the average investment in inventory.

Two facts concerning these costs are relevant here. First, the administrative, accounting, and labor costs associated with any order are far more significant than many people realize. Indeed, the cumulative acquisition costs from numerous orders can exert a significant downward effect on earnings. Second, the individual acquisition costs remain relatively constant regardless of the size of the order involved.

Holding costs. This category of costs is associated with holding or storing goods in inventory. It is this cost that most people associate with inventory. Included in this category would be:

- The costs of maintaining and managing warehouses or other storage facilities.
- The costs of safety systems for guarding inventory.
- The costs of inventory shrinkage that might occur from spoilage, theft, or obsolescence.
- The cost of company funds tied up in inventory (opportunity costs or interest charges).

Holding costs rise as the size of inventory increases. Since annual inventory carrying costs rise as the average size of an investment increases, each component of these costs should be examined with a view to keeping them at a minimum.

In contrast to acquisition costs, holding costs may be viewed as variable costs in the sense that more units held in inventory result in an increase in these costs. The financial or opportunity costs increase in exact proportion to the size of the investment. However, other carrying costs also increase, although the proportions are less precise. Therefore, as investment is increased, warehouse costs also increase because the firm needs more space to store more inventory. As the investment grows, the firm will also experience rising insurance and maintenance costs, as well as an increase in expenses from deterioration or obsolescence. Estimates of holding costs ranging from 20 to 30 percent of the value of inventory are not uncommon. The basic economic ordering quantity equation states that the ideal reorder quantity is as follows:

$$\text{EOQ} = \sqrt{\frac{2 \times (\text{order cost}) \times (\text{yearly demand})}{(\text{annual carrying cost for one unit})}}$$

If a business sells 5,000 units of product per year, the ordering costs are $50.00 per order, and the carrying costs are $0.80 per unit per year, we find that the company should reorder 790 units each time it places an order. The calculation is as follows:

$$\text{EOQ} = \sqrt{\frac{2 \times \$50.00 \times 5,000}{\$0.80}} = 790 \text{ units}$$

Table 10.7 shows the total ordering and holding costs for ordering different quantities during the year. Column 1 shows the number of orders the company can place during the year; it ranges from one to ten orders. Column 2 presents the number of units it would have to order each time an order is made. For example, by placing five orders, the company would order 1,000 units each time. Column 3 indicates the annual cost for placing the orders. For example, ordering five times during the year would cost the company $250.00 ($50.00 × 5). Column 4 shows the average number of units that the company would have in its warehouse, depending on the number of orders it places. For instance, if only one order or 5,000 units is placed during the year, the average number of units the company would have in stock would be 2,500 (5,000 ÷ 2). Column 5 presents the average dollar investment per unit. For example, if the holding cost per unit, which includes maintenance, spoilage, interest charges, etc., is $5.35, the average dollar investment if the company places one order per year is $13,375 (2,500 × $5.35). Column 6 shows the annual holding costs, which can be calculated in two ways. The first is to multiply 15 percent, which represents the annual holding cost, by the average dollar investment and obtain $2,006 ($13,375 × 15%). The second is

TABLE 10.7 Advantages and Disadvantages of Subordinated Debts

1	2	3	4	5	6	7
Number of Orders	Order Quantity (units)	Annual Order Cost (at $50.00 per order)	Average Unit Inventory (2) ÷ 2	Average Dollar Investment (4) × $5.35	Annual Holding Costs (5) × 15%	Ordering Cost + Holding Cost (3) + (6)
1	5,000	$ 50	2,500	$13,375	$2,006	$2,056
2	2,500	100	1,250	6,688	1,003	1,103
5	1,000	250	500	2,675	401	651
6	833	300	416	2,231	335	635
8	625	400	312	1,675	251	651
10	500	$500	250	1,337	201	701

to multiply the annual holding cost per unit of $0.80 by the average unit inventory and obtain the same answer, $2,006 (2,500 × $0.80). Column 7 shows the sum of column 3 (ordering cost) and column 6 (annual holding cost). As shown, 833 units (closest to 790) is the combination that costs the least ($635.00).

Inventory Replenishment

Another extension of the EOQ is the decision related to replenishment of inventory. Supposing that the company decides to order 790 units each time it places an order. The next decision is to decide the frequency of the orders. **Figure 10.3** shows graphically the factors that are taken into account for replenishing inventory. The key factors to take into account for determining inventory replenishment are:

- The minimum and maximum levels of inventory the business will want to have in stock prior to the point of placing a new order.
- The total time it takes from the purchase to the receipt of the goods (LT).
- When the order should be placed (RP).

Managing Current Liabilities

The management of current liabilities is also part of working capital management. Current liabilities are the credit obligations that fall due within a 12-month period. For a business, it is important to determine which assets should be financed by short-term liabilities and which by long-term sources. A business should always maximize the use of its accounts payable and accruals as sources of financing,

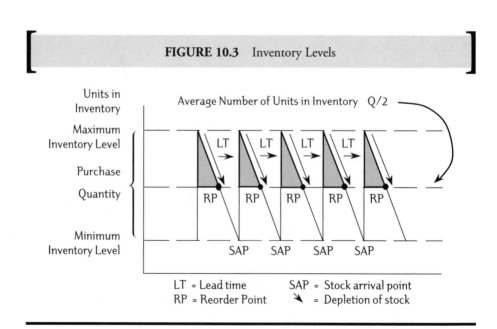

FIGURE 10.3 Inventory Levels

because they are spontaneous and self-adjusting. This means that these accounts can expand and contract with changes in the levels of sales. When more sales are made, accounts payable increase in roughly the same proportion. Similarly, when more people are on the payroll, wages and salaries payable increase.

The main objective of managing payables and accruals is to provide the business with a spontaneous source of financing at no cost. Some of the more popular sources and forms of short-term financing were discussed in Chapter 9.

This section deals with sources of working capital financing. Leverage is the extent to which a firm's assets are supported by debt. We will deal here with short-term leverage: the funds that can be derived from suppliers (accounts payable), various accruals, and working capital loans obtained from commercial banks. The intent of this section is to examine the benefits of leverage and how this type of financing can help realize higher earnings.

Accounts Payable

Several guidelines must be respected if credit is to be used effectively. First, the sales budget should be prepared in order to find out when the raw materials financing will be required. Second, the manufacturing budget should also be established in order to ascertain salary and wage payments. Third, the suppliers that offer the best products and services are selected, and the credit terms that best meet the company's needs are determined. Finally, when and how invoices should be paid are determined.

Managing accounts payable requires a good relationship between the company and its suppliers. This means that when bills arrive, they should be paid according to the agreement, on the appropriate date. This allows a firm to maintain a good credit standing with its suppliers and ensures that they will continue to sell goods and provide services to it.

However, nothing prevents a firm from taking advantage of cost-free funds, such as accounts payable. It is a matter of deferring the payment of the accounts' bills, and ensuring, at the same time, that the suppliers maintain confidence in the firm as a "slow, but sure, payer."

A supplier contributes financing to a firm any time account credit consideration is extended. This trade credit allows a business to defer cash payment for a purchase in accordance with the supplier's selling terms. Conceptually, trade credit provides the same benefits to a business as any other form of leverage: It increases a company's cash capability and enables it to satisfy objectives that might remain out of reach in the absence of external financing. However, it is more closely connected with the cash flow cycle than any other form of financing; therefore, its use calls for deliberate cash planning which focuses on the following four points:

◆   The link between trade credit and cash capability.
◆   Benefits the firm can derive from an alternative supplier's selling terms.

- The relationship between trade credit and the cash flow process with the help of the average payment period calculation and the period that contributes positively to cash flow.
- Good working relations with suppliers.

Link Between Trade Credit and Cash Capability. Trade credit is a significant source of financing for most businesses and, if it is properly administered within the planning and purchasing functions, can help a business increase its cash capability and obtain interest-free, permanently revolving loans in the form of an infinite series of single-payment loans.

The goal of accounts payable management is to provide as much spontaneous financing as possible at zero cost to a business. A major advantage of trade credit is the flexibility it gives a business. It is at management's discretion to determine whether a cash discount should be taken or not, or whether it should stretch its accounts payable beyond the credit period. "Leaning on credit" involves postponement of payment beyond the credit period. The opportunity cost of leaning on credit is a possible deterioration of a company's credit rating.

Credit is directly related to purchasing and is not an isolated activity; it is part of a comprehensive process that touches on the effective scheduling of products and services for sale to customers. In order to determine the amount of trade credit a business requires, management must know how many units it needs to buy and when to buy them. The key activities related to purchasing are as follows:

- Preparation of a sales budget
- Preparation of a production budget
- Determining what and when to purchase
- Determining which suppliers to use
- Determining what credit terms to accept
- Receiving purchases and ensuring quality
- Determining when and how to pay invoices

Benefits Derived from Alternative Supplier Selling Terms. Delaying disbursements generates more cash capability in a firm and increases profitability. The maximum cash disbursement period comes from two complementary management practices: liability management and float management.

In either instance, the objective remains the same—the retention of all cash in a business as long as possible. A business should not pay its bills before they become due. This is the guiding principle of liability management. Of course, a business should never abuse a creditor's consideration, nor should it exceed the requirements set by the suppliers' required payment terms. But, if management experiences a tight cash flow, it can delay cash disbursements beyond the credit terms.

In some industries, such as electronics and printing, the practice of stretching payables is common. In other industries, such as steel and food commodities, failure to observe supplier terms can eliminate any future credit consideration. Certainly, management should know where it stands before deferring any payment beyond its due date.

As indicated earlier, extending the average payable period, which is the relationship between trade credit and the cash flow process, increases cash capability and earnings. Average payable period measures the average length of time each dollar of trade credit is used. A common characteristic of trade credit is that it is spontaneous, or self-adjusting. As sales expand, a business necessarily purchases more materials and parts, hence payables increase. Trade credit involves the acquisition of materials, parts, and supplies needed, and a delay between the date of their acquisitions and the date of payment to the creditors increases your cash capability and earnings.

To calculate the average payable period and to find how it contributes to positive cash flow, accounts payable is divided by the average daily purchases. For example, if the accounts payable shown on a balance sheet are $300,000 and the average daily purchases are $10,000, the average payment period is 30 days. Thus, each dollar of trade credit consideration contributed to a business remains in the bank account for 30 days before being returned to the supplier in the form of a cash payment. If the average payment period is extended to 45 days, accounts payable increase to $450,000 ($10,000 × 45 days), which gives an extra on-time $150,000 in cash.

Two important factors should be considered here:

- Payments to suppliers should not be extended to a point where relationships and goodwill are damaged.
- Cash discounts should be considered before making payments.

Relationship Between Trade Credit and Cash Flow. A trade discount can help increase profitability at the expense of cash flow; therefore, it is a matter of figuring out the trade-off. Many businesses offer various types of trade discounts if a supplier wants to increase its cash flow position. A business can reinvest its accelerated cash flow rapidly and thus increase profitability. The earnings that the supplier loses from today's discounts could benefit it more in the future.

When a company decides to offer a trade discount, it may mean that its average collection period is long (45, 60, or even as high as 90 days). If this is the case, a company may offer trade discounts to get its customers to pay faster. This accelerates cash flow and increases profitability.

If a supplier offers a trade discount, the business should take advantage of it, as long as the cost of borrowing from the bank is less than the supplier discount. Here is the effective cost of various early-payment discounts when annualized:

Discounts allowed for payment in ten days	Annualized cost to the supplier
0.5%	9%
1	18
2	37

This means that if a supplier offers a 2 percent discount, net 30 day payment option, the 2 percent discount translates into a 37 percent annual borrowing cost. The following shows how this percentage was calculated.

$$\text{Annualized Interest cost} \left(\frac{\text{Discount percent}}{100 - \text{Discount percent}} \right) \times \left(\frac{365}{\text{Credit limit} - \text{discount period}} \right) =$$

$$\left(\frac{2\%}{100\% - 2\%} \right) \times \left(\frac{365}{30 - 10} \right) =$$

$$\left(\frac{2\%}{98\%} \right) \times \left(\frac{365}{20} \right) = 37.2\%$$

Working Relationship with Suppliers. A favorable working relationship with suppliers has a direct influence on a firm's cash capability. A good working relationship affects both the amount and the terms of the credit consideration a business receives. One may argue that making a major purchase from any supplier involves considerations that proceed beyond any potential credit consideration. To be sure, price structures, product lines, delivery schedules, and service capabilities remain relevant.

However, most businesses eventually establish on-going relationships with their major suppliers; once such relationships are established, a business should seek to develop and maintain the maximum potential cash capability from each supplier's credit consideration.

Two management practices contribute to good supplier relations.

First, *practice consistent payment patterns.* Erratic payments upset even the most patient suppliers. As long as they know when to expect payment for purchases, even if persistently late, they can feel comfortable with the relationship.

Second, *keep the lines of communication open.* The more a supplier knows about a business, the more one can respond to the company's needs. After all, the business's purchases presumably are profitable sales for the supplier. The better the supplier responds to a business's needs, the more it can improve its own bottom line.

Opening lines of communication can help a business in two ways. First, by informing the suppliers of projected requirements for credit considerations, management may obtain an increased line of credit. In this way, a business can lay the groundwork for approval by giving suppliers the information that will facilitate the credit decision process. Second, it can help a business slip unscathed through a cash flow problem.

Accruals

Accruals such as salaries and taxes payable are similar to trade credit in that they are spontaneous sources of financing. They differ from trade credit in that they are much less a decision variable; that is, a business is relatively constrained in what it can do to influence accruals as a source of financing. However, some techniques can be used to improve cash flow and profitability.

Salaries and Wages Payable. Some managers may not realize that they, together with their fellow employees, are a source of financing to their firm. Indeed, all employees help finance their firm since they are not paid for their services on a day-by-day basis. Instead, they are paid at the end of the week, every two weeks, or perhaps at the end of the month.

For firms operating seasonal businesses, wages and salaries payable represent a spontaneous and flexible source of financing. During the busiest part of the year, when more employees are hired in the production process, the amount of financing available from wages and salaries payable increases. From a management perspective, there is not much flexibility with this source of financing. However, some leeway exists when a firm may choose to pay its employees (including management) less frequently—for example, monthly rather than semi-monthly. But, because there are laws that dictate how frequently employees must be paid, there is a limit to the amount of additional financing that can be obtained this way.

Also, a business may pay its employees by draft rather than by a negotiable check, thus delaying payment even further. Employees receive their checks just as quickly, but the funds will remain on the balance sheet for a longer period until the bank draft works its way back to your bank and the cash account is decreased. This procedure creates additional, zero-cost financing for the business.

Taxes Payable. Taxes payable are also a potential free source of financing. They sometimes should be delayed beyond the due date if the interest charges are less than the interest charged by banks. Taxes that are owed to various governments constitute another accrual that becomes part of short-term financing. Property taxes and income taxes (state and federal) do not become due at the moment they are incurred; rather, their payment is delayed until a later date.

Taxes payable are a free source of financing since governments do not charge interest on outstanding balances. However, if management must accumulate funds in a special checking account in anticipation of a future tax payment, there is an opportunity cost since those funds cannot be used for anything else.

Since the timing of tax payment is specified by government agencies, including the Internal Revenue Service, there is little that a business can do to manipulate this free source of short-term financing. An exception would occur if management deliberately decided to delay tax payments beyond the due date, even though a known penalty would result. There have been reported cases in foreign countries where firms have deliberately avoided paying taxes to their government, recognizing that the penalties for late tax payments were less than the interest rates charged by bank and other lenders on comparable amounts of financing.

Another point that should be taken into account is this: Penalties or interest charges made by governments are not tax-deductible expenses. If this is the case, it may be more economically attractive to pay the taxes on the due date.

If the cost recovery rate for tax purposes on the purchase of assets is higher than the internal depreciation rate, management should take advantage of it, since it represents an interest-free government loan. The acquisition of an asset affects the bottom line in two ways: depreciation and cost recovery rate. As explained in Chapter 2, depreciation is the internal rate used by a business and represents the estimated decrease in the book value of capital or long-lived assets, computed annually (usually with the straight-line method). For accounting purposes, depreciation is treated as an expense which appears on the income statement.

Cost recovery using the MACRS system is the Internal Revenue Service's equivalent of depreciation. Irrespective of the method of depreciation used to calculate the income of a business, the IRS establishes a set of percentages for different groups of assets that must be used to determine the amount of taxes to be paid by a business.

Given that the MACRS rate is usually higher than the internal rate of depreciation in the early years of an asset's life, and that MACRS is used to calculate the taxes a firm should pay, the higher deduction will allow the company to defer paying its taxes. Here is how the arithmetic works. If a business buys a truck for $50,000 and MACRS allows a 40 percent MACRS rate (declining basis), while the internal rate of depreciation is 10 percent (straight line), the company would pay $5,000 less in taxes in the first year. Since this amount has to be paid at a later date, management may wish to put the money in the bank at 10 percent and earn $500 each year (before taxes) in interest from the bank. The MACRS amount for the first year is $10,000 [($50,000 × 40%) ÷ 2] and the depreciation amount is $5,000 ($50,000 × 10%).

Working Capital Loans

In order not to waste its time and that of lenders, management should always make sure to match the sources of financing to the appropriate assets. (This topic was also covered at some length in Chapter 9.)

As mentioned earlier, leverage is another term used for money borrowed from bankers. Since bank credit is a significant element in cash flow management, it is important to review the more common bank lending methods which offer the maximum impact on a firm's profitability and cash capability.

Basically, management should use short-term credit (that with a maturity of one year or less) to finance seasonal current assets and long-term credit to finance permanent assets. It is important to match the maturities of sources and the maturities of uses of funds. Also, since there are so many different forms and sources of financing, management must ensure that they approach a lender that will meet their specific need, such as a short-term loan, term or installment loan, or revolving loan.

Decision-Making in Action

When Bill Lui, controller of Pickford Electronics Inc., attended the annual financial planning meeting with his management group, he made the observation that the company's profitability could be improved if all working capital accounts moved faster. He continued his explanation by stating that if the turnover of Pickford's accounts receivable and inventory moved faster, and accounts payable slower, the company would improve its profitability, have more cash to work with, and be in a much better financial position.

Bill was not a line manager and could not do anything to improve the company's cash performance. However, he made the point that all line managers should take time and be more cautious in the way that the cash flow of the company was managed. As he pointed out, extra cash could be reinvested into the company to help Pickford grow at a faster pace. Jamika Simmons, the general manager thought that the point should be discussed further to determine how this cash flow idea could be implemented.

After several meetings between Jamika and Bill, it was agreed that all managers should become sensitive to the importance of cash flow management and be given some training that would help them find solutions to improve the company's cash conversion cycle. During one of the management meetings, Jamika pointed out that a portion of the future budgeting and financial planning meeting should be devoted to objectives that had to do with the function of cash management.

It was therefore decided that all line managers at Pickford attend a two-day course on the topic of working capital management. This course would be given by an expert in the field of working capital management. All line managers would have to attend this two-day training session. This course would be given to groups of fifteen managers at a time over a two-month period. After the training sessions, Jamika held a meeting for all line managers at which Bill Lui explained the financial targets to be incorporated in Pickford's financial plan, namely the days of working capital and the cash conversion efficiency ratio. Bill pointed out that if all current asset and current liability accounts were improved, which is the responsibility of all managers, these two financial targets could be improved. He also indicated that once the operating budgets and the projected income statement and balance sheet were completed, he would present to them the improvements in the various working capital accounts, and particularly, the results related to the days of working capital and the cash conversion efficiency targets. He also added that if the cash flow objectives were not met all operating budgets and plans would have to be redone until the targets were achieved.

A month later, Bill Lui presented a summary of the year-end 2000 and 2001 financial targets. Both he and Jamika were pleased with the results as he pointed out that the cash flow from operations for the years 2000 and 2001 showed a $99,000 increase, which is a 50 percent improvement. The make-up of the cash flow is as follows:

Cash flow	2000	2001
Income after taxes	$127,000	$179,000
Depreciation/amortization	80,000	97,000
Change in net working capital	− 10,000	+ 20,000
Net operating cash flow	$197,000	$296,000

As shown, the overall cash flow improvement was due to an increase in three operating activity accounts: income after taxes, depreciation/amortization, and net change in working capital. The following paragraphs show how each cash flow item is calculated. As shown below, the income after tax improvement was due to two reasons. First, sales revenue increased by 15 percent and return on sales jumped from 8.5 to 10.4 percent.

Income statement	2000	2001
Sales revenue	$1,500,000	$1,725,000
Cost of goods sold		
Purchases	735,000	784,000
Manufacturing expenses	315,000	337,250
Subtotal	1,050,000	1,121,250
Gross margin	450,000	603,750
Other expenses and taxes	323,000	424,750
Income after tax	$ 127,000	$ 179,000
Return on sales	8.5%	10.4%

The return on sales improvement is due to improvements in the expense accounts at both levels, cost of goods sold, and other expenses and taxes. Here is the vertical analysis for the key expense items shown on the income statement for the years 2000 and 2001.

Vertical Analysis	2000	2001
Sales revenue	100.0%	100.0%
Cost of goods sold	70.0	65.0
Gross margin	30.0	35.0
Other expenses including taxes	21.5	24.6
Income after taxes	8.5%	10.4%

The net change in working capital accounts in 2000 shows a net increase over 1999 in cash flow in the amount of $10,000, and a decrease in 2001 in cash inflow of $20,000. The favorable cash flow performance in 2001 is due in large measure to the acceleration in the cash conversion cycle, that is, a faster payment in accounts receivable, an improved inventory turnover, and a slow-down in the payment of accounts payable.

Working Capital Accounts	1999	2000	2001
Accounts receivable	$150,000	$155,000	$150,000
Inventory	120,000	125,000	120,000
Subtotal	270,000	280,000	270,000
Accounts payable	110,000	110,000	120,000
Net working capital	$160,000	$ 170,000	$ 150,000
Change in working capital	—	+$10,000	−$20,000

As shown, Pickford invested an additional $10,000 in working capital in 2000 and plans to reduce it by $20,000 in 2001. Bill Lui indicated that the favorable cash flow performance would help the company significantly increase its days of working capital from 41.4 days to 31.7 days and its cash conversion efficiency ratio from 13.1 to 17.2 percent.

By using a flip chart, Bill Lui explained how these working capital accounts would be improved and the impact it would have on the company's cash flow position. He indicated that the net working capital between the years 2000 and 2001 is expected to drop by $20,000 (from $170,000 to $150,000) despite the fact that the average daily sales will show an increase of $617 or 15 percent. This change will have a positive effect on the days of working capital by 10 days (from 41.4 days to 31.7 days). Bill Lui further explained this improvement with the following calculations:

Days of working capital

Year 2000

$$\frac{\text{Net working capital}}{\text{Average daily sales}} = \frac{\$170,000}{\$4,110} = 41.4 \text{ days}$$

Average daily sales = $4,110 ($1,500,000 ÷ 365)

Year 2001

$$\frac{\text{Net working capital}}{\text{Average daily sales}} = \frac{\$150,000}{\$4,726} = 31.7 \text{ days}$$

Average daily sales = $4,726 ($1,725,000 ÷ 365)

As Bill Lui pointed out, the reasons why the net working capital dropped from $170,000 to $150,000 are due to improvements in the average collection period in accounts receivable and inventory turnover and the extension of the average daily payables. He gave the following explanation for each.

Average collection period. The average collection period improved from 37.7 days to 31.7 days because of a change in the policies of the collection procedures. Here is the calculation:

Year 2000

$$\frac{\text{Accounts receivable}}{\text{Average daily sales}} = \frac{\$155,000}{\$4,110} = 37.7 \text{ days}$$

Year 2001

$$\frac{\text{Accounts receivable}}{\text{Average daily sales}} = \frac{\$150,000}{\$4,726} = 31.7 \text{ days}$$

Inventory turnover. The inventory turnover will improve from 8.4 times to 9.3 times despite the 6.8 percent increase in cost of goods sold. This inventory turnover's favorable performance is caused by a reduction in inventory level in the amount of $5,000 or 4 percent. This is due to a better method in the way the raw materials will be purchased and the acceleration in the manufacturing process. This is calculated as follows:

Year 2000

$$\frac{\text{Cost of goods sold}}{\text{Inventory}} = \frac{\$1,050,000}{\$125,000} = 8.4 \text{ times}$$

Year 2001

$$\frac{\text{Cost of goods sold}}{\text{Inventory}} = \frac{\$1,121,250}{\$120,000} = 9.3 \text{ times}$$

Average payable period. The average payable period increased slightly from 55 days to 56 days. Bill explained that this small improvement was due to the fact that the purchasing department was able to negotiate better prices and credit conditions with about half of Pickford's suppliers. Here is the calculation:

Year 2000

$$\frac{\text{Accounts payable}}{\text{Average daily purchases}} = \frac{\$110,000}{\$2,014} = 55 \text{ days}$$

Average daily purchases = $2,014 ($735,000 ÷ 365)

Year 2001

$$\frac{\text{Accounts payable}}{\text{Average daily purchases}} = \frac{\$120,000}{\$2,148} = 56 \text{ days}$$

Average daily sales = $2,148 ($784,000 ÷ 365)

The cash conversion efficiency ratio also improved as a result of the 50.3 percent increase in operating cash flow (from $197,000 to $296,000) compared to the 15 percent increase in sales revenue.

Cash conversion efficiency ratio

Year 2000

$$\frac{\text{Operating cash flow}}{\text{Sales revenue}} = \frac{\$197,000}{\$1,500,000} = 13.1\%$$

Year 2001

$$\frac{\text{Operating cash flow}}{\text{Sales revenue}} = \frac{\$296,000}{\$1,725,000} = 17.2\%$$

Bill Lui concluded his presentation by saying that if a major effort had not been made to improve the working capital accounts, the company would probably have had to invest an additional 15 percent or $25,000 instead of experiencing a $20,000 reduction in these accounts. As a result, Pickford will be able to use this incremental $55,000 cash flow amount for investments, expansion, and capital assets.

Summary

Working capital management involves the management of all current assets and current liability accounts. Since these types of accounts vary on a day-to-day basis, managing this current portion of business activities is time-consuming. The objective of working capital management is to manage individual current accounts and to ensure a proper balance between all asset accounts and all liability accounts. Also, there must exist a balanced relationship with other balance sheet items such as capital assets and long-term debt.

Managing current assets focuses on cash, marketable securities, accounts receivable, and inventory. The essence of managing cash is to ensure an adequate reservoir of cash to enable a business to conduct its ordinary operating activities, handle emergencies, and take advantage of specific opportunities. The preparation of a cash budget helps management find what level of cash is needed and when. There are two ways that a firm can speed up cash receipts: by changing the paying habits of customers and by reducing the negative float.

Managing marketable securities consists of investing surplus cash in profit-making investments, such as Treasury bills, bank deposits, or bonds. Six different approaches can be used for managing marketable securities; it is a matter of selecting the one that best responds to the needs of a business.

Managing accounts receivable involves six activities: setting credit terms; granting credit to customers; billing; monitoring payments made by customers; applying the necessary measures to maintain or reduce the average collection period; and obtaining proper credit insurance.

Managing inventory consists of replenishing stocking points in such a way that associated order and holding costs are kept at a minimum. Keeping inventory low helps to improve profitability. Three methods used to manage inventory are material requirements planning (MRP), just-in-time (JIT), and the economic order quantity (EOQ).

Management of current liabilities consists of using current debt, such as accounts payable, accruals, and working capital loans, as effective sources of financing.

CHAPTER 11

Business Valuation

After three years of operations, CompuTech Inc. was doing extremely well in terms of meeting its financial goals. The Edwards were now moving their business into another phase of its development, that of opening several retail stores. The retail concept that they had conceived had caught on very well with the general public and CompuTech was generating greater earnings than competing firms.

The Edwards had two options in terms of growth. First, to grow slowly by opening a retail outlet every two years by using internally generated funds over the next ten years. The second option was to approach a risk capital investor interested in their retail concept who would be interested in investing in the business. This option would help them grow more rapidly. It is a strategy that would enable the Edwards to open five retail outlets in year 2004 and more the year after. However, this strategy would require equity participation in CompuTech Inc. by a venture capitalist. If this option is chosen, the Edwards would have to share business ownership.

After discussing these options with their advisors Bill Murray and Jeff Irwin, both agreed that attracting risk capital was a viable option. Bill made the following points:

"Private investors are very demanding and require a substantial return on their investment. The investment proposal will have to be very complete and clearly demonstrate the key points. First, these investors want to see evidence that the investment opportunity generates a return commensurate with the risk—usually 25 percent to 40 percent compounded and adjusted for inflation. Second, they seek a good management team. Since most risk capital investors claim that management is the single most important aspect of a business opportunity, they regard reputation and quality of the team as "key." Third, they will be looking for a viable exit strategy and options to realize their investment. Since these types of investors usually want to liquidate their investments in three to seven years, they want to be assured that you will have thought about how to comply with their wishes. This may require going public or selling their shares to another buyer. They might even want you to buy back their shares. Fourth, these investors will want to monitor and control their investment by having a voice on your board of directors, such as suggesting who should sit on your board, receiving monthly financial statements and having a say in hiring key managers."

Jeff Irwin added the following points regarding the strategy for approaching private investors.

"You have to understand that these types of private investors often reject investment opportunities because entrepreneurs do not understand the needs, requirements, and specialization of the particular investor. If you approach the wrong investor, you run the risk of being rejected. The best approach to contacting private investors is to make sure that they will be able to provide the amount of capital that you require. Also, you will have to verify that they are familiar with the industry that you are in and most important, that they are located in your region. This is particularly important if they want to take an active part in your business. Another key criteria when selecting a private investor is to pick one who is a leader in the investment community and able to give you sound advice about your business. In this type of deal you should complement one another. The business offers a good investment opportunity in terms of a return and the investor offers the capital the business needs to realize your dreams."

The Edwards realize that the investment proposal will have to be very convincing and address their needs if they are to attract venture capital funds. It will have to be very clear in providing information about the financing needs, financial requirements, investment potential, and management capabilities.

This chapter looks at three key topics:

- The type of information that should be incorporated in an investment proposal.
- How financial statements can be restated to show the real market value of a business.
- How investors go about determining the real value of a business opportunity.

Introduction

Throughout this book, we have talked about book value—what a business owns and owes—that is, the value of a business' assets and liabilities. There was no mention of the market value of a business—that is, how much it would be worth if the business were sold.

For example, the book value of a house bought in Dallas in the early 1970s for $40,000 would be considerably less than what the owner could sell it for today. When the house was purchased, the value of the land was $5,000 and the house itself was $35,000. Today, since the house has lost some value because of wear and tear (depreciation), it could now be worth only $10,000 "on the books." However, because the house appreciated in value over the years, the market value of that house and land, or their real worth, is $400,000. This example illustrates the point that there is a difference between the value of assets shown in the books and the real value of these assets if they were put up for sale on the market.

If we examine Eastman Technologies Inc.'s 2000 balance sheet shown in **Table 2.5** of Chapter 2, we see that the company's total assets amount to $1,800,000 and total liabilities to $1,245,000 ($445,000 in current liabilities and $800,000 in long-term debts). In this case, Eastman's book value, being the difference between the asset and liability components of the balance sheet, is $555,000. If the owners were to sell Eastman at book price, they would sell the assets for what they are worth in the books ($1,800,000), transfer to the new owners the liabilities ($1,245,000), and ask for a $555,000 check. To be sure, if Eastman's owners were to sell the business, they would not sell it for book value, but for what it is worth on the market. They would therefore assess the true market value of the business, as an ongoing concern, and sell it for a price that, like that of the house, would probably be different from what is shown on the books.

As shown in **Figure 11.1**, this chapter explores various topics dealing with the process of buying an ongoing business, more specifically, market valuation. We will begin by looking at the meaning of price level accounting and current value accounting, that is, the difference between book value and market value. We will then turn to valuation methods that organizations and investors use to determine

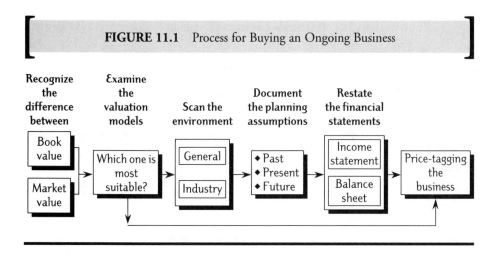

FIGURE 11.1 Process for Buying an Ongoing Business

the value of businesses. The rest of the chapter looks at how to put a price tag on privately owned ongoing businesses. In particular, the process includes scanning the environment, documenting the planning assumptions, restating financial statements, and three methods used to price-tag ongoing businesses: asset valuation, net present value, and industry multipliers. The chapter ends with a brief examination of price-tagging publicly owned businesses.

Market Value Versus Book Value

To business persons, it may not make much sense to report information on financial statements that does not really reflect the "true" or "real" market value of assets. For example, **Table 11.1** presents a balance sheet showing the house that was purchased in 1970. The table indicates that after some 30 years, the $40,000 house, after allowing for depreciation, would only have a $10,000 value on the books. As shown in the table, however, the "real value" of the house is $400,000. If the owner wants to borrow $200,000, his or her balance sheet would look absurd (upper portion of the table) because the liability side of the balance sheet would be $190,000 more than the **book value** of the house. However, as shown on the lower portion of the table, if the **market value** of the house was shown on the balance sheet, the owner's financial structure would be more appropriate. The owner could have done different things with the $200,000 mortgage money. The money could have been:

1. Deposited in a bank account.
2. Used to make major alterations to the house.
3. Used to buy other assets such as a cottage, a car, or a trailer.
4. Used to make a one-year first-class trip around the world with the family.

If the homeowner picked the fourth option, that mortgage money would have simply been spent and not shown on the asset side of the balance sheet. If that

TABLE 11.1   Book Value versus Market Value

Balance Sheet (based on book value)

House:			
Original cost	$40,000		
Depreciation	30,000		
Net book value	$ 10,000	New mortgage	$200,000

Balance Sheet (based on market value)

House:			
Market value	$400,000	New mortgage	$200,000

had been the case, the balance sheet would have shown $10,000 on the asset side and $200,000 on the liability side, similar to the amounts shown in **Table 11.1**.

Because of the difference between book values and market values, some individuals would challenge the validity of the traditional accounting practices and ask the following question: Do financial statements prepared according to traditional accounting principles present fairly the financial position of a company in a period of inflation? Many would say no! For this reason, over the past decades, accountants have attempted to deal with this issue in order to present information on financial statements in a more sensible way. They have come up with two suggestions: price level accounting and current value accounting.

Price level accounting means that the numbers on financial statements be restated in terms of current purchasing power. Thus, if an asset such as a building was purchased five years ago for $1,000,000 at a time when yearly inflation was 4 percent, the value of the building the next year would be reported as $1,170,000.

Current value accounting is based on what it would currently cost a business to acquire an asset with the same capability or capacity as the one it presently owns. In the above example, if the asset were to be purchased today at a cost of $1,200,000 that would be the value that the existing asset would be reported on the balance sheet.

Take the example of Eastman Technologies Inc.'s 2000 balance sheet shown in **Table 2.5**. The balance sheet shows the owners' equity to be $555,000. This is known as the book value and is based on the original or historical purchase price of all assets, adjusted for depreciation (total $1,800,000), less the amount of money owed to lenders, which amounts to $1,245,000.

If Eastman's owners were to sell their business for book value, they would sell the assets for what they are worth on the books, transfer the liabilities to the new owners, and ask for a $555,000 check. However, the company could be worth more than $555,000 for two reasons. First, Eastman's assets listed on the balance sheet are *historically based*. This means that if the company purchased in 1995 a piece of machinery for $100,000, the transaction provides an objective measure of the asset's value, which is what is shown on the company's balance sheet. However, this 1995 value may not have much relevance today. In fact, the asset could be worth much more or much less.

Second, the assets of the company could generate excellent earnings. These earnings are not reflected in the balance sheet. However, if the earnings produce a 20 percent or 25 percent annual return, anyone wanting to sell such a business would certainly take the level of productivity of these assets into consideration.

Some may argue that accountants should disregard the purchase price of capital assets and use a more meaningful current value in financial statements. The problem with this is that for many assets, objectively determinable current values do not exist. Therefore, accountants have opted for *objective historical cost values* over *subjective estimates* of current value.

Also, the United States government has serious reservations about having company officials re-appraise capital assets higher than historical values. The reason is simple: the original $100,000 used to calculate MACRS would be increased and consequently reduce the amount of income taxes that the company would pay to the government. Furthermore, what organization would be responsible for policing the activity of determining whether assets shown on balance sheets reflect the true market value? Also, balance sheets would have to be adjusted each year to reflect inflation or the changing prices of the capital assets. Also, how would these changes be reflected on the right side of the balance sheet?

To solve the valuation problem, the *American Institute of Certified Public Accountants (AICPA)* recommended that all U.S. enterprises whose securities are traded in public markets disclose in their annual reports, whenever appropriate, supplementary information about the effects of changing prices. In other words, if the value of a building is shown in the books at $600,000 (after depreciation) and the market value is $1,200,000, the annual report would comment on this difference through an appropriate footnote.

Valuation Models

Different models can be used to value businesses. So far, we have talked about the book value and the market value. In Chapter 7, we examined the present value and the discounted cash flow methods to determine the value of an investment in capital assets. The time value of money approach can also be used for business valuation purposes. Depending on the reason for valuing a business, organizations use different approaches.

In his book *Techniques of Financial Analysis,*[1] Erich Helfert identifies several valuation models. There is the *economic value* that has to do with the ability or capacity of an asset to produce a stream of after-tax cash flows. For example, a person who invests $100,000 in U.S. Savings Bonds does so in order to earn future cash receipts in the form of interest payments. However, the person may invest $100,000 in a capital asset for additional savings through productivity or for increased sales revenues. The investor would therefore compare the worth of the future receipts (cash inflows) to the original investment (cash outflows). The economic value approach is a future-oriented concept that is based on the principles of *trade-off* and *risk*. For example, how much would one expect to earn from U.S. Savings Bonds—4 or 5 percent, or in a revenue-generating business asset— 15, 20 or 25 percent? The investor would also examine the risk factor related to that particular investment. For example, the investor might be prepared to accept a 7 percent economic return on the relatively risk-free investment, or 25 percent in a revenue-generating business venture that is riskier. Risk is the price tag on the sought-after economic return. The economic value concept therefore looks at future cash flow expectations and the relative risk associated with the investment.

The second approach is based on market value, that is the worth of an asset traded on the market between a buyer and a seller without duress. The stock market is a classic example of market value. At a particular point in time, some buyers would be prepared to buy (and others sell) a share for what each party believes it is worth. By using this approach, the buyer and the seller are able to arrive at a mutually acceptable value for the commodity in question. A consensus is built between the two parties, where the value of a commodity is therefore subject to individual preferences, and the psychological climate that exists at the time of the transaction. Both the economic value method and the market value approach deal with theoretical values, based exclusively on estimates. Unless the commodity is actually transferred between two parties, the market value is considered hypothetical. Consequently, one can establish a minimum and a maximum value of a commodity if a seller considers trading it on the market on a particular date.

We have already mentioned the third approach, the *book value* method. As already mentioned, this method deals with the worth of an asset recorded on the balance sheet, based on generally accepted accounting principles. Book value can be described as the historical value of an asset represented by its purchase price (original cost of the asset) less the accumulated depreciation.

The **liquidation value** shows the worth of specific assets when sold separately. Liquidation means that a business must sell an asset under duress in order to obtain some cash. The liquidation value does not reflect the real worth of an asset or a business. In most cases, it is substantially below the economic value, the market value, and even the book value of an asset.

The **replacement** or **reproduction value** is the cost of replacing an existing capital asset with an identical asset. This is a good approach for measuring the worth of an ongoing business because it is based on engineering estimates and judgments. However, this approach has a flaw since it does not take into consideration the real worth of the management team, the reputation of the business, the strength of the organization, and the value of its products. Furthermore, it is difficult to equate the value of assets of an ongoing plant with so-called "equivalent assets." For example, what appears to be a "duplicate asset" may, in fact, have a higher or lower rate of productivity. With the passage of time, most physical assets are subject to some technological and physical wear and tear.

To secure their loans or other types of credit, lenders use the *collateral value* approach. This method is based on the premise that maximum credit will be allowed to a particular business against identifiable assets. Generally, in order to allow for a margin of safety, lenders will set a lower value than what the asset is worth on the market.

Municipal governments use the **assessed value** approach for property taxation. The rules to determine the assessed value vary widely between municipalities and do not necessarily reflect market values. The prime purpose of the assessed value is to levy tax revenues. Such values have little connection with other market values.

Economic value is the "price" that is placed on a business as an *ongoing entity*. For example, you will surely pay more for a retail store that is operating (ongoing) than a similar business that is on the brink of declaring bankruptcy. For the ongoing business, you would have to pay for the goodwill that includes the customers, reputation, patents, employees, image, etc. This approach compares the cash outflow to future cash inflows. The final section of this chapter will explore how to calculate values of ongoing businesses through time value of money yardsticks such as the internal rate of return and the net present value approach.

Before looking at the process of putting a price tag on an ongoing business, let's examine several broad steps that an investor will want to go through. This includes the scanning of the environment, documenting the planning assumptions, and restating the financial statements.

Scanning the Environment

As shown in **Figure 11.1**, the first thing to look at in the valuation process is the nature of the industry in which a business operates and the competition it faces. This is commonly referred to as scanning the environment. If the business operates in an extremely volatile and competitive environment, this affects its viability and profitability. Its risk is higher and the cash and earnings generated by the business may be more difficult to predict.

Scanning the environment means formulating assumptions on which the purchase decision will be based. Here, we are talking about assessing the general and industry environments and formulating planning assumptions that could be expressed in quantitative and qualitative terms. *Quantitative* results such as the GNP, labor rates, market demand, supply capability, imports, unemployment rate, and prevailing interest rates help to profile the conditions under which the business operates and to prepare the detailed operating plans related to marketing, manufacturing, research and development, engineering, and production.

Qualitative factors examine additional important perspectives such as government regulations and controls, labor activities, consumer preferences, and so on. The general environment includes economic, political, social/ethical, technological, and international conditions. Industry conditions include such factors as the profile of the consumers, number and power of suppliers, the competitive climate (rivalry among competing sellers), the threat of substitute products, potential entry of new competitors, and growth patterns.

Documenting the Planning Assumptions

The next step is to document the planning assumptions that will help prepare the pro-forma financial statements. Investors will want to examine a company's past performance, determine whether the existing resources will be adequate to realize the new owners' strategic intentions, and also look at the company's pro-forma financial statements (i.e., income statement and balance sheet), which will be discussed later in this chapter.

Past Performance

Looking at the track record of a business for the previous four or five years is always important for investors. A history of healthy past performance supports the decision to purchase. A company's track record can be gauged in terms of overall performance, operating performance, and market performance.

Overall performance is a measure of how a company has used its resources in the past. Useful ratios to gauge overall performance may be grouped under two headings: those measuring financial conditions, such as current ratio, acid test ratio, and debt ratios; and those measuring profitability, such as return on sales and return on equity.

Operating performance is a measure of managerial and technical competence. This is important in determining to what extent the existing management team is able to make the business profitable. Pertinent information on managerial performance relates to the major organizational functions. For example, under marketing—product acceptability, distribution efficiencies, sales performance; under manufacturing—operating expenses, cost of raw material, utilization of plant capacity, capital assets turnover, inventory turnover, and accounts receivable turnover; and under human resources—labor turnover, quality of the workforce, and general working conditions.

Market performance is a measure of a firm's position within its industry. Did it lose, maintain, or improve its market position? Was it able to manage its business under adverse environmental or industry conditions? How? Why? By how much? A number of firms compile industry data against which historical company performance can be compared. For example, *Dun & Bradstreet*, *Standard & Poor's*, and several commercial banks disclose, through written reports or web sites, pertinent industry ratios based on financial and taxation statistics. *Dun & Bradstreet* provides very comprehensive and essential financial data on company and industry key ratios related to solvency, efficiency, and profitability. Also, *Standard & Poor's Compustat Services* provides online information related to industry and company financial performance. Examples of this type of information are presented in chapter four in **Table 3.7**, *Benchmarking the Corporation*.

Present Capability

If a business is purchased, the purpose of analyzing its present capability is to objectively review the company's strengths and weaknesses and determine what needs to be done in order to carry out the new strategic and operational plans. It is also appropriate to specify how any deficiencies could be resolved. If, for instance, market share and profitability have been declining steadily, the new investors may strive to reverse this trend by introducing new products, modifying some existing products, and changing production processes to eliminate waste and inefficiencies.

The purchase of a business may call for a different direction and orientation of the resources. Therefore, the analysis of present capability focuses on the following questions: Can the resources be extended? By how much? What new resources must be added in order to make the business more profitable? How will existing and new resources be integrated? Is there a need to redefine the company's mission, objectives, and priorities? The new owners may have to plan in detail the new business's capabilities in the following areas:

- Human resources (technical and managerial)
- Financial resources
- Machinery, equipment, facilities
- Sources of raw material (suppliers)
- Know-how (techniques, programs, systems)
- Internal relations (employees)
- External relations (union, image, financial community, community relations, government relations, associations)
- Organizational structure

Future Cash Needs and Profitability

This segment of the analysis is the most time-consuming and demanding. It is difficult because, unlike analyzing past performance and diagnosing existing operating functions such as marketing, production, and research and development, looking into the future involves establishing a series of assumptions underlying the purchase decision. The point of the analysis is not only to justify the purchase, but also to determine how much the business is really worth and what plans will be required to make the business achieve its strategic, operational, and financial objectives.

Restating the Financial Statements

The key documents investors examine when buying a business are its financial statements, that is, the income statement and the balance sheet. On the balance sheet, they look at the book value of a company's assets and how much the business owes to creditors on these assets. By examining each item individually, they can put a price tag on each asset to determine how much each is "actually worth"—that is, its "market value."

However, looking at the balance sheet is not enough. The investor will also examine the income statement to determine the company's existing and potential earning power. The true value of a business is directly related to its ability to generate earnings, and the income statement is the starting point for arriving at this number. However, the existing earnings the owners are able to generate may be different from what the new owners will be able to realize. Therefore, as with the balance sheet, there is a need to assess the individual components of the income statement to determine, for example, if more sales revenue can be generated and if there could be improvements in operating efficiencies in order to improve the bottom line. Each expense account on the income statement is examined to determine whether cost savings could be realized through economy, downsizing, and increased productivity.

Financial ratios are used to analyze financial statements to assess a company's liquidity, leverage, operating, and profitability performance. Typical questions that investors ask include:

◆ Have these financial statements been audited?
◆ Is the business carrying too much debt?
◆ What is the real worth of the physical assets?
◆ Is the company profitable?
◆ Are the operating costs reasonable? Inflated? Out of line?
◆ Is the business carrying too much accounts receivable compared to sales revenue? Too many inventories compared to the cost of goods sold? What is the real worth of these assets?
◆ How much is the reputation of the business worth?

After looking at a company's financial statements, the investors will formulate planning assumptions for each item included in the financial statements in order to help produce the pro-forma income statement and balance sheet.

Let's now examine how each element shown on the income statement and the balance sheet can be restated to determine the real worth of a business.

Restating the Income Statement

Looking at only one year's income statement does not give enough information to gauge the full meaning of a company's operating performance. The company's historical financial and operating performance will be analyzed in some detail. Several years must be analyzed to determine how consistent a company is in generating revenues and earnings, and how each cost element has performed in the past. Specific things to look for are the following: Has sales revenue been on the increase? Are the operating expenses, such as cost of goods sold and selling and administration expenses, consistent from year to year? If we were to buy this company, would we be able to increase sales revenue? Reduce costs? If so, how would we be able to achieve such improvements?

Let's assume that an investor wants to purchase Eastman Technologies Inc. The potential investor would want to analyze the company's existing income statement, and by exploring some of the questions mentioned earlier, could restate the numbers. In other words, every account on this statement would be examined in terms of how the business would operate under the new owners.

Eastman Technologies Inc.'s 2000 actual income statement and pro-forma statement are shown in **Table 11.2**. Comments related to the more important segments of the income statement follow.

Sales Revenue. In 2000, the company sold $2,500,000 worth of goods, and the new owners estimate $4,000,000, a 60 percent increase. The new owners' marketing plan would determine how this growth will be realized. The so-called "marketing variables," which include selling, advertising, promotion, distribution, product, market finance, and market definition, have a direct influence on that all-important figure in the pro-forma income statements—sales revenue. Miscalculating the number of units to be sold and the selling price could severely affect profitability.

Predicting the mood of the consumer calls for a thorough investigation of wants or needs. The marketing plan usually includes the following:

◆   Marketing philosophy
◆   Description of the market (size and trends)
◆   Objectives (volume, price, share of market, and product mix)
◆   Consumer profile
◆   A list of the more important customers that will buy from the company (Who are they? Where are they located? Are they wholesalers? Retailers? Government organizations?)
◆   Marketing functions (strengths and weaknesses)
◆   Product description (features, patents, packaging, market test results, etc.)
◆   Marketing programs (sales promotion, sales organization, distribution, credit, and warehousing facilities)
◆   Competitive advantage
◆   Selling costs as a percentage of sales
◆   Advertising and promotional budget
◆   Service arrangements
◆   Pricing strategies
◆   Warranties on products

Cost of Goods Sold. Based on a marketing plan, each expense item included in the expense accounts shown on the income statement is examined carefully. For example, even though the cost of goods sold shows one figure, the new buyers would want to examine the many different costs that are included in the $1,900,000 to determine whether efficiencies can be obtained through purchasing, freight, and manufacturing. Most expenses are incurred at the manufacturing level, through plant expenses, manufacturing costs, maintenance, raw material purchases, insurance, cost of inventory, and utilities.

This plan focuses on efficiencies and shows production at competitive prices. Manufacturing's prime objective is to make a product that meets the needs of marketing (its selling agent) at the best possible price. The total manufacturing

TABLE 11.2   The Restated Income Statement

Eastman Technologies Inc.
Income Statement for the Year Ended December 31, 2000
and the Buyer's Estimates

	Actual 2000		Buyer's 2001 Estimates	
Net sales	$2,500,000	1.00	$4,000,000	1.00
Cost of goods sold	1,900,000	.76	2,400,000	.60
Gross margin	**600,000**	.24	**1,600,000**	.40
Operating expenses				
Selling expenses:				
Sales salaries	140,000	0.05	245,000	0.06
Advertising expenses	20,000	0.01	85,000	0.02
Total selling expenses	160,000	0.06	330,000	0.08
Administrative expenses:				
Office salaries	170,000	0.06	190,000	0.05
Rent	20,000	0.01	30,000	0.01
Depreciation	40,000	0.02	150,000	0.03
Total administration expenses	230,000	0.09	370,000	0.09
Total operating expenses	390,000	0.16	700,000	0.18
Operating income	**210,000**	0.08	**900,000**	0.23
Other income	20,000	0.01	32,000	0.01
Other expenses (interest)	35,000	0.01	194,000	0.06
Net	15,000	0.00	162,000	0.05
Income before taxes	195,000	0.08	738,000	0.18
Income taxes	97,500	0.04	369,000	0.09
Income after taxes	**$ 97,500**	0.04	**$ 369,000**	0.09

concept should incorporate the most modern techniques, equipment use, material handling, storage, inventory control, traffic, record keeping, and costing. Production scheduling should be integrated with sales.

Calculating the break-even points for several future years of operation could highlight the relationship between revenue and costs (fixed and variable) and is considered a valid yardstick to determine level of risk. Several sensitivity checks can estimate the margin of safety regarding a price or volume drop, or an increase in operating expenses with no corresponding change in selling price.

Planning assumptions related to cost of goods sold and manufacturing expenses include the following:

- Production operation (job-shop or mass production)
- Plant layout
- Production runs (capacity and forecast of utilization rate)
- Fixed and variable cost estimates (break-even point)
- List of equipment (auto equipment, trucks, and vehicles)
- Raw material costs and reliability
- Maintenance costs
- Government regulations (health and security)
- Economics of a two- or three-shift schedule
- Quality control procedures

As shown in **Table 11.2**, vertical analysis helps to determine to what extent the new owners would be able to improve manufacturing efficiencies. Under the present owners, cost of goods sold as a percentage of sales is 76 percent (or $0.76 for each $1.00 worth of sales), and the new owners would show a $0.16 improvement, down to 60 percent (or $0.60 for each dollar's worth of sales). Because of this exceptional improvement in cost of goods sold, the gross margin jumped from 24 to 40 percent.

Selling Expenses. The assumptions related to selling expenses can be covered in the marketing plan and reflect the planning assumptions related to sales and advertising. As shown in the table, despite the 60 percent increase in sales revenue, selling expenses will be increased by 106 percent, reflecting the emphasis that the new owners may put on selling their products and services. As shown, selling expenses as a percentage of sales increase from 6 to 8 percent.

Administrative Expenses. As shown in the table, administrative expenses include office salaries, rent, and depreciation. There is a 61 percent increase in these expenses, which is equivalent to the sales revenue increment. Because of this, total administrative expenses as a percentage of sales are maintained at 9 percent. Individually, office salaries increased by 12 percent, rental charges by 50 percent and depreciation expense by 275 percent; the latter increase is due to the significant increase in capital assets.

Total operating expenses, which include both selling and administrative, increased by 79 percent, and as a percentage of sales, they increased from 16 to 18 percent. Because of the significant improvement in sales revenues and costs of goods sold, operating income increases by 328 percent; as a percentage of sales, it improves from 8 to 23 percent.

Other income and interest expenses show a substantial increase. The interest expense reflects a huge increase in liabilities to finance the purchase of the assets.

The Bottom Line. As a result of the changes in the revenue and expense accounts, the income after taxes reaches $369,000, which represents a 278 percent increase. As a percentage of sales, income after taxes increases from 4 to 9 percent. This means that in 2001, for every $1.00 of sales, the company made $0.09 in after-tax income, compared to $0.04 in 2000.

The acquisition of the business by the new owners will therefore make the business more profitable. The new owners are expected to earn $369,000 in profit after taxes and $519,000 in cash flow (income after taxes plus depreciation).

Now that we know the potential earning power of the business, the next question: Based on the income statement projections, how much is the business worth? Restating the balance sheet will give us this information.

Restating the Balance Sheet

Table 11.3 shows Eastman Technologies Inc.'s balance sheet of the present owners, and the buyers' estimated value of individual assets and liabilities. The buyers' estimated market value represents the new owners' pro-forma balance sheet. For this reason, items such as accounts receivable, inventory, net capital assets, and retained earnings reflect what the investors would really buy from the present owners and how these assets would be financed. Let's look at the various components of the balance sheet.

Current Assets. Based on the market value, the worth of the current assets is estimated at $502,000. The value of both cash ($22,000) and prepaid expenses ($60,000) shows their actual worth. Based on a detailed audit of the company's accounts receivable and inventory accounts, they have been reduced to $250,000 and $170,000 respectively.

Capital Assets. Capital or fixed assets, which include land, buildings, equipment, and machinery, are valued at $3,000,000 for an increase of 123 percent over the book value of the seller's assets. Presumably, both the investor and the seller asked their respective real estate agents and engineers to estimate the market value of the individual assets shown on the balance sheet. Since we are dealing with the opening balance sheet, there is no accumulated depreciation. At the end of the first fiscal year, however, this account would show an amount of $150,000 (drawn from the income statement) for the use of the capital assets.

Goodwill. Goodwill is a special asset that appears on a balance sheet when a business is sold. It represents the value of the reputation, faithful customers, and good name of the existing company. It is the excess paid for a business over the fair market value of the assets, less the liabilities just prior to the purchase. In the case of Eastman, the new owners might pay $400,000 for the name and reputation. Like capital assets, this $400,000 can be amortized over a period of years, and the amortization expense, just like depreciation, would be included in the buyers' income statement.

Current Liabilities. All items reported under current liabilities are brought forward from the seller's balance sheet to the new owners' opening. In **Table 11.3**, current liabilities amount to $445,000.

TABLE 11.3   The Restated Balance Sheet

Eastman Technologies Inc.
Balance Sheets as at December 31, 2000
and the Buyer's Opening Balance Sheet

	Actual 2000		Buyer's Estimated Value Opening Balance Sheet	
Assets				
Current assets				
Cash	$ 22,000	0.01	$ 22,000	0.01
Prepaid expenses	60,000	0.03	60,000	0.02
Accounts receivable	300,000	0.17	250,000 ✓	0.06
Inventory	218,000	0.12	170,000 ✓	0.04
Total current assets	**600,000**	0.33	**502,000**	0.13
Capital assets (at cost)	1,340,000	0.74	3,000,000 ✓	0.77
Accumulated depreciation	140,000	0.08	—	0.00
Capital assets (net)	**1,200,000**	0.67	**3,000,000**	0.77
Goodwill	—	—	400,000 ✓	0.10
Total assets	$ 1,800,000	1.00	$ 3,902,000	1.00
Liabilities				
Current liabilities				
Accounts payable	$ 195,000	0.11	$ 195,000 ✓	0.05
Notes payable	150,000	0.08	150,000	0.04
Accrued expenses	20,000	0.01	20,000	0.01
Taxes payable	80,000	0.04	80,000	0.02
Total current liabilities	**445,000**	0.25	**445,000**	0.11
Long-term debts	**800,000**	0.44	**2,000,000**	0.51
Total liabilities	1,245,000	0.69	2,445,000	0.63
Common shares	300,000	0.17	1,457,000	0.37
Retained earnings	255,000	0.14	—	—
Owners' equity	**555,000**	0.31	**1,457,000**	0.37
Total liabilities and equity	$ 1,800,000	1.00	$ 3,902,000	1.00

✓ Denotes items that are taken into consideration for the purchase of the business.

Long-term Debts. As shown in the table, the buyers will borrow $2,000,000 to purchase the current and fixed assets.

Common Shares. Common shares represent the amount of cash that the buyers would have to put up in order to buy the business. An amount of $1,457,000 would be invested in the business by the new owners and represents 37 percent of the total liabilities and owners' equity.

Price-tagging an Ongoing Business

Now that we have created the projected income statement and opening balance sheet, we can determine how much the business is worth as a going concern. Three techniques will be used to make that calculation: asset valuation, net present value, and industry multipliers.

Asset Valuation

The asset valuation method is to look at the buyer's restated balance sheet (**Table 11.3**) and select the items that the buyer is interested in purchasing. These items are shown in **Table 11.4**. The only assets that are of interest to the new owners are accounts receivable, inventory, capital assets, and goodwill. As shown, the buyer will probably keep the accounts payable (sometimes accrued expenses) since they are used to finance current assets such as accounts receivable and inventory. Based on the re-appraised value, the buyer will purchase the seller's working capital for an amount of $225,000.

The other assets include capital assets such as the land, buildings, equipment, machinery, and tools. These assets would be listed in detail at book price and market price. The value of these assets is $3 million. The other asset that the buyer will purchase is the goodwill. As shown, this is valued at $400,000.

The seller is therefore asking $3,625,000 for the business. The question is this: Based on the pro-forma income statement, is the asking price worth it? The

TABLE 11.4   NPV Based on Cost of Capital and Hurdle Rate

Accounts receivable	$ 250,000
Inventory	170,000
Total current assets	420,000
Less: accounts payable	195,000
Net working capital	225,000
Capital assets	3,000,000
Goodwill	400,000
Purchase price	$3,625,000

potential buyers could invest $3,625,000 in investment securities at 10 percent a year (before tax) and earn $362,500 a year. If they buy the business instead, they should expect larger earnings because of the risk factor.

Net Present Value Method

The net present value method is based on the time value of money concept and takes into account cash inflows and cash outflows. (This topic was covered in Chapters 7 and 8.) As shown in **Table 11.5**, the net present value is calculated by taking into account both the cost of capital and the hurdle rate. The seller's asking price is $3,625,000. This is the amount of cash that the buyer would have to pay and includes working capital, capital assets, and goodwill (**Table 11.4**).

The next step is to determine the amount of cash that would be generated over the life of the project. From the buyer's income statement shown in **Table 11.2**, the cash inflow is estimated at $519,000. This is made up of the income after taxes of $369,000 plus depreciation of $150,000. If we assume that the owner will want to keep the business for a period of ten years, after which he or she will want to sell it for $6,000,000, the net present value of the purchase, using a 10 percent cost of capital discount rate, is a positive $1,877,287. This means that the buyer would earn 10 percent on the investment plus $1,877,287 over the ten-year period.

If cost of capital was used as the rate for approving the purchase, the buyer would certainly buy the business. However, because of the risk involved, if the

TABLE 11.5   Cost of the Business

	Cost of capital 10%	Hurdle rate 20%
Purchase price (outflow)	− $3,625,000	− $3,625,000
Cash inflows		
Cost of capital $519,000 × 6.1446	+ 3,189,047	
Hurdle rate $519,000 × 4.1925		+ 2,175,908
Sale of business		
Cost of capital $6,000,000 × .38554	+ 2,313,240	
Hurdle rate $6,000,000 × .16151		+ 969,060
Net present value	+ $1,877,287	− $ 480,032

buyer's hurdle rate on the investment is 20 percent, the net present value would be negative, that is, −$480,032. In this case, the buyer would earn less than the expected 20 percent. He or she would probably not buy the business for the $3,625,000 asking price. However, if the buyer insists on making a 20 percent return, a counter-offer of $3,144,968 ($3,625,000 − $480,032) could be made— which, in this case, would make the cash outflow equal to the cash inflow. At that price, the IRR would be 20 percent. On the other hand, if the buyer still purchases the business for the $3,625,000 asking price, an internal rate of return of only 17.2 percent would be made.

Industry Multipliers

The other approach to putting a price tag on a business is the use of industry multipliers. Here, the buyer or seller would refer to a list of multipliers that applies to a particular industry. Although many individuals use multipliers, some (particularly buyers) refrain from using them because they focus too much on gross sales, rather than income after taxes. The argument is this: It's not the top line that counts, but the bottom line.

Table 11.6 presents a list of typical industry multipliers. Although some of them are accurate in some industries, they should still be used with caution because they tend to simplify, to a large extent, the worth of a business. Nevertheless, these multipliers can be used as a complementary tool to obtain a rough estimate of an asking price. By using these multipliers with another technique such as NPV, you may arrive at roughly the same asking price. If that's the case, then the valuation price would be in the ball park.

Because of a wide variation in gross sales from year to year, it may be wise to calculate the asking price by using the company's last three or four years' income statements. You may also want to average out the last three years' gross sales revenue to calculate the asking price.

Times Multiple Earnings

In the case of Eastman Technologies Inc., a times earnings multiple can also be used to determine the value of the company. A times multiple earnings is equal to the inverse of a capitalization rate. For example, if the investors want to use an 11 percent capitalization rate, the times multiple earnings would be 9.1 (100 ÷ 11%) If they want to use 13 percent, the times multiple earnings would be 7.7 (100 ÷ 13%). To determine the company's market value by using the times multiple earnings, the investor would therefore have to determine the appropriate capitalization rate and multiply this rate by maintainable after-tax cash flow which in the case of Eastman is $519,000 ($369,000 + $150,000). If the investors want to use a 13 percent capitalization, the value of the business would be $3,996,300 ($519,000 × 7.7).

If the investors buy 40 percent ownership of the business, than they would be entitled to only 40 percent of the $3,996,300 or $1,598,520.

$$\left[\quad \textbf{TABLE 11.6} \quad \text{Industry Multipliers} \quad\right]$$

Industry	Multipliers
Travel agencies	.05 to .1 × annual gross sales
Advertising agencies	.75 × annual gross sales
Collection agencies	.15 to .2 × annual collections + equipment
Employment agencies	.75 × annual gross sales
Insurance agencies	1 to 2 × annual renewal commissions
Real estate agencies	.2 to .3 × annual gross commissions
Rental agencies	.2 × annual net profit + inventory
Retail businesses	.75 to 1.5 × annual net profit + inventory + equipment
Sales businesses	1 × annual net profit
Fast food (non-franchise)	.5 to .7 × monthly gross sales + inventory
Restaurants	.3 to .5 × annual gross sales, or .4 × monthly gross sales + inventory
Office supply distributors	.5 × monthly gross sales + inventory
Newspapers	.75 to 1.5 × annual gross sales
Printers	.4 to .5 × annual net profit + inventory + equipment
Food distributors	1 to 1.5 ×annual net profit + inventory + equipment
Building supply retailers	.25 to .75 annual net profit + inventory + equipment
Job shops	.5 × annual gross sales + inventory
Manufacturing	1.5 to 2.5 × annual net profit + inventory (including work in progress)
Farm/heavy equipment dealers	.5 × annual net profit + inventory + equipment
Professional practices	1 to 5 × annual net profit
Boat/camper dealers	1 × annual net profit + inventory + equipment

Source: Richard W. Snowden, *Buying a Business* (New York: AMACON, 1994), pp. 150–151.

Market Value of Publicly Traded Companies

To calculate the value of publicly traded companies, analysts would have to use the number of common shares issued and the share market price. Here, in order to calculate the market value of the shareholders' equity, one has to multiply the number of outstanding common shares by the share price on the last day that the shares were traded on the stock market.

Let's assume that Eastman Technologies Inc. is a publicly traded company and has 30,000 shares outstanding. With a $555,000 net worth, that means that the book value of each share outstanding would be $18.50 ($555,000 ÷ 30,000).

However, if the shares were traded at $25.00, the market value of the company, or the equity portion of the balance sheet, would be $750,000 ($25.00 × 30,000). In this case, the ratio of the market value to the book value would be 1.35 times.

Decision-Making in Action

Robin Pedwell, CEO of Amoco Sauna Inc., is considering launching a new product line in the United States market by the early part of 2000. The company is in the process of completing a prototype beauty care product—a compact, portable, and multifunctional facial sauna. If Amoco is successful in the U.S., Pedwell would then market the product line in the Canadian and European markets.

The development of the multifunctional facial sauna began in 1998, when the company's marketing research department studied the market opportunities for health and beauty care products. The favorable market results encouraged Pedwell to design and develop a new line of products—a "family of products"—for health and beauty care. The leading product, called "Beauty Facial Sauna," was a portable, hand-held, and steam-generating apparatus.

The only obstacle to Pedwell's dream was the shortage of cash he needed to complete his research on the facial sauna in 1999, and promotional funds to market the new product line in the early months of 2000. Because of the nature of the business venture, he was aware that conventional lenders would not be interested in financing his project. He realized that his only option was to obtain funds from high risk capital investors. He was aware that obtaining funds from these types of investors would be a very difficult, time-consuming process, and also very expensive.

Therefore, Pedwell approached a long-time friend and financial advisor with excellent connections in the high risk capital markets, Norm Woodstock. He would help Pedwell develop an investment proposal and develop a strategy on how to approach high-risk investors. The first thing that Woodstock suggested was to determine the value of the business as a *going concern* several years after the launching of the new product line. In other words he was asking the question: What will Amoco's financial statements look like several years from now? Woodstock knew that high-risk investors are particularly interested in investing money in highly successful ventures, those that offer very high returns (somewhere in the 25 to 35 percent range). Also, these types of investors want to make sure that they have a clear option about how they would go about making their exit from the company, that is, selling their shares four to five years after their initial investment. An exit strategy could take the form of a public offering or the possibility that Pedwell himself would buy back the investor's share.

Before going through the detailed calculation and preparing the investment proposal, Woodstock analyzed Amoco's financial statements and indicated to Pedwell the different methods that could be used to determine the value of his company. He pointed out four methods: the book value, the liquidation value, the going concern value, and the discounted cash flow (DCF) method.

Woodstock pointed out that the DCF method is the most suitable method to determine the *real value* of Amoco. However, he decided to calculate the value of the business by using all methods just for the sake of getting some idea about Amoco's different economic values.

Book Value. As Woodstock pointed out to Pedwell, the book value of Amoco is the company's net worth or shareholders' equity that is based on generally accepted accounting principles. By simply subtracting the liabilities from the book value of Amoco's assets, it gives the economic value called *shareholders' equity* or *net worth*. **Table 11.7** shows Amoco's book value for the year-end 1999. As shown, the estimated book value of the company is $700,000.

Liquidation value. Woodstock explained that the liquidation value would only be useful if Amoco was sold in order to satisfy its creditors. By using this approach, tangible assets such as land usually have a liquidation value close to their market value. Inventories and accounts receivable, on the other hand, are usually

TABLE 11.7

Amoco Sauna Inc.
Estimated Balance Sheet
December 31, 1999

	Book Value	Liquidation Value
Assets		
Current assets		
Accounts receivable	$ 300,000	$ 125,000
Inventory	200,000	200,000
Other current assets	150,000	100,000
Total current assets	650,000	425,000
Total net capital assets	900,000	700,000
Other assets	50,000	20,000
Total assets	$1,600,000	1,145,000
Liabilities and owners equity		
Total current liabilities	$ 600,000	600,000
Total long-term debts	300,000	300,000
Total liabilities	900,000	900,000
Total shareholders' equity	700,000	245,000
Total liabilities and shareholders' equity	$1,600,000	$1,145,000
	Book value	Liquidation value

valued at less than what is shown in the books. He also added that in order to determine the liquidation value, all of Amoco's assets would be assigned a distressed value while all debts would be listed at book value. As he pointed out, most of the assets sold under duress are discounted from their book value. The difference between the distressed value of the assets and the actual or book value of the liabilities is considered the *liquidation value*. This value would not reflect Amoco's real worth.

In most instances, however, a liquidation value is substantially less than the market value and book value. This method would be used only if Amoco was in serious financial trouble and had to liquidate its assets to pay the creditors. As shown in **Table 11.7**, Amoco's liquidation value is estimated at $245,000. The book value of the company's assets is reduced by $455,000 or 28% while the liabilities (both current and long-term) remain the same at the $900,000 level.

Going Concern Value. Woodstock indicated that the going concern value was a more relevant approach for determining a price tag for an ongoing business since it was related to the ability or capacity of Amoco to produce a stream of after-tax cash flows. This method would show the pro forma income statements after the new sauna product line was introduced in the U.S. As indicated to Pedwell, this forecast would require the help of many managers in the company involved in marketing, production, research and development, administration, accounting, etc. Woodstock indicated that a high-risk investor would base his or her investment decision on sales revenue, marketing and manufacturing costs, income after taxes, and cash flow estimates. Most important, the investor would want to be confident about the reliability of all revenue and cost estimates contained in the income statement.

As Woodstock pointed out, typical non-risk investors are prepared to accept a 5 percent return if money is invested in relatively risk-free investments. However, high-risk investors, that is, those prepared to invest in companies such as Amoco, expect to earn a return between 25 to 35 percent for such a revenue-generating business that presents some risk. Woodstock further explained that the level of risk is the price tag that helps determine a sought-after economic return. Therefore, the going concern value has the ability to look at *future cash flow expectations* and the *relative risk* associated with an ongoing business.

Table 11.8 presents Amoco's income statement for the year 2000, that is, the year that Amoco expects to launch the new product line. As shown, Amoco anticipates earning $450,000 in income after taxes and $550,000 in after-tax cash flow ($450,000 + $100,000). If a potential investor wants to earn 20 percent, Amoco's going concern value would be $2,750,000 million ($550,000 ÷ 20%). The $550,000 amount represents the maintainable, perpetual, or indefinite cash flow that Amoco expects to generate. A capitalization rate is a discount rate used to find the present value of a series of future receipts. In this particular instance, a 20 percent capitalization rate is the required rate of return expected by risk capital

[

TABLE 11.8

 ]

Amoco Sauna Inc.
Pro-Forma Income Statement
For the Year Ended December 31, 2000

In 000's of dollars

Sales revenue		$5,000
Total cost of goods sold		2,960
Gross margin		2,040
Operating expenses		
Total selling expenses	800	
Total administrative expenses	500	
Total operating expenses		1,300
Operating income		740
Other income/charges		90
Income before taxes		650
Income taxes		200
Income after taxes		450
Add back depreciation and amortization		100
After-tax cash flow from operations	$ 550	$ 550
Divided by capitalization rate	20%	30%
Going concern value	**$2,750**	**$ 1,833**

investors from Amoco. Woodstock indicated that this rate is based on a number of subjective factors and conditions at the time of valuation.

If the risk capital investors found Amoco's venture extremely risky and wanted to earn 30 percent, the cash flow receipts of the $550,000 would give a $1,833,000 ($550,000 ÷ 30%) present value. **Table 11.8** shows that the higher the capitalization rate (20% versus 30%) the lower is the present value ($2,750,000 versus $1,833,000).

Discounted Cash Flow Method. The more appropriate approach for calculating the value of Amoco is the discounted cash flow method (DCF). The primary benefit of the DCF method is that it allows for fluctuations in future cash flows over a period of time.

The following lists the four steps involved in calculating Amoco's value by using the DCF method. Each step is explained in the next several pages.

Step 1:   Calculate Amoco's yearly after-tax cash flow.
Step 2:   Calculate Amoco's projected residual value.

Step 3:   Calculate Amoco's estimated market value.

Step 4:   Calculate the investor's before- and after-tax return.

Step 1: Calculate Amoco's Yearly After-tax Cash Flow

The first step for calculating Amoco's market value is to determine its after-tax cash flow forecast for the years 2000 to 2004. As mentioned earlier, these estimates are based on Amoco's management team and business-related experts in the field of sauna products.

Amoco hopes to have completed the research activities of the sauna's new product line by the end of 1999 and be ready for market distribution in the U.S. by early 2000. If the product line is well accepted in the United States (which is what Pedwell expects to realize), Amoco would than be ready to launch the product line in the Canadian market. As shown in **Table 11.9**, the cash flow from operations generated by Amoco jumps from $550,000 (the detailed calculation for this figure is shown in **Table 11.8**) in 2000 to $1,450,000 in 2004. This represents a $900,000 growth over a five-year period for a substantial 164 percent increase.

After adding the investments in capital assets and incremental working capital to the after-tax cash flow from operations, Amoco shows a negative $850,000 cash flow in 2000 and positive cash flows between years 2001 and 2004 from $200,000 to $950,000. As shown, a 20 percent discount rate to be considered by investors for this type of venture is used to determine the present value of the projected cash flows. This discount factor reflects the risk associated with Amoco's new product line. As shown, the projected present value cash flow loses more value proportionately to the undiscounted net cash flow (NCF) as it reaches the end of the forecast period. This is due to the fact that smaller discount factors are used in later years to reflect the loss of value as a result of time. The present

---

TABLE 11.9   NPV Calculations

In 000's of $	2000	2001	2002	2003	2004
Cash flow from operations	$ 550	$ 800	$ 900	$1,200	$1,450
Capital investments	(1,200)	(400)	(400)	(300)	(300)
Incremental working capital	(200)	(200)	(200)	(200)	(200)
Subtotal	(1,400)	(600)	(600)	(500)	(500)
NCF	(850)	+200	+300	+700	+950
Factor @ 20%	.83333	.69444	.57870	.48225	.40188
Present value	(708)	+139	+174	+338	+382
NPV	+$ 325				

value of the cash flow for each year is than added to determine the net present value (NPV). The net present value for the five-year forecast, using a 20 percent discount rate, is $325,000.

The above shows that after making the initial $1.4 investment, Amoco's venture will still produce a positive net cash flow to the extent of $325,000 during the 5-year period.

By taking into account only the above five-year cash flow forecast, the business venture would generate an internal rate of return of 36.9 percent. If the company's last year's $950,000 was maintained indefinitely and capitalized by using 18 percent (this will be discussed in step 2 under the heading Calculate Amoco's Projected Residual Value), this would give an additional inflow of cash in the amount of $5.3 million. If this amount were incorporated in the return calculation, the company's internal rate of return would jump to 78.6 percent with a $2.1 million NPV using a 20 percent discount rate.

As pointed out by Woodstock, this is a very lucrative venture if the projected cash flow is realized. The only obstacle and concern is to convince risk-capital investors of the feasibility of realizing these cash flow estimates.

Step 2: Calculate Amoco's Projected Residual Value

This step determines the residual value of a business. This is important to risk capital investors since they want to compare the amount of money that they will invest in the business today to what the business will be worth once it reaches maturity. In the case of Amoco, Pedwell is looking for $600,000 from private investors. He will have to demonstrate that the investment will multiply many-fold and earn a return that will offset the risk. This is what this step in the valuation process explores.

At the end of the forecast period, that is in 2004, Amoco will likely remain viable and continue to generate $950,000 in net cash flow for an indefinite period of time. Basically, the *residual value* is the present value of projected after-tax *maintainable* cash flow expected beyond year 2004. As shown in **Table 11.9**, the maintainable cash flow from operations for the year 2004 is $1,450,000. Also, capital spending for each year after 2004 is estimated at $300,000 in addition to a $200,000 increase in working capital resulting from the anticipated introduction of the sauna product line in the U.S. market and possibly the European market. It is assumed here that Amoco will maintain its level of operations based on the year 2004 performance (a realistic estimate according to Pedwell).

When calculating the residual value, a capitalization rate has to be determined. Using capitalization is similar to discounting a *maintainable* cash flow in *perpetuity*. To calculate this figure, the maintainable after-tax cash flow amount of $950,000 is divided by an acceptable capitalization rate. In this case, the capitalization rate used for Amoco is 18 percent instead of the previous 20 percent. The difference between the discount rate and the capitalization rate is that the rate is adjusted for inflation, for growth and for risk. By using this capitalization rate, the value of Amoco in 2004 would be $5.3 million ($950,000 ÷ 18%). Furthermore, the present value of this amount will be discounted to 1999 by using a 20 percent discount rate, that is the year that the investor will advance the $600,000 to Amoco. Amoco's present value of the residual value totals $2,121,033 ($5,277,778 × .40188). Here is how it is calculated:

	2004
Cash flow	$1,450,000
Investments	−500,000
Net cash flow	950,000
Capitalization rate @ 18%	$5,277,778
Present value factor @ 20%	.40188
Prevent value of the residual value	$2,121,033

Step 3: Calculate Amoco's Estimated Market Value

This step in the valuation process involves the calculation of Amoco's estimated fair market value. As shown below, Amoco's fair market value is estimated at $2,444,030 and reflects Amoco's five-year after-tax discounted cash flow of $325,000 (step 1) and the estimated residual value of $2,121,033 (step 2).

Present value of cash flow from operations	$ 325,000
Present value of the residual value	2,121,033
Estimated fair market value	$2,446,033

Step 4: Calculate the Investor's Before-tax and After-tax Return

This last step in the process involves the calculation of the investor's return on investment on a before-tax and after-tax basis. Pedwell will be seeking a $600,000 amount from a risk capital investor. This cash will be used to finalize the research and development on the sauna product line and help to fund a marketing program to launch it.

This investment will be required by the middle of 1999. Here, capitalization will also be used to determine Amoco's residual value. The total value at exit must be determined by multiplying the maintainable after-tax cash flow by a multiple. Here, the multiple is equal to the inverse of a capitalization rate. In this case, 12.5 percent capitalization rate is used and equals 8.0 (100 ÷ 12.5%) times earnings multiple. As shown in **Table 11.10**, by using the 8 times multiple, the value at exit is estimated to be $7,600,000 ($950,000 × 8 times). It is assumed that the risk capital investor has a 40 percent equity participation in the company and represents $3,040,000 in gross proceeds that will be paid to him or her in 2004.

As shown in **Table 11.10**, by using a 38.34 percent discount rate, the present value of the $3,040,000 would be equivalent to the $600,000 investment made by the risk capital investors.

TABLE 11.10   Before-tax IRR on Investment

In 000's of dollars	1999	2000	2001	2002	2003	2004
Before-tax return						
Initial investment	−600	—	—	—	—	—
Total value at exit						
After-tax cash flow	—	—	—	—	—	950
Multiple	—	—	—	—	—	8
Total value at exit	—	—	—	—	—	7,600
Investor's share (40%)	—	—	—	—	—	3,040
Initial investment	−600					
Total cash flows	+600					3,040
Before tax IRR on investment	38.34%					

The discount rate would therefore be considered the investor's before-tax internal rate of return (IRR) on investment. As shown in **Table 11.11**, similar calculations would have to be done to calculate the investor's IRR on an after-tax basis.

Assuming that the after-tax cash flow is $2,125,000 at exit, the investor's after-tax IRR on investment would be 28.78 percent. By using a 28.78 percent discount rate, the present value of the $2,125,000 received in year 2004 would be equivalent to the $600,000 investment made by the risk capital investor today. This discount rate would therefore be considered the investor's after-tax internal rate of return (IRR).

The return on investment by the investor would be earned only when he or she sells his shares at the planned exit in year 2004. The exit could be made in one of the following ways:

- Initial public offering
- Sale of all the shares of the company
- Sale of the investor's shares to a third party
- Buyback of the investor's shares by Pedwell

TABLE 11.11   Net After-tax Proceeds to Investor

In 000's of dollars

Gross proceeds received on exit	$ 3,040
Initial investment	(600)
Capital gain on investment	2,440
Taxable portion (75%)	1,830
Investor's tax payable (50%)	915
Gross proceeds received on exit	$ 3,040
Investor's tax payable	915
Net after-tax proceeds to investor	$ 2,125

In 000's of dollars	1999	2000	2001	2002	2003	2004
Before-tax return						
Initial investment	$(600)	—	—	—	—	—
Total value at exit After-tax cash proceeds to investor	—	—	—	—	—	$2,125
Initial investment	(600)					
Total cash flows	600					2,125
After-tax return on investment	28.78%					

Summary

The book value of a business is what a business is worth on the books—that is, the difference between total assets and total liabilities. Market value is what a business is worth to a buyer as an ongoing entity. Because financial statements do not necessarily reflect the true market value of a business, accountants have attempted to resolve this issue through price level accounting and current value accounting.

Different valuation models exist. They include economic value, market value, book value, liquidation value, replacement value, collateral value, assessed value, and going concern value.

When buying a business, it is important to scan the environment and to document the planning assumptions in order to construct a pro-forma income statement and pro-forma balance sheet.

Price-tagging a business can be done through the asset valuation method, which is the difference between the market value of the assets of an ongoing business and its liabilities; the net present value method, which takes into consideration cash outflow (purchase price of the business) and cash inflows (profit plus depreciation) and the potential resale value of the business at a later date; and industry multipliers, which reflect a percentage of the sales revenue.

APPENDIX A

Interest Tables

TABLE A

INTEREST FACTORS $F_n = P(1 + i)^n$ FOR CALCULATING F, FUTURE VALUE OF A SUM

Year	1%	2%	3%	4%	5%	6%	7%	8%
1	1.010	1.020	1.030	1.040	1.050	1.060	1.070	1.080
2	1.020	1.040	1.061	1.082	1.103	1.124	1.145	1.166
3	1.030	1.061	1.093	1.125	1.158	1.191	1.225	1.260
4	1.041	1.082	1.126	1.170	1.216	1.262	1.311	1.360
5	1.051	1.104	1.159	1.217	1.276	1.338	1.403	1.469
6	1.062	1.126	1.194	1.265	1.340	1.419	1.501	1.587
7	1.072	1.149	1.230	1.316	1.407	1.504	1.606	1.714
8	1.083	1.172	1.267	1.369	1.477	1.594	1.718	1.851
9	1.094	1.195	1.305	1.423	1.551	1.689	1.838	1.999
10	1.105	1.219	1.344	1.480	1.629	1.791	1.967	2.159
11	1.116	1.243	1.384	1.539	1.710	1.898	2.105	2.332
12	1.127	1.268	1.426	1.601	1.796	2.012	2.252	2.518
13	1.138	1.294	1.469	1.665	1.886	2.133	2.410	2.720
14	1.149	1.319	1.513	1.732	1.980	2.261	2.579	2.937
15	1.161	1.346	1.558	1.801	2.079	2.397	2.759	3.172
16	1.173	1.373	1.605	1.873	2.183	2.540	2.952	3.426
17	1.184	1.400	1.653	1.948	2.292	2.693	3.159	3.700
18	1.196	1.428	1.702	2.026	2.407	2.854	3.380	3.996
19	1.208	1.457	1.754	2.107	2.527	3.026	3.617	4.316
20	1.220	1.486	1.806	2.191	2.653	3.207	3.870	4.661
21	1.232	1.516	1.860	2.279	2.786	3.400	4.141	5.034
22	1.245	1.546	1.916	2.370	2.925	3.604	4.430	5.437
23	1.257	1.577	1.974	2.465	3.072	3.820	4.741	5.871
24	1.270	1.608	2.033	2.563	3.225	4.049	5.072	6.341
25	1.282	1.641	2.094	2.666	3.386	4.292	5.427	6.848

Year	9%	10%	11%	12%	14%	16%	18%	20%
1	1.090	1.100	1.110	1.120	1.140	1.160	1.180	1.200
2	1.188	1.210	1.232	1.254	1.300	1.346	1.392	1.440
3	1.295	1.331	1.368	1.405	1.482	1.561	1.643	1.728
4	1.412	1.464	1.518	1.574	1.689	1.811	1.939	2.074
5	1.539	1.611	1.685	1.762	1.925	2.100	2.288	2.488
6	1.677	1.772	1.870	1.974	2.195	2.436	2.700	2.986
7	1.828	1.949	2.076	2.211	2.502	2.826	3.185	3.583
8	1.993	2.144	2.305	2.476	2.853	3.278	3.759	4.300
9	2.172	2.358	2.558	2.773	3.252	3.803	4.435	5.160
10	2.367	2.594	2.839	3.106	3.707	4.411	5.234	6.192
11	2.580	2.853	3.152	3.479	4.226	5.117	6.176	7.430
12	2.813	3.138	3.498	3.896	4.818	5.936	7.288	8.916
13	3.066	3.452	3.883	4.363	5.492	6.886	8.599	10.699
14	3.342	3.798	4.310	4.887	6.261	7.988	10.147	12.839
15	3.642	4.177	4.785	5.474	7.138	9.266	11.974	15.407
16	3.970	4.595	5.311	6.130	8.137	10.748	14.129	18.488
17	4.328	5.054	5.895	6.866	9.276	12.468	16.672	22.186
18	4.717	5.560	6.544	7.690	10.575	14.463	19.673	26.623
19	5.142	6.116	7.263	8.613	12.056	16.777	23.214	31.948
20	5.604	6.728	8.062	9.646	13.744	19.461	27.393	38.338
21	6.109	7.400	8.949	10.804	15.668	22.575	32.324	46.005
22	6.659	8.140	9.934	12.100	17.861	26.186	38.142	55.206
23	7.258	8.954	11.026	13.552	20.362	30.376	45.008	66.247
24	7.911	9.850	12.239	15.179	23.212	35.236	53.109	79.497
25	8.623	10.835	13.586	17.000	26.462	40.874	62.669	95.396

Year	22%	24%	26%	28%	30%	32%	34%	36%
1	1.220	1.240	1.260	1.280	1.300	1.320	1.340	1.360
2	1.488	1.538	1.588	1.638	1.690	1.742	1.796	1.850
3	1.816	1.907	2.000	2.097	2.197	2.300	2.406	2.515
4	2.215	2.364	2.520	2.684	2.856	3.036	3.036	3.421
5	2.703	2.932	3.176	3.436	3.713	4.007	4.320	4.653
6	3.297	3.635	4.002	4.398	4.827	5.290	5.789	6.328
7	4.023	4.508	5.042	5.630	6.275	6.983	7.758	8.605
8	4.908	5.590	6.353	7.206	8.157	9.217	10.395	11.703
9	5.987	6.931	8.005	9.223	10.605	12.167	13.930	15.917
10	7.305	8.594	10.086	11.806	13.786	16.060	18.666	21.647
11	8.912	10.657	12.708	15.112	17.922	21.199	25.012	29.439
12	10.872	13.215	16.012	19.343	23.298	27.983	33.516	40.038
13	13.264	16.386	20.175	24.759	30.288	36.937	44.912	54.451
14	16.182	20.319	25.421	31.691	39.374	48.757	60.182	74.053
15	19.742	25.196	32.030	40.565	51.186	64.359	80.644	100.713
16	24.086	31.243	40.358	51.923	66.542	84.954	108.063	136.969
17	29.384	38.741	50.851	66.461	86.504	112.139	144.804	186.278
18	35.849	48.039	64.072	85.071	112.455	148.024	194.038	253.338
19	43.736	59.568	80.731	108.890	146.192	195.391	260.011	344.540
20	53.358	73.864	101.721	139.380	190.049	257.916	348.414	468.574
21	65.096	91.592	128.169	178.406	247.064	340.450	466.875	637.261
22	79.418	113.574	161.492	228.360	321.184	449.394	625.613	866.675
23	96.890	140.831	203.480	292.300	417.539	593.200	838.321	1178.680
24	118.205	174.631	256.385	374.144	542.800	783.024	1123.350	1603.000
25	144.210	216.542	323.045	478.905	705.640	1033.590	1505.290	2180.080

TABLE B

INTEREST FACTORS $P = F\left[\dfrac{1}{(1 + i)^n}\right]$ FOR CALCULATING P,

PRESENT VALUE OF A SUM

N	1%	2%	3%	4%	5%	6%	7%	8%
1	0.99010	0.98039	0.97007	0.96154	0.95238	0.94340	0.93458	0.92593
2	.98030	.96117	.94260	.92456	.90703	.89000	.87344	.85734
3	.97059	.94232	.91514	.88900	.86384	.83962	.81630	.79383
4	.96098	.92385	.88849	.85480	.82270	.79209	.76290	.73503
5	.95147	.90573	.86261	.82193	.78353	.74726	.71299	.68058
6	.94204	.88797	.83748	.79031	.74622	.70496	.66634	.63017
7	.93272	.87056	.81309	.75992	.71068	.66506	.62275	.58349
8	.92348	.85349	.78941	.73069	.67684	.62741	.58201	.54027
9	.91434	.83675	.76642	.70259	.64461	.59190	.54393	.50025
10	.90529	.82035	.74409	.67556	.61391	.55839	.50835	.46319
11	.89632	.80426	.72242	.64958	.58468	.52679	.47509	.42888
12	.88745	.78849	.70138	.62460	.55684	.49697	.44401	.39711
13	.87866	.77303	.68095	.60057	.53032	.46884	.41496	.36770
14	.86996	.75787	.66112	.57747	.50507	.44230	.38782	.34046
15	.86135	.74301	.64186	.55526	.48102	.41726	.36245	.31524
16	.85282	.72845	.62317	.53391	.45811	.39365	.33873	.29189
17	.84438	.71416	.60502	.51337	.43630	.37136	.31657	.27027
18	.83602	.70016	.58739	.49363	.41552	.35034	.29586	.25025
19	.82774	.68643	.57029	.47464	.39573	.33051	.27651	.23171
20	.81954	.67297	.55367	.45639	.37689	.31180	.25842	.21455
21	.81143	.65978	.53755	.43883	.35894	.29415	.24151	.19866
22	.80340	.64684	.52189	.42195	.34185	.27750	.22571	.18394
23	.79544	.63416	.50669	.40573	.32557	.26180	.21095	.17031
24	.78757	.62172	.49193	.39012	.31007	.24698	.19715	.15770
25	.77977	.60953	.47760	.37512	.29530	.23300	.18425	.14602

N	9%	10%	11%	12%	13%	14%	15%	16%
1	0.91743	0.90909	0.90090	0.89286	0.88496	0.87719	0.86957	0.86207
2	.84168	.82645	.81162	.79719	.78315	.76947	.75614	.74316
3	.77218	.75131	.73119	.71178	.69305	.67497	.65752	.64066
4	.70843	.68301	.65873	.63552	.61332	.59208	.57175	.55229
5	.64993	.62092	.59345	.56743	.54276	.51937	.49718	.47611
6	.59627	.56447	.53464	.50663	.48032	.45559	.43233	.41044
7	.54703	.51316	.48166	.45235	.42506	.39964	.37594	.35383
8	.50187	.46651	.43393	.40388	.37616	.35056	.32690	.30503
9	.46043	.42410	.39092	.36061	.33288	.30751	.28426	.26295
10	.42241	.38554	.35218	.32197	.29459	.26974	.24718	.22668
11	.38753	.35049	.31728	.28748	.26070	.23662	.21494	.19542
12	.35553	.31863	.28584	.25667	.23071	.20756	.18691	.16846
13	.32618	.28966	.25751	.22917	.20416	.18207	.16253	.14523
14	.29925	.26333	.23199	.20462	.18068	.15971	.14133	.12520
15	.27454	.23939	.20900	.18270	.15989	.14010	.12289	.10793
16	.25187	.21763	.18829	.16312	.14150	.12289	.10686	.09304
17	.23107	.19784	.16963	.14564	.12522	.10780	.09293	.08021
18	.21199	.17986	.15282	.13004	.11081	.09456	.08080	.06914
19	.19449	.16351	.13768	.11611	.09806	.08295	.07026	.05961
20	.17843	.14864	.12403	.10367	.08678	.07276	.06110	.05139
21	.16370	.13513	.11174	.09256	.07680	.06383	.05313	.04430
22	.15018	.12285	.10067	.08264	.06796	.05599	.04620	.03819
23	.13778	.11168	.09069	.07379	.06014	.04911	.04017	.03292
24	.12640	.10153	.08170	.06588	.05322	.04308	.03493	.02838
25	.11597	.09230	.07361	.05882	.04710	.03779	.03038	.02447

N	17%	18%	19%	20%	21%	22%	23%	24%
1	0.85470	0.84746	0.84034	0.83333	0.82645	0.81967	0.81301	0.80645
2	.73051	.71818	.70616	.69444	.68301	.67186	.66098	.65036
3	.62437	.60863	.59342	.57870	.56447	.55071	.53738	.52449
4	.53365	.51579	.49867	.48225	.46651	.45140	.43690	.42297
5	.45611	.43711	.41905	.40188	.38554	.37000	.35520	.34111
6	.38984	.37043	.35214	.33490	.31863	.30328	.28878	.27509
7	.33320	.31392	.29592	.27908	.26333	.24859	.23478	.22184
8	.28478	.26604	.24867	.23257	.21763	.20376	.19088	.17891
9	.24340	.22546	.20897	.19381	.17986	.16702	.15519	.14428
10	.20804	.19106	.17560	.16151	.14864	.13690	.12617	.11635
11	.17781	.16192	.14756	.13459	.12285	.11221	.10258	.09383
12	.15197	.13722	.12400	.11216	.10153	.09198	.08339	.07567
13	.12989	.11629	.10420	.09346	.08391	.07539	.06780	.06103
14	.11102	.09855	.08757	.07789	.06934	.06180	.05512	.04921
15	.09489	.08352	.07359	.06491	.05731	.05065	.04481	.03969
16	.08110	.07078	.06184	.05409	.04736	.04152	.03643	.03201
17	.06932	.05998	.05196	.04507	.03914	.03403	.02962	.02581
18	.05925	.05083	.04367	.03756	.03235	.02789	.02408	.02082
19	.05064	.04308	.03669	.03130	.02673	.02286	.01958	.01679
20	.04328	.03651	.03084	.02608	.02209	.01874	.01592	.01354
21	.03699	.03094	.02591	.02174	.01826	.01536	.01294	.01092
22	.03162	.02622	.02178	.01811	.01509	.01259	.01052	.00880
23	.02702	.02222	.01830	.01509	.01247	.01032	.00855	.00710
24	.02310	.01883	.01538	.01258	.01031	.00846	.00695	.00573
25	.01974	.01596	.01292	.01048	.00852	.00693	.00565	.00462

N	25%	26%	27%	28%	29%	30%	31%	32%
1	0.80000	0.79365	0.78740	0.78125	0.77519	0.76923	0.76336	0.75758
2	.64000	.62988	.62000	.61035	.60093	.59172	.58272	.57392
3	.51200	.49991	.48819	.47684	.46583	.45517	.44482	.43479
4	.40960	.39675	.38440	.37253	.36111	.35013	.33956	.32939
5	.32768	.31488	.30268	.29104	.27993	.26933	.25920	.24953
6	.26214	.24991	.23833	.22737	.21700	.20718	.19787	.18904
7	.20972	.19834	.18766	.17764	.16822	.15937	.15104	.14321
8	.16777	.15741	.14776	.13878	.13040	.12259	.11530	.10849
9	.13422	.12493	.11635	.10842	.10109	.09430	.08802	.08219
10	.10737	.09915	.09161	.08470	.07836	.07254	.06719	.06227
11	.08590	.07869	.07214	.06617	.06075	.05580	.05129	.04717
12	.06872	.06245	.05680	.05170	.04709	.04292	.03915	.03574
13	.05498	.04957	.04472	.04039	.03650	.03302	.02989	.02707
14	.04398	.03934	.03522	.03155	.02830	.02540	.02281	.02051
15	.03518	.03122	.02773	.02465	.02194	.01954	.01742	.01554
16	.02815	.02478	.02183	.01926	.01700	.01503	.01329	.01177
17	.02252	.01967	.01719	.01505	.01318	.01156	.01015	.00892
18	.01801	.01561	.01354	.01175	.01022	.00889	.00775	.00676
19	.01441	.01239	.01066	.00918	.00792	.00684	.00591	.00512
20	.01153	.00983	.00839	.00717	.00614	.00526	.00451	.00388
21	.00922	.00780	.00661	.00561	.00476	.00405	.00345	.00294
22	.00738	.00619	.00520	.00438	.00369	.00311	.00263	.00223
23	.00590	.00491	.00410	.00342	.00286	.00239	.00201	.00169
24	.00472	.00390	.00323	.00267	.00222	.00184	.00153	.00128
25	.00378	.00310	.00254	.00209	.00172	.00142	.00117	.00097

TABLE C

INTEREST FACTORS $W = R\left[\dfrac{(1 + i)^n - 1}{i}\right]$ FOR CALCULATING W,

FUTURE VALUE OF AN ANNUITY

N	1%	2%	3%	4%	5%	6%	7%	8%
1	1.000	1.000	1.000	1.000	1.000	1.000	1.000	1.000
2	2.010	2.020	2.030	2.040	2.050	2.060	2.070	2.080
3	3.030	3.060	3.091	3.122	3.153	3.184	3.215	3.246
4	4.060	4.122	4.184	4.246	4.310	4.375	4.440	4.506
5	5.101	5.204	5.309	5.416	5.526	5.637	5.751	5.867
6	6.152	6.308	6.468	6.633	6.802	6.975	7.153	7.336
7	7.214	7.434	7.662	7.898	8.142	8.394	8.654	8.923
8	8.286	8.583	8.892	9.214	9.549	9.897	10.260	10.637
9	9.369	9.755	10.159	10.583	11.027	11.491	11.978	12.488
10	10.462	10.950	11.464	12.006	12.578	13.181	13.817	14.487
11	11.567	12.169	12.808	13.486	14.207	14.972	15.784	16.646
12	12.683	13.412	14.192	15.026	15.917	16.870	17.889	18.977
13	13.809	14.680	15.618	16.627	17.713	18.882	20.141	21.495
14	14.947	15.974	17.086	18.292	19.599	21.015	22.551	24.215
15	16.097	17.293	18.599	20.024	21.579	23.276	25.129	27.152
16	17.258	18.639	20.157	21.825	23.658	25.673	27.888	30.324
17	18.430	20.012	21.762	23.698	25.840	28.213	30.840	33.750
18	19.615	21.412	23.414	25.645	28.132	30.906	33.999	37.450
19	20.811	22.841	25.117	27.671	30.539	33.760	37.379	41.446
20	22.019	24.297	26.870	29.778	33.066	36.786	40.996	45.762
21	23.239	25.783	28.677	31.969	35.719	39.993	44.865	50.423
22	24.472	27.299	30.537	34.248	38.505	43.392	49.006	55.457
23	25.716	28.845	32.453	36.618	41.430	46.996	53.436	60.893
24	26.974	30.422	34.427	39.083	44.502	50.816	58.177	66.765
25	28.243	32.030	36.459	41.646	47.727	54.864	63.249	73.106

N	9%	10%	11%	12%	14%	16%	18%	20%
1	1.000	1.000	1.000	1.000	1.000	1.000	1.000	1.000
2	2.090	2.100	2.110	2.120	2.140	2.160	2.180	2.200
3	3.278	3.310	3.342	3.374	3.440	3.506	3.572	3.640
4	4.573	4.641	4.710	4.779	4.921	5.066	5.215	5.368
5	5.985	6.105	6.228	6.353	6.610	6.877	7.154	7.442
6	7.523	7.716	7.913	8.115	8.536	8.977	9.442	9.930
7	9.200	9.487	9.783	10.089	10.731	11.414	12.142	12.916
8	11.029	11.436	11.859	12.300	13.233	14.240	15.327	16.499
9	13.021	13.580	14.164	14.776	16.085	17.519	19.086	20.799
10	15.193	15.937	16.722	17.549	19.337	21.322	23.521	25.959
11	17.560	18.531	19.561	20.655	23.045	25.733	28.755	32.150
12	20.141	21.384	22.713	24.133	27.271	30.850	34.931	39.581
13	22.953	24.523	26.212	28.029	32.089	36.786	42.219	48.497
14	26.019	27.975	30.095	32.393	37.581	43.672	50.818	59.196
15	29.361	31.773	34.405	37.280	43.842	51.660	60.965	72.035
16	33.003	35.950	39.190	42.753	50.980	60.925	72.939	87.442
17	36.974	40.545	44.501	48.884	59.118	71.673	87.068	105.931
18	41.301	45.599	50.396	55.750	68.394	84.141	103.740	128.117
19	46.019	51.159	56.940	63.440	78.969	98.603	123.413	154.740
20	51.160	57.275	64.203	72.052	91.025	115.380	146.628	186.688
21	56.765	64.003	72.265	81.699	104.768	134.840	174.021	225.026
22	62.873	71.403	81.214	92.503	120.436	157.415	206.345	271.031
23	69.532	79.543	91.148	104.603	138.297	183.601	244.487	326.237
24	76.790	88.497	102.174	118.155	158.659	213.977	289.494	392.404
25	84.701	98.347	114.413	133.334	181.871	249.214	342.603	471.981

N	22%	24%	26%	28%	30%	32%	34%	36%
1	1.000	1.000	1.000	1.000	1.000	1.000	1.000	1.000
2	2.220	2.240	2.260	2.280	2.300	2.320	2.340	2.360
3	3.708	3.778	3.848	3.918	3.990	4.062	4.136	4.210
4	5.524	5.684	5.848	6.016	6.187	6.362	6.542	6.725
5	7.740	8.048	8.368	8.700	9.043	9.398	9.766	10.146
6	10.442	10.980	11.544	12.136	12.756	13.406	14.086	14.799
7	13.740	14.615	15.546	16.534	17.583	18.696	19.876	21.126
8	17.762	19.123	20.588	22.163	23.858	25.678	27.633	29.732
9	22.670	24.713	26.940	29.369	32.015	34.895	38.029	41.435
10	28.657	31.643	34.945	38.593	42.620	47.062	51.958	57.352
11	35.962	40.238	45.031	50.399	56.405	63.122	70.624	78.998
12	44.874	50.895	57.739	65.510	74.327	84.321	95.637	108.438
13	55.746	64.110	73.751	84.853	97.625	112.303	129.153	148.475
14	69.010	80.496	93.926	109.612	127.912	149.240	174.065	202.926
15	85.192	100.815	119.347	141.303	167.286	197.997	234.247	276.979
16	104.935	126.011	151.377	181.868	218.472	262.356	314.891	377.692
17	129.020	157.253	191.735	233.791	285.014	347.310	422.954	514.661
18	158.405	195.994	242.586	300.252	371.518	459.449	567.758	700.939
19	194.254	244.033	306.658	385.323	483.973	607.473	761.796	954.278
20	237.989	303.601	387.389	494.213	630.165	802.864	1021.810	1298.820
21	291.347	377.465	489.110	633.592	820.214	1060.780	1370.220	1767.390
22	356.444	469.057	617.278	811.998	1067.280	1401.230	1837.100	2404.650
23	435.861	582.630	778.771	1040.360	1388.460	1850.620	2462.710	3271.330
24	532.751	723.461	982.251	1332.660	1806.000	2443.820	3301.030	4450.010
25	650.956	898.092	1238.640	1706.800	2348.800	3226.850	4424.380	6053.010

TABLE D

$$\text{INTEREST FACTORS } B = R \left[\frac{1 - (1 + i)^{-n}}{i} \right] \text{ FOR CALCULATING B,}$$

PRESENT VALUE OF AN ANNUITY

Year	1%	2%	3%	4%	5%	6%	7%	8%
1	0.9901	0.9804	0.9709	0.9615	0.9524	0.9434	0.9346	0.9259
2	1.9704	1.9416	1.9135	1.8861	1.8594	1.8334	1.8080	1.7833
3	2.9410	2.8839	2.8286	2.7751	2.7232	2.6730	2.6243	2.5771
4	3.9020	3.8077	3.7171	3.6299	3.5459	3.4651	3.3872	3.3121
5	4.8535	4.7134	4.5797	4.4518	4.3295	4.2123	4.1002	3.9927
6	5.7955	5.6014	5.4172	5.2421	5.0757	4.9173	4.7665	4.6229
7	6.7282	6.4720	6.2302	6.0020	5.7863	5.5824	5.3893	5.2064
8	7.6517	7.3254	7.0196	6.7327	6.4632	6.2098	5.9713	5.7466
9	8.5661	8.1622	7.7861	7.4353	7.1078	6.8017	6.5152	6.2469
10	9.4714	8.9825	8.5302	8.1109	7.7217	7.3601	7.0236	6.7101
11	10.3677	9.7868	9.2526	8.7604	8.3064	7.8868	7.4987	7.1389
12	11.2552	10.5753	9.9539	9.3850	8.8632	8.3838	7.9427	7.5361
13	12.1338	11.3483	10.6349	9.9856	9.3935	8.8527	8.3576	7.9038
14	13.0038	12.1062	11.2960	10.5631	9.8986	9.2950	8.7454	8.2442
15	13.8651	12.8492	11.9379	11.1183	10.3796	9.7122	9.1079	8.5595
16	14.7180	13.5777	12.5610	11.6522	10.8377	10.1059	9.4466	8.8514
17	15.5624	14.2918	13.1660	12.1656	11.2740	10.4772	9.7632	9.1216
18	16.3984	14.9920	13.7534	12.6592	11.6895	10.8276	10.0591	9.3719
19	17.2261	15.6784	14.3237	13.1339	12.0853	11.1581	10.3356	9.6036
20	18.0457	16.3514	14.8774	13.5903	12.4622	11.4699	10.5940	9.8181
21	18.8571	17.0111	15.4149	14.0291	12.8211	11.7640	10.8355	10.0168
22	19.6605	17.6580	15.9368	14.4511	13.1630	12.0416	11.0612	10.2007
23	20.4559	18.2921	16.4435	14.8568	13.4885	12.3033	11.2722	10.3710
24	21.2435	18.9139	16.9355	15.2469	13.7986	12.5503	11.4693	10.5287
25	22.0233	19.5234	17.4131	15.6220	14.0939	12.7833	11.6536	10.6748

Year	9%	10%	11%	12%	13%	14%	15%	16%
1	0.9174	0.9091	0.9009	0.8929	0.8850	0.8772	0.8696	0.8621
2	1.7591	1.7355	1.7125	1.6901	1.6681	1.6467	1.6257	1.6052
3	2.5313	2.4868	2.4437	2.4018	2.3612	2.3216	2.2832	2.2459
4	3.2397	3.1699	3.1024	3.0373	2.9745	2.9137	2.8550	2.7982
5	3.8896	3.7908	3.6959	3.6048	3.5172	3.4331	3.3522	3.2743
6	4.4859	4.3553	4.2305	4.1114	3.9976	3.8887	3.7845	3.6847
7	5.0329	4.8684	4.7122	4.5638	4.4226	4.2883	4.1604	4.0386
8	5.5348	5.3349	5.1461	4.9676	4.7988	4.6389	4.4873	4.3436
9	5.9852	5.7590	5.5370	5.3282	5.1317	4.9464	4.7716	4.6065
10	6.4176	6.1446	5.8892	5.6502	5.4262	5.2161	5.0188	4.8332
11	6.8052	6.4951	6.2065	5.9377	5.6869	5.4527	5.2337	5.0286
12	7.1607	6.8137	6.4924	6.1944	5.9176	5.6603	5.4206	5.1971
13	7.4869	7.1034	6.7499	6.4235	6.1218	5.8424	5.5831	5.3423
14	7.7861	7.3667	6.9819	6.6282	6.3025	6.0021	5.7245	5.4675
15	8.0607	7.6061	7.1909	6.8109	6.4624	6.1422	5.8474	5.5755
16	8.3125	7.8237	7.3792	6.9740	6.6039	6.2651	5.9542	5.6685
17	8.5436	8.0215	7.5488	7.1196	6.7291	6.3729	6.0472	5.7487
18	8.7556	8.2014	7.7016	7.2497	6.8399	6.4674	6.1280	5.8178
19	8.9501	8.3649	7.8393	7.3658	6.9380	6.5504	6.1982	5.8775
20	9.1285	8.5136	7.9633	7.4694	7.0248	6.6231	6.2593	5.9288
21	9.2922	8.6487	8.0751	7.5620	7.1016	6.6870	6.3125	5.9731
22	9.4424	8.7715	8.1757	7.6446	7.1695	6.7429	6.3587	6.0113
23	9.5802	8.8832	8.2664	7.7184	7.2297	6.7921	6.3988	6.0442
24	9.7066	8.9847	8.3481	7.7843	7.2829	6.8351	6.4338	6.0726
25	9.8226	9.0770	8.4217	7.8431	7.3300	6.8729	6.4641	6.0971

Year	17%	18%	19%	20%	21%	22%	23%	24%
1	0.8547	0.8475	0.8403	0.8333	0.8264	0.8197	0.8130	0.8065
2	1.5852	1.5656	1.5465	1.5278	1.5095	1.4915	1.4740	1.4568
3	2.2096	2.1743	2.1399	2.1065	2.0739	2.0422	2.0114	1.9813
4	2.7432	2.6901	2.6386	2.5887	2.5404	2.4936	2.4483	2.4043
5	3.1993	3.1272	3.0576	2.9906	2.9260	2.8636	2.8035	2.7454
6	3.5892	3.4976	3.4098	3.3255	3.2446	3.1669	3.0923	3.0205
7	3.9224	3.8115	3.7057	3.6046	3.5079	3.4155	3.3270	3.2423
8	4.2072	4.0776	3.9544	3.8372	3.7256	3.6193	3.5179	3.4212
9	4.4506	4.3030	4.1633	4.0310	3.9054	3.7863	3.6731	3.5655
10	4.6586	4.4941	4.3389	4.1925	4.0541	3.9232	3.7993	3.6819
11	4.8364	4.6560	4.4865	4.3271	4.1769	4.0354	3.9018	3.7757
12	4.9884	4.7932	4.6105	4.4392	4.2785	4.1274	3.9852	3.8514
13	5.1183	4.9095	4.7147	4.5327	4.3624	4.2028	4.0530	3.9124
14	5.2293	5.0081	4.8023	4.6106	4.4317	4.2646	4.1082	3.9616
15	5.3242	5.0916	4.8759	4.6755	4.4890	4.3152	4.1530	4.0013
16	5.4053	5.1624	4.9377	4.7296	4.5364	4.3567	4.1894	4.0333
17	5.4746	5.2223	4.9897	4.7746	4.5755	4.3908	4.2190	4.0591
18	5.5339	5.2732	5.0333	4.8122	4.6079	4.4187	4.2431	4.0799
19	5.5845	5.3162	5.0700	4.8435	4.6346	4.4415	4.2627	4.0967
20	5.6278	5.3527	5.1009	4.8696	4.6567	4.4603	4.2786	4.1103
21	5.6648	5.3837	5.1268	4.8913	4.6750	4.4756	4.2916	4.1212
22	5.6964	5.4099	5.1486	4.9094	4.6900	4.4882	4.3021	4.1300
23	5.7234	5.4321	5.1668	4.9245	4.7025	4.4985	4.3106	4.1371
24	5.7465	5.4509	5.1822	4.9371	4.7128	4.5070	4.3176	4.1428
25	5.7662	5.4669	5.1951	4.9476	4.7213	4.5139	4.3232	4.1474

Year	25%	26%	27%	28%	29%	30%	31%	32%
1	0.8000	0.7937	0.7874	0.7813	0.7752	0.7692	0.7634	0.7576
2	1.4400	1.4235	1.4074	1.3916	1.3761	1.3609	1.3461	1.3315
3	1.9520	1.9234	1.8956	1.8684	1.8420	1.8161	1.7909	1.7663
4	2.3616	2.3202	2.2800	2.2410	2.2031	2.1662	2.1305	2.0957
5	2.6893	2.6351	2.5827	2.5320	2.4830	2.4356	2.3897	2.3452
6	2.9514	2.8850	2.8210	2.7594	2.7000	2.6427	2.5875	2.5342
7	3.1611	3.0833	3.0087	2.9370	2.8682	2.8021	2.7386	2.6775
8	3.3289	3.2407	3.1564	3.0758	2.9986	2.9247	2.8539	2.7860
9	3.4631	3.3657	3.2728	3.1842	3.0997	3.0190	2.9419	2.8681
10	3.5705	3.4648	3.3644	3.2689	3.1781	3.0915	3.0091	2.9304
11	3.6564	3.5435	3.4365	3.3351	3.2388	3.1473	3.0604	2.9776
12	3.7251	3.6060	3.4933	3.3868	3.2859	3.1903	3.0995	3.0133
13	3.7801	3.6555	3.6381	3.4272	3.3224	3.2233	3.1294	3.0404
14	3.8241	3.6949	3.5733	3.4587	3.3507	3.2487	3.1522	3.0609
15	3.8593	3.7261	3.6010	3.4834	3.3726	3.2682	3.1696	3.0764
16	3.8874	3.7509	3.6228	3.5026	3.3896	3.2832	3.1829	3.0882
17	3.9099	3.7705	3.6400	3.5177	3.4028	3.2948	3.1931	3.0971
18	3.9279	3.7861	3.6536	3.5294	3.4130	3.3037	3.2008	3.1039
19	3.9424	3.7985	3.6642	3.5386	3.4210	3.3105	3.2067	3.1090
20	3.9539	3.8083	3.6726	3.5458	3.4271	3.3158	3.2112	3.1129
21	3.9631	3.8161	3.6792	3.5514	3.4319	3.3198	3.2147	3.1158
22	3.9705	3.8223	3.6844	3.5558	3.4356	3.3230	3.2173	3.1180
23	3.9764	3.8273	3.6885	3.5592	3.4384	3.3254	3.2193	3.1197
24	3.9811	3.8312	3.6918	3.5619	3.4406	3.3272	3.2209	3.1210
25	3.9849	3.8342	3.6943	3.5640	3.4423	3.3286	3.2220	3.1220

NOTES

Chapter 1

1. Shawn Tully, "America's Wealth Creators," *Fortune,* November 22, 1999, p. 275.
2. Much of the arithmetic done in the rest of this chapter may be overwhelming. However, it is included in this chapter to show how business decisions can be calculated. These calculations will be explained in more detail in later chapters.
3. The income statement is presented at the center of the balance sheet in **Figure 1.5** strictly for illustration purposes. It shows how net income (or profit) increases the shareholders' equity on the balance sheet.
4. This percentage is equivalent to what the shareholders could earn if they were to invest these funds elsewhere; it is sometimes called the opportunity cost.

Chapter 2

1. T-accounts are not used in the formal bookkeeping system, but they are a convenient way to analyze transactions.
2. Managers often use the term "profit and loss statement" when referring to the income statement internally. However, it is not used in *external documents* such as the annual report for a simple reason: the word "profit" is considered by many as greedy and selfish. Also, the term profit suggests an excess of surplus on top of what is really needed for the business to operate.

Chapter 10

1. Linda Corman, "Cash Masters," CFO, July 1998, vol. 14, no. 7, p. 30.

Chapter 11

1. Erich A. Helfert, *Techniques of Financial Analysis,* 6th edition (Homewood, IL.: Richard D. Irwin, Inc., 1987), pp. 337–342.

GLOSSARY

Accounting. Process of recording and summarizing business transactions on a company's financial statements.

Accounting cycle. Steps involved in processing financial transactions for preparing financial statements.

Accounting equation. *Assets = Liabilities + Equity* or *Assets − Liabilities = Equity.*

Accounting methods. Calculation of the book value rate of return by using data presented on financial statements.

Accrual method. Accounting method that considers sales when made and expenses when incurred, regardless of when the transactions takes place.

Activity-based costing. Accounting system that focuses on the analysis of overhead costs to determine how they relate to different products, services, or activities.

Administrative expenses. Expenses that are not directed related to producing and selling goods or services.

Aging of accounts receivable. A process of sorting accounts receivable by how long they have been outstanding.

Amortization. It is a tax-deductible expense that applies to intangible assets such as goodwill and trademarks.

Annuity. A series of payments (or receipts) of fixed amount for a specified number of years.

Assessed value. Value set on assets by municipal government for determining property taxes.

Asset-management ratios. Evaluate how efficiently managers use the assets of a business.

Assets. Resources that a business owns to produce goods and services (e.g., cash, accounts receivable, buildings).

Asset valuation. Reappraising selected assets of a business.

Auditor's report. Report prepared by an independent accounting firm that is presented to a company's shareholders.

Average collection period. Measures how many days it takes for customers to pay their bills.

Balance sheet. Financial statement that shows a "snapshot" of a company's financial condition (assets, liabilities and equity).

Benchmarking. Process of searching for the best practices by comparing oneself to a competitor's excellent performance.

Benchmarks. Industry norms for comparing one's financial ratios.

Bond. Long-term loan with regular payments of interest and principal that could be secured or unsecured (20 to 30 years).

Bookkeeping. Activity which involves collecting, classifying, and reporting accounting transactions.

Book value. The accounting value of an asset—that is, the original cost minus total depreciation deductions made to date. This is a firm's assets shown on the financial statements.

Break-even chart. Graph that shows the effect of change in both revenue and costs on profitability.

Break-even point. Level of production where sales revenue equals total costs.

Break-even wedge. Method that helps managers determine the most appropriate way of structuring their operating costs (fixed versus variable).

Budgeting. Process by which management allocates corporate resources, evaluates financial outcomes and establishes system to control operational and financial performance.

Business risk. Has to do with the uncertainty inherent in projecting the level of sales revenue and income.

Cs of credit. Factors that banks look at to gauge the creditworthiness of a business: character, collateral, capacity, capital, circumstances, coverage.

Capital assets. Balance sheet accounts such as land, buildings, equipment, machinery that are to be used over an extended period of years.

Capital assets turnover. Measures how intensively a firm's capital assets are used to generate sales.

Capital budgets. Budgets that show how much will be spent for the purchase of capital assets.

Capital investment. Project that requires extensive financial resources (cash outflow) made for the purpose of generating a return (cash inflows).

Capital structure. Represents the permanent financing sources used to buy capital assets.

Cash. Cash on hand and short-term deposits.

Cash break-even point. Number of units or sales revenue that must be reached in order to cover total cash fixed costs (total fixed costs less depreciation).

Cash conversion cycle. Periodic transformation of cash through working capital and capital assets and back to cash.

Cash conversion efficiency ratio. Ratio that measures how fast a business converts sales revenue to cash flow within its operations.

Cash flow. Result of the income after taxes plus depreciation.

Cash inflows. Represents the receipt of money generated by sales revenue less expenses or the cash receipts generated by a capital project.

Cash insufficiency. Not enough cash generated by a capital project to pay for fixed charges.

Cash method. Accounting method of recording business transactions when sales are made and expenses incurred.

Cash outflows. Represents cash disbursements for the purchase of assets.

Chart of accounts. Categorization of accounts used to record transactions.

Combined leverage. Financial technique used to calculate both operating and financial leverage.

Committed fixed costs. Costs that must be incurred in order to operate a business.

Common size ratios. Method of reducing (1) all numbers on the balance sheet as a percentage of total assets and (2) all numbers on the income statement as a percentage of sales revenue.

Complementary budgets. Budgets that complement operating budgets by presenting data differently and in more detail.

Compound interest. Interest rate that is applicable on the initial principal and the accumulated interest of prior periods.

Comprehensive budgets. Projected financial statements such as the income statement, the balance sheet, and the statement of cash flows.

Compulsory investments. Investments made in capital assets that do not require in-depth analytical studies.

Conditional sales contract. Agreement made between a buyer and a seller regarding the purchase of an asset such as on a time payment basis.

Confirming institution. Organization that finances inventory.

Contribution margin. The difference between sales revenue and variable costs.

Controllable costs. Costs that operating managers are accountable for.

Controller. Person responsible for establishing the accounting and financial reporting policies and procedures.

Cost accounting. Accounting system that provides information about costs to managers to make informed decisions.

Cost of borrowed funds. Effective after-tax cost of raising funds from different sources (lenders and shareholders).

Cost of capital. Deals with the cost of borrowing funds from investors (creditors and shareholders) to finance a business.

Cost of common shares. Cost of common shares includes dividends paid to shareholders, flotation costs, and growth rate.

Cost of debt. Debt financing includes interest charges less income taxes.

Cost of financing. Represents how much it costs (%) a business to finance all assets shown on a company's balance.

Cost of goods sold. Cost incurred in making or producing goods that are sold.

Cost of preferred shares. Cost of preferred shares includes fixed dividends paid to shareholders and the flotation costs.

Cost of retained earnings. Cost of retained earnings includes dividends and growth rate.

Cost-volume-profit analysis. Tool used for analyzing how volume, price, product mix, and product costs relate to one another and affect profit levels.

Credit. Accounting entries recorded on the right side of an account.

Credit insurance policy. Insurance to cover losses suffered from a firm's accounts receivable that become uncollectible.

Credit policies. Decisions about the extent of credit to be provided to customers.

Credit-scoring system. System that assigns weights to characteristics of a customer to determine a score of creditworthiness.

Credit terms. How fast a customer is required to pay its account.

Current assets. Balance sheet accounts such as cash, accounts receivable, and inventory that are expected to be turned into cash (usually in one year or less).

Current liabilities. Debts that a business must pay within one year (e.g., accounts payable).

Current ratio. Current assets divided by current liabilities.

Current value accounting. Accounting method used to restate assets on financial statements in terms of what they would be worth if purchased.

Days of working capital ratio. The number of days in working capital a business holds to meet average daily sales requirements.

Debit. Accounting entries recorded on the left side of an account.

Debt-to-equity ratio. Measures the proportion of debt used compared to equity to finance all assets.

Debt-to-total-assets ratio. Measures how much debt a business uses to finance all assets.

Deferred taxes. Future tax liability resulting from the difference between depreciation and MACRS.

Demassing. Recession-driven technique to remove management layers from organizational charts to cut costs.

Depreciation. Estimated decrease in the value of capital assets due to wear and tear and/or obsolescence.

Direct costs. Costs that are directly related to a specific activity, product, or objective.

Discounted payback. The number of years required for a capital investment to generate enough discounted cash inflow to just cover the initial cash outflow.

Discounting. The process of finding the present value of a series of future cash flows.

Discretionary fixed costs. Costs that can be controlled by managers.

Double-entry accounting. System for posting financial transactions so that the accounting equation remains in balance.

Du Pont System. Presentation of financial ratios in a logical way to measure return on investment (ROI).

Earnings per share. Measures how much net income is available to each outstanding share.

Economic life. Number of years that a capital asset or investment opportunity will last.

Economic ordering quantity (EOQ). Inventory management technique that determines the optimum (least cost) quantity of goods that should be ordered at any single time.

Economic value. Value of a business determined by the ability or capacity of an asset to generate cash.

Economic value added (EVA). Tool that measures the wealth a company creates for its investors.

Efficiency. The relationship between profits (outputs) generated and assets employed (inputs).

Expense investment. A fully tax deductible cost that should produce favorable effects on the profit performance.

External financing. Funds obtained from investors (long-term lenders and shareholders).

Factoring. Selling accounts receivable to a financial institution.

Feedback controls. System that helps to focus on variations of past performance.

Financial health score. Linear analysis in which five measures are objectively weighted to give an overall score that becomes the basis for classifying the financial health of a business.

Financial lease. Lease for a specified time period that is fully amortized.

Financial leverage. Financial technique used to determine the most favorable capital structure (debt versus equity).

Financial management. Activity involved in raising funds and buying assets in order to obtain the highest possible return.

Financial needs. The amount of money (and for what reasons) a business needs to finance its operations.

Financial ratios. Comparison or relationship between numbers shown on financial statements.

Financial risk. Has to do with the way that a business is financed (debt versus equity).

Financial statements. Financial reports, which include the income statement, the statement of retained earnings, the balance sheet, and the statement of cash flows.

Financial structure. The way to finance a company's assets by the entire right-hand side of the balance sheet (short-term and long-term financing).

Financing activities. Portion of the statement of cash flows that shows how much cash was provided (or used) from external sources (e.g., sale of shares, borrowing or repaying a mortgage, payment of dividends).

Financing decisions. Decisions related to borrowing from lenders and shareholders.

Financing mix. Proportion of funds raised from lenders and shareholders.

Financing requirements. Sources of money (shareholders and lenders) to finance a business.

Fixed-charge-coverage ratio. Measures to what extent a business can service all its fixed charges (e.g., interest, leases).

Fixed costs. Costs that remain constant at varying levels of production.

Float. The amount of funds tied up in checks that have been mailed but are still in process and have not yet been collected.

Forms of financing. Financing instruments used to buy assets (e.g., term loans, bonds, common shares).

Future value. The amount to which a payment or series of payments will grow by a given future date when compounded by a given interest rate.

Generally Accepted Accounting Principles (GAAP). A broad set of rules governing how various transactions will be reported on financial statements.

Government financing. Funds obtained from government institutions (direct or indirect) to finance a business.

Gross margin. Difference between sales revenue and cost of goods sold.

Holding costs. Category of costs associated with the storing of goods in inventory (e.g., insurance, rent).

Horizontal analysis. Shows percentage change of accounts shown on two consecutive financial statements.

Hurdle rate. Capital budgeting technique used to rank the financial desirability of capital projects according to their cost of capital.

Income. The excess of revenues over expenses.

Income after taxes. Difference between the income before taxes and income taxes.

Income statement. Financial statement that shows a summary of revenues and expenses for a specified period of time.

Indemnification policy. Insurance a business takes against the catastrophic loss in cash.

Indirect costs. Costs that are not associated with a specific activity, product, or objective.

Industry multipliers. Standard used to determine the value or worth of a business in a particular industry.

Inflation. Represents a price rise in the average cost of goods characteristic of periods of prosperity.

Instrument risk. Has to do with the quality of security available to satisfy investors.

Intangible assets. Items that are not tangible but represent some value to a business (e.g., trademarks, patents).

Interest tables. Numbers found in compound or discount interest and annuity tables.

Interim financing. Loan made to a business to help finance the construction of a new plant until regular financing is obtained.

Internal financing. Funds obtained from retained earnings, depreciation, and a reduction in working capital accounts.

Internal rate of return (IRR). The specific interest rate used to discount all future cash inflows so that their present value equals the initial cash outflows.

Inventory turnover. Measures the number of times a year a company turns over its inventory.

Investing decisions. Decisions related to the acquisition of assets (current and capital).

Investing activities. Portion of the statement of cash flows that shows how much cash was provided (or used) to buy or sell assets (e.g., purchase or sale of a building).

Investments. Assets such as bonds and shares purchased from other businesses.

Investment securities. Funds invested in short-term deposits such as treasury bills, Fed funds, bank deposits, etc.

Job order costing. Accounting system that helps to allocate direct costs related to producing a specific good.

Journalizing. Process of recording transactions in a journal (e.g., sales journal, cash payments journal).

Just-in-time inventory management. An inventory management technique that obtains materials from suppliers just when they are needed.

Labor variance. Variance in costs between standards and actual performance due to changes in the amount of time and rate used to make a product.

Lessee. One who gets to use an asset without owning it.

Lessor. One who lends an asset to someone (lessee).

Leverage. Technique used to determine the most suitable operating and financial structure that will help amplify financial performance.

Leverage ratios. Measure the capital structure of a business and its debt-paying ability.

Liabilities. Represents the debts of a business.

Line of credit. A formal or written agreement between a bank and a borrower regarding the maximum amount of a loan that will be extended during a year.

Liquidation value. Worth of an asset if sold separately under duress.

Liquidity. Ability of a firm to meet its short-term financial obligations.

Liquidity ratios. Measure the ability of a firm to meet its cash obligations.

Lockbox system. Using post office boxes in different cities to receive customer payments with deposits managed by a local bank.

Long-term debts. Debts that are not due for a least one year.

Long-term loan. Loans to finance capital assets for a long period of time (five years or more).

MACRS. A depreciation method that accelerates depreciation and reduces taxes in the early years of an asset's life.

Marginal cost of capital. Represents the additional cost for borrowing new funds.

Market performance. Measure of the efficiency and effectiveness of management within the industry in which it operates.

Market value. The price at which an item can be sold today.

Market-value ratios. Measurement tools to gauge the way investors react to a company's market performance.

Matching principle. Process of selecting the most appropriate financing source when buying an asset.

Material requirements planning (MRP). Method for developing a schedule to help coordinate and execute resources in production.

Material variance. Variance in costs between standards and actual performance due to changes in quantity of materials used and changes in the price of the materials used.

Mortgage. Loan obtained against which specific real property such as a building is used as collateral.

Net future value. The difference between the future values of two different future values.

Net present value (NPV). The present value of the future cash flows of an investment less the initial cash outflows.

Net sales. What a business earns for the sale of its products and/or services.

Net working capital. The difference between current assets and current liabilities.

Non-controllable costs. Costs that are not under the direct control of operating managers.

Non-operating section. Section of the income statement that shows income or expenses that are not directly related with the mainstream activities of a business (i.e., interest income, extraordinary expenses, non-recurring items).

Operating activities. Portion of the statement of cash flows that shows how much cash was provided (or used) from internal sources (i.e., income after taxes, depreciation).

Operating budgets. Budgets prepared by operating managers.

Operating decisions. Decisions related to accounts appearing on the income statement (i.e., sales revenue, cost of goods sold, selling expenses).

Operating income. Difference between gross margin and operating expenses.

Operating lease. A lease that is cancelable by the lessee at any time upon due notice.

Operating leverage. Financial technique used to determine to what extent fixed costs are used relative to variable costs.

Operating performance. Measure of the efficiency and effectiveness of management at the operating level (e.g., marketing, production).

Operating section. Section of the income statement that shows a company's gross margin and operating income.

Opportunity cost. The income sacrificed by pursuing the next best alternative.

Opportunity investments. Investments made in capital assets that are of a strategic nature and usually have far-reaching financial implications.

Ordering costs. Category of costs associated with the acquisition of goods (e.g., receiving, inspecting, accounting).

Overall performance. Measure of how well a business is deploying its resources.

Overhead variance. Variance in costs between standards and actual performance due to changes in indirect costs.

Owners' section. Section of the income statement that shows the amount of money left to the shareholders (i.e., income after taxes).

Payback method. Calculation of the number of years required for a capital investment to generate enough undiscounted cash inflow to just cover the initial cash outflow.

Payback reciprocal. Capital budgeting technique that gives a rough estimate of the return on investment of a capital project.

Performance indicator. How an organizational unit should be measured.

Performance standards. Quantitative measurements used as benchmarks to compare results with performance.

Planned downsizing. Systematic way of cutting overhead costs.

Posting. Process of transferring recorded transactions from the journals to the appropriate ledger accounts.

Present value. The value today of a future payment or stream of payments discounted at an appropriate rate.

Preventive controls. System that helps to guide actions toward intended results.

Price/earnings ratio (P/E). Indicates how much investors are willing to pay per dollar of reported profits.

Price level accounting. Accounting method used to restate assets on financial statements in terms of current purchasing power (inflation).

Process costing. Accounting system that helps to allocate direct and departmental overhead costs in organizations that produce goods on a continuous basis.

Productivity indicators. Ways of measuring organizational performance such as return on assets.

Profitability. The ability of a firm to grow in all segments of a business.

Profitability index. Ratio of the present value of the cash inflows to the present value of the cash outflows discounted at a predetermined rate of interest.

Profitability ratios. Measure the overall effectiveness of a business.

Profit break-even. Number of units or sales revenue that must be reached in order to cover all fixed costs plus a profit objective.

Profit margin on sales. Measures the operating efficiency of a business.

Pro-forma financial statements. Projected financial statements (i.e, income statement, balance sheet).

PV ratio. The contribution margin expressed on a per-unit basis.

Quick ratio. Shows the relationship between the more liquid current assets and all current liabilities.

Ratio analysis. Helps readers of financial statements to assess the financial structure and performance of a business.

Regional bank. Location where a company maintains an account to receive customer payments to shorten mail delays.

Relevant costs. Cost alternatives that managers can chose from to operate a business.

Relevant range. Costs (fixed and variable) that apply to a certain level of production.

Residual value. Represents the estimated remaining value of an asset at the end of its useful life.

Responsibility center. Organization unit headed by a manager accountable for results.

Retained earnings. Amount of money kept by a company after paying dividends to its shareholders.

Return. Amount of income earned by a unit of some other financial statement item.

Return on equity. Measures the yield shareholders earn on their investment.

Return on sales. Measures a company's overall ability to generate profit from each sales dollar.

Return on total assets. Gauges the performance of assets employed in a business.

Revenue break-even point. Sales revenue that must be reached in order to cover total costs.

Revolving credit. Maximum amount of a loan a bank agrees to provide a business (borrower).

Risk. Represents the level of expectations (probabilities) that something will happen in the future.

Risk analysis. Process of attaching probabilities to individual estimates in capital project's base case.

Risk capital investors. Individuals or institutions that provide money to business to finance a business that have much risk.

Rule of 72. Calculation that shows the approximate number of years it takes for an investment to double when compounded annually.

Sale and leaseback. Arrangement made by someone to sell an asset to a lessor, then lease it back.

Screening controls. System that helps to monitor performance while work is being performed.

Secured loan. Loan that is guaranteed with a pledge of collateral.

Self-liquidating loan. Funds used to finance temporary or fluctuating variations in working capital accounts (e.g., accounts receivable, inventory).

Selling expenses. Cost incurred by a marketing organization to promote, sell and distribute its goods and services.

Semi-variable costs. Costs that change disproportionately with changes in output levels.

Sensitivity analysis. Capital budgeting technique that involves the identification of profitability variations as a result of one or more changes in a project's base case to certain key elements of a capital project.

Sensitivity evaluation. Technique that shows to what extent a change in one variable (i.e., selling price, fixed costs) impacts the break-even point.

Shareholders' equity. Funds provided in a business by its shareholders (i.e., shares, retained earnings).

Short-term financing. Sources of financing obtained for a period of less than one year (e.g., trade credit, line of credit).

Solvency. Ability to service or pay all debts (short and long-term).

Sources of financing. Institutions that provide funds (i.e., commercial banks).

Stability. Relationship between debt and shareholders' equity.

Statement of cash flows. Financial statement that details the sources and uses of cash in three sections: operating activities, financing activities, and investing activities.

Statement of retained earnings. Financial statement that shows the amount of income retained in a business since it was started.

Subordinated debt. Loan that is more risky for which investors expect higher interest rates.

Sunk costs. Investment costs that have been incurred prior to making the decision to proceed with a capital project.

Supplier credit. Financing obtained from suppliers (accounts payable).

Sustainable growth rate. Rate of increase in sales revenue a company can attain without depletion of financing resources, excessive borrowing, or new stock issue.

Term loan. Loan made to buy capital assets and repaid in a series of payments of interest and principal.

Times-interest-earned ratio. Measures to what extent a business can service its interest on debt.

Time value of money. Rate at which the value of money is traded off as a function of time.

Total assets turnover. Measures how intensively a firm's total assets are used to generate sales.

Treasurer. Person responsible for raising funds and regulating the flow of funds.

Trend analysis. Analyzing a company's performance over a number of years.

Trial balance. Statement that ensures that the general ledger is in balance (debit transactions = credit transactions).

Unit break-even point. Number of units that must be sold in order to have sales revenue equal to total costs.

Variable costs. Costs that fluctuate directly with changes in volume of production.

Variance analysis. Accounting system that compares standards to actual performance.

Venture capital. Risk capital supplied to small companies by wealthy individuals (angels), partnerships, or corporations, usually in return for an equity position in the firm.

Weighted cost of capital. Product of the proportion of a source of capital relative to the total capital structure and the cost of that source.

Working capital. Accounts appearing on the current asset and current liability portion of the balance sheet.

Working capital management. Managing individual current asset and current liability accounts to ensure proper interrelationships among them.

Zero-based budgets. Budgets based on the premise that every budget dollar must be justified.

SELECTED READINGS

The following is a list of books that can be used to supplement and extend the material covered in this book.

Bernstein, Leopold A., and John J. Wild. *Analysis of Financial Statements*. New York: McGraw-Hill, 2000.

Brimson, James A. *Activity Accounting*. New York: McGraw Hill, 1991.

Butler, Robert E., and Donald Rappaport. *A Complete Guide To Money and Your Business*. New York: New York Institute of Finance, 1987.

Covello, Joseph A., and Brian J. Hazelgren. *The Complete Book of Business Plans*. Naperville, Ill.: Sourcebooks, Inc., 1994.

Elgers, Pieter, T., and John J. Clark. *The Lease/Buy Decision*. New York: The Free Press, 1980.

Ernst & Young Staff. *Ernst & Young Management Guide to Mergers and Acquisitions*. New York: Wiley, 1991.

Fallek, Max. *Finding Money for Your Small Business*. Chicago, Ill.: Enterprise, Dearborn, 1994.

Finney, Robert G. *Basics of Budgeting*. New York: AMACOM, 1994.

Finney, Robert G. *Every Manager's Guide To Business Finance*. New York: AMACOM, 1994.

Finnerty, Joseph E. *Planning Cash Flow*. New York: AMACOM, 1993.

Finnerty, Joseph E. *How to Manage Corporate Cash Effectively*. New York: AMACOM, 1991.

Griffin, Michael P. *Intermediate Finance and Accounting for Nonfinancial Managers*. New York: AMACOM, 1991.

Helfert, Erich, A. *Techniques of Financial Analysis*. Homewood, Ill.: Richard D. Irwin, Inc., 1987.

McLaughlin, Thomas A. *Financial Basics for Nonprofit Managers*. New York: John Wiley & Sons, Inc., 1995.

Mancuso, Joseph R. *Mancuso's Small Business Resource Guide*. New York: Prentice-Hall, 1996.

Margolis, Neal, and N. Paul Harmon. *Accounting Essentials*. New York: Wiley, 1991.

Massarella, Gregory, J., Patrick D. Zorsch, Daniel D. Jacobson, and Marc J. Ritenhouse. *How to Prepare a Results-Driven Business Plan*. New York: AMACOM, 1993.

Miller, B., and D. Miller. *How to Interpret Financial Statements for Better Business Decisions*. New York: AMACOM, 1990.

Milling, Bryan E. *Cash Flow Problem Solver*. Radnor, Penn.: Chilton Book Company, 1981.

Orsino, Philip S. *Successful Business Expansion*. New York: John Wiley & Sons, Inc., 1994.

Perry, William E. *Controlling the Bottom Line*. New York: Van Nostrand Reinhold Company, 1984.

Plewa, Franklin J., and George T. Friedlob Jr. *Understanding Cash Flow*. New York: John Wiley & Sons, Inc., 1995.

Plewa, Franklin J., and George T. Friedlob Jr. *Understanding Income Statements*. New York: John Wiley & Sons, Inc., 1995.

Ritchie, John C. *The Fundamentals of Fundamental Analysis*. Chicago: Probus Publishing Company, 1993.

Shim, Jae K., and Joel, G. Siegel. *Budgeting Basics & Beyond*. Englewood Cliffs: Prentice Hall, 1994.

Snowden, Richard W. *Buying a Business*. New York: AMACOM, 1993.

Tomasko, Robert M. *Downsizing*. New York: AMACOM, 1987.

Tracy, John, A. *How to Read a Financial Report*. New York: John Wiley & Sons, 1999.

INDEX

About the Author

Pierre G. Bergeron is Professor at the Faculty of Administration, University of Ottawa and former Secretary, Associate Dean (External Relations) and Assistant Dean (Undergraduate Programs) at the same university. He is president of Budgeting Concepts Inc., a management and business consulting firm, and is a highly skilled educator with more than 25 years of experience. Mr. Bergeron has occupied the position of Director in such federal government agencies as Industry Canada (Incentives Division) and Human Resources Canada. In the private sector, he worked at Imperial Oil Limited in the Quebec Marketing Region and at the company's head office in Toronto in market analysis and capital project evaluation. He was also Director, Financial Planning, at Domtar Limited.